CURT PRÜFER

Curt Prüfer, 1931

CURT PRÜFER

German Diplomat from the Kaiser to Hitler

Donald M. McKale

THE KENT STATE UNIVERSITY PRESS
Kent, Ohio and London, England

88000899.2

All photographs used courtesy of Olaf Prüfer, private collection.

© 1987 by The Kent State University Press, Kent, Ohio 44242
All rights reserved
Library of Congress Catalog Card Number 87-4114
ISBN 0-87338-345-1
Manufactured in the United States of America

The paper in this book meets the guidelines for permanence and durability of the Committee on Production Guidelines for Book Longevity of the Council on Library Resources.

Library of Congress Cataloging-in-Publication Data

McKale, Donald M., 1943–
    Curt Prüfer, German diplomat from the Kaiser to Hitler.

    Bibliography: p.
    Includes index.
    1. Prüfer, Curt Max, b. 1881. 2. Diplomats—Germany—Biography.
3. Germany—Foreign relations—Near East. 4. Near East—Foreign relations—
Germany. 5. Germany—Foreign relations—20th century. I. Title.
DD247.P73M35   1987   943′.08′092′4 [B]   87-4114
ISBN 0-87338-345-1 (alk. paper)

British Library Cataloguing-in-Publication data are available.

For
Donald V. and Mildred Wedd McKale
and
Georgia, Coleene, and Ellen

Contents

Preface

THE dividing line between patriotism and pride on the one hand and arrogance and racism on the other is a narrow one, and Germany clearly crossed it from 1933 to 1945 under Adolf Hitler and the Nazis. That should be a reminder to us all. How one of Germany's political and social elite, a leading diplomat, crossed that line is the theme of this study. For nearly forty years, Curt Max Prüfer served as a specialist for Arab and Middle Eastern affairs in the foreign service of three German governments. Born and educated in the Kaiser's Germany, he developed an unbending loyalty to the state and a belief in the power of the German people; he survived the Reich's defeat in World War I and the Weimar republic, which he detested, to support Hitler's fanatical nationalism, military aggrandizement, and anti-Semitism.

Recent studies have shown how such traditional German conservatives and nationalists in the upper and upper-middle classes as Prüfer, most of them highly educated and involved in the professions and business, provided a crucial ingredient in Hitler's power base during the Third Reich. They not only voted for the dictator and joined his party in its drive to power, but also remained in their jobs and offices, which many had entered during the period of Imperial Germany, to serve the Nazi regime after 1933.[1] That held particularly true for the most conservative and elitist government bureaucracy, in which Prüfer worked, the German foreign ministry (*Auswärtiges Amt*, or AA), which by its nature represented an inevitable target for Nazi encroachment.[2] Even as late as the autumn of 1944, with World War II nearing its end and the Nazi government contemplating a massive purge of the AA in the aftermath of the July plot to kill Hitler—the conspirators included several diplomats—numerous careerists who had entered the ministry prior to the Nazi regime still retained their jobs. That included Prüfer, sent on leave in 1943 to Switzerland. A study of the "personnel questionnaires" completed in 1944 by 330 of the diplomats, Prüfer among them, reveals that many had careers that paralleled his.[3]

This data is not meant to suggest any unusual significance for Prüfer; neither he nor his colleagues in the second echelon of the foreign ministry ever determined foreign policy, either before Hitler or during the Nazi era. What the career data fails to tell us, moreover, is whether the lesser diplomats, in whose hands lay the day-to-day operation of the foreign service and who have not been examined individually by historians, acted in serving the Nazi regime because of opportunism and naïveté, as many conservatives maintained after World War II, or because of conviction.[4] As this study of Prüfer will show, he acted for each of these reasons, but the overwhelming portion of his behavior resulted from the principles or attitudes that he had in common with the Nazis.

In explaining why Hitler had so much success in attracting the support of the professional bureaucracy, Prüfer's example both confirms and augments previous scholarship. On the one hand, it substantiates much of what we know about how the culture of the Kaiser's Germany, the loss of World War I, the Versailles treaty, and the frustration with the Weimar republic combined to persuade "respectable" Germans to support Nazism.[5] On the other hand, his career adds a further dimension to some of these issues. It sheds light on the intense loyalty to the state that could be felt by a member of the new middle class (*neuer Mittlestand*) in Imperial Germany, comprised of civil servants and other white collar employees who owed their prominence to higher education (*Bildung*) and property (*Besitz*). It also illustrates how a lesser bureaucrat survived the leftist revolution of 1918–19 in Germany and yet remained unscathed in his position through the Nazi seizure of power in 1933.

The study, moreover, reveals that Prüfer's bitterness at the loss of World War I made him reject the peace settlement even before it was concluded and that the AA opposed more in the Versailles treaty than its clauses concerning Europe. The ministry's Middle Eastern section, in which Prüfer worked, secretly refused to accept the postwar situation in Egypt, the primary country in the Orient (defined in this book as the Middle East, the region stretching from Tunisia in the west through such countries as Egypt, Arabia, and Turkey to Afghanistan in the east) where Britain was still deeply involved after 1919. Furthermore, the section violated the democratic principles of the Weimar republic and supported the anti-Semitism (defined as hatred of Jews) of the Nazis against foreign criticism even before Hitler became chancellor.

Hence, the following pages offer evidence for the controversial historical generalization that the Second Reich of Bismarck and Kaiser William II produced attitudes and policies that continued, with variations, into the Third Reich.[6] The book especially shows how the goals of German policy in the Middle East remained essentially unchanged from the Kaiser's Germany to Hitler's, and why Germany failed to mobilize Arab support. The Reich government kept its activities in the Orient subordinate to its policy in Europe, developed little that offered the Arabs a chance for self-determination, and instead aimed in varying degrees at weakening British influence and increasing Germany's in the Arab world. The hatred that Prüfer developed for England before and during World War I stayed with him until the end of his life.

He felt similarly about the Jews. His example provides a glimpse, however limited, into the attitude of the upper classes towards them. He belonged to the large group of old-fashioned anti-Semites, whose loathing of Jews stemmed from numerous sources, mainly political, economic, and religious in nature. Although scholars have portrayed this group as relatively moderate in comparison to the rabid racial anti-Semites,[7] Prüfer's career illustrated the intensity, crudeness, and brutality of this traditional brand of anti-Semitism and how it accepted, indeed supported, the Nazi persecution of the Jews. Prüfer backed Hitler in 1933 not only because he believed that the dictator would be controlled or moderated by the responsibilities of power, but also because he expected Hitler would do what he said about removing the alleged Jewish influence from German politics and the economy. Not even the catastrophe of World War II changed his mind; he responded to the news of his government's extermination of the Jews with a mixture of indifference and opportunism. His example supports those historians who have concluded that public enthusiasm among Germans for anti-Semitism continued throughout the Nazi regime, even among persons who appeared unconcerned about what was happening.[8] Moreover, in Prüfer's case, Germany's defeat in the war heightened his venomous hatred of Jews after 1945.

The following pages, therefore, show that Prüfer's long and distinguished career was most important for the failure it reflected. In this respect, his life mirrored that of his nation. His prejudices, arrogance, and sense of superiority, the products of his early family life and the narrow and illiberal culture of Imperial Germany, dominated his personal relationships. Such attitudes limited his knowledge of the Middle East to a superficial level, despite his ability with Oriental languages and his credentials as a scholar and diplomat. A genuine appreciation or understanding of the region and its problems eluded him; he possessed little sympathy for its peoples and no vision of their future without significant German or other European influence. His associates—whether Arab or German, personal or professional—were nearly always people with whom he felt comfortable, but who were less capable than himself and outside the mainstream of politics. Consequently, he pursued ill-conceived policies that rarely produced success. The greatest disaster resulting from his thinking, however, was his collaboration with the Nazis, whom he also considered beneath him and the sociopolitical milieu to which he belonged.

Clemson, South Carolina
March 18, 1987

Acknowledgments

MANY people have helped me with advice and encouragement since I began collecting material for this book in 1980. The inspiration for the study came from Olaf H. Prufer of Kent, Ohio, for which I thank him. He generously provided me with his father's diaries and many other documents. I am also indebted to him for his kindness and patience in answering my endless questions in letters and interviews. As a testimony to his memory, the other records used in the study support his recollections of his father. Whatever errors of judgment, interpretation, or fact appear in the book, however, are my responsibility.

I also wish to express my gratitude to Paul H. Rohmann, the former director of the Kent State University Press, who had a hand in guiding me to this project. A large part of the study is based on unpublished records of the German foreign ministry and Nazi party. My thanks particularly extends to the Clemson University Faculty Research committee for several grants and a Provost research award that enabled me to purchase many of these documents on microfilm. I would also like to express my appreciation to the National Endowment for the Humanities for a grant that made possible the completion of my research in Germany and England.

During my visits to Germany, I received valuable help from Dr. Klaus Weinandy, Dr. Sareyko, and Frau Magka at the *Politisches Archiv des Auswärtigen Amts* in Bonn; Daniel P. Simon at the Berlin Document Center; and the staffs at the *Bundesarchiv* in Koblenz and *Institut für Zeitgeschichte* in Munich. I also wish to thank Mr. T. R. Padfield and the staff of the Public Record Office in London for their courtesy and help-fulness. For their correspondence, I owe much to Nehama Chalom of the Weizmann Archives in Rehovot, Israel; John Mendelsohn and George Wagner of the National Archives and Records Service in Washington, D.C.; Dina Abramowicz of the Yivo Institute for Jewish Research in New York; and Jehuda Reinharz of Brandeis University. I particularly wish to thank, moreover, Marian Withington, Dale Simmons, and Julie Penneba-ker of the interlibrary loan department at the Cooper Library of Clemson University.

Several of my colleagues in the field of Nazi studies, including Kenneth R. Calkins, Earl R. Beck, and Alan F. Wilt, read all or parts of the completed manuscript and advised me on points that needed revision. I owe a special word of thanks to Gerhard L. Weinberg, who made valuable suggestions for improvement. A colleague at Clemson University, Ronald H. Nowaczyk, provided me with insights into the personality of Curt Prüfer. For their support of the research grants and a sabbatical leave that helped me complete this project, I wish to thank my dean, Robert A. Waller, and department heads, John R. Wunder and Alan Schaffer.

The greatest debt of gratitude, however, is that owing to my wife, Janna, and my children, Emily, David, and Susan; they have supported this long endeavor in every sense of the word. Without them it could have been neither begun nor completed.

one

Introduction:
Early Years and the
Road to Egypt

"THE German tragedy began with William II," Curt Max Prüfer recorded in his diary on 27 January 1947. "He was a precursor of Hitler's in spirit, not in deed and will. He dreamed of fame, triumph, and splendor like Hitler. He did not possess the iron-willed courage to realize his dreams, which Hitler unfortunately did." Prüfer, writing in Switzerland following the devastating defeat of his beloved Germany for the second time in a quarter of a century, reflected on its political failure and frustration during his lifetime.

Because he had served in the German foreign ministry (*Auswärtiges Amt*, or AA) from 1907 to 1945 and owed his career and social status to the German state, its decline and ruin through two world wars obsessed him. As he considered what had gone wrong, however, he refused to acknowledge the share of the German people, including himself, in the responsibility for the calamities that befell the Reich. Instead, he blamed a small clique of Nazis around Hitler for allegedly misleading the people and accused the foreign enemies of Germany who, he argued, included the Jews and Western democracies, of purposely seeking the nation's destruction. "Only fools," he declared, "are still unable today to see that the Allies, i.e., the Jewish avengers, loyal to the law of Moses, want the annihilation of the German people, just as Hitler, this arch-villain and destroyer of Germany, attempted to annihilate the Jews. He did not accomplish that because there were Jews throughout the world, powerful Jews, who mobilized this world against Hitler."[1]

The origins of Prüfer's hatred and prejudice lay in his early career during Imperial Germany and World War I. Born on 26 July 1881 into a lower middle class (*kleinbürgerliche*) Protestant family in Berlin, Prüfer had rejected the idealism and liberalism of his father, a school teacher, in favor of the intoxicating and exciting nationalism, growing power, and global aspirations (*Weltpolitik*) of Kaiser William II's Germany. The earliest Prüfers dated back several centuries to the tiny German principality of Weissenfels-Querfurt, where they had received the family name by producing wine tasters (*Prüfer* is the German word for "tester") for the local dukes. By the nineteenth century the Prüfers had become successful German burghers. Most of the family worked as artisans, except for Carl Prüfer, born in 1848.[2]

Prüfer's parents, Carl and Agnes, about 1870

Though he fought in the Franco-Prussian war in 1870–71 and considered preparing for a career in politics, the elder Prüfer decided for idealistic reasons to teach primary school. The opposite of many fellow *petit bourgeoisie* who admired the new German empire and its authoritarian monarchy, Carl Prüfer believed in education, the liberal concept of human dignity, and democracy. His only son, Curt, attended the Askanisches Gymnasium in Berlin in the years following the secondary school reform of 1892; the Kaiser and other rabidly conservative forces pushed for the new regulation, which aimed at "the stimulation of patriotic feelings" among students by lessening the study of classical languages in favor of courses in German history and language. This may help explain why, following his exit exam (*Abitur*) in 1900, he clashed with his father over his choice of career. The younger Prüfer bitterly resented his father's suggestion that he follow his example and teach school. The son later recalled that his father encouraged him to pursue moderation and conquer ambition, which would allow him to live "as if on a high mountain, in the pure air, like an Olympian god, without the haze or fog of earthly (personal) wishes or desires." The boy, however, rejected the advice, terming it a "swindle" and denouncing the Greek gods and goddesses.[3] The tense relationship between father and son may also have resulted from Curt's childhood ailments, which included kidney disease, tuberculosis, and a bout with diphtheria that shortened his breath, led to an operation on his esophagus, and left him with a quiet, whisperlike voice. The father's criticism of the son's laziness, sloppiness, and lack of manners was probably related to the boy's physical infirmities and certainly heightened his alienation.

Moreover, Curt's mother, Agnes Köcher Prüfer, did not take much interest in him. Nor did he possess childhood friends; his first friendships emerged much later with his fellow soldiers in World War I. The fierce attachment which Curt Prüfer had to his only sibling, an older sister, Helene, undoubtedly represented his effort to compensate for the lack of affection from his parents. One can only speculate about the impact of his childhood alienation and physical problems on his personality; it will be clear here, however, that as an adult he exhibited an unyielding arrogance towards non-Germans and persons of lower status, a ruthlessness in exploiting others for his own gain, and a fanatical loyalty to the German state.[4] He especially became obsessed with hatred for the British and Jews, and anyone whom he disliked he often labeled a "homosexual."[5] His homophobia and his constant need for sexual affairs with women suggest serious feelings of inadequacy. The haughty and insolent society of Imperial Germany reinforced such tendencies.

Prüfer at age 13

Unhappy at home, the young Prüfer left soon after his early schooling and toured Italy.[6] He returned to Germany still at odds with his father. He did not reject the latter's advice entirely, however; convinced that his best opportunity for a professional career and social advancement lay in education, he entered the University of Berlin, studying law and attending the seminar for Oriental languages. His impressionable student years coincided with the enrollment explosion in the German universities, a product of the prestige Germans traditionally accorded such institutions and of the rapid changes in the German economy, society, and political system since the formation of the Reich in 1871.

Conservative Prussia's conquest and unification of Germany, Bismarck's blocking of responsible self-government, and the onset of the industrial revolution had exacerbated latent tensions among the social classes. Conflict existed not only between the ruling landed aristocracy and the new upper middle class (*Oberer Mittelstand*) of industrialists, professionals, and higher civil servants, but also between these groups and the wage-earning masses. Sandwiched between the upper classes and workers was the social entity to which Prüfer belonged, the remainder of the middle class. It included the traditional elements of the self-employed (small and intermediate merchants, craftsmen, and peasants), often threatened by the competition from industrialism, and a newly emerging group of salary-dependent professionals (low- and mid-level employees and civil servants). The government sought to paper over the problems with a policy of constant compromises. It concluded alliances between the agrarian and industrial elites against the alleged revolutionary danger of the workers and their representative in the German parliament (*Reichstag*), the Social Democratic party (*Sozialdemokratische Partei Deutschlands,* or SPD). Bismarck's system of protective tariffs united the upper classes as did the later construction by William II of a powerful new navy and his embarkation on a "world policy" in foreign affairs.

Prüfer grew up in a rigidly stratified society that discouraged upward mobility beyond one's class, which aggravated the social tensions. The upper classes reacted against what they perceived as dangerous "leveling" forces in industrialization and urbanization. They maintained social barriers and denied recognition to those who had acquired the wealth for entry into their ranks. The government and the military also kept themselves closed to such minorities as Jews and to persons suspected of not being staunchly monarchist and conservative, especially those with a working-class background.[7]

One of the few hopes for advancement for a son of the lower middle class such as Prüfer, therefore, lay in education. Large numbers of students from the professional, propertied, and commercial bourgeoisie entered the universities; after 1900, the lower middle class provided nearly half of the university enrollments. Because of Prüfer's health, his archeologist's love of adventure and investigation, and his attraction to Oriental culture, he left Berlin and spent the winter of 1903 studying languages at universities in Palermo and Cairo; a year later he again visited Egypt and traveled to Turkey and Greece. While in Egypt, he met Frances Pinkham, a member of the family of the Massachusetts elixir manufacturer; they married in April 1906 in Berlin. Although the marriage lasted until their

Prüfer at the University of Berlin, 1901

divorce in 1927, it was an unhappy one, marred by Prüfer's philandering and by the couple's differences over World War I.[8]

Prüfer's interest in Egypt reflected a growing activity there among German scholars in the nineteenth century. The "golden age of Egyptology" lasted from the 1880s until World War I and resulted from the romantic fascination of Europeans with Orientalism and from the rivalry for em-

Prüfer's first wife, Frances Pinkham, 1906

pire, discussed later in this chapter, in the Middle East and Africa. German Egyptologists completed the deciphering of hieroglyphics, conducted archeological excavations among ancient Egyptian ruins, and established research institutes in Cairo. They also participated in the leadership of the Egyptian national library, founded in 1870 by the Khedive, the prince who governed Egypt for its nominal ruler, Turkey.[9]

Prüfer completed his doctoral dissertation, in which he studied an ancient Egyptian shadow play, at the University of Erlangen in 1906; the university, although growing rapidly in enrollment, was fairly new and did not rank as one of the important German institutions in science and scholarship. Shortly thereafter, he made a third trip to Egypt, stopping on the way in Rumania and Constantinople.[10] The visit to Egypt produced contacts with members of the German consulate general in Cairo, particularly the *Dragoman* ("translator"), Walter Zechlin, and resulted in Prüfer's publication of articles on Arab culture in German newspapers.[11] He displayed an extraordinary ability for languages, which contributed to his later success as a diplomat and intelligence agent. Eventually, he achieved fluency in French, English, Italian, and Arabic, and could understand Turkish, Russian, Spanish, and Portuguese. Prüfer, said one of his fellow Arab scholars later, "possessed a phenomenal linguistic talent; there were only a very few Arabists in Germany at the time who could speak and write modern Arabic and be active in the Arab press like him."[12]

But the much-heralded neohumanist and liberal education in the universities, while producing scholars such as Prüfer, in fact strengthened the nationalistic and authoritarian attitudes of German society. Research has shown that the universities, instead of caring for the emotional and social needs of the students and making them well-informed citizens, treated them solely as scholars, emphasizing value-neutral learning stripped of humane principles and critical analysis of society and politics. The universities prepared students for careers in the civil service by encouraging their sense of elitism as an educated class and instilling the idea that they owed unconditional loyalty to the monarchy and should function as patriotic officials "above political parties." Nationalism, anti-Semitism, Social Darwinism, a fear of socialist revolution, and an enthusiastic support of German military power and Weltpolitik also flourished in the universities.[13]

Prüfer's commitment to the German state intensified in February 1907, when the AA admitted him to its consular service as a Dragoman. The ministry sent him to replace Zechlin at the German consulate general in Cairo. Young, ambitious, and intelligent, but from the petit bourgeoisie, he was an "outsider" who could not qualify for a position in the heavily aristocratic, elitist, and socially connected diplomatic service of the ministry. Like other European foreign services, sharp distinctions existed between the diplomatic and consular departments. State secretaries and their leading officials in the ministry's Berlin headquarters, and ambassadors and ministers abroad constituted the diplomatic branch. Consular officials, while they were also a part of the higher strata of the foreign service and had to complete rigorous language and civil service examinations, were junior diplomats of lesser social status who hoped for transfer to the diplomatic service.

That Prüfer now owed his career and social standing to the upper classes made the aspiring young consular official, as will be noted in ensuing chapters, even more zealous in his dedication to such exclusive groups and the Empire they ruled. Like many others in the foreign service, he absorbed the professional ethos that characterized it and that resulted from the narrow education, professional training, and experience of its members. While those in the foreign service were committed to serving the *Rechtstaat,* a government based on law, such service did not mean responsibility to the German constitution, the political leaders, or the citizens, but rather to the state itself.

Moreover, the position of Dragoman represented for Prüfer the possibility of a move into the diplomatic service. Some Dragomen held appointments as consuls and won promotions to the coveted superior branch. Although most European diplomatic agencies in the Middle East advertised their translators as unpolitical and merely students of Orientalalism, such claims rarely corresponded to reality. The Dragomen, because of their familiarity with Oriental languages and culture, studied local laws and customs and engaged in political activities that included pursuing various intrigues, spreading propaganda, and gathering intelligence.[14]

Prüfer's pride in entering the AA and thus identifying with the state also resulted from the security which belonging to the civil service provided in Imperial Germany; once appointed to the bureaucracy, one received lifetime tenure, a steady advancement according to service rendered, and various other privileges. This factor also intensified the view accepted by Prüfer and other diplomats that the authority of the AA originated in the ministry's history and its leadership and not in the Reich's constitution or people. As a child, for example, Prüfer had met Bismarck, an event that left a steadfast impression on the boy. From the beginning of his career in the Wilhelmstrasse (the street in Berlin where the AA's headquarters were located), he viewed himself as part of the foreign service that Bismarck had created.[15]

By the time of his appointment at Cairo, bitter conflict over Egypt had raged for a quarter of a century among the great powers of Europe. Much of Prüfer's fascination for the Orient and Arab culture stemmed from his interest in Germany's political clashes in the Middle East with England and other powers. His knowledge of and experiences with the British in Egypt before World War I, which are discussed in chapter 2, left him with a lifelong hatred of the English.

A consummate imperialist, he believed that the Reich's place among the European powers did not equal its potential as the most industrialized country on the continent. The English, in his view, did not deserve the empire they possessed; Germany, however, was entitled to more territory overseas. Prüfer denounced Britain's claims that its control of Egypt was legal and temporary. Instead, he maintained, England's rule there and in the Sudan enabled London to dominate Asia and Africa and purposely thwart German colonial ambitions. "England cannot relinquish Egypt," he wrote at the end of World War I, "without placing its entire Asiatic and African policy on another level." Prior to the war, he continued, "the Anglicization of Africa occurred. Only the German colonies prevented it, and indeed from Egypt there soon appeared an anti-German propaganda against German rule in East Africa. Without Egypt, India would be threatened and the penetration of Africa would be cut off from its northern base."[16]

Before examining Prüfer's personal role in the "Egyptian question," it is necessary to survey Germany's steady involvement in it and the consequences for Anglo-German relations. The land of the Nile river had been transformed into a classic arena of imperialist rivalries by England's occupation in 1882.[17] Britain needed to protect its route through the Suez canal to India from disruption both by other European powers taking advantage of the bankrupt Khedive's regime and by the growth of an antiforeign nationalist movement in Egypt. France, which had extended its imperial rule into North Africa and had invested heavily in Egypt since Napoleon's day, felt particularly cheated by the British move. Paris attempted to inhibit British rule by collaborating periodically with the other European states—especially Germany—in using its power on the International Debt Commission (*Caisse de la Dette Publique*) in Egypt, which represented the financial interests of the European powers (including Germany) and dominated Egyptian finances.[18] Confusion increased because Egypt, while occupied by British troops and governed *de facto* until 1907 by Lord Cromer, the British commissioner or resident in Cairo, remained an autonomous state within the Ottoman empire governed by its viceroy, the Khedive. In practice, the Khedive and his Egyptian officials held varying degrees of authority from the British.[19] Although the latter steadily expanded their influence over all branches of Egyptian government before World War I, their control was far from total, and they never ruled directly.

Germany had initially favored Britain in the latter's estrangement from Paris over the Egyptian question, but by the end of the 1880s Bismarck's entry into the race for overseas colonies led him to ally with the French against England.[20] This encouraged the British to make concessions to Germany in Southwest Africa, the Cameroons, Togoland, and islands that included Zanzibar, New Guinea, and Samoa.[21] Despite a brief rapprochement with London during Bismarck's last years, however, Germany's relations with England declined dramatically under William II, the young and belligerent Kaiser. Not only did he refuse to renew Bismarck's treaty with Russia, which resulted in the Franco-Russian alliance of 1892–94, but hoping to blunt the Socialist opposition to his regime by unifying the German middle and upper classes around the ideal of the Reich's military might, the emperor set forth to make Germany a world power. The resulting Weltpolitik greatly influenced Prüfer and his generation. The policy was often arrogant, however.[22] It produced sharp clashes with other nations, particularly England, over colonial territories in the Far East and Africa.[23] Both Britain and Russia, moreover, felt menaced by the sudden rush of German activity in the Middle East, which included the Kaiser's tour of the holy land and a speech in Damascus in November 1898, where he assumed the role of protector of the world's 300 million Muslims. The Reich also began construction of the Baghdad railroad, dispatched a military mission to Turkey, and its emperor tried unsuccessfully to encourage a war in 1898 between England and France during their brief armed confrontation at Fashoda in the Sudan.[24]

But the major reason for the conflict with Britain centered on Germany's construction after 1898 of a huge battle fleet, which German leaders, the press, and nationalist groups like the Pan German League (*Alldeutscher Verband*) and Colonial Union (*Kolonialverein*) hoped would force concessions from England. Many Germans, including Prüfer, wholly accepted the nationalists' view that England was responsible for the antagonism between the two countries.[25] Building the fleet, however, ended in disaster by producing an isolation of Germany that its leaders interpreted in hysterical fashion as an "encirclement" or "iron ring" imposed on the country from the outside.

When the Kaiser and his advisers rejected England's feelers for an alliance with Germany, London settled its colonial differences with France in 1904 and Russia in 1907, thus completing the Triple Entente that enveloped the Reich. Although Bismarck's Triple Alliance with Austria-Hungary and Italy in 1882 had formed the first major alliance in Europe during the period leading up to World War I, the Entente heightened Germany's paranoia. Berlin attempted new and unsuccessful diplomatic ventures aimed at splitting the Western powers, such as the first Moroccan crisis of 1905–06.[26]

The Anglo-French *entente cordiale* represented a severe blow for German diplomacy in Egypt. France agreed to limit the authority of the Egyptian Debt Commission and to support an eventual reform of the capitulations, the legal privileges granted by the Khedive's regime to Europeans in Egypt, thus virtually abandoning the administration of the country to England. This made obsolete the old German device of exploiting Anglo-French tension over Egypt to acquire colonial cessions from Britain. The setback shocked the Germans, who tried to recover by asking London to compensate them for what had happened in Egypt.

Although the remaining European powers on the Debt Commission agreed quickly to the changes in alliances, German assent came only in July 1904 after long and bitter negotiations that left much ill feeling on both sides. An agreement between the German and Egyptian governments provided that the mixed tribunals hearing cases involving the capitulations would continue, that a German would retain leadership of the Egyptian national library, and that German cultural and trade interests would remain protected.[27]

Curt Prüfer's arrival in Egypt thus coincided with an intensifying of the divisions and fears among Germany and its rivals. Now deprived of using Egypt to its advantage in the colonial sphere, Berlin involved itself more directly in Egyptian affairs, hoping thereby to enhance its economic and political interests in the Orient and intensify its pressure on England and France. With little regard for its consequences, Prüfer and his superiors at the German consulate general in Cairo played a central role in the new policy.

two

Dragoman in Cairo, 1907-13

"FOR the last nine years," declared *The Times* of London shortly after the beginning of World War I, "the German Government has set itself to weaken British power and prestige in Egypt by politico-financial and political propaganda actively supported by the German Agency at Cairo." The paper implied that the German activity represented a major justification for England's part in the war against the Reich. As one of the culprits in the German campaign in Egypt, the paper identified "the Oriental Secretary of the Agency, Dr. Pruefer, a retiring little man, a fine Arabic scholar, who had travelled not a little in Syria."[1]

The Times overestimated the contribution of German policy in Egypt to the war's origins. However, it correctly linked Prüfer, a slightly built man with grayish-brown eyes, pointed nose, and thinning hair, and his notorious mentor in Cairo, Max Freiherr von Oppenheim, to the intrigue. German activity along the Nile after 1907 suffered from the usual inconsistency, lack of direction, and fuzzy motives that characterized much of foreign policy under the Kaiser. Disagreement existed within the consulate general in Cairo over what policy should be followed. On the one hand, its leaders, Johann Heinrich Count von Bernstorff and his successor, Hermann Count von Hatzfeldt, while supporting a more active German presence in Egypt, wished to limit it and not antagonize the British into establishing more rigid controls, thus damaging Germany's economic opportunities. On the other hand, the subordinate officials in the agency, particularly the Dragoman, Prüfer, and his immediate superior, Baron von Oppenheim, were extreme Anglophobes who pursued political activities aimed at undermining British rule in Egypt. Oppenheim in particular encouraged the idea of a German-inspired "holy war" of the Muslims against England; as early as 1898, his views had impressed William II and prompted the latter's anti-British speech in Damascus.

With few exceptions, the AA permitted such divisions; although it periodically counseled caution in Egypt,[2] it deferred to the Kaiser and the requirements of Weltpolitik. German leaders especially wished to use incidents such as the Moroccan crises of 1905–06 and 1911 to force compensation from the Western powers in the colonial regions of Central Africa (*Mittelafrika*), which Berlin hoped to link with Germany through the latter's economic and political penetration of the Ottoman empire (e.g., the Baghdad railroad). Nor was the concept of going to war to settle the Reich's differences with its enemies, both abroad and at home, new among German military and political leaders.[3]

Anti-British Politics and Oppenheim's Example

Prüfer, on assuming his duties as Dragoman in February 1907, spent much of his time translating official documents, acting as interpreter for the consul general, Bernstorff, in the latter's meetings with Egyptian leaders, and studying the capitulations, the special agreements granting extraterritorial rights to Europeans in Egypt.[4] Although Berlin had agreed in July 1904 to support an eventual revision of the capitulations, it continued to demand that they remain unchanged, viewing them as necessary for protecting the limited German trade in the country.[5]

Prüfer and other German officials further defended the capitulations on the basis of their belief in the virtues of European, and especially German, imperialism. Despite his knowledge of Arab culture, Prüfer showed little genuine sympathy for it or for Islam. Sharing a social Darwinian view widely held in the West, he portrayed the Muslims in newspaper articles which he published in Germany as backward, superstitious, and inferior to Europeans. He criticized the Muslims' family life and education and argued for their Europeanization; the most praiseworthy aspects of Arab marriages, he maintained in an article in *Der Tag,* existed in their "perpetuation of the race" and their society's penalizing of families without children.[6] Change would only come to the Arabs, he concluded, through extensive European influence.

By the spring of 1907, however, Bernstorff feared that the aging and authoritarian Lord Cromer, the British resident in Egypt, intended to abolish the capitulations, thereby restricting foreign activity and tightening British control over the Egyptian nationalist movement. That movement, while confined to the minority of educated and professional classes and suffering from internal divisions, nevertheless agitated in newspapers and schools for the removal of British rule and formed its own political parties in 1907 in response to the major crises of the previous year at Akaba and Dinshawai. The nationalists demanded some form of self-government, greater participation in Egypt's parliamentary bodies, and a reform of the capitulations.[7]

Cromer agreed only with the last nationalist demand. German opposition to any change in the capitulations took various forms; though Bernstorff carefully avoided discussion of the matter in meetings with Cromer, he warned the Wilhelmstrasse and Reich chancellor, Bernhard Prince von Bülow, of the suspected British action.[8] Articles also appeared in the German press, rousing public opinion against removal of the capitulations and claiming bitterly that Englishmen received preferences in Egyptian trade and government contracts. Such accusations irritated London, which complained to the Reich foreign minister through its ambassador in Berlin.[9] That the British made no effort to abolish the capitulations, however, resulted less from the German attitude than from Cromer's resignation in April 1907 and replacement by the less ruthless Sir Eldon Gorst.

The German policy that most angered Cromer and his successors, however, was the consulate general's relationship with the nationalists and the Khedive, the Austrian-educated Abbas Hilmi II, whose influence had been steadily eroded by the British since his assumption of the throne and earliest rebellions against them in 1892 and 1893. In addition to working with Bernstorff, Prüfer also worked for another powerful official in the consulate general, Baron von Oppenheim, known to the British as "the Kaiser's Spy." Prüfer learned much from the Baron about intriguing with the Arabs against England. Oppenheim, a former Jew who had converted to Christianity, the son of a Cologne banker, and a passionate archeologist, had traveled and studied extensively in the Orient and Africa and served as an attaché in Cairo since 1896. He spoke Arabic fluently, but with a bad accent. Obsessed with rising from the consular to the prestigious diplomatic service, a goal he never achieved because of the German government's discrimination against him on the basis of his Jewish background, the Baron spent much of his time and personal fortune in acquiring influence with various Arab sheikhs, Egyptian nationalists and journalists, and the notoriously anti-British Turkish high commissioner in Cairo, Mukhtar Pasha, in the hope of persuading his government to promote him.[10]

Dressed in Arab garb and using the pretext of excavating ancient ruins and archeological sites in the desert, Oppenheim and Prüfer visited Bedouin tribes in Egypt and Syria.[11] They presented the sheikhs with gifts and denounced the British. Their visits also confirmed Oppenheim's long-held view that Germany should encourage Pan-Islamic ideas as a means for subverting the Muslim subjects of the Reich's potential enemies. Oppenheim repeatedly prophesied to the AA the rise of Egyptians against British rule if troops of the leader of Islam, the Ottoman Sultan, appeared at the Suez Canal, or if a war began in Europe that involved England.[12] During 1908 and 1909, he maintained that the revolution of the nationalist Young Turks in Constantinople strengthened Pan Islam, and he urged radical Egyptian nationalists to unite with the Young Turks against the British. The Baron also continually proclaimed to the extreme nationalist press in Egypt that Europe, particularly England and France, threatened Islam with extinction. Germany, he declared, was the only European power friendly to Muslims because it had befriended the Turkish Sultan-Caliph, the leader of the Islamic world and last hope of the faithful followers of the prophet Muhammad.[13]

Oppenheim especially cultivated ties to the Egyptian nationalists and the Khedive, hoping to encourage them to form an anti-British alliance.[14] He introduced Prüfer to such circles, and the Dragoman eventually developed strong contacts with the nationalists. As early as 1905 Oppenheim had organized a large reception in Berlin for Mustafa Kamil, the leader of the most radical nationalist faction, the *al-Hizb al-Watani*. The Baron claimed that his interviews with Kamil especially irritated Lord Cromer, who placed the German's house under surveillance and even sought unsuccessfully through the AA to achieve Oppenheim's removal from Egypt. But according to Ronald Storrs, the Oriental secretary of the British residency in Cairo, Oppenheim "was not, save as a genial host and an enterprising rather than a profound archaeologist, taken very seriously by the British or indeed by the Germans either."[15]

Following Cromer's resignation, however, the new British resident, Gorst, made Oppenheim's activities even less effective. Seeking to blunt the outburst of nationalism against Cromer's coercive tactics, he pursued a policy of reconciliation with the Khedive, thereby discouraging further Abbas Hilmi's friendship with the nationalists and exploiting their differences over the form of Egyptian government they wanted. The calls of some nationalists for a constitution and a parliamentary regime threatened the Khedive's position and family even more than British rule had.[16]

Oppenheim's lack of success may have been a factor in his resignation from the consulate general at the beginning of 1910 to pursue his excavation of an ancient Hittite city, Tell Halaf, which he had discovered in Syria. Another probable cause was continuing conflict with Bernstorff; the Baron repeatedly corresponded with the Reich chancellor, Bülow, over the indignant head of the consul general. The latter disliked Oppenheim's independence and underground activities, fearing their use by the British as a pretext for establishing a protectorate over Egypt and eliminating foreign activity (including Germany's) entirely. Bernstorff, moreover, sharply disagreed with Oppenheim's enthusiastic estimates of the Pan-Islamic movement or what Egypt would do in a European war.[17] But Oppenheim apparently knew the Kaiser, who called him the "feared spy"; the latter helped shape William's belief in Pan Islam and its usefulness in fomenting revolts among Muslims in the Anglo-French colonies.[18]

Probably the most important reason for Oppenheim's departure from Egypt and the German consular service, however, involved his usefulness to German policy in the Syrian and Mesopotamian sectors of the Ottoman empire. Advertising himself as a private citizen and archeologist, he conspired during 1911 with the former head of the Egyptian national library, Professor Moritz, to purchase the support of Arab and Kurdish tribal chiefs in the Khabur valley region for the Baghdad railroad, Germany's main project for expanding its influence in the Middle East. The German agents also pitted the Arab tribes against each other, hoping thereby to eliminate those who opposed construction of the railroad through their land.[19]

Intrigue: The Nationalists and the Libyan War

Even before Oppenheim left Cairo, however, the Wilhelmstrasse replaced Bernstorff with Count von Hatzfeldt. Although Hatzfeldt also discouraged activities that might antagonize the British, such as articles in the German press critical of English policy in Egypt, he felt less restrained than his predecessor and allowed anti-British intrigue to take a sharper turn.[20] Oppenheim's pupil, Prüfer, stood at the center of it. Despite Hatzfeldt's wish to limit the German press's comment on Egyptian affairs, the Dragoman was permitted to publish articles in Berlin and Hamburg papers advertising the importance of the Suez Canal in the world economy and urging Germany to rival Britain by expanding German trade and cultural influence in Egypt.

In other articles Prüfer decried the weakening of a potential anti-British movement in Egypt, caused by divisions between the Egyptian nationalists and the Khedive. He condemned the nationalists' attacks on Abbas Hilmi, maintaining that the Khedive, whose power had been "stripped from him" by the "absolute but irresponsible foreign rule" of England, represented the "last obstacle to the total merging of the land of the Nile into the *Imperium Britannica.*"[21] The nationalist movement, he suggested, had failed to educate the Egyptian masses about their exploitation by Britain, leaving them "to insult the inactive government or call for foreign help." Such education, Prüfer concluded, must come from out-side Egypt. "Here there indeed exists a rich field for European activity," he wrote in the *Hamburger Montagsblatt* in January 1911. "France and Italy have recognized for a long time the great advantages of founding schools and spreading their languages in Egypt for their trade and politi-cal influence. . . . The establishment of German activity in this region, which must naturally remain free of any political coloration, would only be desired."[22]

Despite Prüfer's disagreement with the nationalists and support of the Khedive, he developed intimate ties to the former during 1910 and 1911. As Dragoman, he was the channel through which the German consulate general communicated with Egyptian leaders. His activities reflected the German—and his own—antagonism towards Britain far more than any concern for the Egyptians. He wore Arab dress on many occasions, espe-cially when he visited the Al Azhar University in Cairo, where he met with nationalist students. He held numerous interviews with the most radical anti-British leaders of the national party, including Muhammad Farid, Ali Fahmy Kamil (brother of the deceased Mustafa Kamil, one of the founders of the nationalist movement), and the fiery Sheikh Abdul Aziz Shawish.

Prüfer also attended meetings of the nationalists with Hatzfeldt at the latter's residence. The Germans spent much time seeking to use their guests to improve Germany's position in the Ottoman empire.[23] Many of the Young Turks, prior to their revolution and seizure of power in Con-stantinople during 1908–09, had taken refuge in Egypt because it was distant from Turkey and it offered them relatively greater freedom under British administration. The revolutionaries made contacts with Egyptian nationalists, and when the rebels replaced the despotic Sultan, Abdul Hamid II, with his benign brother, Muhammad V, promising to create a government that granted equality for Turk and non-Turk alike, the Egyp-tians responded with enthusiastic support for the new regime.

The Young Turk government resulted at first in a lessening of German and Russian influence in the Ottoman empire and a sharp rise in the popularity of England, which the new rulers in Constantinople identified with political liberty.[24] Hatzfeldt and Prüfer, in their talks with the Egyp-tian nationalists, emphasized the Reich's friendship for both Turkey and Egypt; moreover, the German officials declared, Berlin was "so inter-ested in the Egyptian question that the Emperor holds the Nationalist party in high esteem." Hatzfeldt encouraged the nationalists to arouse public opinion in Egypt against an alliance between Britain and Turkey and suggested that each of the nationalist parties emphasize the idea in its press.

The German consulate general also funneled money and favors to the radical nationalists. It supported a nationalist school in Cairo, paid for the education of fifty Al Azhar University students in the Reich, and arranged for asylum in Germany of Al Ghayali, a nationalist exiled to Turkey for publishing a seditious pamphlet. The Germans, furthermore, permitted the national party to send its mail by Reich diplomatic courier to and from Constantinople and to Europe, thus avoiding surveillance or censorship by the Egyptian government and aiding the movement's foreign contacts. The consulate general even contributed cash to the party.

In return for the favors, Hatzfeldt asked not only for the nationalists to agitate in Turkey against Britain but also to help Germany expand its economic position in Egypt. He stressed the necessity of persuading wealthy Egyptians to deposit their money in the recently established German Orientbank and urged the party to publicize that the bank made loans at a cheaper rate than either the French bank, the Credit Foncier, or the Egyptian national and agricultural banks. Muhammad Farid, the leader of the nationalists, agreed in November 1911 to dispatch members of the movement "into the provinces at the expense of the German Agency, to enlarge upon the advertising of the Deutsche Orient Bank."[25]

While such efforts apparently produced little success for the Germans in either the Egyptian economy or in Turkey, the enormous political and military problems of the new Ottoman government eventually reestablished Berlin's influence in Constantinople. Turkey's loss of much of Libya to Italy in the war of 1911–12 and its losses in the Balkan wars greatly concerned Germany's leaders, who viewed Turkey as the crucial link between Germany's future domination of Europe and expansion into Asia and Africa.

During the Turco-Italian war, Berlin faced the dilemma of which of its allies to support. Tied to Italy through Bismarck's Triple Alliance of 1882 and to Turkey by extensive political and economic relations with the Sublime Porte (the Ottoman government, named from the gate of the Sultan's palace), Berlin ultimately backed both sides and accused England of instigating the war to divide the Reich from its allies.[26] As a part of the aid to Turkey, the German agency in Cairo collected money from Egyptians and recruited Bedouins as soldiers to help their fellow tribesmen and Turkish forces in Libya fight the Italians. Hatzfeldt created an Egyptian pro-Turkish relief committee that deposited its money in the German Orientbank, which forwarded the funds to Turkish diplomats in Paris and Tripoli.

Prüfer served as a principal figure in enlisting the Egyptian fighters. Apparently influenced by his friend, Oppenheim, he attempted to exploit Pan-Islamic feelings to persuade the Egyptians to help their coreligionists to the west. Though the Dragoman himself held little genuine respect for Arab or Islamic culture, he portrayed the Libyan conflict as another example of the alien and infidel Europe attacking the Islamic world. A leader of one of the Pan-Islamic movements, Muhammad al-Sherei, arranged meetings for Prüfer with tribesmen from the Libyan frontier who brought intelligence information and discussed the amount of assistance which the Egyptians could provide. Working through a relative of the Khedive, Prince Omar Tussoun, and a recruitment office in Cairo headed by a Turk, Gaafar Bey Hamad, Prüfer enrolled Egyptian volunteers, promising them money and gifts both when they enlisted and when they crossed the border into Libya.

Although the campaign raised far less money and fewer volunteers than the Germans planned and had a miniscule effect on the course of the war, the Ottoman defeats in Libya and the Balkans in 1912–13 prompted a coup in Constantinople that placed Young Turks in power who were more conservative, nationalistic, and pro-German.[27] Enver Pasha, their leader, had served as a military attaché in Berlin and admired German power and efficiency. In May 1913, the Turks asked that Germany renew its military mission to the Ottoman empire to reorganize the Turkish army;[28] a few months later, a group of forty German officers led by Liman von Sanders arrived in Constantinople. The mission particularly damaged Germany's relations with Russia, which feared the German military presence next to its southern border and the Black Sea straits. Amid the other diplomatic crises on the eve of World War I, Germany's ties to Turkey drove St. Petersburg even closer to its anti-German allies, Britain and France.

The involvement of Hatzfeldt, Prüfer, and other German officials in enlisting the aid of Egyptians in the Turco-Italian war and in promoting anti-British sentiment in Turkey did not escape the attention of the British administration in Egypt. German intrigue with the Egyptian nationalists concerned Britain because of the anti-British outburst of the nationalists in 1910 and 1911. Tensions between the nationalists and the substantial minority of Coptic Christians exploded with the assassination of Egypt's Coptic prime minister, Butrus Ghali, by a young nationalist fanatic. Britain's unease was increased when one of the Egyptian parliamentary bodies condemned its government's agreement to extend the Suez Canal concession to Britain for forty years.

"Dr. Pruefer is evidently impossible"

These events resulted in the appointment of a new British resident, Lord Herbert Kitchener, the hero of Britain's conquest of the Sudan and a notoriously autocratic leader. He revived the ruthless policies of Cromer, dealing harshly with the Khedive by decreasing the latter's authority over even ceremonial matters and threatening to depose him. Kitchener also sought to weaken the nationalist movement by playing on its divisions; he collaborated with its moderate party, but refused to tolerate the leaders of the extremist faction, whom he imprisoned or exiled. Many of the radicals took refuge in Constantinople, Paris, and Switzerland by 1913.[29]

Kitchener's crusade also touched the Germans. He unleashed a controversy with Hatzfeldt and the German government in September 1911 by refusing their suggestions that the Egyptian national library appoint the Dragoman, Prüfer, as its new director and that the Cairo museum name a German as its second in command. A German official, Professor Moritz, whom the British labeled as "anti-English," had held the leadership of the library until his transfer by Berlin to Syria with Oppenheim.[30] Moreover, the German agreement with Egypt in July 1904 had stipulated that the directorship of the library should remain in German hands.[31]

The prestigious library appointment promised to enhance the young Prüfer's career significantly. That the Cairo government would pay his salary, thereby necessitating his resignation from the AA, would be a supreme recognition of his talent in the fields of Arab culture and Egyptology. Furthermore, his position would contribute to German influence in each subject and provide the new library director with easy access to leading Egyptian cultural and political figures. The German consulate general could exploit such contacts to increase its ties to the nationalists and other officials. Heading the library thus offered Prüfer the opportunity to fulfill his ambition of rising in the German sociopolitical hierarchy by using his intellectual abilities.

The appointment became mired in politics, however. When a representative of the consulate general, Baron von Richthofen, proposed Prüfer as the replacement, portraying him as a brilliant Arab scholar and claiming "that there was no other person in the whole of Germany suitable for the post," Kitchener responded that while the agreement of 1904 had designated that a German should head the library, nothing implied that the Reich government should be consulted about his appointment. "If the Germans could not find a suitable candidate," Kitchener told Richthofen, "the Egyptian Government, on their part, were confident that they would have no difficulty in doing so." The resident reported Prüfer's anti-English ventures to the Foreign Office in London and concluded: "These facts seem to be sufficient evidence that Dr. Pruefer's activities are those of a confidential political agent, rather than those of a student of Arabic as Baron Richthofen endeavors to represent." An official in the office's eastern department agreed and observed, apparently with some exasperation: "Dr. Pruefer is evidently impossible."[32]

A month later, Hatzfeldt visited Kitchener and pressed further for Prüfer's appointment. Even Sir Edward Grey, the British foreign minister, received a visit from the German ambassador in London, Paul Count von Wolff-Metternich. The ambassador, said Grey, "deprecated" the objection taken to Prüfer's appointment. "Dr. Pruefer was a man of much tact and learning," Grey quoted the German ambassador as saying, "who got on well with Europeans and natives. If there were any facts of a political or personal nature on which objection was taken to him, Count Metternich hoped that I would inform him of them, in which case an explanation would be given."[33]

Despite the British opposition to Prüfer, the Germans persisted with his candidacy. Hatzfeldt complained to Kitchener again, adamantly defending the Dragoman and noting that the affair had resulted in "a certain note of personal unpleasantness" for the diplomats involved. The consul general judged correctly. A low-ranking official in the British Foreign Office, Robert Vansittart, complained: "As to Pruefer, his relations with the Nationalists are simply undeniable, and it is foolish of the Germans to go on vowing that he is calumniated."[34] Storrs, the Oriental secretary at the British residency in Cairo, recalled later: "I knew and liked Dr. Prüfer, but the more I learnt of his talents and activities the less suitable a candidate did he seem for a position which would maintain him, *ex officio,* in close and daily contact with the Intelligentsia of Young Egypt [the nationalists]."[35] Kitchener soon received an opinion from the Egyptian government; the latter agreed with the English assessment of Prüfer, supplied Kitchener with a lengthy report on the Dragoman's relations to Oppenheim and the Egyptian nationalists, and urged that the library appoint an Egyptian as its new director.[36]

The Egyptian view provided the British with a convenient escape, which they used, along with a French request that one of their Egyptologists receive an appointment in the Cairo museum, as further reasons to deny Prüfer the position. Hatzfeldt, however, persisted; in January 1912, he wrangled a compromise from Kitchener. In exchange for naming an Egyptian to head the national library, Germany received several concessions that included the post of assistant director in the library, which did not go to Prüfer; the headship of the less prestigious Cairo museum; a position in the Egyptian public health department; and a public award for Prüfer from the Khedive. Kitchener also agreed on a job in the museum for a Frenchman.

Kitchener's deal with the Germans dismayed his colleagues in the Foreign Office, however; one lamented, "The Germans got three posts instead of one . . . and a decoration for a man whom we know has been intriguing against us."[37] In the end, Berlin rejected the British offers because they did not "equal" the directorship of the Khedivial library. The Germans persisted in declaring that Prüfer interested himself only in Oriental scholarship and literature and not in politics. Consequently, the Cairo government gave the library position in 1913 to Ahmad Lutfi al-Sayyid, a leading Egyptian political philosopher and editor of the newspaper published by a moderate nationalist party. Lutfi welcomed British and western influence in developing Egypt and rejected the idea of Egyptian nationalism based on Pan Islamism and on an Arab or Turkish lineage.[38]

The affair left both sides resentful. It probably encouraged Kitchener to take further measures against suspected German influence, which included the forced removal in the fall of 1913 of the pro-German Yussuf Saddik Pasha as secretary to the Khedive.[39] The AA soon replaced Hatzfeldt with the former counselor at the German embassy in Constantinople, the scholarly and cultivated Hans von Miquel. Because the library incident had revealed damaging information about German activity in Egypt, the new consul general apparently refrained from mingling with the nationalists, many of whom were in prison or exile. Miquel met frequently with the Khedive, however. The Khedive, apparently because of the harsh treatment accorded him by Kitchener and the series of military defeats suffered by Turkey, the legal and historical source from which he derived his position, cultivated relations with Miquel. Not knowing what the future held, he tried to offset his precarious relationship with the British by courting German support.[40]

The library incident also destroyed Prüfer's credibility with the British administration and the Egyptian government and severely limited his political and intelligence activity. One can only guess how much his rejection by the Egyptians and the British, whom he clearly considered inferior, intensified his search for personal success and fulfillment through service to the German state. His work and that of the other diplomats at the consulate general provided examples of the worst features of Germany's Weltpolitik: its insistence on exploiting each diplomatic crisis, no matter how unimportant, by demanding concessions from its rivals while offering them little in return. Berlin, with more significant consequences, followed such a policy towards Russia in 1909 during the Bosnian crisis and towards France and England in the second Moroccan affair in 1911.

The effort to wring advantages from Britain along the Nile, however, resulted partly from a lack of unified goals towards Egypt and partly from the ambition of men like Prüfer and Oppenheim to make their reputation in Berlin with little regard for the impact of their actions. Such behavior irritated the British and possibly contributed, along with the more important Moroccan conflict and the Reich's continued naval buildup, to Germany's failure in 1911 and 1912 to negotiate an agreement with London establishing Britain's neutrality in the event of a European war.[41]

Prüfer's experiences with the British, furthermore, shed light on the policies they employed to govern Egypt and protect their interests there. The British residents carefully manipulated the Egyptian government and played it off against the other European powers. When forced to do so, as in the library affair, the British changed their previous agreements with the other powers or interpreted them to their own advantage. The Anglo-German clash involving Prüfer also illustrated how German behavior in colonial confrontations with England exasperated the London Foreign Office, whose officials disliked the Reich's policies. Moreover, the German stubbornness in demanding Prüfer's appointment to the library encouraged the British to cooperate with France by granting the latter's request that one of its officials receive a position in the Cairo museum.

Prüfer left the foreign service on 12 November 1913.[42] No records survive to explain his relationship to the AA or whether his withdrawal resulted from a genuine frustration with his experience in Egypt and a wish to devote the immediate future to his scholarly interests. Possibly, like Oppenheim previously, his separation from official duty provided him with a new cover for further intrigue. Not only had he contributed to the failure of German diplomats to enhance their nation's position in Egypt, but he had also suffered a bitter personal setback when snubbed by the British and Egyptians for the prestigious library position. Prüfer traveled for the next seven months along the Upper Nile River with the German painter, Richard von Below, whose etchings from the trip appeared after World War I. Prüfer enriched Below's art with anonymous translations of Arabic poems from Abdul-'Ala al-Ma'arri, the gifted and blind poet from the tenth century.[43] He also published extensively on Egyptian culture in newspapers and in *Bädekers Ägypten,* the famed German travel guide.

Returning to the Reich in the summer of 1914, he lectured privately on Oriental languages in Munich.[44] Only a few weeks later, however, the assassination at Sarajevo of the heir to the Austro-Hungarian throne, Franz Ferdinand, ignited war in the Balkans that soon pitted the partners of the Triple Alliance, Germany and Austria-Hungary, against England and its allies, France and Russia. The conflict prompted Prüfer's sudden return to the foreign service and the Middle East.

three

The "Holy War" that Failed, 1914-15

LIKE most Europeans, Prüfer greeted the news of the war in August 1914 with excitement and enthusiasm. He immediately offered his services to the AA for "inciting unrest in Egypt" against the British. "The possibility of destroying the British occupation forces in Egypt that would lead easily to the blocking of the Suez canal," he suggested to the government, existed for Germany if it appealed to the Egyptian "mixture of unsatisfied greed and distaste for rulers who are of an alien religion."[1] Confident of victory and the contribution he could make to it, Prüfer soon rejoined the AA, which dispatched him to Turkey to help organize the subversive operation that he had suggested.

His strategy mirrored that of many in his government—the Kaiser, the chancellor, Theobald von Bethmann Hollweg, the chief of the general staff, and top officials in the Wilhelmstrasse, including the undersecretary of state, Arthur Zimmermann. Their grandiose war aims included stopping the erosion of popular support for the monarchy inside the Reich by destroying the British, Russian and French empires and replacing them with German hegemony; one means by which the German leaders intended to achieve this goal involved promoting revolution among Muslims and other peoples within the far-flung European empires.[2] As war engulfed Europe, the Central Powers of Germany and Austria-Hungary concluded an alliance with Turkey on 2 August 1914, hoping to make Constantinople the base for unleashing a Pan-Islamic movement and "holy war" (*jihad*) against the British in India and Egypt and the Russians and British in Persia.[3]

The AA, to conduct its revolutionary activities in the Islamic world, quickly recalled Oppenheim to service.[4] He soon headed a newly created special information bureau for Middle Eastern affairs (*Nachrichtenstelle für den Orient*) in the ministry.[5] The bureau collaborated with the political section of the army reserve general staff in Berlin during the remainder of 1914 and 1915 in sending a series of expeditions to Persia, headed by the Reich consul there, Wilhelm Wassmuss, and to Afghanistan, led by Oskar von Niedermayer and Werner Otto von Hentig.

These ventures, poorly organized and unsuccessful, aimed at persuading both countries to enter the war on the German side. Other operations, equally abortive, focused on inciting anti-British and anti-French activities among the Senussi tribes in Libya, the Bedouins in Arabia, and the Ethiopians, Arabs, and Berbers in North Africa.[6] The leaders of the campaigns, promoted by postwar political writers, later advertised themselves in romantic fashion as the German version of the legendary "Lawrence of Arabia."[7]

Prüfer, although he, too, fell far short of the British colonel's success in helping mobilize Arab support for England, was also described after the war as a "German Lawrence."[8] Such exaggerated comparisons notwithstanding, he contributed significantly to organizing the Reich's other major (and unsuccessful) expedition in the Middle East, the German-Turkish military operations against the Suez Canal in February 1915 and August 1916, and in other positions later in the war. His value especially rested on his ability to speak fluent Arabic and to move easily among the Bedouins dressed as one of them, a rarity among the hundreds of German officers in wartime Turkey.[9]

Arrival in Constantinople

Barely a week after the declaration of war in Europe and two months before the Porte joined in the conflict, the AA issued Prüfer a passport. He left Berlin by train for Constantinople on the morning of 28 August 1914 with hastily conceived orders to organize an anti-British revolt in Egypt by spreading reports there that the leader of Islam, the Sultan-Caliph of Turkey, intended soon to join Germany in the war. The extravagant plan included liquidating the British officer corps in the Egyptian army, blocking the Suez Canal, and blowing up railroads and important port installations.[10] Until Turkey entered the war on 2 November, Berlin had little hope of conducting a military operation against the canal.

Prüfer, on passing through Vienna during his journey to Turkey, noted an "enthusiastic war mood" in the city, and while traveling toward Rumania he observed "great enthusiasm" among the many trainloads of

Austro-Hungarian troops moving from the Serbian to the Russian front.[11]
He arrived in Constantinople on 3 September 1914 and met the next day
at the German embassy with the ambassador, Baron Hans von
Wangenheim, and Captain Humann, the Reich naval attaché, to discuss
Prüfer's assignment. Prüfer immediately noticed problems. Personal ri-
valries and "a lack of cooperation" characterized the relations between
Wangenheim and the German military mission in Turkey, headed by Li-
man von Sanders.

The meeting also revealed to him the divisions in the Porte over
whether to join Germany in the war; he discovered, moreover, that Humann and other officials feared the military weakness of the Turks, including a lack of defenses in the Dardanelles. Despite such misgivings, he
received the impression that his colleagues wished to force the Turks into
the war by "precipitating events with an action of the *Goeben,*" one of
two German cruiser ships that had entered the Dardanelles, had been sold
fictitiously to Turkey, and which could be launched across the Black Sea
against Russia. The meeting, furthermore, left Prüfer and Wangenheim
with an instant dislike for each other. While the former represented the
view of the authorities in Berlin, who urged the utmost pressure on the
Turks, the ambassador counseled caution and delay, noting the hesitancy
of Enver Pasha, the pro-German Turkish war minister, and the lack of
support among other ranking Turks for intervention in the war.

German dignitaries in Turkey just before World War I. Prüfer is second from
right.

Wangenheim, nevertheless, introduced Prüfer to Robert Mors, the principal agent in his mission to sabotage the British in Egypt until a Turkish expedition could be approved and organized to attack the Suez Canal. Mors was a lieutenant of German descent in the Alexandria police on leave in Constantinople.[12] Prüfer and Mors met in the following days with Omar Fauzi Bey and Suleiman Askeri, officials in the Porte's ministry of war who promised to cooperate with the Germans. They devised a plan to send secret agents to Egypt to organize bands (*comitaji*), each numbering ten to fifteen Egyptian marauders recruited from among criminals, to attack railroads and British property and force the English to scatter their troops throughout the country. Moreover, Fauzi intended to form groups of fifty Bedouins to raid British posts along the Suez Canal and fire on ships steaming through it.[13]

Prüfer, however, learned quickly that implementing the plans for a "revolution" in Egypt would not be as easy as he had thought a month earlier when he had offered his services to the AA for the project. The difficulties he faced in recruiting agents to carry out such operations increased because of the Turkish reluctance to allow the Germans to operate freely in their territories and because of the traditional mistrust and rivalry between the Turks and Arabs in the Ottoman empire.[14] Relations with the Egyptians were not improved when officials in the German war ministry denounced Sheikh Shawish, the exiled Egyptian nationalist in Constantinople, as a "gossiper whose service is worthless," when Prüfer reported that Shawish had offered to send secret emissaries to Egypt.

Enver and other Ottoman leaders also feared and mistrusted the Khedive, who had settled briefly in Constantinople, and rejected his offer to cooperate with the Germans in organizing the revolt in Egypt. By the end of 1914, Abbas Hilmi left for Europe, where he negotiated with other exiled Egyptian nationalists. He requested their support for his eventual return to his position in Egypt and intrigued with both the Central Powers and Entente.[15] The Turks even mistrusted the pro-Turkish prince in Central Arabia, Ibn Rashid, and discouraged Prüfer from approaching him for help.[16]

Such problems notwithstanding, Enver Pasha confirmed the plans worked out by his officials and Prüfer for triggering a revolt in Egypt and agreed to ship large batches of anti-British propaganda pamphlets there. The war minister impressed Prüfer; following their meeting on 7 September 1914, the German described Enver in his diary: "A man of stone. A beautiful face, rigidly set and well-ordered like a woman's. Groomed to the utmost. With it a trait of unmatched toughness: 'We are able to be more cruel than the English.' The man wants something; it doesn't matter what the 'something' is."[17]

The same day German chancellor Bethmann approved the even more radical project of the AA and German general staff to organize a combined German-Turkish military expedition against the canal.[18] The German military mission in Constantinople began immediate preparations. Prüfer learned of the directive in a 9 September meeting with the mission leader, Liman, who also complained bitterly about Wangenheim. The ambassador, Liman told Prüfer, had informed the AA incorrectly about Liman's views on Turkey and Germany. Liman was not as eager for the Germans to attack the Russians as Wangenheim implied to Berlin; according to Sanders, a "landing on the Russian coast of the Black sea [would be] achieved with difficulty, because the naval power [is] insufficient to protect the transports under all circumstances."[19]

Wangenheim continued to press for a cautious Reich policy, suspecting that German preparations for an operation against Egypt might alienate Germany's partner in the Triple Alliance, Italy, which had chosen to remain neutral in the war. The Italians feared any political or military action by the Turks or Central Powers in North Africa that could undermine Italy's already unstable position in Libya.[20] Wangenheim also interfered with Prüfer's activities. He urged the AA to send Prüfer to Jaffa and refused to authorize the agent's request for money to pay Sheikh Shawish to send four followers to spy in Egypt.

Nevertheless, Prüfer managed to dispatch Mors with dynamite, propaganda leaflets, and several Egyptian cohorts on a ship to Egypt. He instructed Mors to assist a Turkish officer already in Alexandria to carry out the planned comitaji operations in the city. Those accompanying Mors included an Egyptian military officer appointed as a comitaji leader.[21] During the first half of September, Prüfer had received his first information on the alleged strength of British forces in Egypt. One of his spies reported that four thousand troops had left for the Sudan and of the forty to fifty thousand remaining, London had shipped thirty thousand to France; the agent could not account for the whereabouts of the others. The report, while probably inaccurate on the figures, appeared to reflect Britain's transfer of Egyptian soldiers to the Sudan and its shipment of units from India to Egypt and to France.[22]

Problems with the Turkish Expedition

The situation soon changed for Prüfer. With William II's approval of the Egyptian expedition added to that of Bethmann Hollweg, and with Enver Pasha's increasing confidence in Turkey's defenses along the Dardanelles, marked by his inching closer to a war with Russia, the Turks agreed to allow the Germans to help prepare the Eighth Corps of the Fourth Turkish Army for the campaign against Egypt. The AA assigned Prüfer as a political adviser and intelligence agent to the Bavarian colonel, Friedrich Freiherr Kress von Kressenstein, the chief of staff of the corps, who left Constantinople on 20 September 1914 with Turkish and other German officers for the corps headquarters in Damascus.[23]

After a grueling week on trains and riding horse-drawn lorries over poor roads through the snow-covered Taurus mountains, the group arrived in Damascus. With the help of Loytved-Hardegg, the German consul in Haifa and administrator of the consulate general in Damascus, Prüfer and several other German officers feverishly assembled Bedouins, camels, and horses for the expedition. Enver had ordered the creation of a special Bedouin auxiliary unit within the Eighth Corps. Prüfer cultivated friendly relations with influential sheikhs, other Arab notables, and Ottoman officials and bribed them with "gifts and decorations." Abdin Rahman Bey, a senator in the Turkish parliament, and Sheik Essad Shukair aided Prüfer in winning Bedouin support around Damascus. At the beginning of October, Prüfer visited the Turkish governors (vali) and police chiefs of Damascus and Beirut and a family of notables near Nablus, who agreed to supply recruits for the expedition. He helped Muntaz Bey, an Arab officer in the Turkish army, enroll fifteen hundred volunteers, but the number fell far short of the several thousand which the Germans hoped for, and many, Prüfer observed, were "unreliable."[24]

In addition, Prüfer continued seeking spies to enter Egypt, including some to participate in the planned comitaji units. His efforts generally failed, however, because his dubious plan of recruiting Bedouin criminals from Lebanon displeased Turkish leaders, who delayed releasing some from prison, and because money proved insufficient to transform the new recruits into trustworthy agents. Conflicts between comitaji leaders also undermined the enterprise. Prüfer even experienced difficulties with the Mufti of Haifa, the city's religious leader, who had agreed to travel to Egypt and return with reports for the Germans.[25] The insistence of Wangenheim that Prüfer stop sending his reports directly to the AA and instead route them through the embassy in Constantinople added to his woes.[26]

Meanwhile, the British authorities in Egypt noted the problems created by the German activities. On 16 October, Sir John Maxwell, the new head of Britain's troops in Egypt, informed Kitchener: "There is rather more nervousness in Egypt, but everything is quiet. It is part of the German propaganda that a revolution in Egypt is imminent, and that there are agents all over the country fomenting the natives against the British. We can find little evidence in support of this."[27] Nevertheless, said Maxwell, he had recently captured "an undoubted spy of Enver's. He is a

German and an officer of the Alexandrian police, and he had on him when arrested a secret code, maps of the Suez canal, and two boxes of detonators."

The arrest of Mors, the German agent, and his trial in Cairo at the end of October 1914 provided the British with extensive information about Prüfer's activities in Syria.[28] London immediately announced a reward for the capture of Prüfer, Kress, and the other German officers associated with the Egyptian expedition.[29] Only a few days after Mors's trial, the British foreign minister, Sir Edward Grey, sent an official warning to the Turks "that a military violation of [the] frontier of Egypt will place them in a state of war with three allied Powers," and he included Prüfer in his complaints about the Turkish and German preparations to assault Egypt. "Dr. Prueffer [sic]," Grey informed the Porte, "who was so long engaged in intrigues in Cairo against the British occupation, and is now attached to the German Embassy in Constantinople, has been busily occupied in Syria trying to incite the people to take part in this conflict."[30]

Several days later, the Turkish fleet made coastal raids on Russian harbors, shelling and mining them. On 2 November 1914, the tsarist regime officially declared war on Turkey, and England and France soon followed. These events did little to change Prüfer's fortunes; his difficulties in recruiting reliable spies for Egypt and Bedouins for the military expedition persisted. The British established martial law in Egypt; the Egyptian government reported arresting seven hundred "Turkish, Khedivist and Nationalist agitators," and retiring "practically all German and Austro-Hungarian subjects . . . from the Egyptian Public Service."[31] A month later, Britain declared a protectorate over Egypt, deposed the Khedive, and made his uncle, Hussein, the new Egyptian ruler with the title of Sultan.

Neither the official proclamation on 14 November by the Turkish Sultan-Caliph of holy war against the Entente, which unleashed Pan-Islamic demonstrations in Constantinople, nor the appointment of the ruthless Ottoman naval minister, Djemal Pasha, as head of the fourth Turkish army improved matters for Prüfer, the remainder of Kress's staff, and Loytved-Hardegg. Conflicts between Prüfer and a leading Turkish officer, Sabih Bey, undermined the German's bargaining with the chief camel dealer near Damascus, Bassam Bey, who produced only two thousand animals for an expedition that required many more. The Bedouins, Prüfer reported to Oppenheim, "preferred either to wander off into the desert or even to sell their camels to the higher paying English in Egypt."[32]

Further, antagonism between the Germans and the Porte's governor of Damascus caused Prüfer endless difficulties in securing the Turks' release of the Bedouin criminals whom the Germans wished to use for smuggling weapons and propaganda into Egypt. Similar problems arose in procuring arms for the smugglers; apparently unable to acquire them from the Turks or his own army, Prüfer had to pay Arab agents who promised to find them in Lebanon.[33]

The first of the smugglers left for Egypt on 6 December, but only a few achieved their destination; many took payment from the Germans and then disappeared or fled into the desert because of fright when they neared Egypt. A handful may have reached the Gulf of Suez and laid a mine there which the British later recovered. Two groups rode into the Sinai. A Cherkesse, Ismirli Escref Bey, led one band that occupied part of the center of the desert. Muntaz Bey headed another that approached the Suez Canal but, when fired on, retreated in disarray to Al Arish near the Egyptian-Palestine border. "His Bedouins," Prüfer complained later, "scattered themselves to the wind."[34]

Prüfer also organized one of the earliest attempts of the Germans and Turks to raise the Senussis in Libya against Egypt. He sent two Senussi sheikhs to the Red Sea, where they planned to cross into Upper Egypt and proceed to Libya. But one sheikh quit, exhausted from the strenuous camel ride across the desert, and left on a pilgrimage to Mecca, while the other joined a Hungarian, Ungar Gondos, recruited by Prüfer to blow up British petroleum tanks in Upper Egypt. Gondos's mission also failed, however, when the British fired on his boat in the Red Sea. He tried again—unsuccessfully—in December with the objective of dynamiting the main railroad bridge across the Nile at Nag Hamadi, about five hundred kilometers south of Cairo.[35]

Similar work in Arabia also encountered troubles. In addition to the AA sending the Orientalists, Moritz and Alois Musil, there, Prüfer directed agents to the Hejaz along the Red Sea, especially two Indian brothers with orders to influence Indian and Egyptian pilgrims visiting the Muslim shrines at Mecca and Medina. The reports he received from there persuaded him by October and November that Hussein Ibn Ali, the Grand Sharif of Mecca and the guardian of the holy cities, was pro-British and untrustworthy. He also judged Ibn Saud, one of the main Arab princes in the Nejd in Central Arabia and a foe of the Sharif, and the Idrissi, the Emir of Asir (along the southern seaboard), similarly.

Although the Turks pressured Hussein to join the holy war against the Entente, the Sharif's secret contacts with Britain about his possible support in exchange for England's backing of his independence from Turkey, apparently unknown to the Germans, proved the accuracy of Prüfer's suspicions.[36] Not only did German intelligence fail to uncover the Sharif's activities, but Prüfer also appeared not to realize the Sharif's political ambitions. He underestimated the prince's power and thought that the new Ottoman governor of the Hejaz, Wehib Bey, controlled Hussein. A bit arrogantly, Prüfer informed Oppenheim on 3 November 1914 that the Sharif "is thoroughly English, but luckily powerless and in our hands." The AA and Oppenheim ignored still another of Prüfer's warnings at the end of December about the Sharif and later believed him a loyal propagandist for the German and Turkish cause.[37]

The Abortive Attack on the Canal

The lack of information about Egypt concerned Oppenheim and was even more disquieting to the Wilhelmstrasse; even as Oppenheim decried the insufficient number of German Orientalists available to send to the Middle East, he proposed establishing an official intelligence bureau in Turkey and Persia.[38] Information was so scarce that when the Turks brought the flag (*sanjak*) of the prophet Muhammad from Medina to Jerusalem to symbolize the beginning of the jihad and the bulk of the Turkish expedition, numbering 20,000 men, left from Beersheba during mid-January 1915 to cross the Sinai to attack the Suez Canal, the force's leaders possessed no accurate estimates of the canal's defenses. They knew little except that Indian troops passed through the canal; at the end of October 1914, Prüfer had received a report estimating British strength in Egypt at 11,000 soldiers, with half guarding the canal. But by the time of the move on the Suez, more Indian detachments and the first Australian and New Zealand units had arrived, and Egypt possessed a considerable garrison approaching 70,000 troops, greatly outnumbering the Turks.[39]

Kress later acknowledged the failure to construct an effective intelligence system.[40] Indeed, the lack of information may have contributed to the decision of the Turks and Germans to launch the expedition, despite its severe deficiencies in troops, modern weapons, and supplies (especially water) and in transportation across the Sinai desert. Kress, Prüfer, and the other German officers in the expedition realized such problems and even feared the outcome of the operation.

Nonetheless, Prüfer argued to Kress and Djemal Pasha against the suggestion of the German reserve general staff in Berlin to delay the attack until supply lines improved. Although the German high command overruled the proposal and pressed Enver to carry out the expedition immediately, Prüfer's views are interesting in that they reflect how, despite his misgivings about the holy war, he still misjudged its effect on the Egyptians and was willing to risk the entire operation on it. He informed Oppenheim on 31 December 1914 that "the enthusiasm for the holy war in Syria and Palestine . . . is artificial" and if one "were to delay the march, so undoubtedly the carefully manufactured enthusiasm would disappear and the old indifference, if certainly not hostility, take its place." Even worse, he added, the failure of the Turks to attack "would be tantamount to the total discouragement of the Egyptians, who are cowards anyway."[41]

Further uncertainties about the jihad must have resulted from the meeting Prüfer and several other German officers held with Hussein's son, the Emir Abdullah, as they left Palestine with the expedition on 11 January 1915. They met near Hebron, and Prüfer appeared uneasy about what he saw and heard. "The sharif invited us to tea," he recorded in his diary, "which made no special impression on me. He gossiped much and emphasized to excess his friendship for the Ottomans. With crossed legs, we sat on carpet in front of the colored tent of the holy man, who was surrounded by a small band of companions and his brother. Among other things, he said that he had been a burden for Lord Cromer in Cairo."[42]

It took the Turkish expedition two weeks to cross the nearly one hundred miles of desert. The force included nine batteries of field artillery and a battery of howitzers; its principal units were the Arab Twenty-fifth Division, a regiment of the Twenty-third Division, the Tenth Division, a cavalry regiment, and several camel companies and the auxiliary unit of mounted Bedouins. Some 10,000 camels accompanied the troops to carry supplies, water, and ammunition. The Turks, and particularly the German officers, deserved credit for merely transporting such a huge force through the desert.

Djemal Pasha sent the main invasion body through a central route in the Sinai. To secure its flanks and deceive the British about the real line of attack, however, he moved two smaller detachments along a northern road parallel with the Mediterranean Sea and a southern route through Nekhl to the city of Suez. The central path led most directly to the main Turkish goal: the invasion of Egypt by seizing control of the Sweet Water Canal that ran from the Nile River at Cairo to Ismailia, where it branched north and south into the Suez Canal to the cities of Port Said and Suez. Once holding Ismailia, especially the gates and sluices there, the invader could cut off the water to Port Said and Suez and damage the position of the British forces to the north and south.

Kress's advisers, including Prüfer, traveled with the main body, marching by night to avoid the heat and hoping to conceal themselves.[43] Enduring the cold and stormy nights, sleeping on blankets without tents, and marching seven hours at a time exhausted the troops. Not only did Kress and his staff often dispute strategy with Djemal Pasha, but the Germans also resented the Ottoman commander's arranging comforts for himself that no one else had. Following Djemal's criticism of a German doctor for failing to transport enough medical supplies, for example, Prüfer angrily

Prüfer during the Suez campaign, 1915

observed: "This ambitious Napoleon in the waistcoat takes magnificent tents, hat stands, commodes, beds etc. into the desert and we sleep in the open!"[44]

As the main force reached the small village of Ibni in the eastern Sinai, Bedouin riders arrived with two prisoners, an English and an Egyptian officer. Hopes rose in the camp of acquiring useful information from them. Prüfer's interrogation of the two in front of Kress, however, achieved little, except perhaps to reinforce the Turks' low estimates of enemy troop strength. "Only Australians, New Zealanders, and Indians are in Egypt," Prüfer concluded. "No heavy guns."[45]

On 24 January 1915, the troops reached Chabra II, an oasis formed from a tiny lake situated between massive sand dunes and located forty kilometers from the canal. Early the next morning, Kress, Prüfer, and sixty others left by camel on a reconnaissance patrol to a high ridge about ten kilometers from the Suez, which yielded a view of the canal from Ismailia northward to the south end of the Bitter Lakes. Unlike the Turkish camel patrols, however, the British used airplanes for their reconnaissance and had kept themselves well informed of the Turkish advance. British planes bombed the expedition repeatedly, which frightened both Turks and Germans. The initial raids even impressed the normally daring Prüfer, who noted on 26 January: "I immediately found Kress. I confess that the smashing of the bombs, the powerful detonation, and black smoke horrified me somewhat, although I was concerned to hide."[46]

For the next two days, which included the "Kaiser's birthday" as Prüfer remarked in his diary, the Turks feigned attacks along the northern and southern extremities of their advance. They did not deceive the English. Further patrols to areas near the canal on 28–29 January filled Prüfer with a mixture of excitement and discouragement as the attack drew nearer. On the one hand, the sight of the canal full of ships and British cruisers in the Great Bitter Lake and Lake Timsah made him "determined to lead men to the battle line." Still, when the Turks discovered that the enemy had stationed no troops on the eastern bank of the canal but had heavily fortified the opposite side, he found it "almost eerie, this lack of activity," and even began doubting the outcome of the expedition. "A disaster appears to me nearly inevitable," he jotted in his diary. "The enemy cruisers in the lakes see the situation . . . completely. We will be destroyed without even generally reaching the canal."[47]

His prophecy came true. When the attack, delayed for a few hours by a sandstorm, began early on the morning of 3 February, Prüfer received orders to await the course of the struggle on a hill overlooking the canal, and when the moment appeared right, to lead a column of soldiers to Tussum to block the waterway with sacks of sand.[48] How they would acquire the thousands of sacks needed for such a dubious scheme remained unclear. Along with another German officer, he listened to the ever louder roar of the guns and caught brief glimpses of the enemy cruisers firing on the Turks from the canal. During the early afternoon, the battle intensified; shells continually landed around them. The British shelling of the Turkish field hospital, which Prüfer witnessed, especially angered him, as did reports of the ambush and destruction of two Turkish companies on Lake Timsah and the massacre of forty Turks who had succeeded in reaching the heavily defended west bank of the canal by pontoon.

Prüfer learned near evening from his colleagues on Kress's staff "that the attack had failed along the entire line." [49] Total Turkish losses numbered at least fifteen hundred; British casualties neared one hundred fifty. The Turkish retreat into the Sinai, ordered by Djemal Pasha, began immediately, "because continuing the struggle was impossible, considering the enemy's superior power." Kress, hoping to make the best of the fiasco, quickly assembled his advisers and informed them, according to Prüfer, "that the entire affair should be considered a major reconnaissance [mission]. One will hold Ibni, Arish, Bir Hassan, and Nekhl and renew the attack in the autumn with stronger forces." [50] The Turks retreated through the desert without difficulty; Prüfer arrived in Jerusalem on 11 February 1915.

The attack on the canal failed for many reasons, some already discussed here. Although the Porte organized and led the expedition, much of the blame for its outcome rested with the Germans, who pushed their allies into a premature operation without providing them with adequate weapons and supplies. Moreover, the German leaders had deceived themselves more than their Ottoman counterparts, like Djemal Pasha, by expecting the appearance of the Turks near the canal to set Egypt ablaze in the holy war against Britain.

In Prüfer's view, however, the Germans held little responsibility for what happened. He blamed others for the disaster at the canal, including those whom he considered inferior to the Germans—the Arabs, Egyptians, Turks, even the English, who had relied heavily on troops from India, Australia, and New Zealand to defend the canal. In a report to Wangenheim, for instance, he portrayed the result of the attack in significantly more favorable terms than Kress had the morning following the battle. "Although the Turkish losses are severe," he told the ambassador, "there can be no talk of a catastrophe, indeed of a defeat." He also denounced the Bedouins he had recruited as intelligence agents, calling them "cowardly" and "unqualified, because they were unable to survey the military situation correctly. We could not establish whether a revolutionary movement had arisen in Egypt." [51]

Reporting to Oppenheim, he found little fault with himself or German policies and instead blamed the Orientals for the collapse of both the jihad

and the assault on the canal. "The holy war is a tragicomedy," he declared. "The Egyptians are even cowardly in desperation and lack any
genuine love of fatherland. On the contrary, there are spectacular cases of
treason among the Egyptian officers who served with us. Also the Syri-
ans and Palestinians were of no use. The old hostility towards the Turks
stirred itself again among the officers. . . . With the first machine-gun
fire, all fled to the rear. That left only the defensive."[52]

His report concluded with a plea that Berlin send heavier artillery and
airplanes for a new assault on the canal in the fall of 1915. It also reflected his insolence and resentment towards his Turkish counterparts,
when he urged the removal of the latter from the leadership of the expedition: "The Turkish officers in command slept the entire day if they were
not bothered; their energy was only enough to offer passive resistance to
us Germans, because they felt that our work was an annoying disturbance
of their peace."[53] In a second memorandum to Oppenheim he noted "that
in fact a certain strained atmosphere exists among the Turks and the
Germans," exacerbated by German officers who had gone to Turkey "to
make a quick career or money."[54]

The failure of the expedition to secure a foothold near the canal and the
fact that the Turkish advance triggered neither a native uprising in Egypt
nor any anti-British activities among the Senussis in the western desert
caused equal disappointment in the German high command. Nevertheless, Berlin felt relieved that the operation had not been a rout like that
suffered by the Turks against the Russians a month before in the Transcaucasus. The Germans also soon concluded that the assault on Suez had
served the purpose of alarming the British sufficiently for the latter to
transfer additional troops to Egypt, which removed such forces from
availability for the Western front in Europe.[55] The German and Turkish
commands agreed for the moment not to resume large-scale operations
from Palestine. However, while the main body of the Eighth Turkish
Corps withdrew to Beersheba, Kress remained in the desert with a force
of several battalions, artillery, and a unit of armed camel riders; the force
kept British anxieties alive through minor raids on the canal, culminating
with one in August 1916. Kress's chief intelligence and political officer,
Prüfer, would participate in that attack, too.

four

From Frustration to Defeat, 1915-18

THE failure of the canal expedition to raise a revolt in Egypt against the British did not lessen the interest among leading officials in the AA in seeking an Islamic "holy war" to defeat the Entente in the Orient and establish German rule there.[1] Such plans continued during 1915 and 1916 to face major obstacles, however. Turkish fortunes were eroded by rivalries between German and Turkish leaders, the Ottoman Empire's economic backwardness and underdeveloped transportation system, and the heterogeneity of the population and doubtful loyalty of its ethnic and religious groups, such as the Arabs, Greeks, Jews, and Armenians. The excessive repression of these peoples by the Turks, far more than needed for internal security, fanned discontent and led to revolts, especially among the Arabs. It also resulted in the brutal campaign that murdered over a million Armenians in 1915 and 1916. Germany and Austria-Hungary, fearing that alienation of the Turks might result from opposition to such policies, revealed a moral callousness towards the Armenian tragedy by refusing to insist that it stop.[2]

Nevertheless, during April 1915 Enver Pasha complained to Wangenheim that the German consuls and agents like Prüfer, by favoring some among the population in Syria and Palestine and giving them "money and promises of decorations" to collaborate in the canal expedition, had angered local Turkish officials. They accused Germany of seeking to establish "some kind of protectorate" over the Ottoman state and of trying to "win Islamic elements for the German cause, not for the cause of Turkey."[3] Furthermore, Enver told the Germans, he saw little promise for victory in provoking revolt among the Egyptians; instead, he had sent his brother, Nuri Bey, to incite the Senussis in Libya to attack Egypt.[4]

Jews as German Spies

Ignoring the Porte's complaints, the AA and army reserve general staff in Berlin tried even more zealously to infiltrate Egypt and kindle a holy war. On 1 March 1915, Prüfer suggested to Oppenheim major changes for gathering intelligence information inside Egypt. Noting that the results from "the use of native Egyptians as intelligence agents have not been very satisfactory" and that Turks or Germans could only be sent to Egypt with great difficulty, he recommended dispatching Jews to Egypt as spies. "A considerable number" of Jews in Palestine, he said, possessed "astuteness and self-control" and, "naturally for a good reward, are ready to make a trip to Egypt to furnish us with military and political news."

He outlined an elaborate scheme for creating espionage networks of Jews in Alexandria and Cairo, the former comprising male agents, the latter, females. According to the plan, they would file reports through intermediaries or directly with the German embassy in Rome and possess full authority "to eliminate" treasonous agents "by any means possible." Prüfer intended for the spies to acquire information from prominent Jewish families in Egypt "who were on excellent terms with the leading English functionaries" there. Revealing the view that the Jews should be tools for Germany in the war and that women existed primarily for sexual purposes, he directed that "the female agents . . . be young" and engage in affairs with their male counterparts, if necessary, to achieve their goal.[5]

Several factors, particularly German policy towards Zionism and the growing Jewish settlement in Palestine, prompted his proposal to employ Jews. Many of the 85,000 Jews in Palestine by 1914 had come from Russia, fleeing persecution by the tsarist government; some were Zionist, others orthodox and assimilationist. Between 10,000 and 12,000 lived in agricultural colonies; the remainder resided in Jerusalem, Jaffa, Haifa, and smaller cities like Hebron. Before the war, Zionism had appealed to William II's anti-Semitism and nationalism. He viewed Palestine as a place where German Jews might be encouraged to emigrate, but eventually he feared that the Reich's support of Zionism could endanger its relations with Turkey.[6] The Turks believed erroneously that certain Zionists sought to create an independent Jewish state in Palestine and sever it from the Ottoman empire.[7]

When the war began, the Zionist World Congress, headquartered in Berlin, declared its neutrality. But one of its leaders, Chaim Weizmann,

identified with Britain and worked for a Jewish Palestine independent of
Turkey; others retained ties to the Central Powers. The war's impact on
trade impoverished the Jews in Palestine, the Porte classified the roughly
50,000 Jews who held Russian citizenship as enemy aliens, and the viru-
lently anti-Jewish Djemal Pasha, the commander of the fourth Turkish
army in Syria and Palestine, persecuted them.[8]

The German government feared that the Turkish action would alienate
public opinion abroad, especially American Jews, whose influence Berlin
believed significant in world finance. At the urging of Zionist leaders,
Germany cooperated in 1914 and 1915 with the American and Italian
governments in persuading the Turks to moderate their policy.[9] Essentially, however, the Reich's attitude towards Jewish settlement in Palestine
remained the same as before the war. Most Germans believed that Zionism did not have much political significance; the Pan Germans and other
anti-Semites, who despised the small minority of Jews in Germany for
economic, religious, and racial reasons, applauded the settlement because
of its potential for removing the Jews from the Reich.[10]

Some in the AA, especially those who hoped to employ Zionism to
foment revolts by Jews inside the tsarist empire, thought Jewish coloniza-
tion in Palestine useful to German interests because it would enhance the
economy of the province and thereby strengthen Berlin's ally, Turkey. But
other officials, such as Wangenheim and Zimmermann, mistrusted the
alleged "international character" of Zionism and remained fearful that
supporting it might add to Berlin's problems with the Turks. Nevertheless, Wangenheim suggested in February 1915 to the German chancellor,
Bethmann, that Germany seek to exploit to its advantage the hatred of the
Russian Jews in Palestine for the tsar's regime.[11]

Prüfer's attitude towards Jews and Zionism reflected a view widespread
in Imperial Germany. He disliked Jews because of his fanatical nationalism, lack of respect for foreigners, and association of Jews with "international" finance and influence. His study of Arab culture and friendships
with Arabs fueled his prejudices. Just as the war heightened German anti-
Semitism and the belief that the Reich had fallen prey to "war profiteers"
tied to "international Jewish finance," so it hardened Prüfer's anti-Jewish
views, particularly as his awareness of Zionism increased. He recorded in
his diary in December 1914 that a German-American doctor in Jerusalem
had warned him of the "Zionist danger," and he called Zionist leaders in
Palestine "very anti-Turkish and anti-German."[12] In a report to the AA a
week later, he denounced "Jewish newspapers" in Jerusalem for their
pro-Entente views and claimed that the Turkish censorship in Syria and
Palestine "lay previously almost entirely in Jewish-Zionist hands," but
had finally been "entrusted exclusively to people with a reliable political
direction."[13]

Prüfer's hostility towards Jews did not prevent his mingling with them in Palestine. He developed such relationships, however, only to benefit himself, his work, and Germany's cause in the war. While in Damascus, for example, he joined the German consul, Loytved Hardegg, in furthering German interests by befriending the director of a Jewish technical school in Jerusalem who agreed to help open a German school in Damascus.[14] During April and May 1915, he also began carrying out his plan to use Jews as German spies and, as Wangenheim had urged, exploiting the hatred of local Russian Jews for tsarism.

He sent at least three Jews on missions to Egypt: two Jewish-Americans in Palestine, Moritz Rothschild and Isaak Cohn, and a young Russian émigré in Jerusalem, Minna Weizmann.[15] Rothschild and Cohn traveled successfully to Cairo and established contact with a tiny German spy cell in a major hotel for British officers, Shepheard's. They reported to the German embassy in Rome or returned to Palestine with information, usually exaggerated, about troop numbers in Egypt. Rothschild, who spoke seven languages and had lived ten years in the United States, continued his espionage activity after November 1915 in Holland and Switzerland at the suggestion of Kress and the German embassy counselor in Constantinople, Constantin von Neurath.[16]

Hiring Jews for such work, however, proved risky. Some in Palestine worked for British intelligence, like Aaron Aaronsohn, a Zionist who founded an agricultural experiment station near Haifa and who believed a Jewish *modus vivendi* with Turkey impossible. Moreover, the British eventually learned of the spy ring at Shepheard's Hotel in Cairo and of the activities of Prüfer's other Jewish spy, Minna Weizmann.[17] The youngest sister of Chaim Weizmann, who had cast his lot and the fate of Zionism from the beginning of the war with an Entente victory, Minna had left her native White Russia, studied medicine in Zurich and Berlin, and emigrated in 1913 to Palestine, where she worked as a physician. She had met Prüfer in Jerusalem during January 1914; although one cannot be certain of the nature of their relationship, she bid him farewell in a local hotel the day he departed on the Turkish expedition to the Suez Canal.[18] One can also only conjecture about her motives in spying for the Germans. From the sketchy details of her early life, it appears that she immersed herself with much idealism and passion in the Russian revolutionary movement against tsarism and its Jewish persecution. She disagreed with the Zionist solution of her brother, Chaim, however, and joined the Jewish socialist organization in Russia, the Jewish workers' *Bund,* at the age of thirteen; the Bund officially rejected Zionism and sought to transform Jewish life in Russia itself.[19]

However, the Bundists and some Zionists with socialist leanings shared both a common opposition to middle-class Jews and conservative rabbis and a common rejection of the alien Russian society. After the failure of the 1905 revolution in Russia, Minna Weizmann possibly joined other Bundists in moving toward the Zionist vision of a Jewish socialism carried beyond the hostile Russian environment to the ancient homeland of Palestine, which would be redeemed through a rebirth of Jewish spirit and labor. The frightful pogroms conducted against Jews in 1903 by the Russian government and the failed revolution two years later prompted the second major wave of Jewish migration from Russia to Palestine, as well as to the United States.[20] Minna Weizmann left for study in Germany and Switzerland, and eventually proceeded to Palestine. She may have cooperated with the Germans because of Berlin's efforts during 1914 and 1915, despite their purely self-serving nature, to slow the Turkish persecution of Palestine Jews.

Whatever her intentions, she traveled for Prüfer to Egypt in May 1915. Through her work in large hospitals in Cairo and Alexandria, in which she met leading British, Russian, and French personalities, she gathered information for Germany. She accompanied a severely wounded Frenchman from Cairo to Naples, during which journey she visited the German embassy in Rome. A Russian official apparently observed her activities, however, and betrayed her to the Entente authorities. On her return to Cairo, they removed her from the hospital staffs, confiscated her possessions and officially condemned her to the British prison on Malta. But for unknown reasons, they displayed an extraordinary leniency by expelling her from Egypt and sending her to Russia in the fall of 1915.[21]

The German government supplemented Prüfer's attempts to organize a Jewish espionage network in Egypt by sending Bulgarian and other agents there. Berlin also relied on him to establish the reliability of Egyptian nationalists, whom it planned to sneak into Egypt. The proposal of the reserve general staff in Berlin to dispatch Prüfer to the Sudan to organize Bedouin traders for disrupting railroad communications with Egypt never materialized because Djemal Pasha and Kress insisted that Prüfer remain with the Fourth Turkish Army in Syria and Palestine. Kress telegraphed Wangenheim about Prüfer: "He is indispensable to me as head of the intelligence service and interpreter. Furthermore, cultivating public opinion is more necessary than ever."[22]

Another Attempt at Holy War: The Oppenheim Mission

Kress's allusion to "public opinion" reflected the growing preoccupation of German leaders by the spring of 1915 with the lack of success of their propaganda among the Arabs. The AA reacted to this concern by assigning Prüfer to another project for inciting the Muslims to undertake a jihad against the Entente: the Oppenheim mission.

The Sharif of Mecca's withholding of his endorsement of the holy war appeared to give creditability to Prüfer's warnings about the trustworthiness of Hussein and his sons.[23] Oppenheim received approval from his superiors in the AA, including Zimmermann, to visit the Arab and Persian regions of the Ottoman empire to revitalize German and Turkish propaganda.[24] It was perhaps indicative of the lack of planning and logic which dominated much of Germany's wartime policy in the Middle East that Berlin dispatched a former Jew who had converted to Christianity to persuade the Arabs to give their lives for the cause of the Reich, a cause about which many Arabs knew little and which could offer them only continued Turkish rule and repression.

The German approach to the Arabs stood in sharp contrast to the highly secret negotiations during 1914 and the beginning of 1915 between Britain and Hussein and other Arab leaders. They discussed Britain's proposal to support Arab aspirations for political autonomy in return for the Arabs' concluding a wartime alliance with England and rebelling against the Turks.[25] Oppenheim arrived in Constantinople in April 1915. He met there at the end of the month with the Sharif's son, Faisal, sent by Hussein to Constantinople to complain to the Turks about his conflict with the Porte's governor of the Hejaz, Wehib Bey. In reality, however, Faisal met secretly in Damascus on his father's order with Arab nationalists, many of them officers in the Turkish army who belonged to secret Arab societies, to discover their attitude towards England's proposal.[26] Oppenheim, in his discussions with Faisal, often used Ahmed Pasha Khafik, an Egyptian agent of the ex-Khedive, as an emissary; Khafik apparently had met Faisal during Abbas Hilmi's pilgrimage to Mecca in 1910.

The ex-Khedive's role in the negotiations was mysterious.[27] A master at intrigue and extortion, the ex-Khedive had failed to re-establish his influence in Constantinople and had been unable to resume his throne or place his eldest son, Abd al Moneim, on it. He turned to Germany for support and found a sympathizer in Oppenheim, who believed Abbas Hilmi could provide valuable help spreading German propaganda in Turkey and Egypt. Much of the money the ex-Khedive obtained, both from Germany and from his properties in Turkey and Egypt, he squandered in paying corrupt advisers and political intriguers in his entourage. When Oppenheim suggested to Gottlieb von Jagow, the state secretary in the AA, that the Kaiser officially receive the ex-Khedive, Jagow and Wangenheim refused, fearing that such a meeting would anger the Turks and complicate an already tense relationship.[28] Undaunted, Oppenheim persisted in his contacts with Abbas Hilmi and used his agent, Ahmed Pasha, in the meeting with Faisal.

One must doubt whether Faisal negotiated seriously with Oppenheim; he apparently sought to use the meeting to pressure the Arab nationalists in Damascus to join the Sharif in a revolt against the Turks. Whatever his motives, he agreed on behalf of his father that the Sharif would assume responsibility for German and Turkish "propaganda in the entire Islamic world as well as providing regular reports from Mecca" for the Turks. While Wangenheim hailed the agreement as a great success for the Reich and claimed that Enver supported it, the Wilhelmstrasse appeared skeptical. It informed the embassy in Constantinople that, based on reports from Prüfer and other German agents in Arabia (e.g., Moritz, who had just returned to Berlin, and Musil), "it appears doubtful whether the promises of the great Sherif [sic] of Mecca bring much trust."[29] The ministry's unease proved justified. Faisal continued negotiating with the Arab officers in Damascus, and in July 1915, despite the poor showing of the Entente at Gallipoli and elsewhere in the Middle East, Hussein resumed discussions with the British.[30]

The AA, its fears about the loyalty of the Sharif notwithstanding, allowed Oppenheim to remain in the Middle East and allocated a half million marks for the rest of his mission.[31] Accompanied by Prüfer, the Egyptian nationalist Sheikh Shawish, and several Indian Muslims, Oppenheim addressed assemblies of Dervishes and religious notables in Constantinople and elsewhere; the group traveled for several months in Syria, Palestine, and Mesopotamia. Hoping to raise Pan Islamic feeling against Britain, but revealing amazing insensitivity to Turkish and Arab culture, they preached monogamy, abandonment of the fez (the national headdress of the Turks), and practice in using arms for war against the Entente. But such exhortations did not impress those who heard them, nor did the fact that Oppenheim had once been Jewish.[32]

Oppenheim's plan to send Indian sheikhs to Arabia to spread propaganda among Indian pilgrims visiting the Muslim holy places in the Hejaz did not bear fruit. Few Indians visited the shrines, especially owing to restrictions placed on them by the British government in India. Furthermore, Prüfer persuaded Oppenheim of the unreliability of the Indian official whom the Germans hoped to send to Mecca.[33] Nothing indicated during the summer and fall of 1915 that the Sharif of Mecca was developing a pro-German and Turkish propaganda campaign among fellow Muslims. The closest Oppenheim's group came to Arabia was the Sinai, including territory there occupied by the British, which the German agents visited in September and October 1915. The AA soon received another warning from one of its experienced spies, Moritz, who called Hussein pro-British but "relatively decent" and Faisal "a complete rogue."[34]

Nevertheless, Oppenheim served (as usual) as his own best promoter. At the beginning of November 1915, he boasted to Bethmann, the Reich chancellor, that he had created an intelligence and propaganda network "throughout all provinces of European and Asiatic Turkey." His mission, he continued, established seven new Turkish newspapers and founded special propaganda rooms in the major cities, where Muslims could view photographs and news releases from Germany. This organization would soon be extended to Persia and Bulgaria. Oppenheim, furthermore, claimed full cooperation from the Porte's ministry of war for constructing movie theaters and from the Turkish leaders, Enver and Djemal.[35]

But the long-awaited Muslim holy war with which Prüfer, Oppenheim, and other German leaders hoped to raise a new attack on Egypt never transpired. The Oppenheim mission failed not only because of its weaknesses, but also because of Turkish policy, and particularly that of Djemal Pasha, who, suspecting the Arabs of treason after the failed Turkish expedition to Egypt, unleashed a wave of terror against Arab leaders in the fall of 1915. The intelligence staff of Djemal's Fourth Army failed to assess the situation accurately, just as it had in the attack on Egypt. While the intelligence staff had an ear for rumors, its nose failed to pick up the scent. The treason that Djemal suspected was real enough, but his military intelligence lacked the skill to trace it to any of the plotters.[36] His intelligence failures also included Prüfer, who journeyed at Djemal's directive through Syria and Palestine during November and the beginning of December 1915, disguised as an Arab traveler, to establish "whether the internal political situation, above all the hostile mood of the Arabs towards Turkey, made necessary the creation of a military-political security service separated from the civilian authorities."

Prüfer concluded in his report for the Ottoman commander that the majority of the population, ranging from the Christian minority to the Arabs, possessed little fervor for an anti-Turk revolution. "The anti-Turk movement . . . directed towards Arab independence," he declared, "seems to be significantly weakened. Among the middle classes reformism has barely any supporters and among the small landowners, merchants, and workers, who constitute the bulk of the population, the cause of the Ottoman government is very popular." An Arab uprising also had little chance of success, he maintained, because of the "cowardice and frivolousness of the population."[37]

On the other hand, Prüfer revealed in his report a greater contempt than previously for the Jews and Zionism. He mocked the Russian Jews "coming from Polish ghettos" to Palestine; they saw themselves, he told Djemal Pasha, as "the protectors of civilization and liberal thought." On the contrary, he declared, they possessed "a cowardly nature and no initiative" and "will never give up subversive activities unless an enemy's armed force is present already in this country." He rated Zionism "the most important party" among the Jews in Palestine. Describing it incorrectly as a monolithic global movement which sought political autonomy for the Jews by supporting the Entente, he insisted that Zionism worked in the war for the defeat of the Central Powers and dismemberment of Turkey. "We can certainly not trust their program on the subject of their alleged Ottomanism," he informed Djemal Pasha.

"I cite only some facts," he continued, "that prove obviously the double-dealing of this international movement." He noted the formation in the British army of the Zion Mule Corps, a tiny force of Jews expelled from Palestine who participated in the Anglo-French attack on the Dardanelles. "In the Ententist press," he added, "Zionists discussed the future of Palestine in the event of a conquest of that country, while arguing for Jewish autonomy. We cannot doubt then that this autonomy is the final goal hidden in the bottom of every Zionist heart."[38]

One should not attach too much importance to the impact of Prüfer's views on Djemal Pasha or on the Porte's policy towards the Arabs and Jews. His allegations of Zionist intentions to establish Jewish autonomy through the dismemberment of Turkey may have helped undermine the effort of Wangenheim and other German officials who sought to moderate the Turkish persecution of the Jews. A few months later, in the summer of 1916, the Turks renewed their attack against both Zionism and the Arabs.[39] Djemal's oppressive rule, together with the traditional animosities between Arab and Ottoman and the British encouragement of the Arabs to rebel against the Turks to achieve autonomy, contributed directly to the final alienation of the Arabs. The Sharif of Mecca refused to grant passage through Arabia to the Yemen for a German intelligence expedition whose task included in part "securing German East Africa," and Hussein even arrested the agent Moritz.[40] On 9 June, the Sharif began the Arab revolt.

The Fliegerabteilung and a Second Defeat at the Canal

By the summer of 1916, the Turks had defeated the Entente armies in the Dardanelles, but the war in the Middle East also involved several other theaters. The Turks battled the Russians in the Transcaucasus and Persia, the British in Mesopotamia, and the Arab revolt in the Hejaz. Such events naturally affected the Ottoman plans towards Egypt. With the end of the battle for the Dardanelles, which had claimed much of Turkey's forces in 1915, and with Britain transferring more troops from Egypt to Europe in the belief that the Turks had abandoned their invasion of Egypt, the German high command pushed Enver for another attack against the Suez Canal.[41] Kress and Djemal stubbornly held to the belief that the appearance of Turkish troops at the canal would unleash a rebellion by the Egyptians as well as an attack on Egypt from the West by the Senussis, and they demanded massive German military support for their plans.

Whether Prüfer, the chief German intelligence officer for Kress and Djemal, influenced their views, is uncertain. Both Prüfer and Oppenheim urged the AA to speed preparations for a new Turkish attack on Egypt; Oppenheim recommended that Germany invite Djemal Pasha to Berlin to discuss the latter's supplying of war materials for the venture. Prüfer's report to the ministry on 6 August 1915 illustrated his and Oppenheim's rabid imperialist aims in Africa; their goals represented nothing new in the war aims policy of Reich leaders.[42] Prüfer pushed for a large-scale invasion of Egypt in the hope of opening German penetration into the rest of Africa. He called for Germany to commit extensive heavy artillery, motorized vehicles, and equipment to build roads and dig wells in the desert, and for more German and Turkish troops to replace Arabs.

Furthermore, he no longer considered the original Turkish goal of attacking and obstructing the Suez Canal of value to the Central Powers. A canal held by the Turks would not hurt Britain's transport of troops from the Far East appreciably. "The sea route around the Cape of Good Hope," he declared, "means no more than a three-week loss of time at the most in relation to the Suez canal route." The objective of the attack on Egypt, in his view, had become "the conquest of Egypt and the Sudan" as "an object of equalization against the British occupation of our colonies and as a door for invading Uganda and British East Africa."[43]

The chief of the German high command, General Erich von Falkenhayn, however, discarded such plans for a massive invasion of Egypt. He believed that they cost too much and doubted their success; Germany was suffering tremendous losses in Europe and did not possess the resources for such an expedition. Neither did the Turks, whose troops mounted a campaign in 1916 against the Russians in Armenia and were forced by the Arab revolt in June to take military measures in western Arabia at the expense of an attack on Egypt. Falkenhayn, therefore, agreed to a far more limited assault on the canal which would utilize a large contingent of German and Austro-Hungarian troops. The mission received the code name of "Pasha."

The first of the assault units, which included pilots and fourteen planes of the German 300th Flight Detachment (*Fliegerabteilung*), arrived in April 1916. But the usual colossal problems which the Turks faced in the war involving transportation, desert heat, and water supplies slowed the assembling of the remaining Pasha troops and war materials from the Central Powers and delayed final preparations for the expedition. In the interim a small air war developed in the Sinai in May and June, as the

German airplanes raided the canal and Port Said and British planes retaliated by bombing Turkish posts at Al Arish and elsewhere. Prüfer participated in this campaign as an air reconnaissance observer; he joined the Fliegerabteilung 300 and took his first flight in a two-seater Aviatiks on 5 May, recording that evening in his diary: "Contrary to expectations, I have no troubles or feelings of anxiety. We stayed in the air for twelve minutes. . . . The landing was not very dazzling, nearly into a wall."[44]

From the flight unit's quarters outside Beersheba, he flew training missions to Gaza and Jaffa and took instruction in machine gunning, telescopic sighting, photography, and airplane motor repair. On 28 May 1916, he received word that the British had allegedly condemned him to death.[45] The danger which the German airmen faced during the day gave way in the evening to heavy drinking and carousing among the officers, with whom Prüfer developed a camaraderie and acquaintance with such flyers as Adolf von Arnim, Karl Kettenbeil, Erich Heiden, Helmut von Langenn-Steinkeller, Erik von Witzleben, Tiller, and the commander of the Fliegerabteilung, Captain Hans-Eduard von Heemskerck, that lasted for his lifetime.

But morale among the German and Turkish forces in the desert soon plummeted at news of the revolt of the Arabs on 9 June, the failure of the battle of Verdun in France, the great Russian offensive of June and July which broke the Austrian front at Lutzk, and the damage to newly transferred German planes at Al Arish by a British bombing raid on 18 June. "I was right to warn about the Sharif," Prüfer observed of the Arab rebellion; as it spread, he lamented a month later in a rare example of his feeling for his mentor: "Poor Oppenheim." Of the troubles involving the Russians, he declared on 22 July, just before the Turks launched their second major assault on the canal, "No one is talking about peace."[46]

The Turkish expedition, including the German Pasha corps and totaling 18,000 soldiers and nearly as many camels, attacked the main British outpost east of the canal at Romani on the morning of 4 August 1916. But the fighting ended within the day. British air reconnaissance anticipated the main Ottoman thrust, the defenders counterattacked with well-provisioned cavalry forces and with heavy artillery from warships in the nearby Mediterranean Sea, and the Turks suffered from the fatigue caused by stifling heat, scarce water, and climbing over steep sand dunes.

Prüfer was ill when the battle began, but nevertheless he participated in the air bombing of British units at Bir Etmale, a few miles west of Romani. He had expected the failure of the Turkish attack, fearing as it began "that the favorable moment has passed for it." As the fighting ended, an officer in the Fliegerabteilung suggested that its planes fly behind the enemy lines and bomb Port Said, but Prüfer privately denounced the proposal. "With the present ratio of strengths," he observed in his diary, "that is unheard-of nonsense."[47] Under the cover of darkness, the Turks quickly retreated into the Sinai, many sleeping as they rode. The retreat was uneventful; the exhausted British had retired to Romani and Kress had had the foresight to prepare successive lines of defense for the withdrawal.

The failure of this second expedition against Egypt represented a considerable British victory. Total casualties among the Turks amounted to nearly nine thousand, the enemy's barely a thousand. The battle marked the end of the Turco-German campaign to take the canal and Egypt from England. Britain now seized the initiative; in the ensuing months, its forces steadily and methodically drove the Turks eastward across the Sinai to the Egyptian frontier between Al Arish and Gaza and invaded Palestine.

Prüfer arrived back in Jerusalem on 14 August, apparently suffering from cholera, which had killed seventy members of the Turkish expedition to Romani. He received a leave to return to Germany for the first time since the war began. Extremely ill, he survived a difficult and uncomfortable journey to Constantinople and from there to Berlin. He recuperated for four months while working in the cartographic department of the reserve general staff in Berlin.[48] By January 1917, however, Oppenheim had returned from his mission to the Middle East and, supported by the new German ambassador in Constantinople, Richard von Kühlmann, appointed Prüfer head of the intelligence bureau at the embassy and the network of propaganda centers Oppenheim had established in the Turkish provinces.

German Imperialism in Turkey

Prüfer's new position resulted not only from his weakened physical condition, which was aggravated by tuberculosis, and from the collapse of the Turkish war against Egypt, but also from a new thrust by Germany in 1917 to exploit Turkish economic resources for gains in both the war effort and the future beyond the war. Since the outbreak of the war, German political, military, and industrial leaders had steadily expanded their prewar Weltpolitik. Beginning with the war aims program of the chancellor, Bethmann, in September 1914, they advanced various extravagant schemes for exploiting their planned defeat of the Entente to expand the German empire into a vast Central European (*Mitteleuropa*) and Russian one.

As for the Middle East, the German leaders envisioned making Turkey and the Baghdad railroad the bases for the postwar German domination of the Persian Gulf, Afghanistan, India, and much of the African continent.[49] But for a variety of reasons, German business had made little progress in penetrating the Ottoman Empire since 1914; in some instances, the war eroded German economic activity there. The Porte refused Berlin's pressure during the spring of 1917, prompted by the German army's increasing need for raw materials, to persuade the Turks to liquidate Anglo-French businesses and grant the Reich mining, railroad, and oil concessions.

The impetus and planning for much of the campaign to exploit Turkey's resources developed in the AA. Oppenheim, who returned to Germany in 1916, and others in the Oriental section proposed to Bethmann that the Reich use a private organization, financed in large measure by German industry but controlled by the ministry, to act as a front for the propaganda activities of the German embassy in Constantinople.[50] To recruit the backing of German industry for the project, Oppenheim published a pamphlet which argued incorrectly that the war had greatly enhanced German economic influence in Turkey and that German-Ottoman relations offered the prospect of massive profits for German business in Turkey and neighboring lands after the war.[51]

In appointing Prüfer head of the embassy's intelligence bureau and hence of the new propaganda campaign, the AA had sent out a fanatical adherent to German imperialism in the Orient. Together with Kühlmann, the new Reich ambassador, and Otto von Wesendonk, a counselor in the ministry's Oriental section, Prüfer negotiated during the spring of 1917 with Heinrich Rötger, an official of heavy industry's powerful association, the General Federation of German Industrialists (*Centralverband Deutscher Industrieller*), and arranged for one of its agencies, the German Overseas Service (*Deutsche Überseedienst*), to act as the front organization in Turkey for the embassy's propaganda.[52]

Prüfer arrived in Constantinople at the end of March. He criticized Germany's previous propaganda policies in Turkey and proposed major reforms in the network of reading rooms and propaganda centers established by Oppenheim in the provinces and supplied by the embassy.[53] First, he urged that the leaders of the centers reach the Turks, Arabs, and other populations in their cities or regions by aggressively forwarding the propaganda materials to surrounding schools, clubs, hotels, and newspapers. He suggested that the embassy persuade the Porte to demand that its subjects visit the reading rooms and that Turkish military offices disseminate "our materials."

Second, he laid greater emphasis on producing Turkish language publications that discussed subjects of interest to Turks. In a memorandum to the AA of 12 April 1917, he noted that the Turks had censored German propaganda in regions where they considered it too heavily German and non-Muslim in nature. German pamphlets, he declared, should "deal more with Turkish affairs and show greater tact in self-importance. To write much about the war, its origin, enemy atrocities etc., appears futile to me. We will not change the opinion of the generally war-weary and pretty pessimistic population by forever protesting our innocence in the war and describing the execution of Mohammedans in India and Egypt."[54]

His proposals, generally agreed to by the AA, produced little but frustration, however. Despite the efforts to camouflage the embassy's shipment of propaganda through the Deutsche Überseedienst, Turkish suspicions and censorship intensified, and Germany lacked specialists on Turkish affairs to write the propaganda materials.[55] In addition, new differences emerged among the two allies over Turkey's hesitancy in declaring war on the United States and over peace feelers from America and the Pope. Nor did Prüfer's difficult trip from May through July, staying each night in dirty, flea-infested hotels, visiting the reading rooms in the provinces, improve prospects for the Reich's propaganda.[56]

During his travels, Prüfer gathered intelligence information, observed what he termed "miserable" relations between German and Turkish officers, and had little sympathy for the "dubious pro-Armenian propaganda" of a Catholic priest who administered to Armenian prisoners of war in a camp near Aleppo.[57] He also arranged for North African and Egyptian delegates (including the nationalist, Muhammad Farid) and the Syrian politician loyal to Constantinople, Shekib Arslan, to attend via Berlin the international socialist congress in Stockholm. There the group served German propaganda interests by denouncing British and French plans to conquer Mesopotamia, Syria, and Palestine.[58]

Courting the Ex-Khedive

Prüfer was one of the first to receive a visit in Constantinople from Abbas Hilmi when the ex-Khedive of Egypt arrived in the Turkish capital in October 1917 after living nearly three years in Austria and Switzerland.[59] Abbas Hilmi's political intrigue with both the Entente (or Allies, as the coalition became known by 1917 and 1918) and Central Powers, in which he hoped to retain a measure of influence with whoever won the war, helped explain Prüfer's assignment to his entourage during much of 1918. The principal task of the German diplomat-spy, a long-time acquaintance of the ex-Khedive, involved ensuring his loyalty to Germany in the event the Central Powers emerged triumphant and he returned to the throne in Egypt.

By the summer of 1915, Abbas Hilmi had found himself opposed by the Turks and by Egyptian nationalists exiled in Switzerland, including Sheikh Shawish and Muhammad Farid. Although he remained in the pay of the Germans, they refused him a reception with the Kaiser.[60] Reports soon surfaced among German diplomats in Switzerland, where Abbas Hilmi had moved, that he had secretly contacted his old nemesis, Britain, apparently hoping to pressure the Germans and Turks into a more favorable attitude and to negotiate other advantages for himself from London.[61] The reports turned out to be true; the British minister in Bern, Grant Duff, met Abbas Hilmi privately in December 1915.

London only wished, however, to keep the ex-Khedive from a reconciliation with the Turks and Germans. The British also hoped to persuade him to accept a pension and settlement from his Egyptian property in exchange for his public acceptance of the Egyptian regime of his uncle, the Sultan Hussein, who governed under the authority of the British protectorate. Abbas Hilmi and his son, Abd al Moneim, made numerous overtures to Britain during 1916, but the English knew that the ex-Khedive was also negotiating with the Central Powers and, wishing to avoid problems with the jealous and insecure Hussein, rejected all agreements the former prince proposed.[62]

The Germans, including the ex-Khedive's contacts, Freiherr Gisbert von Romberg, the German minister in Switzerland, and Matthias Erzberger, the Center party leader in the German parliament, viewed Abbas Hilmi as their future ally in Egypt once the Reich defeated and ousted Britain. The AA feared the rumors of his rapprochement with England and tried without success to convince him to return to Turkey and settle his differences with the Porte.[63] During the spring of 1917, however, several changes in the Ottoman government lessened the tension with the ex-Khedive, and encouraged anew by Berlin, he began negotiating for his return. Furthermore, events in Egypt changed significantly. The death of Sultan Hussein, his replacement by Mehmed Fuad, a younger brother, and the first signs of anti-British feeling in Egypt during the war, made Berlin even more determined to safeguard its future candidates for the throne by reconciling the ex-Khedive and the Turks and preventing his son from befriending the English. As Abbas Hilmi returned to Constantinople in the fall of 1917 and the Germans intensified their efforts to lure Abd al Moneim to the Reich and potentially out of British hands, the AA detailed Prüfer to the ex-Khedive's entourage.[64]

The improved military situation for Germany, at least at the beginning of 1918, when the new Bolshevik regime in Russia had surrendered, also appeared to warrant the attention lavished on the ex-Khedive. But the Central Powers were steadily defeated during the summer and fall in both

Europe and the Middle East; whatever slim chances the ex-Khedive had had of returning to the Egyptian throne were destroyed, and much of Prüfer's time with the entourage involved unimportant affairs. He kept Abbas Hilmi's bickering advisers, who denounced each other as "English spies," under surveillance, and counseled the ex-Khedive on his difficulties with his son, his three former wives, and a French mistress.[65] Prüfer also published propaganda articles in the German press, which condemned Britain for its prewar imperialism in Egypt and demanded the ex-Khedive's restoration to the throne.

Prüfer's zealous support of German expansion persisted, however. Even as the Reich's offensive in France slowly collapsed, he applauded rumors circulating among the last wartime German ambassador to the Porte, Johann Count von Bernstorff, and Werner Otto von Hentig, an embassy official, about an alleged British peace offer to divide the Middle East with Germany and Turkey. Believing that "the offer is genuine" and hoping for a way for Germany to gain in the Middle East from the war, he suggested eliminating the Reich's alliance with Turkey and splitting that territory with Britain. "Divide Turkey into 2 spheres," he declared in his diary on 30 June 1918, "Arabic for England, Turanian (North Persian, Turkestan) German."[66]

Thus, only a few months before Germany's defeat and surrender, Prüfer appeared to suffer from the same aura of unreality and vision of final victory and world power that dominated the Reich's high command and many other reactionary Germans, including the Pan Germans and the new Fatherland party.[67] His accompaniment of the ex-Khedive to Germany in July and August reflected a similar air of fantasy. The visit followed the Porte's agreement to return Abbas Hilmi to the Egyptian throne once the war had ended and resulted in the removal of England from the land of the Nile. The ex-Khedive requested, as he had done unsuccessfully in 1915, an audience with the Kaiser; this time the response was positive, and Abbas Hilmi arrived in Berlin hoping he would receive official German support for his claims.

Despite the lavish reception given his entourage by the AA on its arrival, Abbas Hilmi's visit to German high command headquarters in Belgium and the meeting with William II on 31 July 1918 in Spa were meaningless; not only had the emperor lost most of his political authority to General Erich Ludendorff, the army's *de facto* chief of staff, but he lacked interest in what was happening. Although, as Prüfer observed about the meeting to the AA, "Oriental policy, especially Egyptian, appeared not to have been discussed," the Kaiser received "the best impression" of Abbas Hilmi. William, in his parting reply to Prüfer, which the latter proudly reported to the AA, declared: "I request that you see me next time in a free Egypt."

Prüfer, however, possibly fearing the negative reaction in Berlin towards himself and Abbas Hilmi, did not inform the ministry that the ex-Khedive "was somewhat disillusioned" with what he saw in Belgium and his long-awaited visit with William II. He knew that the military dictators running the government executed "defeatists" or sent them to the front.[68] Nor did he discuss with his superiors Abbas Hilmi's growing mood of depression as the ex-Khedive visited the Imperial estate at Marienburg and traveled in mid-August to Munich, where the king of Bavaria received him.

From there the ex-Khedive's party went to Garmisch, where it remained until the end of August 1918, fraternizing with the Kaiser's sister, Princess von Schaumburg-Lippe, with Prince and Countess Montgelas, and a friend, Herr von Hrugrzka, whom Prüfer labeled "a Jew and political shyster."[69] As the bad news arrived from the Western front with the Allied armies sweeping forward in every sector, the evenings degenerated into debauched and scurrilous behavior. Prüfer described it in his diary: "Monotony in Garmisch. Increasing intimacy with the Princess and Countess Montgelas and Selime v. Schlotheim. Evenings hitting the bottle, dancing, and flirting; knees-up and similar. . . . The whole world is very depressed over the Entente offensive."[70]

Not only did Abbas Hilmi and those around him sense the impending defeat of the Central Powers, but the ex-Khedive's relations with his son had also broken down completely. Abd al Moneim, he informed Prüfer, received money from England and hoped to marry the daughter of the Egyptian Sultan, Fuad, to persuade the British of his worthiness as a successor to the Egyptian throne. Although Britain had no interest in the young prince and steadfastly refused to deal with him, the ex-Khedive's story brought himself and his son renewed attention in Berlin.[71] In a scheme hatched by the prince and one of his advisers, Achmed Nureddin Effendi, probably to bilk the German government out of more money, the AA dispatched Prüfer to Switzerland at the end of September to attempt to bribe Abd al Moneim into moving to Germany and away from the alleged English influence. By the beginning of October, however, Prüfer's mission had failed; the prince, seeing more clearly than his suitors that they represented a losing cause, chose to remain in Zurich.[72]

In addition to the German defeat in France, the dissolution of the Central Powers had begun in Eastern Europe. Allied troops at Salonica attacked and breached the Bulgarian lines and began a headlong advance into Serbia. The Bulgars immediately sued for an armistice at the end of September. Allied armies converged on Turkey and its government hastened to follow the Bulgarian example. Even before these defeats, the Austrians informed Germany that they could fight no longer and had begun diplomatic exchanges with the Allies. When the ex-Khedive returned to Turkey during October, the AA assigned Prüfer to its headquarters in Berlin to identify and arrange for the large number of Egyptian nationalists and other pro-German Arabs, such as the Syrian, Shekib Arslan, arriving from Turkey to obtain German passports for settlement in neutral Switzerland.[73] A few weeks later, however, the events of November 1918 stunned Prüfer, as they did the millions of other Germans who had supported the Imperial government so fanatically and who felt threatened by its sudden defeat and demise.

five

New Reasons to Hate, 1918-25

"THE Jewish slogan, 'shed no blood,' " Prüfer wrote in his diary after the war, "made a farce of the revolution of 9 November" 1918. Fearful and uncertain about his own future as well as Germany's, he responded with bitterness and resentment towards the Reich's defeat, the collapse of the Imperial regime, the abdication of the Kaiser, and the revolutionary events that created the new democratic republic fashioned at Weimar in 1919.[1] The Free Corps, special units hired by the SPD government after November 1918, brutally murdered several thousand Spartacists (German Communists), including Karl Liebknecht and the Polish-German Jewess, Rosa Luxemburg, but Prüfer observed that he would have used even greater violence to suppress the entire revolution and save the old regime he so passionately loved—and upon which rested his career.

Numerous studies show how conservatives and nationalists like Prüfer, who comprised Imperial Germany's bureaucratic elite, despised and rarely accepted the events of 1918 and 1919. Such officials later admitted their anti-republican feelings in memoirs, but they also glossed over the fact that few lost their jobs because of the defeat and revolution.[2] The fear in the new Socialist government that radical changes would plunge the country into Bolshevik chaos similar to that in Russia severely limited the changes it produced.

Reformers launched a major effort to change the AA, possibly the most difficult ministry to alter because of its aristocratic background and strongly nationalistic character. The attempt ultimately failed, however.

Demands that the ministry be changed had begun even before the war and intensified in its final months.[3] Although the Weimar constitution of 1919 established in the Reichstag a special Committee for Foreign Affairs through which the legislature scrutinized foreign policy, reforms initiated by Edmund Schüler, the director of the AA's personnel division, were short-lived. He abolished the old political division in the AA, combined the diplomatic and consular services as well as the political and economic divisions, and divided the latter into three regional groups (*Länderabteilungen*). Four other divisions remained in the AA, dealing with legal, cultural, personnel, and press affairs.

Schüler intended the reorganization, together with new admission requirements that included passing rigorous foreign service and language examinations, to dislodge the aristocracy, which had dominated diplomatic posts and the AA's political desks, and to allow new men from outside the ministry to reach its upper levels.[4] He only partially succeeded, however; numerous capable outsiders received positions as division heads and ambassadors, but few remained for very long because of the resentment towards them among the professional diplomats. Because of the AA's need for a trained staff, which had been significantly depleted by the war, a substantial group of such middle-aged and younger careerists as Romberg, Bernstorff, and Hans-Heinrich Dieckhoff either stayed in the service or, as in Prüfer's case, left the ministry and were later rehired.[5]

Surviving the Revolution

Prüfer's experience partly reflected the course of the revolution. The AA placed him in charge of dissolving the Nachrichtenstelle für den Orient, the special office created in the ministry to coordinate its war propaganda and other activities in the Middle East. When the Nachrichtenstelle closed in March 1919, however, the AA placed Prüfer on leave. It is unclear why. Possibly he requested the leave because he could not persuade himself to serve the revolutionary government; other young officials in the ministry had done so. His fate, however, may also have resulted from the confusion in the AA produced by the Schüler reforms, which had just begun in December 1918.[6] Whatever the reason for his leaving the ministry, Prüfer soon found himself destitute and fearful about the future.

The war, furthermore, provided the final strain that destroyed his marriage; not only did Prüfer's wife resent his continued infidelity, but also her American background and his fanatical devotion to Germany caused them to differ sharply over the war. They had separated at the war's beginning, though he received letters in Palestine from her; their attempt at reconciliation in 1919 and 1920 failed.[7] He moved to Munich; there he was arrested for twelve hours by the Communist regime that briefly ruled the city during the spring of 1919. In Munich he also collaborated with Kress, who had been his wartime boss in Palestine and who, following the suppression of the Communists in May, was the minister of war in the Bavarian government. Despite opposition to their activities from the republican government, Kress and Prüfer headed the Berlin and Munich branches of an organization Enver had founded during the war for camouflaging the settlement of former Turkish officers, some of whom were wanted by the Western allies and new Turkish government for war crimes, in Germany and Switzerland.[8]

Prüfer, already plagued by marital, financial, and professional problems, experienced even more embarrassment when his meager circumstances persuaded him to accept help from the wife of a friend, Dr. Moritz Sobernheim. The Jewish Sobernheim headed a new desk in the AA for "Jewish-political affairs" which the ministry hoped would influence foreign Jewish leaders and public opinion in Germany's favor regarding the peace settlement. In accepting help from the Sobernheims, Prüfer exhibited attitudes like those of other old-fashioned German anti-Semites, who held stereotypes or images of Jews, motivated largely by political and economic fears, that characterized them as immoral, greedy financial manipulators who were liberal and Bolshevik and thus part of a powerful international movement opposed to Germany. The Germans who based their prejudice on such political and economic stereotypes, unlike the racial anti-Semites and the Nazis, were willing to exempt certain Jews from such classifications. Traditional anti-Semites believed in the ability of some Jews, for example, to rise above their alleged nature although, the Jew-haters claimed, their "Jewishness" remained a fact that was hostile to all that the Germans stood for. Jews could assimilate into German society by embracing Christianity, by taking up an "honest trade," and by becoming good German patriots.[9] Sobernheim, in the view of the old-style anti-Semite Prüfer, had made himself an acceptable citizen by joining the AA. Prüfer's reliance on Sobernheim further exemplified how he could make friendships with nearly anyone without developing genuine feelings for them; Prüfer cultivated few relationships that did not serve his purposes.

Ironically, however, although he accepted help from the Sobernheims, the war and events of 1918 and 1919 had dramatically intensified his anti-Jewish attitudes. He despised both the sudden appearance of Jewish politicians in the provisional governments and revolutionary councils and their affiliation with the socialist parties. The lost war, while it destroyed Imperial Germany and therefore broke a major barrier to the assimilation of Jews into public life, thrust them into politics at an inauspicious moment. Prüfer, accepting the myth that the Jews played the dominant role in the revolution and establishment of the republic, associated them with wartime opposition and revolutionary politics, despite the fact that Rosa Luxemburg and the revolutionaries in Bavaria in 1919, Kurt Eisner and Ernst Toller, were exceptions. The overwhelming majority of Jewish leaders shunned revolution, wanted to restore the rule of law and democratize Germany's institutions, and were critical of the Communists.

But neither Prüfer nor many other Germans took notice of their position. Instead, Prüfer viewed them as a threat to control the only area in which he had enjoyed success and identity—the Reich government. His idea that Jews and Zionism were inferior global forces that sought the destruction of Germany fueled his fear and hatred. So did England's issuing of the Balfour declaration, which expressed the intention to create a national home for the Jewish people.[10]

Prüfer's attitudes towards the Jews and other alleged enemies hardened during 1920, as his personal difficulties persisted and political violence still plagued the Reich. The AA, partly because of its need for specialists in Arab affairs and partly because of the completion of the Schüler reforms, rehired Prüfer in the spring and eventually took back such Orientalists as Kurt Ziemke and Fritz Grobba. Their readmission provided an example of how weak the commitment was in the AA to genuine reform. The ministry eventually assigned them to its newly established fifth regional division (*Abteilung V*, which became the third division, *Abteilung III*, in 1921), responsible for Anglo-American and Middle Eastern affairs and headed by the veteran diplomat and friend of Schüler, Romberg.

Prüfer, much to his disappointment, received little pay and held the lowly post of assistant (*Hilfsarbeiter*) and specialist for affairs involving the British colonies in the Middle East. Six months later the ministry granted him a promotion to legation counselor (*Legationsrat*), which brought him a substantial salary increase. Prüfer was also discontented in that he bitterly disapproved of Schüler and his reforms which, he believed, had created chaos in and had weakened the AA. His complaints resounded with anger. "We in the English division, since my entry about 14 days ago," he wrote in his diary on 19 March 1920, "have had nothing, positively nothing to do!" Of Schüler and the state secretaries in the AA, Adolf Boye and Edgar Haniel von Haimhausen, he declared: "Never were such disgusting reptiles leaders of a people. The activity of the English division consists meanwhile in solving questions about space and room. But any hotel porter would develop more prudence than our chief."[11]

He also reacted with indignation to the continued chaos in the country caused by Communist-led workers in the Ruhr and other industrial regions, and to the failure by Wolfgang Kapp and General Walther Freiherr von Lüttwitz in March 1920 to overthrow the Weimar republic. He denounced as "rabble" the workers of the Communist party and Independent Socialist party (*Unabhängige Sozialdemokratische Partei Deutschlands,* or USPD) in the capital whose strike and demonstrations helped foil the putsch. "The fear of Bolshevism is, it appears, enormous," he observed in his diary during the uprising, and he attacked Kapp for being spineless and not shooting the "howling mobs." He also condemned the army leader for not having secured prior support for the revolt from the government bureaucracy, and particularly the AA: "The venture was undertaken with unbelievable foolishness. One had not prepared a single ministry. The foreign ministry is still unoccupied! The most favorable opportunity for the rightists is there. The U.S.P.D. will have the advantage."[12]

The breakdown of public services in the city and signs of disaffection in some of the Berlin army garrisons for the coup bewildered him. On 20 March, three days after the collapse of the putsch and during the peak of the Communist disorders in the Ruhr, where a "red army" of thousands had captured the main industrial centers, he lamented what he called "The decline of the West!"[13] He reached the depth of depression the next day. While the German high command dispatched the vicious Free Corps to crush the Ruhr revolt and disturbances continued in Berlin, Prüfer blamed the Jews for the uprisings. In a passage that illustrated his identification with the "old" Germany and his despising of the "new," he recorded in his diary:

> Took a walk in the morning to Steglitz. Also groups there are standing around debating everywhere. The speakers are nearly exclusively Jews, behaving as if they were friends of the people. It is repulsive to see how the stupid Germans allow themselves to be ensnared by international Jewry.
>
> [Gustav] Bauer, Hermann Müller, and other heroes have returned [from Stuttgart]. The call, distributed on a massive scale, designates [Eugen] Schiffer (Jew) [chancellor] for the Reich and [Paul] Hirsch (Jew) for Prussia. We have come apart beautifully. The English, who fear that the Bolshevik danger will achieve the end of the strike, work in alliance with them.
>
> Took a walk in the afternoon with Fr[ances] to the Garrison cemetery. Tears came to me as I saw all the graves of those who died for Germany. Meanwhile, the chattering of a M[achine] G[un] from the direction of Neukölln in the Jewish affair [i.e. the strike].[14]

The Kapp putsch failed, but it affected German politics significantly; in the Reichstag elections of 6 June 1920, the major republican parties (the SPD, Democratic, and Catholic Center) lost votes while the right-wing conservative parties doubled theirs and one, the German People's party (*Deutsche Volkspartei,* DVP), helped form a new coalition government. Prüfer observed: "Our internal situation after the elections has become even more ridiculous than before. We cannot find the necessary majority to form a government, which proves that in Germany parliamentarianism has no right to exist." [15] The subsequent political and economic crises, which reached their zenith in 1923 with massive inflation and attempts by both the extreme right and left to overthrow the republic, undermined the government even more.

The Peace Settlement

The culprits weakening and dividing the Reich, Prüfer maintained, extended beyond republicanism, Bolshevism, and "international Jewry." They included the Western Allies who, he and millions of his countrymen believed, had purposely imposed a hypocritical and unfair peace settlement on Germany in June 1919 in Paris. The Allies, he argued, failed to base the Versailles treaty on the principle of "national self determination," as suggested by the fourteen points program of the American president, Woodrow Wilson. His bitterness towards the Allies, however, had long predated the signing of the treaty.

Like the majority of Germans, the defeat in the war had not persuaded him of the falsehood of the view, disseminated by the Imperial government, that Germany's enemies had been responsible for starting the war and that an encircled Reich had fought for its survival. The AA's propaganda and the censorship during 1918 and 1919 of the government's records regarding the outbreak of the war, moreover, reaffirmed the view. In a long letter to his estranged American wife in February 1919, he denounced the Allies for charging Germany with unilateral war guilt, which the victors had not done nor would do in the treaty they eventually drafted. [16] Although he called it "a foolish venture" to assess war guilt, he illustrated his obsession with the issue by condemning Russian Pan-Slavism and British imperialism and protesting Germany's innocence.

Ignoring his own imperialist ambitions and similar views widespread in German politics and society during the war, Prüfer claimed that only a few leaders in Germany had seen "the war as a welcome opportunity to acquire territory" and that from "the beginning onward the people believed they were leading a war of defense." The Allies, especially England, he declared, had victimized the "patient, good-natured, sentimental, and disciplined people" with "a devilishly clever propaganda" about German atrocities. Yet he admitted that German "government policy slid increasingly toward the Pan Germans and soldiers" at the end of the war, as shown in the treaty of Brest Litovsk in which Germany seized huge chunks of Russian territory. "The world," he conceded further, "began with justification to fear the German victory."

Prüfer, however, fully subscribed to the "stab-in-the-back" legend already popular in postwar Germany, which claimed that the German Socialists, Communists, and Jews, not the Allies, had defeated the German army with the revolution in November 1918. Asserting that the peace movement in the Reich had also included the *de facto* head of the army, General Erich Ludendorff, who "demanded the quickest armstice," Prüfer portrayed Ludendorff as a benevolent leader allied with the masses of his people. But this was untrue. In desperation, Ludendorff sought to democratize the government in October 1918 with only one goal in mind: to find scapegoats among the popularly elected civilian politicians on whom the Imperial regime's abysmal failure could be blamed, thereby allowing those instrumental in helping unleash the war and then in conducting it to escape responsibility and remain in power.

Prüfer concluded the letter by adding other supposed villains to the "stab-in-the-back" myth.[17] On the one hand, he denounced the Allies, who, he alleged, intended to betray and cripple Germany at the Paris negotiations by rejecting a peace settlement formulated on Wilson's fourteen points. Similar to the AA, which developed a passionate propaganda appeal to world opinion to protect German interests against the Allies at Paris, he placed an interpretation on Wilson's program that favored Germany's claims everywhere.[18] Anticipating the decisions of the Allies in the Versailles treaty, he attacked them for not permitting the union (*Anschluss*) of Germany and Austria, for creating a Czechslovakia that governed Germans, and for removing the Reich's colonies.

On the other hand, he blamed much of the German revolution on the country's economic suffering and inflation, results, he argued, of the English blockade of Germany that continued after the war and encouraged the spread of Bolshevism. Prüfer mentioned nothing, however, of how the inflation had started during the war. Nor did he discuss the Allied agreement to lift the blockade and how further delay in removing it occurred as much from Germany's unwillingness to employ its idle ships and pay for food imports with its own gold as from Allied reluctance to grant credit to the Germans.

Revealing a fervent nationalism that blinded him to the misery of the German masses, the final lines of his letter to his wife declared that "it is too late" for reconciliation between the victors and losers. "We do not

want a couple more tons of foodstuffs or a couple million less in debts,"
he argued. "We want our complete freedom in the council of peoples."
On the subject of responsibility for the war, he demanded: "We also want
for you to acknowledge that your imperialist governments, as cleverly as
they too forever hide behind the democratic mask, have guilt in the war,
the same guilt as our imperialists, and that thereby no people has the right
to speak of guilt and atonement to the other."[19]

Prüfer's frame of mind as the Allies met in Paris, therefore, probably
precluded his acceptance of the Versailles treaty no matter what its content. He later joined millions of his countrymen in erroneously condemning the agreement for having left the Reich in ruin and having unjustly
accused Germany of war guilt in the treaty's reparations section, which
contained article 231 affirming the financial liability of Germany and the
other Central Powers for Allied damages suffered during the war.[20] Especially because of his interest in Arab affairs, he resented the treaty's
expulsion of the Reich from the Middle East; in signing the agreement,
Germany liquidated its investments overseas (article 119) and, specifi-
cally, in the former Ottoman empire (articles 155 and 434) and Egypt
(articles 147–54).[21] Little remained of the once widespread German activity in the region. Especially following the conference at San Remo in
April 1920, Britain dominated much of the Arab area, Egypt, Palestine,
and Transjordan either directly or indirectly, and France controlled Syria
and Lebanon. Even in such non-Arab countries as Turkey, Afghanistan,
and Persia, ruled by fiercely nationalist governments, Germany's rivals
held greater influence and possibilities of action.

Reestablishing Relations with the Middle East

With its investments and trade removed and no navy to exert political influence in the Middle East, Germany clearly viewed that region as
peripheral to its immediate sphere of national interest. Nor did the Orient
play a crucial role in the foreign policy of the Weimar government. The
Reich leaders' objectives, which reflected the feelings of an overwhelming
majority of the German people, instead centered on the revision of the
Versailles settlement in Europe, which included changing the clauses in
the treaty on German disarmament, the Reich's eastern borders with the
newly created Poland, and the payment of reparations. However, revisionism necessitated a cautious policy of avoiding antagonizing England and
France in the Middle East lest they be given a reason to frustrate German
efforts in Europe.[22] Such caution resulted in a consistent, if at times somewhat critical, German endorsement of the Anglo-French position in the
Middle East.

When Prüfer returned to the AA in 1920, this policy was impressed on him by his superiors in the Anglo-American division (Abteilung III)—first Romberg and then the feared, rude, and pro-British bureaucrat, Carl von Schubert, a later state secretary in the ministry. Shortly after the Kapp putsch began on 13 March, Romberg sent Prüfer to the British embassy in Berlin to announce Romberg's planned visit to the English ambassador to report on the uprising. Prüfer despised the gesture, much as he did Germany's entire postwar relationship with Britain. Harboring the views of a hardline revisionist, he complained in his diary: "The visit was to have a soothing effect, showing 'that there still are reputable people in Berlin.' Weakness, wherever one looks."[23] A few months later, he again berated his government's policy. Praising the opposition of the new nationalist government of Turkey against the peace settlement fashioned by the British, French, and Italians, he declared: "The Turks still resist the Entente. The people we call primitive are more virile than we who do not support them."[24]

If Prüfer and others in the Wilhelmstrasse deeply resented Germany's position and hoped eventually to reestablish the nation as a world power, it was also true that despite its wartime alliance with Turkey, it had not lost the goodwill of many Arabs, who considered Germany a fellow victim in the postwar peace settlement and the only major European power without imperial ambitions in the Middle East. Arab leaders approached the Weimar government for help on several occasions against Anglo-French rule, but the AA often refused material or diplomatic assistance.[25]

Even when the ministry provided the slightest aid to the Arabs, it carefully avoided the appearance of such activity. During 1920, a number of Egyptians, North Africans, Indians, and Persians in Germany, most of them enemies of Britain or France, asked it for help. Prüfer, who handled the requests from the refugees for Abteilung V, informed his superiors that because of "the obligations of the peace, all official relations to these people have been broken off." Nevertheless, he noted, the ministry aided such persons by giving them money and passports and recommending that for further assistance they contact the German Oriental Institute (*Deutsche Orient Institut*), "a kind of concluding station for our war ties to local Orientals."[26]

The AA also proceeded cautiously with the contacts made in Berlin during 1921 and 1922 by the new government of Afghanistan and by the Zionists. Prüfer, while he disliked the ministry's circumspection, was nevertheless significantly involved in both instances and scrupulously executed the policy. The Afghan regime of the Emir Amanullah, having won its independence from Britain in 1919 in the third Anglo-Afghan war, sought confirmation of its new status by establishing diplomatic relations with as many nations as possible, especially with the distant European powers. For this purpose, the Emir dispatched a diplomatic mission headed by Muhammad Wali Khan, his minister plenipotentiary, to visit Russia, Europe, and the United States.

The proposed visit to Germany made the AA nervous; Schubert, who possessed a strong regard for British interests, feared that London might view it with mistrust because of the Reich's attempts in the war to persuade the Afghans to attack India.[27] But the ministry decided to issue the visas and reassure the British that Germany did not intend to support anti-English activities in Afghanistan or elsewhere in the Orient. The Afghan delegation arrived in Berlin on 8 April 1921; Prüfer planned the visit, which brought him into contact with both the mission and leading barons of German industry, and arranged for the main reception for the guests at the Hotel Kaiserhof in Berlin. Prüfer and other officials from the AA including Hentig and Grobba from Abteilung III attended, as did the Reich foreign minister and the representatives of industry and finance, Walter Rathenau (who served as foreign minister in 1922 until his assassination by right-wing zealots), F. W. von Siemens, and Herbert Guttmann.

The mission asked Germany to establish immediate diplomatic and trade relations, to send technicians and engineers to Afghanistan, and to receive Afghan students. But Schubert continued to fear the British reaction; on his instructions, Prüfer informed the German embassy in London that in "regard to the difficult situation in which we find ourselves, considering the English suspicion toward such 'wishes,' the Afghans have been given in the friendliest form a generally dilatory and evasive answer." The ministry told the Afghans that Germany would welcome one of their diplomatic representatives to Berlin but that dispatching a German diplomat to Kabul would have to wait "because we [must] first begin slowly with the recovery of our foreign relations."[28]

The visit proved successful for both countries. In September 1922, the Emir sent one of the mission's members, the twenty-six-year-old Ghulam Siddiq, as Afghan minister to Berlin. Having impressed the Germans with his knowledge of German literature and command of English as the "most intelligent" of the Afghan delegation, he quickly developed close relations with Schubert, Prüfer, and the others in Abteilung III. Prüfer arranged with the Berlin police and other Reich authorities for the arrival of Afghan students, and at the end of 1922 a consortium of German industries sent a trade mission to Kabul. A year later, following Grobba's appointment as German minister to Afghanistan, growing numbers of German engineers, scientists, and officers arrived there; by 1928, next to Turkey, the Reich possessed the largest foreign colony in the country.[29] While one should not overestimate the significance of such ties, particularly because of their poor results for German investment, Germany nevertheless became the third power in Afghan relations, along with the traditional influence of the British and the Russians.

The AA also proceeded with caution towards Persia.[30] In addition, the AA deemed it in Germany's best interest to accept the spirit and intent of the Balfour declaration as well as relations with and nominal support for the Zionist movement in Germany and Palestine. German leaders no longer viewed Zionism as a function of German policy towards Turkey. Because of Berlin's intention to revise the Versailles treaty, its attitude regarding Zionism was dictated by its policy towards Britain, the United States, and world Jewry. The AA, as evidenced by its appointment of Sobernheim to head a special section in the ministry for "Jewish-political affairs," aspired to develop connections with the Jews through the Zionist movement. By appealing to Jews in America and Britain, the Germans hoped to gain Anglo-American sympathy, which Berlin believed essential for achieving the military and territorial changes it wished in Europe.

Prüfer, despite his bitter antagonism towards the Jews and Zionism, faithfully helped execute the German policy. He and Schubert, receiving dispatches from the German embassies in London, Paris, and Rome and information from German Zionist groups funneled through Sobernheim's office, carefully monitored the Anglo-French conflict regarding the Palestine mandate and the opposition of Zionists to growing Vatican influence there. In 1920 the League of Nations, the international organization created by the Paris peace conference, had assigned the mandate to England.[31]

During 1922 Prüfer met Chaim Weizmann, the president of the World Zionist Organization, while the Jewish leader visited Berlin. Weizmann held the view that Germany and Zionism had a common enemy, France, which openly supported the Arab opponents of the British and Zionism. Because of the Balfour declaration and Britain's control over Palestine, Weizmann believed that Zionism should help Britain in its struggle with France over the Middle East. Not only would that support enable Britain to overcome its difficulties with the Arabs, he reasoned, but Germany should be interested for its own political purposes in giving Britain a hand against the French. Weizmann apparently met few major German leaders; only at Albert Einstein's house one evening did he meet Rathenau, a Jewish industrialist who had become foreign minister and who plunged into an argument against Zionism. Prüfer, for his part, left no record of his response to Weizmann's proposals, probably because the AA focused its attention almost exclusively on European problems and did not wish to take a stand on issues that did not directly concern Germany.[32]

The German view towards the Middle East remained essentially constant, despite Berlin's rapprochement with the Soviet Union, which became public during 1922. The Reich's friendlier relation to Russia was a product of their mutual hatred of Poland and hope of eventually making that country disappear by taking former German and Russian territories from it. The decision by the League of Nations to award most of Upper Silesia to Poland intensified the determination of German leaders in this regard. Other factors that improved relations with Russia included the Reich's resentment towards the Western Allies for refusing to lessen the reparations payments and Russia's interest in ending its postwar isolation.[33] In addition, the German army (*Reichswehr*) conducted secret negotiations with the Red army that eventually provided German soldiers with weapons and training in specialties denied them by the Versailles agreement. Finally, Germany signed a treaty of friendship with the Soviet Union at Rapallo in April 1922.[34]

Still, because German leaders feared and despised Bolshevism—particularly the periodic attempts by the Moscow-based Communist International to use the German Communist party to foment revolution in the Reich—and viewed the relations with Russia as primarily a counterweight to the West, not a replacement of Germany's pro-Western emphasis, the AA's policy towards the Middle East changed little. Most historians correctly emphasize the economic nature of the German activities in the Orient; the AA focused nearly exclusively on rebuilding trade rather than political influence in the region.[35] An example of this policy was Berlin's establishment of diplomatic and economic ties with the nationalist government of Mustapha Kemal in Turkey. To make the initial contact with Kemalist leaders attending the Lausanne conference in 1923, in which the Turks negotiated with Britain and the other European powers a revision of the Allied peace settlement with Turkey, the treaty of Sevres of 1920, the AA employed Prüfer's vast experience in Turkish affairs.[36]

Carrying the best wishes of his government for the Turks in their negotiations with the Allies, Prüfer arrived in Lausanne on 21 July 1923. An acquaintance from the war, Ahmed Ihsan Bey, the press chief of the Turkish delegation, arranged for the German emissary to meet the Kemalist foreign minister and chief negotiator, Ismet Pasha. Prüfer told the minister that he wished to "dispel any misunderstandings" that suggested Germany had little interest in "Oriental matters." His government, he informed Ismet Pasha, believed "that Germany and Turkey have much to give and supplement each other in a future peaceful economic and cultural exchange and that the promotion of these relations would be the task of our future [diplomatic] representatives."[37]

Turkey, replied the foreign minister, laid great value on Germany's assistance and agreed that shortly after the Allied powers had opened their embassies in Turkey diplomatic relations could be restored with the

Reich. Ismet Pasha continued the cordial discussion, noting that his government believed "that Germany would soon find a way out of its present difficulties. The German question becomes increasingly a struggle between England and France, and there is little doubt about who will remain victorious in this battle. England pursues towards France a policy of slow but certain attrition and isolation. As it has triumphed in the Orient, so it will also keep the upper hand in Europe."[38] Prüfer concluded the meeting by stressing that German policy "will probably be determined by similar trains of thought" and that "this common ground in the political attitude toward the great European powers should promote a successful development of German-Turkish relations."[39]

He judged correctly. German-Turkish contacts grew steadily following the conclusion of the treaty of Lausanne, in which the European allies acknowledged Turkish autonomy. The AA assisted Turkish exiles from the war living in Germany to return to their native land "to become active there," in Prüfer's words, "for economic relations between Turkey and Germany." In November 1923, Abteilung III arranged for Ihsan Bey, the Turkish press official, to visit the Reich.[40] The AA, moreover, showed its interest in Turkish friendship by attempting unsuccessfully to suppress, at Prüfer's urging, the publication in Germany of a book by a Venezuelan, Rafael de Nogales y Mendez, *Vier Jahre unter dem Halbmond (Four Years Beneath the Crescent),* recounting the author's experiences in Turkey in World War I.

"The entire work breathes of hostility against Turkey," Prüfer noted to his superiors, adding that the book criticized the Turkish leadership in the war and mentioned "the otherwise blatantly exaggerated atrocities against the Armenians." He reiterated his ruthless view that the political interests of the German state far outweighed considerations of human dignity or morality. Although offering no proof for the assertion, he claimed that the book's author was Jewish and advised the ministry: "In my view, not the smallest basis exists for us to offer a hand in reopening the Armenian question which, fortunately for us, has finally been buried, and just as little the slandering of statesmen of the Turkey allied to us during the war."[41]

The increased contacts soon resulted in the AA's dispatch of a German mission to Turkey to negotiate a treaty of friendship, which was signed on 3 March 1924, establishing diplomatic relations and trade between the two countries. The Reich sent officers, technicians, and German industrial equipment, primarily from a consortium organized by the Krupp works, to Turkey. The AA, including Prüfer, participated in such activities; during 1925, for example, Schubert's successor as director of Abteilung III, Walter de Haas, and Herbert von Richthofen, head of the division's Oriental section, presided over negotiations with the Turkish government for Germany to build an armaments plant there.

Despite conflicts between the AA and Reichswehr ministry and intense competition among German firms—including Otto Wolff (represented by Baron von Oppenheim, who had retired from the AA), Junkers, and Rheinmetall-Borsig—for the contracts to build the plant, the two governments finally reached agreement on the project in December. Although one should not overemphasize the economic opportunities for Germany in Turkey, a backward and sparsely populated country, the Reich achieved first place by 1930 in supplying Turkey's imports.[42]

Egyptian Policy: The Plot to Restore the Ex-Khedive

If the policy towards Turkey, Persia, Palestine, and Afghanistan reflected Germany's intention not to interfere in the political interests of the Allies in the Orient for fear of jeopardizing German demands in Europe, the AA's activities regarding postwar Egypt indicated otherwise. The policy towards Egypt showed how significantly the old guard had reestablished its power in at least one part of the AA, the Anglo-American and Oriental division, and how much more aggressive the ministry might have been in the Middle East had Germany possessed greater influence there. The Egyptian policy also illustrated how such men as Prüfer and Richthofen resented Germany's position in the Middle East, secretly rejected the peace settlement of 1919 and 1920, and attempted to affect the situation through less-than-moderate means. Even the strongly pro-British Schubert sanctioned the Egyptian policy.

The attitude of Berlin towards Egypt resulted from several factors. Unstable postwar conditions along the Nile and the Reich's wartime alliance with the ex-Khedive, Abbas Hilmi, whom the British had removed from the Egyptian throne in 1914, provided Germany with political opportunities that its leaders could not resist and that the Reich did not possess elsewhere in the Middle East.[43] By secretly aiding the ex-Khedive to regain the throne, the Germans might expand their influence in a strategic country or, failing that (and returning to Bismarck's practice), they could use the Egyptian question to apply pressure on Britain to be more receptive to Germany's claims elsewhere.

The British protectorate over Egypt and the economic dislocation caused by the war had intensified Egyptian nationalism and hopes of autonomy. Anti-British disturbances during the last years of the war exploded in widespread violent disorders in March 1919 and worsened when the British failed to negotiate a settlement in Paris with an Egyptian delegation that included Saad Zaghlul Pasha, the head of the leading nationalist movement, the *Wafd* party.[44] The chaos in Egyptian politics apparently persuaded the Germans to continue their traditional anti-British agitation, which began before the war, with the Egyptian nationalists and the ex-Khedive.

Prüfer and others in the AA welcomed the reports of the Egyptian revolt in 1919; he prophesied, moreover, that Egyptian and Arab nationalism would produce a unified state in North Africa. In a letter to the ministry, apparently outlining a basic theme for its propaganda campaign against the Allied peace settlement, he demanded that the Allies be made to apply, according to "Wilson's 14 points," the "right of self determination" to Egypt and the other North African lands. "Egypt, Tripoli, Tunis, Algiers, and Morocco as a United States of North Africa," he declared, "would certainly be an idea suitable for preparing a headache for the Entente."[45]

On his return to the AA in 1920, he watched closely the negotiations between the British and Egyptian nationalists. He encouraged nationalists in Germany and Switzerland to go to Paris to seek French support for Egyptian demands against England.[46] Despite his denunciations of continued British rule in Egypt and his forecast of further Egyptian opposition, however, he scrupulously followed Reich policy by refusing requests from the nationalists for financial aid in founding a newspaper in Cairo.[47]

But Berlin's anti-British activity regarding Egypt centered mainly around the ex-Khedive, Abbas Hilmi, who intrigued after 1920 throughout Europe and the Mediterranean to place himself back on the Egyptian throne. He had lived in Constantinople since the end of the war, but eventually he traveled to Italy and Switzerland, contacting Egyptian, Arab, and Turkish supporters exiled there and beginning preparations to return to Egypt. In April 1920, following the birth of a son to the Egyptian Sultan Fuad, London sought to strengthen his position and remove attention from his rivals, including Abbas Hilmi, by officially recognizing the prince, Farouk, and his heirs as successors to the throne.[48] Several months later, the English liquidated most of the ex-Khedive's remaining properties in Egypt, from which (ironically) he received a large sum of money that enabled him to conspire further against them.[49]

Abbas Hilmi's travels in Europe in the spring of 1921 coincided with his purchase of weapons, which he began smuggling from Greece to his supporters in Egypt. He also visited Germany incognito during the summer and autumn of 1921, using a German intermediary to withdraw a substantial amount of money, which was deposited in a bank in Kiel and then sent to Switzerland. It is unclear whether the money helped purchase weapons. Because of the curious nature of the withdrawal and because the ex-Khedive later secured arms in Germany, it is not implausible that the money paid for guns. When the German police investigated the transaction, the AA protected Abbas Hilmi; Prüfer informed the police of the "legality" of the ex-Khedive's German agent and claimed that the agent had actually transferred the money to a Munich bank. Moreover, at Abbas Hilmi's request through Prüfer, the AA succeeded in canceling the ex-Khedive's war debts to the Reich government.[50]

As renewed violence spread in Egypt because of the deadlocked negotiations with Britain, Abbas Hilmi tried desperately at the beginning of 1922 to reach Egypt through Italy. He sailed to the Sicilian port of Syracuse before the Italian authorities, acting on pressure from England, stopped him. Meanwhile, the British concluded a compromise agreement with the Egyptian government on 28 February 1922.[51] It removed the protectorate and declared Egypt a sovereign state; protection of British communications through Egypt, of Egypt itself against foreign aggression, and of foreign interests and minorities remained Britain's responsibility.

Although the agreement ended Britain's wartime policy of governing Egypt virtually as a crown colony, it did not change the British claim to be the paramount foreign power there. While the German minister in Cairo, Josef Mertens, carefully avoided political problems with the Egyptians and reassured the English of Germany's intention to cooperate with them, the clandestine tie between the AA and the ex-Khedive intensified.[52] The British elimination of the protectorate in Egypt, instead of discouraging further intrigue by the ex-Khedive and his suitors, prompted just the opposite.

Schubert, Prüfer, and Abteilung III began studying the changed legal position of Egypt and concluded that the British liberation of the country had not produced a new Egyptian state, but rather had restored the Khedivial regime that existed prior to the world war and establishment of the protectorate. The Abteilung based its interpretation on the view that, despite the protectorate, Egypt had remained at peace with the Central Powers, the ex-Khedive had retained his vassalage to Turkey, and Germany and Austria-Hungary had not relinquished the capitulations in Egypt. Furthermore, according to the German reasoning, both international law and the Allied failure to list Egypt as a partner in the Versailles treaty made the Egyptian protectorate merely an "accessory" (*Zubehör*) to the British empire, not a "component" (*Bestandteil*) of it.

Consequently, according to a legal expert hired by the AA, the Versailles agreement lost its validity over Egypt with the removal of the protectorate.[53] The ministry, however, having satisfied itself with the legal argument that Germany was no longer restricted in Egypt by the peace settlement of 1919 and that the Khedivial state and Abbas Hilmi should be returned to power, never challenged England officially. Instead, working mainly through Prüfer, it supported the ex-Khedive secretly and more extensively than before. Whether such collaboration resulted from Prüfer's arrival in Rome on 18 March 1922, during the ex-Khedive's residence there following his unsuccessful attempt to reach Egypt, is unclear. Prüfer's mission, as Lord D'Abernon, the British ambassador in Berlin, reported to London, "is to get in touch with Turks and Egyptians and report upon the position in the Near East." The British official added that the diplomat "would appear not to be a very desirable character" and that "his activities require watching."[54]

Whether intended or not, the Germans thus attracted Britain's suspicion regarding their interest in the Egyptian question, as did the ex-Khedive. During the remainder of 1922, he tried and failed to negotiate with France for the Syrian throne, possibly hoping to legitimize his pretensions to the Egyptian monarchy or to divert British attention away from his adventures involving Egypt. The AA, including Schubert, encouraged Abbas Hilmi's interest in Syria and believed, perhaps as did England, that the French sought to use him against Britain in the persisting contest among the Western powers for influence in the Middle East.[55] Simultaneously, the ex-Khedive reportedly organized a terrorist group in Milan for assassinating Egyptian and British officials.[56]

Such activities formed a prelude to Abbas Hilmi's more extensive preparations, which the Germans assisted, for a coup d'etat in Egypt in 1923 and 1924. The continuing instability in Egyptian politics, centering around King Fuad's lack of popularity with the people and his struggle for power with Zaghlul and the Wafd, on the one hand, and the British, on the other, encouraged the ex-Khedive's plans.[57] Abbas Hilmi failed to realize, however, that Fuad and the Wafd, the latter possessing a majority of control over the newly created Egyptian parliament, were united in their dislike of him; the king feared the ex-Khedive's pretensions to the throne, while the Wafd viewed his authoritarian attitudes with more contempt than they did Fuad's. Nevertheless, Abbas Hilmi intensified the effort to murder officials in Egypt, hoping thereby to persuade the British that King Fuad could not govern Egypt properly and that as long as he occupied the throne the lives of Englishmen would be endangered. His secretary, Hanafi Bey Nagi, arranged for several shootings of Anglo-Egyptian leaders through Sheikh Hag Ahmed, a prominent member of the extremist Egyptian group, the "society of vengeance," which had conducted a campaign of murder since 1920.[58]

As part of the arrangements for the coup, worked out initially during the spring of 1923, the ex-Khedive employed students in Europe and

Egypt to spread Pan-Islamic favorable propaganda that emphasized his fidelity to Egypt and the Caliph during the war, a loyalty that had lost him his throne. His agents, in addition, planted reports in the French and Italian press that predicted a coup in Egypt and maintained erroneously that the ex-Khedive possessed the support of Britain.

Along with the propaganda barrage, however, the conspiracy called for the ex-Khedive to smuggle arms to his supporters in the northern Egyptian port of Tantah; at the right moment, the force would unleash a violent demonstration in favor of Abbas Hilmi. As the revolt spread, supposedly prepared beforehand by propaganda, the ex-Khedive would appear suddenly in the country as its real ruler and "deliverer" from British oppression.[59] He purposely sought, furthermore, the backing of foreign powers for his return to Egypt and, by fostering the rumors of his candidacy for the Syrian throne, to disguise his real ambitions. He tried unsuccessfully to earn the recognition of France, the goodwill of the Turks, and even the support of the major Arab chiefs (especially Faisal, the king of British-controlled Iraq) for an anti-British Arab confederacy, of which Abbas Hilmi would be the leader.[60]

Among those with whom he intrigued, however, Germany provided the most assistance. During June and July 1923, his agents in the Reich acquired the arms intended for the coup. Mehmet Ali Eyublu, an arms smuggler during the Libyan war of 1911–12, and Topal Ismail Hakki, a former official in the Turkish war ministry, purchased 5,000 rifles and large quantities of ammunition and hand grenades. The arms were shipped at the beginning of August from Hamburg through Amsterdam to the Greek seaport of Piraeus, and unloaded. While it is uncertain whether the AA contributed to the operation, it facilitated the conspiracy in other ways and, eventually through Prüfer, attempted to secure more arms for the ex-Khedive.[61]

With the ministry's collaboration, Abbas Hilmi purchased a German yacht. With his greater mobility, particularly in the Mediterranean, he could visit the coasts of North Africa and enhance the impression of his worthiness as a monarch. He intended, furthermore, for the vessel to carry him triumphantly to Egypt once his planned coup began. Prüfer introduced him to Rudolf Wiesner, a former German naval officer, who handled the purchase of the boat, the *Nimet Allah,* and supervised its construction by the Krupp-owned Germania works in Kiel. Wiesner negotiated with Abbas Hilmi in Switzerland, and the ex-Khedive visited Kiel in September 1923. The AA also arranged for shipment of the remains of the ex-Khedive's youngest son, Abd al Kader, buried in Berlin since the boy's death in 1919, for burial in Egypt.[62] Part of Abbas Hilmi's propaganda campaign to arouse Egyptian support for his coup focused on the arrival of the remains in Egypt.

Because the *Nimet Allah* was not completed until 9 October 1923, however, the plot, originally planned for that month, had to be delayed. The ex-Khedive set the new date for the coup for February or March 1924. The yacht, sailing under a German flag and crew of thirty-one hands, left Kiel, stopping at Barcelona and Marseilles and arriving in Monaco on 21 November 1923. It docked in Genoa a few weeks later, heading for the store of arms hidden in Greece. Meanwhile, Abbas Hilmi sent another agent to Germany, his secretary's son, Ali Hanafi Nagi, who purchased more arms with Prüfer's help. But before the weapons could leave Germany, the Berlin police seized them while in the possession of persons suspected of plotting a Communist revolution in the Reich.[63]

Even more serious problems, however, suddenly confronted the ex-Khedive in the Mediterranean. The German crew of the *Nimet Allah*, rebelling against poor pay and treatment, mutinied at Piraeus and refused to sail the yacht to Egypt. The crew protested so bitterly that the affair soon drew the attention of Greek officials. Attempts to settle the conflict through the German legation in Athens, which recommended that the Reich flag be removed from the boat so as not to attract further international notice, failed.

Nevertheless, Prüfer reported to Schubert on 19 January 1924 that the vessel had left Greece flying the Egyptian flag.[64] Although the legation informed Berlin a month later that the grievances of the German seamen had been remedied, the crewmen returned to the Reich in the spring and sued the ex-Khedive for wages owed. A Turkish crew that replaced them proved insufficient for carrying out the plot, and the publicity in Germany regarding the affair and the apparent mistreatment of German workers on Abbas Hilmi's estate in Turkey prevented Wiesner's attempts to hire a new German crew.[65]

Such misfortune persuaded the ex-Khedive to abandon his plans for a coup in Egypt. Although his yacht, carefully watched by the British, continued to move around the Mediterranean, he returned to Switzerland and traveled disguised through Germany in July 1924 to Belgium. Possibly for purposes of liaison with him, the AA assigned Prüfer in the summer to administer the German consulate in Davos, Switzerland. By the fall, however, Prüfer's connections with the ex-Khedive threatened to damage official German-Egyptian relations. Abbas Hilmi was now supported by the new director of the Oriental section of Abteilung III, Richthofen, whose father had known him before the war.

Following the collapse of the negotiations in 1924 between Britain and the Egyptian prime minister, Zaghlul, regarding full autonomy for Egypt, political violence flared anew, fueled by the Wafd demands that Britain relinquish full control of the Sudan to Egypt. In July, Zaghlul nearly fell victim to an assassination attempt, which apparently represented an extremist warning against any compromise with Britain. Several months later, a group of terrorists murdered Lee Stack, the British commander of the Egyptian army and governor-general of the Sudan, as he drove through Cairo.[66] Because of the Wafd hatred for the ex-Khedive, apparently kindled by the attempt on Zaghlul's life and by the widespread knowledge of Abbas Hilmi's intrigue, the Egyptian government bitterly protested the German tie to him.

During September, Egypt's ministers in London, Paris, and Rome denounced the ex-Khedive to their German colleagues as responsible for the attempted assassination of the prime minister, and accused Prüfer and Richthofen of acting for the AA in abetting Abbas Hilmi. As proof, they claimed that the two officials protected the ex-Khedive from the lawsuit against him filed by the German seamen. The Egyptians also attacked the Reich government for permitting a group of anti-Zaghlulist students in Berlin with alleged ties to the ex-Khedive to publish propaganda smuggled into Egypt. Seifullah Yousri, the Egyptian minister in Berlin, demanded that Germany expel the students, especially when the Cairo government implicated several of them in Stack's murder.[67]

Despite the protests of innocence from Prüfer and Richthofen, the Egyptians accused them of complicity, with justification.[68] With the permission of the new director of Abteilung III, de Haas, both Prüfer and Richthofen tried through the former pro-Turkish Syrian politician, Shekib Arslan, living in Switzerland, to persuade the ex-Khedive to pay what he owed the German seamen. However, when that failed, the AA sought to limit the publicity surrounding the trial against him in Germany. Abteilung III resented the republican press's criticism of the ex-Khedive, fearing its negative impact abroad for both him and Germany. Furthermore, Prüfer, following a verdict in the fall of 1925 in favor of the crew, warned Abbas Hilmi of his arrest if he visited the Reich.[69]

While it appears that the affair created embarrassment and some difficult moments for Berlin, it did little to hurt official German-Egyptian relations. The German minister, Mertens, negotiated an agreement in June 1925 in which Egypt granted Germans there equal status with citizens of other countries; the treaty also reestablished trade between Germany and Egypt, which the war had eliminated. During the next five years, Egypt became the Reich's most important Arab trading partner and, although such economic activity was limited in nature, as significant a customer of German goods as Turkey.

Moreover, there is little indication that the incident had much effect on Anglo-German relations. By the spring of 1925, London possessed plenty of evidence of the German assistance to the ex-Khedive and kept a close watch on the movements of his yacht, yet did not seem to be troubled by the German connection.[70] If the AA hoped to use the ex-Khedive to pressure Britain into concessions on issues of far more importance to Germany in Europe, the tactic failed. Although Abbas Hilmi remained a nuisance, the English knew how the Egyptian nationalists and Fuad loathed him and consequently what little chance he had of achieving his ambitions. The British, while steadily continuing to liquidate the ex-Khedive's remaining properties in Egypt and thus eliminating his influence even further, also approved of exploiting his machinations as a lever against the Wafd and Fuad.[71]

Perhaps for these reasons, the episode had a minimal impact on German policy towards Egypt or the remainder of the Middle East. Even as late as 1927 and 1928, the AA refused to cooperate with the *Nimet Allah* crew's lawyers, who requested the ministry's help in learning of the whereabouts of Abbas Hilmi and in convincing him to pay his debts. Not even their threats to inform the Reichstag's Committee on Foreign Affairs about the AA's attitude persuaded the ministry to cooperate.[72]

In this connection, however, the affair illustrated how fiercely at least one division in the AA, Abteilung III, sought to conduct policy solely along lines which it demanded and free of restraints imposed by the Weimar republic. Nor did the appointment of Gustav Stresemann as German foreign minister at the end of 1923 alter the division's policy. Its officials' penchant for secrecy and adventurism had changed little from the Imperial era. What is less clear, however, is whether the Egyptian undertaking and its negligible results, in which Prüfer played the central role, contributed to the AA's new assignment of him to Russia in October 1925.

six

Between Reconciliation and Revision, 1925 - 33

BY the end of 1925 the Reich foreign minister, Stresemann, had achieved a rapprochement with England and France and had involved the United States in Germany's economic recovery through the Dawes plan. Simultaneously, however, he pushed the Western powers for a change in the Versailles treaty by hard negotiation and the preservation of economic, political, and clandestine military ties with the Soviet Union. Prüfer's diplomatic assignments during the next five years reflected this dual nature of German policy. The Wilhelmstrasse sent him to the Soviet Union in 1926 and 1927 and to Ethiopia from 1928 to 1930, where he faithfully executed both sides of Stresemann's strategy.

Although the foreign minister did much towards returning Germany to the status of a world power, Prüfer joined most other Germans in failing to recognize this achievement. Nevertheless, Prüfer's cooperation with Stresemann, a newcomer to the AA, suggested that the old guard in the ministry had much in common with the minister.[1] Each despised the Western powers for the settlement of 1919 and feared Soviet communism, thus mirroring the feelings of most of German society, yet neither shared the *nie wieder Krieg* sentiments of many SPD leaders.

Consul General in Tiflis

Despite the treaty of Rapallo and collaboration between the German and Red armies that violated the peace of 1919, a coolness characterized relations between Berlin and Moscow during 1924 and 1925. One cause was the attempted Communist revolution, inspired by the Soviets, of October 1923.[2] Another was Germany's initiation of discussions for the Locarno agreement with the Western powers, and still another, several incidents involving each government's arrest of several of the other's citizens.[3] The possibility even existed during the summer of 1925 that a break in diplomatic relations would occur; the Germans also feared that the Soviets might blackmail them by threatening to reveal the military cooperation between the two countries, thereby damaging Germany's ties to the West.[4]

Prüfer's assignment to Russia in October 1925 and his arrival as German consul general in Tiflis three months later resulted from the AA's wish to expand its consular activities in the new Soviet republic of Transcaucasia, in order to observe the region's industrial and military development. The German consulate in Tiflis had appointed private German businessmen as honorary consular agents (*Wahlkonsuln*) in nearby Baku, Poti, and Batum, although no agreement existed that made the Soviet government acknowledge the officials. But Moscow never questioned the arrangement, apparently believing there was no need to do so and not relishing the consequences of challenging it for fear of harming German-Soviet relations.

The means for realizing the German plans existed in the consular provisions of the German-Russian commercial treaty signed on 12 October in Moscow, in which German diplomatic personnel in the Soviet Union received enhanced protection from Russian authorities. Before Prüfer reached the consulate at Tiflis and before ratification of the treaty, however, the Soviet police on 13 December suddenly closed the consular agencies, arrested their agents (Theophil Eck, Alexander Schmitz, and Carl Cornehlsen), and confiscated papers from the office in Batum. A few weeks later the Russians added insult to injury by opening a sealed package belonging to the consulate and carried by a German machine foreman traveling from Tiflis to Moscow.[5]

The Soviets accused the arrested agents of engaging in espionage for Britain and Turkey and removed them to Moscow for trial. While the officials apparently did spy for Germany, Russia's paranoia regarding German relations with the West and its desire to push Germany towards a neutrality agreement with Moscow probably accounted more for the incident. Berlin acknowledged that the agents did not possess diplomatic immunity, but it viewed the breaking of the package seal as a grave violation of the consulate's extraterritorial privileges. The AA demanded the return of the package, the punishment of the Soviet authorities responsible for the affair, and an apology from the Russian government.[6]

Amid such tension, however, pressure mounted on Berlin during the first months of 1926 to conclude a neutrality treaty with the Soviets. Partly because the Germans chose to inform their Locarno partners of the negotiations, the talks became increasingly public, heightening the world's expectation of an agreement. Tensions increased when the League of Nations rejected Germany's initial application for membership and the Soviets gestured at allying with France and Poland. Finally, the persistent threat that the unpredictable rulers in Moscow might divulge their secret military ties to Germany, thus possibly destroying the Reich's new relationship with the West, hovered like a sword of Damocles over the Germans.

When Prüfer arrived in Tiflis in January 1926, therefore, he faced the complicated task of simultaneously continuing the surveillance of Soviet industrial and military activities in the Transcaucasus while doing nothing to damage further both German-Russian relations and any chance for concluding the treaty. The AA made his job even more difficult, however, because despite the Soviet action against the German agencies, the ministry permitted the Batum agency to continue operating; an employee of Cornehlsen used the official agency stamp when supplying documents to German citizens, and the sign of the agency remained above the front door.[7] Meanwhile, negotiations unfolded among Ulrich Count von Brockdorff-Rantzau, the German ambassador in Moscow, and Soviet leaders, for the release of the agents and the establishment of mutual consulates in Russia and Germany.[8]

Prüfer was able to overcome these obstacles and develop excellent relations with the local Soviet authorities.[9] Following Moscow's refusal in March to issue temporary permission for establishing consulates in Batum and Baku, however, he came to agree with Brockdorff that to avoid possible future conflicts, the AA should close both agencies. He cautioned the ambassador on 23 March 1926, "Our factual interests are zero in Baku as well as in Batum." Neither city was crucial to the Reich, because it possessed only tiny numbers of Germans whose interests would "be assured without any difficulty from Tiflis." The AA complied and shut down both offices in July 1926.[10]

His main function, however, involved the surveillance of the Soviet petroleum industry near Baku. Prüfer told Brockdorff, however, that "because the anxiety over commercial espionage has blocked all other intelligence sources and would make their usefulness equally dangerous for the consul and his informants," he had to rely for his information on newspapers and local government publications.[11] Prüfer also carefully watched the buildup of Soviet troops along the Russo-Turkish frontier, newly established by the treaty of friendship and neutrality signed by the two countries in December 1925.

Lying on the border with Turkey and Persia, the Transcaucasus offered the German officials in Tiflis a strategic post for contacting Turkish officials and monitoring Russo-Turkish relations. Given Prüfer's long-standing affiliation with Turkish nationalists, one may suspect that his appointment in Tiflis did not result solely from Berlin's considerations regarding its ties to Russia. Yet, through whatever means available, including a request to the AA to suppress a German newspaper in Turkey critical of the Soviet Union, Prüfer sought to restore tranquility to the Reich's relations with the local Russian authorities.[12] His apparent success in the mission contributed to the improved atmosphere that enabled the signing in April 1926 of the treaty of Berlin, the neutrality agreement between Germany and Russia, and to the release of the consular officials and other Reich citizens imprisoned in Russia.[13]

A New Wife and an Appointment in Addis Ababa

The AA recalled Prüfer from Tiflis in the fall of 1927. It sent him—apparently as treatment for his tuberculosis—to Ethiopia and rewarded him a few months later with a promotion to the rank of minister (*Gesandter*). The day he left Berlin for Addis Ababa, 5 December 1927, he married Anneliese Fehrmann, the daughter of a parvenu linen merchant in the Reich capital. Her father, Friedrich Fehrmann, had been a prosperous grocer before the war, but the massive inflation of 1923 had destroyed his business and forced him to begin a new one. Anneliese, attractive and younger than Prüfer by twenty-three years, had met him in 1924 while they both recuperated from tuberculosis in a sanatorium in Davos. She then had accompanied him to Tiflis. Their marriage, also her second, occurred shortly after his divorce from his first wife; during the divorce proceedings he admitted to the court that he had had affairs with other women.[14]

Given Prüfer's political ambition and entry into the upper levels of the middle class, it is curious that he married a woman with Anneliese's social and medical background. Although infatuated with her, he seems to have wed someone over whom he felt dominant and whom he considered no threat to himself. Nevertheless, her lower middle-class origin embarrassed him; he denied her social status by forbidding her parents to visit except at Christmas, and prohibiting her from taking their son, Olaf, born in 1930, to his grandparents. Prüfer, exhibiting a lack of feeling similar to his relationships with others—including his own parents—showed little affection for the child. The son recalled many years later: "My father treated me with emotion only once; although he personally was not violent with me, he beat me severely on one occasion for having shot a toy pistol in the ear of our family's dog, which was sleeping at the time. He loved animals."[15]

Anneliese Fehrmann, Christmas 1924 in Berlin, about the time she and Prüfer met

Furthermore, Prüfer discouraged physical and emotional contact between Anneliese and the boy, reacting with anger towards her when she went against his wishes. He adamantly refused, for example, to allow his son into the parents' bedroom.[16] Because of his behavior, and particularly his continued philandering, which became an obsession with him, Anneliese rarely enjoyed genuine happiness; nevertheless, she obediently endured the indignities and remained faithful to him until his death in 1959. His marriage appeared to be another situation in which his feelings of inadequacy and his tendency to use others for his own ends came to the surface.

Prüfer assumed his new post in Addis Ababa in January 1928. His work there was guided significantly by Germany's relations to the Euro-

Prüfer with his son, Olaf, in Bavaria, 1933

pean powers whose colonial interests dominated East Africa and Ethiopia itself. The improved atmosphere between the Reich and the Western powers after Locarno along with Germany's acceptance into the League of Nations in September 1926 eventually resulted in Stresemann's altering elements of the peace settlement of 1919 regarding disarmament and reparations.[17]

Although such revisions did not impress Prüfer and other German nationalists, including the career diplomats, he nevertheless scrupulously obeyed the directive given him by the AA not to threaten the interests of the Western countries in Ethiopia or jeopardize "the path of negotiation for moderating the conditions of the Versailles treaty."[18] The ministry, which had already eroded the Schüler reforms of 1919 and 1920 and tightened its control over envoys in the field, instructed Prüfer to observe the activities in East Africa by Germany's rivals and, wherever possible, to enhance German trade.

Despite a humiliating loss to the Ethiopians in 1896 at Adowa, Italy had emerged from the scramble among the great powers for African colonies with the major claim to the control of Ethiopia. Avenging the defeat obsessed the Italians, who hoped to unite the sprawling semifeudal country with Italy's other colonies, Eritrea to the north and Somaliland to the southeast. After seizing power in 1922, the Fascist dictator of Italy, Benito Mussolini, regarded the domination of Ethiopia as the first step towards the creation of a colonial empire that would make Italy the most powerful state in the Mediterranean and Middle East.

Initially Mussolini tried diplomacy to advance this end. Ignoring the French, who held a tiny portion of Somaliland on the Red Sea and sponsored Ethiopia's entry into the League of Nations in 1923, Mussolini engaged in negotiations with England. He also established contacts with the ruler of Ethiopia, the chieftain (*Ras*) Tafari, who had been regent and heir to the throne since 1916. Much to Tafari's unhappiness, England agreed in 1925 to recognize Italian economic interests in Western Ethiopia and the area between Eritrea and Italian Somaliland. While Tafari protested to the League that the agreement violated Ethiopian sovereignty, both Rome and London assured the regent of their friendship.[19]

During his first months in Addis Ababa, most of Prüfer's reports to the AA discussed the resentment of the powers towards each other's activities within Ethiopia. The Italians and British, for example, disliked an American company surveying for construction of a dam on Lake Tana, a major source for the Nile; Britain called for a conference to limit arms imports to Ethiopia because of fears that French shipments of weapons might increase Ethiopian defense capabilities and enhance French influence; and each of the powers sought oil concessions from the Ethiopian government by offering it parcels of neighboring lands or use of seaports.[20]

Tafari, especially fearing the Italian designs on his country and trying to consolidate his power at home among the local chieftains, sought to involve as many countries as possible in the rivalry with the hope of maintaining Ethiopia's independence.

Such tactics disgruntled both the British and Italians. Britain, for example, partly for humanitarian reasons and partly to pressure Tafari into greater cooperation, threatened to seek Ethiopia's removal from the League of Nations because it allowed rampant slavery. Prüfer, in a note to the AA, defended the laxity of the Ethiopian government in eliminating the practice of slaveholding among the chieftains and feared instead for Ethiopia's autonomy. While he condemned slavery for its menace to Ethiopian independence, he mentioned nothing of its immorality.[21]

Mussolini began in the fall of 1928 to prepare for a future invasion and conquest of Ethiopia. By signing a treaty of friendship and arbitration with Addis Ababa in August, Italy appeared to be offering a gesture of goodwill towards Ethiopia. But Italy's main goal was to increase its political and economic penetration of the country, and particularly to weaken Tafari by using propaganda and bribery to enflame the opposition against him among the local chieftains. One of the Rases, who feared that the Italian treaty might strengthen Tafari, tried unsuccessfully to overthrow him; following the attempted coup, Tafari tightened his control over the Ethiopian army and proclaimed himself *Negus,* the highest rank below emperor. In addition to the treaty, Rome initiated military and technical measures in Eritrea and Somaliland.

Prüfer, who reported to Berlin that "one is very excited in French circles" against the Italian agreement and that England apparently accepted it "with great calmness," witnessed the Italian preparations firsthand when, after receiving an order from the AA, he toured Northern Ethiopia at the beginning of 1929.[22] His twenty-three person caravan, heavily armed and accompanied by a similar group headed by an Italian diplomat, traveled for three months. They journeyed by mule from Addis Ababa northward through the mountains to the Italian border and by automobile, ship, and railroad through Eritrea, along the Red Sea, and back to the Ethiopian capital.

The group found northwestern Ethiopia poor, thinly populated, teeming with robbers, and feudal in nature; it appeared to Prüfer unsuitable for much German trade. In the widely scattered tribal villages, he reported to Berlin, the "only real passions of the people are the loves for weapons and alcohol." He described the political system as "very confused," dominated by four provincial chieftains hostile to one another and to the Negus. He experienced the bitter struggle for power directly when one of the Rases, Guksa Wolie, viewed the German and Italian envoys as friends of the Negus and detained and imprisoned them for five days. Only when the Italians threatened to stop their secret payments to the Ras did he send the formal apology Prüfer demanded for the "misunderstanding."[23]

Not only did Prüfer learn during the expedition about the Italian subversion among the Rases, but he also observed the close cooperation of the Italians and British, each supplying money and arms to the chieftains and uniting against French interests. The Italian influence was evident in many ways. In Gondar, for example, the Italians had constructed a heavily fortified compound that housed soldiers and colonial officials who traveled regularly to Eritrea. "The entire countryside," Prüfer informed the AA, "is infiltrated by Italian spies, mostly former Eritrean soldiers." During his visit to Eritrea, he noticed the "military character of the colony," as evidenced by "the relatively large crowd of [Italian] soldiers that one generally sees" and by the highway system built for the transport of troops to Ethiopia.

On his return to Addis Ababa in mid-March 1929, Prüfer reacted with ambivalence to what he had seen. On the one hand, he believed that the best prospects for developing German trade in Ethiopia lay with "a European occupation" of the country.[24] On the other hand, his deeply engrained hostility towards the British and his dislike of Italy, which extended back to its opposition to Germany in the world war, prompted considerable sympathy on his part for the Negus and the Ethiopian government. Because Germany, in contrast to the other European powers, possessed little apparent political interest in Ethiopia, a fact which Prüfer repeatedly emphasized to the Negus, the two developed a close friendship. Also enhancing the Negus's confidence were Prüfer's cordial relations with David Hall, an Ethiopian businessman of German ancestry and personal adviser to the ruler. Once, when the Negus told Prüfer of his fears of Italian aggression, he stated that Germany's political position resembled Ethiopia's. "Both countries," he declared, would "only be able to burst the stranglehold that encircles them if they attempt without abandon to transform an enemy into a friend and protector against the others."[25] That prospective ally, the Negus continued, was France. Prüfer's feelings favoring the Negus against the European powers intensified as the German envoy repeatedly avoided intervening in Anglo-French and Italian affairs in Ethiopia; for instance, he urged the AA to prevent German industry from competing with British and American firms for contracts in the construction of the Lake Tana dam.[26]

On several occasions during 1928 and 1929, Prüfer discouraged the retired German major and international arms dealer, Hans Steffen, from concluding agreements with the Negus. Steffen had smuggled a few cases of weapons to the ruler and possessed his full confidence; the Negus's admiration for Steffen also resulted from the major's work as an adviser to several Middle Eastern princes during the 1920s, including King Faisal of Iraq and Ibn Saud of Arabia. In March 1928, as Steffen arrived in Addis Ababa to negotiate the construction of an ammunition factory in Ethiopia and to propose that the Negus conclude a treaty with Ibn Saud, Prüfer demanded that the negotiations "remain secret" and warned the smuggler that his activities were "not completely harmless for himself as well as for our relations to the powers interested in Abyssinia and Arabia." A year later, because of opposition from Britain and Italy, the minister stopped Steffen from selling a commercial airplane to the Ethiopian government.[27]

By the spring of 1930, with Prüfer successfully fulfilling his task in Ethiopia, the AA recalled him to its Berlin headquarters. Perhaps Prüfer's most significant achievement was his personal friendship with the Negus, who, following a final abortive uprising against him by Ras Guksa Wolie in May, crowned himself emperor and took the name of Haile Selassie. As the emperor now consolidated his power over the chieftains, his relationship with Prüfer and the Germans offered Berlin the potential of playing a greater role in Eastern Africa in the future. Even the British minister in Addis Ababa, Sidney Barton, recognized his German counterpart's ability; he described Prüfer to the London Foreign Office on 11 June 1930: "Before and during the war he was head of the German Intelligence Service in the Middle East. He looks it. His real home is in the Wilhelmstrasse, and he is a man of such exceptional cultivation and lively intelligence that he gives the impression that he would be a rising light there but for his ill-health."[28]

On Prüfer's return home, the AA sent him to the small British-controlled land of Yemen to sign a trade treaty between its ruler, the Imam Yahia, and the Reich. The negotiations in Sana, the capital of Yemen, however, collapsed when Prüfer, seeking to avoid violating England's interests, refused to agree to the Imam's demand that Germany recognize Yemen's independence and integrity. While spending a few days in the neighboring British protectorate of Aden and meeting with British officials, he noted "great nervousness" among the English regarding his visit to Yemen. Prüfer was even involved in an incident in Aden in which the police, apparently suspecting him of espionage, questioned him aboard a ship; the British later apologized. To allay Britain's fears, Prüfer urged that the AA forward an official report of the negotiations in Yemen to the British minister in Addis Ababa.[29]

Back at the Wilhelmstrasse:
Abteilung III and the End of the Republic

With his arrival in Berlin in September 1930, Prüfer officially assumed his new post in the Wilhelmstrasse as deputy director (*Dirigent*) of

On the trip to Yemen in 1930. Prüfer is on the left.

Abteilung III, the division for Anglo-American and Oriental affairs. Prü-fer received the appointment for several reasons. First, he had demon-strated a superior talent for obeying and executing the policy directives of his superiors. For example, none of his dispatches from Addis Ababa or Tiflis displayed personal willfulness or any tendency to make suggestions independent of the AA. Second, the ministry had completed the removal of the republican elements infused into its upper levels by the Schüler reforms and replaced them with the veteran diplomats. Generally con-servative, nationalistic, and anti-republican, the career officials, with the exception of Julius Curtius, who became foreign minister on Strese-mann's death in 1929, dominated both the major posts abroad and in Berlin.

The professionals had especially reestablished their influence through the newly defined posts of state secretary (which fell to Bernhard Wilhelm von Bülow in 1930) and deputies to the chiefs of each division (*Ministe-rialdirektoren*). The deputies (*Dirigenten*) possessed extensive authority in both policy and personnel affairs. Like Prüfer, however, most had spent their time in political analysis and reporting rather than in making policy proposals. By 1930, the career men had gained control of the position of chief in most of the divisions, including Abteilung III.[30] The directors and their deputies intensified the bureaucratization and antirepublicanism of the ministry. They insisted on loyalty from their subordinates and reasserted the AA's autonomy against attempts at domination by the divided political parties in the Reichstag, by the Committee on Foreign Affairs, and by interest groups.

Abteilung III, headed after September 1930 by Hans Heinrich Dieckhoff and his deputy, Prüfer, were perfect examples of the new career officers. Both officials had begun their diplomatic careers before the war. Dieckhoff joined the AA in 1912, fought as a cavalry officer in the war, and served in the 1920s at the German embassies in Washington and London. Because of his efforts to prevent war while serving as Nazi Germany's ambassador to the United States during 1937 and 1938, he later received the reputation of being ideologically independent of and even opposed to the Nazi government and its leader, Adolf Hitler.[31]

Before Hitler seized power in Germany in 1933 and the country embarked on a policy of aggression aimed at destroying the Versailles settlement, however, both Dieckhoff and Prüfer indicated their sympathy for such a program. They pursued actions in their division that reflected the harder and more combative revisionism, conservativism, and nationalism that marked the governments of Heinrich Brüning (1930–32) and Franz von Papen (1932). Both tried to solve the domestic crisis during the Depression by ignoring the Reichstag and ruling with decrees issued by the aging Weimar president, Paul von Hindenburg; by pandering to the extreme rightists, particularly Hitler and his National Socialist German Worker's party (*Nationalsozialistische Deutsche Arbeiterpartei,* shortened to NSDAP or Nazi); and by achieving successes in foreign affairs through a more "active" revisionist policy.

Many nationalists in the Reichswehr, AA, and in industry were dissatisfied with Stresemann's achievements in foreign diplomacy. They dreamed of moving Germany beyond a mere alteration of the Versailles settlement and returning it to a position of world power, and they pressed for a vigorous economic and political penetration of southern and eastern Europe. Recent studies have shown that their activities marked the end of the "Locarno era," recalled the traditional imperialist views of Wilhelmine Germany, and provided a beginning for the subsequent expansionist policies of the National Socialists.[32]

Certain activities of Abteilung III and its leaders in dealing both with the republic and with the issues surrounding Germany's relations to the Middle East and Anglo-America mirrored the hard-line attitude. To be sure, in Germany's handling of its everyday relations with England and the United States, little changed after 1930. Dieckhoff supervised American affairs and Prüfer concentrated on British. Among other duties Prüfer handled arrangements for the visits of British leaders to Berlin, carefully monitored diplomatic dispatches arriving from the London embassy, and drafted colorless reports on British politics for Dieckhoff, Bülow, and the foreign minister.[33] Particularly towards those areas of the Middle East where British interests remained the greatest, the division continued the previous policy of fostering German trade at the expense of political activities that could alienate the Western power. Abteilung III, for instance, scrupulously avoided any overt ties with Indian nationalists that might anger Britain.[34]

The division's policy towards Ethiopia remained cautious. Stories circulated in February 1931 that Haile Selassie and the Ethiopian government had received a new shipment of weapons from Steffen, an honorary consul general of Ethiopia and notorious arms dealer in Berlin. Such claims posed potential problems for Germany, since England and Italy, the dominant colonial powers in Selassie's kingdom, had previously signed an arms convention with France and Ethiopia on the sale of weapons to the latter. Dieckhoff and Prüfer quickly secured a written promise of innocence from Steffen. When the European powers and Ethiopia ratified the arms convention in February 1932, the AA informed the other government ministries. Curiously, however, that was the extent of the ministry's inquiry into the rumors; Prüfer and Dieckhoff ignored the Anglo-Italian suspicion about Steffen's role as Ethiopia's official representative in Germany, maintained close relations with the smuggler, and accepted his declaration without further investigation.[35]

On other issues of Middle Eastern policy the division leaders displayed a more aggressive attitude. Prüfer, for instance, bristled at the alleged poor treatment of Germans in French Somaliland. Declaring that "the French colonial regime in Somaliland still forever treats all German travelers and goods with chicanery," he recommended that the Reich establish a consular agency in Djibouti to protect against such behavior. Abteilung III's activities regarding Egypt, moreover, illustrated the persistence of the hopes of some division members for an eventual change in the postwar settlement there.[36] While maintaining the proper diplomatic ties to Cairo, which the Wilhelmstrasse used to encourage German-Egyptian trade, Berlin also retained its connection, mainly through Prüfer, to the ex-Khedive, Abbas Hilmi.

Despite the continued Anglo-Egyptian tensions and the disruption in Egyptian politics caused by the conflict between King Fuad and his Wafd opponents in the parliament, Abbas Hilmi officially renounced his claim to the throne on 12 May 1931 in Lausanne, in return for an annual subsidy from the Cairo government. Prüfer met the ex-Khedive the same day that he signed the documents, and Abbas Hilmi asked the German official to ensure that there be no "unfriendly commentary in the German press."

Although Abbas Hilmi appeared to have removed himself from international politics with the stroke of a pen, he nevertheless managed to keep his name in the news by encouraging rumors about his candidacy for the throne in Syria.[37] Prüfer still harbored the belief that the ex-Khedive might one day be of use to Germany should the political situation change in favor of the Reich and against its Anglo-French rivals in Egypt or elsewhere in the Middle East. Thus Prüfer urged Dieckhoff and Bülow to protect Germany's relations to Abbas Hilmi, even at the cost of infringing on the political freedoms granted by the Weimar republic. During the spring of 1932, the AA asked the police to investigate Egyptian students in Berlin accused of anti-Khedive activities, and the ministry placed pressure on a German newspaper to refrain from criticizing Abbas Hilmi. The ministry also attempted to encourage him to contract with German industry to build him a new yacht. Although no truth existed to the stories about serious French and Turkish support of the ex-Khedive for the Syrian throne, his continued propaganda and intrigue generated concern on the part of King Fuad, as well as continued surveillance by the British.[38]

The nationalist and anti-republican sympathies of the leaders of Abteilung III particularly manifested themselves in the division's policies towards Persia and the mounting criticism abroad against the anti-Semitic movement in Germany. In both instances, the Abteilung's behavior reflected its growing concern for the turmoil in Germany during the Depression. As the Brüning and Papen governments proved incapable of halting the economic disaster, the radical Nazis, promising relief from suffering to the masses and appealing to the latent xenophobia and anti-Semitism in the population, increased dramatically their number of seats in the Reichstag and other political assemblies by 1932. They intensified the nation's fear by provoking a virtual civil war with the Communists. The leaders of Abteilung III, however, worried most about the alleged threat from Bolshevism. This fear was revealed in the crisis that developed by 1931 and 1932 between Germany and Persia, in which the division displayed its hatred of communism and willingness to subvert the democratic principles of the republic to protect German relations with a foreign country.

By 1932, several problems threatened to destroy Germany's hard-won commercial position with Persia. The Depression caused German companies to lose trade in Persia, and a scandal in the Persian national bank involving German officials, including the bank chairman, Kurt Lindenblatt, led to their dismissal and prosecution by the Persian government.[39] A long-standing conflict between Tehran and Berlin over what appeared to the Shah to be the Reich's toleration of Persian Communists and students publishing anti-Shah propaganda in Germany also menaced

German interests in Persia. Fundamental differences between the Weimar and Persian governments lay at the heart of the issue: the former, a democracy, permitted freedom of the press and association, while the latter, an absolute monarchy, allowed few civil rights and brutally crushed its opponents.

Since 1926, Persian Communist and anti-monarchist students had organized political groups in Berlin and published propaganda pamphlets and newspapers, demanding a Persian revolution to overthrow the Shah. They sent much of the material to other anti-Shah elements in Europe and smuggled it into Persia. The Tehran government insisted that Germany expel the students, but the intervention of Rudolf Breitscheid, a Socialist deputy in the Reichstag and member of the parliament's Committee on Foreign Affairs, frustrated any such efforts by Abteilung III and the Prussian ministry of interior. Breitscheid argued that banning the students violated the Weimar constitution and would "contradict the spirit of a democratic republic." Pressure from Tehran continued, however, and in 1930 the Reichstag established a new law providing for the expulsion of foreigners for endangering Germany's relations to other nations.[40]

Shortly after Dieckhoff and Prüfer assumed the leadership of Abteilung III in September 1930, they illustrated their dislike (and that of the AA generally) for having to answer to the Reichstag and other republican institutions (e.g., the press) for their activities by renewing the campaign against the Persian students with zeal. The division persuaded the Berlin police to confiscate much of the propaganda. But in February 1931 it learned that German Communists had infiltrated the student groups, resulting in new anti-Shah publications in Berlin and Munich.[41]

The contacts between the German and Persian Communists disturbed Prüfer and Dieckhoff. Apparently, such ties confirmed their belief in the existence of a global Communist conspiracy.[42] They redoubled their efforts to settle the affair, pushing the German newspapers involved to publish retractions. But the articles had already enraged the Shah, who immediately ordered the recall of his minister, Muhammad Ali Khan Farzine, from Berlin. On 22 October 1931, Prüfer met with Karl Severing, the Prussian interior minister, and pressured him to expel Morteza Alavi, a Persian Communist, and to ban the Berlin newspaper Alavi published. Prüfer argued that the need of Germany to protect its trade and political influence with Persia justified violating the democratic principles of the republic—in this instance, freedom of the press and the Persian publisher's civil rights. Prüfer insisted to the Socialist Severing that continuing to harbor a person "who had grossly abused the hospitality extended to foreigners and who belonged to a radical party" would hurt Germany's relations to Persia, "which would damage the German economy to its utmost, but above all the working classes." After "some hesitation," Prüfer noted in a memorandum summarizing the meeting, Severing agreed to expel Alavi "immediately from Prussian territory."[43]

The expulsion and the prohibition of Alavi's newspaper in Berlin led the Shah to rescind his directive recalling his minister, Farzine, from the Reich capital.[44] Nevertheless, rumors flooded the German press about an impending break in relations between the two countries. Prüfer reported to Dieckhoff that Farzine believed "the facts of the case were not fully understood in Tehran."[45] Subsequent events justified the warning. Tensions remained as the Persian administration released German employees at the beginning of 1932 and closed several German firms in Tehran. At the Shah's request, furthermore, the Reich government introduced legal proceedings against the German communist writer, Dr. Carl Wehner, and the expelled Alavi.

Despite the efforts of Abteilung III to defuse the incident, the Shah mistrusted the German government because of Berlin's delay in acting against his enemies. His suspicions intensified when a new Persian paper, the Communist *Naehzaet (Revolt)*, surfaced in Berlin and attacked him.[46] Abteilung III moved quickly. At its insistence, the Prussian authorities confiscated the paper, arrested its editor and placed him on trial, and searched the home of a Persian friend. The government sentenced the editor in April 1932 to three months in jail, and a few weeks later the Shah demanded the expulsion of other Persians from Germany.[47]

The Shah intensified the pressure on Berlin by releasing more Germans from his administration. Wipert von Blücher, the German minister in Tehran, reported that some Reich citizens considered telegraphing Hitler to request his "intervention" in the affair. On 13 June, Prüfer and other officials from Abteilung III met again with representatives of the Prussian interior ministry. A mood of panic dominated the meeting, during which Prüfer noted the "further sharpening of relations with Persia" because of the "slow progress of the trials" against the German and Persian Communists. The session ended with his request that the interior ministry see to the "quickest possible execution of the proceedings."[48] To encourage the ministry to act rapidly, the AA reported several days later that the Reich president, Hindenburg, requested information on "the situation."[49]

The tactic succeeded. Severing, the Prussian interior minister, immediately ordered the expulsion of another Persian living in Berlin, and a court sentenced the German Communist, Wehner, to six weeks in prison. Prüfer also reported to Dieckhoff on 6 July 1932 that a German writer, Leo Matthias, agreed to retract his anti-Shah articles of the previous year in a Munich paper.[50] These measures significantly improved the Tehran government's attitude towards Germany; nevertheless, even after the establishment of the Nazi regime in January 1933, press matters and German racial policies disrupted relations between the two.[51]

Although in this regard the Abteilung's campaign against both its government's laws and Communism succeeded, the affair received widespread attention in Germany. The liberal press criticized the unjust expulsions of the Persians, while the Nazis attacked the Prussian ministry of interior for its reluctance to ban the "foreigners" and Communists.[52] The Nazi party newspaper, *Der Angriff,* alleged that behind the protection of such outsiders and evil elements, stood an even more sinister force at work against Germany: international Jewry.[53]

Similar reasoning prevailed in Abteilung III, particularly with Prüfer, and such an attitude intensified in 1931 and 1932 because of criticism from abroad about Hitler's rapidly emerging anti-Semitic movement in Germany. The division possessed direct knowledge of Hitler's racism. It ignored, for example, copies of an exchange of letters it received in December 1931 between Chempakaraman Pillai (a leading Indian nationalist in Germany and acquaintance of Prüfer) and Hitler's private secretary. Pillai criticized both Hitler's racism and his remark to the *Times* (of London) that the preservation of British rule in India was in the common interest of Germany and England. The secretary adamantly defended Hitler, noting that the Nazi leader "is still of the conviction that a relinquishing of English rule in India would mean the spread of Bolshevism in India, and thus the preservation of British rule there lies in the interest of the entire civilized world."[54]

Already in the spring of 1931, however, seven months after the Nazis' first startling triumph in Reichstag elections, the Abteilung was trying to blunt negative foreign reaction to Nazism. As in the incident involving freedom of the press for the Persian publisher, the division violated the democratic principles of the republic, this time by trying to restrict the individual freedoms of leading Jewish officials in Germany as well as the publicity abroad surrounding the mounting Nazi attack on the Jews. In April 1931 Jewish leaders in the United States and the German ambassador in Washington, Friedrich Wilhelm von Prittwitz-Gaffron, asked the AA "whether a position could be taken in some form by an authoritative German office against the anti-Semitic propaganda of National Socialism." Such provocation, the ambassador warned, threatened to become "very harmful to German interests in the United States."[55]

Responding to the ambassador's inquiry, Prüfer dispatched Sobernheim, a subordinate and the AA's specialist for Jewish affairs, with Gaffron's telegram to the Reich chancellery to discuss the possibility of the Chancellor Brüning's speaking publicly against the Nazi agitation. The AA files give no indication of why Prüfer sent Sobernheim to Brüning's office; most probably, however, given Prüfer's anti-Semitic views, he did not wish to intervene personally on behalf of the Jews and, trying to downgrade the importance of the subject, sent a subordinate instead. Moreover, because Sobernheim was himself a Jew, his visit to the chancellery would have even less significance. Under such circumstances, Prüfer made certain that the chancellery would not publicly agree to Brüning's defense of the Jews, but would make an altogether different and far less beneficial arrangement for them. Sobernheim, who retained close ties to German-Jewish groups, organized—with the chancellery's agreement—a private meeting of Brüning with officials from the principal German-Jewish agency to rebut anti-Semitism, the *Central-Verein deutscher Staatsbürger jüdischen Glaubens* (Central Association of German Citizens of the Jewish Religion), and arranged for the dispatch of a report of the meeting to Jewish leaders abroad.[56]

During the summer of 1932, the Abteilung again undermined the rights of the German Jews through a concerted effort to limit publicity abroad about the anti-Jewish Hitler movement, as verbal and physical attacks on Jews by the Nazis and their semi-armed thugs, the storm troopers (*Sturmabteilung,* or SA), intensified. Meanwhile, Hitler's followers increased their number of seats in the Reichstag from 107 to 230 in the July election. After Hitler's unsuccessful negotiations with Hindenburg and his advisers, including the new chancellor, Papen, about forming a Nazi government, diplomatic dispatches arriving at the Wilhelmstrasse reflected a steadily growing concern abroad about such events. The German consulate general in Jerusalem, for example, reported to Abteilung III that "the increase in the anti-Semitic movement in Germany has been followed closely by local Jewry." The consulate general in Antwerp noted that "with the clashes on the Kurfürstendamm" in Berlin between Nazis and Jews, "a certain unrest" had come over the city's Jewish community, which numbered "about 40,000." Similar complaints arrived from the German legation in Egypt and the embassy in Paris; the latter mentioned "the call for a boycott of German goods by the Jewish population in North Africa." In addition, David Brown, the publisher of the *American Hebrew* and *Jewish Tribune* newspapers in the United States, asked for permission to visit the Reich "with a view towards ascertaining the true status of Jewish affairs there."[57]

Abteilung III rigorously countered the foreign criticism by trying to control the public statements of German Jews regarding the situation. It ignored the daily reports of Nazi outrages against Jews and agreed with the Reich ministry of interior, which informed the AA that "peace and order governed throughout Germany."[58] In August 1932, Dieckhoff and Prüfer sent Sobernheim, the AA's specialist for Jewish affairs, to observe an international conference of Zionists in Geneva. The meeting featured reports on anti-Semitism by Jewish delegations from North America, Rumania, Germany, Russia, and Palestine, and produced a decision to form a world Jewish congress by 1934.[59] Apparently because he was Jewish, Sobernheim knew the members of the German delegation to Geneva and could therefore watch them closely; Prüfer directed him to accompany the German delegation to Geneva and submit "a thorough report" on its members' behavior and remarks there.

The AA intended Sobernheim's presence to moderate or lessen what the German Jews said at the meeting about the mounting attacks on them in their homeland. The tactic produced satisfaction in Abteilung III. One member of the group was the Berlin banker and leader of a renegade organization among German Zionists, Georg Kareski, who was noted for his contacts with the Catholic Center party and his vigorous demands for opposition to Nazi anti-Semitism.[60] Sobernheim declared about Kareski's remarks: "The third speaker, Kareski, agreed that the situation in Germany was serious, yet one should not overestimate it. The government was determined to protect the Jews; what the future would bring, no one could foresee."[61] The German consulate in Geneva praised Sobernheim's work, observing that because of it "the speeches of the German Jews, but also particularly the press reports, insofar as they could have had a negative effect on Germany, were weakened."[62]

The AA's pressure on the German Jews, however, did not stop with Sobernheim's mission to Geneva. When Kareski allegedly wrote an anti-German, anti-Hitler article in an Antwerp newspaper, *Neptune,* Prüfer questioned the Jewish leader, who denied writing the essay. Furthermore, as Prüfer recorded later, Kareski claimed that he had made his "view on the situation of the Jews in Germany" clear at the Geneva conference, in which "he indeed did not deny the anti-Semitic movement in Germany, but had emphasized the trust of the German Jews in the present government." Kareski also informed Sobernheim that he planned "to protest with *Neptune* in Antwerp against the misuse of his name and also to enlighten the Jewish papers in Antwerp."[63]

It is difficult to judge whether the campaign to muzzle Jewish leaders in Germany lessened the foreign reaction to Nazism. During the fall and winter of 1932, fewer dispatches arrived at Abteilung III from the missions abroad noting criticism of the anti-Jewish movement. The decrease in criticism probably resulted, however, from the decline of the Nazi vote in the Reichstag election in November and the popular opinion that Hitler had lost his political momentum. Nevertheless, defending Germany against criticism from abroad and violating the democratic rights of German-Jewish leaders by seeking to keep them from expressing their views freely on events in their country became major elements of the AA's policy during the early months of the Hitler regime in 1933, when the Nazis were unleashing their official persecution of the Jews.

Moreover, such incidents show that at least one division in the ministry included officials who, even though they did not belong to the Nazi party, worked actively to shield the Nazi prejudice and hatred from being exposed to the world.[64] That, too, became a characteristic of institutions in Hitler's Germany, including the AA, which eventually contributed to the horrors perpetrated by the regime in World War II against the Jews and other "non-Aryans." Such episodes also raised questions about the attitudes of the AA's leaders, foreign minister Constantin von Neurath and state secretary Bülow, towards the Jews and democracy.

While the activities of Abteilung III during the final years of the Weimar republic do not warrant the conclusion that the German foreign ministry played a significant role in the destruction of the democracy, they do illustrate that certain elements in the Wilhelmstrasse refused to content themselves with only revising the Versailles peace settlement. Like other individuals and agencies in the Reich government, they acted to subvert the republic.[65] In this respect, the division's policies contribute another piece of evidence for the view that 1933 was not so sharp a political break in German history as was once believed.

seven

The Nazis Seize Power, 1933-35

"WE, the officials of the foreign service slowly recognized that we were outsiders," Prüfer declared after World War II in describing the relationship of German diplomats to the Nazi regime. "I am certain," he continued, blaming Hitler for the war and absolving his colleagues and himself for responsibility in the Nazi catastrophe, "that . . . the career officials of the foreign ministry were unaware of the concrete details of Hitler's eventual plans for violence."[1] Although he echoed the postwar claims by his fellow diplomats of their innocence in remaining at their posts after 1933 and serving Hitler, the files of the ministry's Anglo-American and Oriental division (Abteilung III) reveal that Prüfer supported from the outset Hitler's promise to Germans that he would destroy the Versailles settlement.[2] The diplomat also immediately and eagerly helped implement the new government's policies that indicated it would achieve its goals both at home and abroad, if necessary, with violence: rearmament, nationalism, dictatorship, terror, and anti-Semitism.

Research has shown that while the career diplomats sympathized with Hitler's early stress on peace, moderation, and anti-Marxism, he also appealed to their desire for more than a mere revision of the post-World War I European order. Neurath and Bülow, for example, longed for a return to the Reich's world power status of the Wilhelmine era, demanding in 1933 a recovery of the frontiers and overseas colonies of 1914, the Anschluss with Austria, and the achievement of "other aims in foreign policy" resulting from "the formation of states in Europe since 1918."[3]

The diplomats also held in varying degrees the authoritarian (i.e., anti-democracy and individual liberty) and anti-Bolshevik attitudes that permeated the Weimar republic and contributed to the widespread German support of Nazism. While admitting after World War II their disdain for democracy, Prüfer and this group of diplomats nevertheless absolved themselves of responsibility for its demise. They noted that few of their number had joined the NSDAP before 1933, that Hitler had disliked them because of their education and social origins, that they had focused their attention abroad and not on domestic affairs, and that they had believed that the Weimar president, Hindenburg, along with other conservatives like Neurath, would control the Nazis.[4] Prüfer, true to the pattern of his personal relationships, viewed himself and the AA's old guard both as superior to the violent, lower-middle-class Nazi leaders and able to exploit them for the ministry's purposes.[5]

Several diplomats, moreover, declared after the war that they had aided the Jews against Nazi persecution. Historians have dated the ministry's cooperation with Nazism from Bülow's memorandum to the AA on the day Hitler took office as chancellor on 30 January 1933; the memorandum urged the diplomats to remain in their posts to exercise a temperate influence on the radicals.[6] But recent evidence has indicated that the anti-Semitism of the ministry's old guard extended further than previously thought.[7] That the anti-Jewish and anti-republican policies of Prüfer and others in Abteilung III predated the Hitler government, as detailed in the preceding chapter, and that such activities continued after the dictator's appointment, augments this conclusion. The existence of such sentiments also suggest that, contrary to what the diplomats wished for the world to believe following the war, at least a few realized the nature of Nazism and accepted its premises—if not also some of its horrible implications—before Hitler became chancellor.[8]

Building Personal and Professional Defenses

Mixing opportunism with his affinity for Nazi philosophy, Prüfer immediately welcomed the new government but hoped that the AA could be guarded from infiltration by the Nazis. Hitler wasted little time in destroying his supposed domestic enemies and in making his first moves towards revising the Versailles treaty, rearming Germany, and transforming the nation again into a world power. These policies appealed strongly to Prüfer's conservatism and nationalism. As early as 1 February 1933 he had changed the tenor of his official communications to foreign missions regarding the Versailles agreement. He declared in a belligerent note to the German legation in Rio de Janeiro that the Versailles settlement had been "imposed on Germany" and that the Reich would assert "all its power to remove the Versailles disarmament clauses." In addition, although Prüfer had no occasion to deal officially with such issues, he admitted after the war that he favored the return of former German territories from Poland and the Anschluss with Austria.[9]

He also expected that Hitler would remove the alleged Jewish influence from Germany. A few months after the dictator's assumption of power, Prüfer explained the Nazi policies towards the Jews to Shekib Arslan, the Syrian nationalist exiled in Switzerland. Prüfer prophesied that the "confessed attitude of the Reich government regarding the Jewish question makes it naturally appear desirable to promote the emigration of the Jews from Germany."[10] His view resulted not only from his deeply rooted anti-Semitism, but also from the brutality so swiftly shown by the Nazi government towards the Jews and other alleged opponents.

Hitler used the burning of the Reichstag building as a pretext to unleash a "reign of terror" against Communists, Socialists, Jews, and "liberals." The military units of the NSDAP, the SA and Heinrich Himmler's "elite guard" (*Schutzstaffel*, or SS), took over the important police positions; the government created a ministry of propaganda headed by Joseph Goebbels; and Hitler received dictatorial power for four years from an intimidated Reichstag. Many persons hostile to the Nazis were sent to concentration camps, and the new rulers initiated the *Gleichschaltung* ("coordination") of the German state governments. The regime outlawed trade unions and political parties, except for the NSDAP.

What especially affected Prüfer and the other diplomats, however, were the government's numerous decrees removing Jews, Communists, Socialists, and Weimar loyalists from the bureaucracy; similar purges occurred in the other professions. On 7 April 1933, the "Law for the Restoration of the Professional Civil Service" authorized the elimination from the government of Jews and political opponents of the Nazi regime. Apparently to satisfy Hindenburg's concern for the honor of the German army, the law exempted officials who had joined the civil service before August 1914 or had fought at the front in World War I. Another law of 28 September prohibited the employment by government authorities of "non-Aryans" or of persons married to them.

Prüfer was able to comply with the directives easily. He secured letters from his commanders in World War I, Kress von Kressenstein and Hans-Eduard von Heemskerck, certifying his participation in the war's fighting.[11] Each civil servant, to retain his position, had to prove "Aryan" descent through birth and marriage certificates stretching back to his grandparents; Prüfer and his wife searched for the records of their families.[12] While they found nothing that endangered them with the regime, they uncovered information that apparently aggravated Prüfer's anti-Semitism. Not only did his wife learn that her family had Jewish members in its distant background, but she also discovered in her research that one of her husband's ancestors five generations back had married a former Jew in Oranienburg, Gustav Wilhelm Hirschfeld, who had converted to Christianity.[13] Prüfer's fanatical hatred for Jews made him conceal this fact by having the records of the forefather removed from the registry office (*Standesamt*) by bribing one of its officials.[14]

Despite the Nazi witch hunt, which ousted large numbers of SPD officials and virtually all Jews from the Prussian civil service and other parts of the bureaucracy, and despite Hitler's personal antagonism towards the diplomats, Prüfer and his colleagues in the AA survived the purge essentially untouched. Hitler's assignment in June of a Nazi official and SS *Gruppenführer* (major general), Josias Erbprinz von Waldeck und Pyrmont, to the ministry may have intimidated the diplomats, but it produced no significant changes and the SS leader was removed a year later.

Waldeck possessed neither the ability nor the experience to enforce his demand, vigorously opposed by Neurath, the conservative foreign minister and favorite of Hindenburg, that Waldeck participate in selecting future officials. Frustrated in his efforts, he bribed a clerk in the ministry to obtain incriminating information on certain persons. When Neurath angrily protested to Himmler, head of the SS and Waldeck's superior, Waldeck no longer appeared in the Wilhelmstrasse. Only a handful of AA officials joined the NSDAP; chief among the mission leaders were Edmund Freiherr von Thermann (Argentina), Otto Reinebeck (Estonia), Ulrich von Hassell (Italy), Prince zu Wied (Sweden), Emil Wiehl (Southwest Africa), Otto Köcher (Switzerland), Heinrich Rüdt von Collenberg (Mexico), and Erich von Luckwald (Albania).

Historians agree that because Hitler needed the diplomats to help him project a peaceful image in foreign affairs and relieve the anxiety of Germany's critics abroad, he saw little reason to bring wholesale changes to the Wilhelmstrasse. Still another reason for his permitting the ministry to continue essentially unchanged centered on the NSDAP's lack of trained and experienced diplomats. Other scholars attribute the AA's record to the "stubborn persistence" of Neurath in protecting his fellow careerists by ignoring the law of 7 April 1933 and claiming that foreign service appointments were the sole prerogative of the president and subject to civil service rules that included clear provisions for careers in the service, employment plans, and regulations for promotions.[15]

Yet the attempt of Neurath and others in the AA to safeguard the ministry from penetration by the Nazis invariably contributed to the diplomats' cooperation with them. Prüfer, for example, possibly with Neurath's blessing as part of a strategy to accommodate the NSDAP without surrendering the AA's autonomy, quickly befriended Ernst Wilhelm Bohle, head of the party's Foreign Organization (*Auslandsorganisation,* or AO). The AO organized and administered small party groups of Reich citizens in foreign countries, and Bohle, a protégé of Hitler's deputy, Rudolf Hess, aspired to become Germany's foreign minister.

Although Prüfer apparently viewed Bohle as an uneducated upstart and parvenu, Prüfer sought to use the AO leader to the advantage of the AA, the institution that had commanded his unswerving loyalty for over a quarter century. For his part, Bohle admired Prüfer, who became a kind of authority figure or "father" to the party official. Prüfer's political attitudes, especially his hatred of Bolshevism and the Jews, resembled Bohle's, and Prüfer's career and training—his position as an "insider" in the AA—appeared to offer Bohle valuable assets for his ambition to head the ministry. Bohle's attraction to the diplomat may also have resulted from the AO leader's birth outside Germany and resulting lack of intimate friends, except for Hess, among the other party leaders.[16]

In the final analysis, however, Prüfer's attitude toward the National Socialists mirrored that of other German conservatives who collaborated with them—they thought that the Nazis could be manipulated. His friendship with Bohle contributed further to compromising him with the Nazis, yet it failed to preserve the independence of the AA. The AO leader, although he received an appointment in the ministry in 1937, never became a significant force in the Nazi leadership; much to the frustration and anger of Prüfer, Neurath, and others in the AA, Hitler would eventually replace Neurath as foreign minister with Joachim von Ribbentrop, the champagne salesman turned foreign policy adviser to the Nazi chief.

One of Prüfer's first meetings with Bohle occurred on 4 July 1933 in Munich, where a group of AA officials met with Hitler and representatives of the AO to discuss "new directives" for the Nazi groups abroad.[17] A few months later, when Hess attempted to propose Bohle for the position of a special state secretary in the AA to supervise the "nazification" of the ministry, Neurath courted Bohle even more intently, hoping the latter would influence Hess and keep extremists like Waldeck out of the AA. Members of the ministry's personnel division, including its director, Werner Otto Freiherr von Grünau, met with Bohle at his headquarters in Hamburg; Neurath agreed to allow Bohle an office in the AA.

The tactic succeeded, at least temporarily; Bohle thought of persuading the AA to transfer Prüfer, one of its own trusted guard, to the ministry's personnel division and use the diplomat to appoint National Socialists from the AO to the ministry. Following Bohle's meeting with Neurath in December, the AO leader informed Hess that he had discussed this possibility with the foreign minister. Both the latter and state secretary Bülow, said Bohle, found Prüfer acceptable, but refused to consider replacing Grünau. "I had expected this opinion," Bohle concluded, "because I made certain that Prüfer's candidacy would not be rejected by the ministry." He promised to "keep the affair under observation." [18]

The party's interest in Prüfer was not misplaced. His star rose steadily in the AA; in 1935, he received added responsibilities for American affairs in Abteilung III. Apparently to acquaint himself with his new duties, he visited the United States and Mexico in March. [19] Then in 1936, as shown in chapter 9 here, Neurath agreed to the party's proposal that he name Prüfer head of the personnel and budget division. Despite Prüfer's failure to join the NSDAP till later and his snobbish disdain for the much less educated and sophisticated Nazis, his conservative, nationalist, and anti-Jewish attitudes made it possible for him to serve his new masters. He misunderstood, however, that such collusion with Nazism on his part and that of his fellow diplomats, which contributed significantly to Hitler's early success both at home and abroad, would undermine and, ultimately, destroy the influence of the institution they so venerated and sought to guard.

Defending and Abetting Persecution

Yet another reason that Hitler retained the established diplomats involved their support—or lack of criticism—of what the Nazis considered most important in 1933 and 1934: the campaign inside Germany against the Jews, Communists, and other alleged enemies of the government. While Hitler mistrusted and repeatedly denounced the professionals in the Wilhelmstrasse, Prüfer's example and the behavior of others in Abteilung III suggest that the ministry gave the dictator little to fear on this crucial issue. Prüfer defended the government's vicious policies against foreign criticism not only because of his desire to protect Germany's national honor, but also because of a strong attraction to Nazi principles, especially the hatred of Jews and Communists.

Although Hitler's first move in revising the Versailles treaty and rebuilding Germany into a world power was his withdrawal of the Reich from the League of Nations and from the Geneva disarmament conference in October 1933, the world reacted with greater hostility against the new government's policies at home. Particularly in the Western democracies, the Nazi suppression of freedom and political dissent, the beatings and other attacks on the Jews, the dismissal of prominent university professors, the abolition of trade unions, the public burning of books, and the campaign against the Christian churches combined to provoke anti-

German sentiment. Much of the respect for Germany that had developed among the Western powers during the Weimar years now reversed itself.

On 3 March 1933, apparently ignoring the spread of physical violence against Jews and the removal of Jewish judges and other professionals from their positions, Neurath assured Sir Horace Rumbold, the British ambassador in Berlin, that the Jews had nothing to fear from the new regime.[20] Similarly, Hitler's vice-chancellor, Papen, emphasized to the press that Jews would be treated like all other German citizens.[21] Bülow, moreover, showed no sympathy towards the Jews and even justified the radical measures against them prior to the anti-Jewish boycott and the first racial legislation in April. In March he joined Neurath in creating the *Referat Deutschland,* the ministry's liaison office with the NSDAP, which was designed to protect Germany against its foreign critics. Neurath and Bülow quickly approved the adoption by Bülow's cousin and the head of the new office, Vico von Bülow-Schwante, of the party's crude anti-Semitic propaganda to combat the opposition abroad.[22] Bülow-Schwante sent the propaganda, which claimed that Jews dominated German life and that a Communist-Jewish world conspiracy existed to ruin the Reich, to Dieckhoff and other division leaders and to the foreign missions.

Prüfer, however, had accepted such views for some time; he continued his efforts with Dieckhoff, begun in Abteilung III before 1933, to blunt foreign criticism of Nazi anti-Semitism. During March 1933 the division received a flood of cables from Leopold von Hoesch, the anti-Nazi German ambassador in London, warning of the damage done to Germany's reputation in England by the Jewish persecution. Dieckhoff, setting the future tone for the division's response, angrily replied to Hoesch on 27 March that the claims of mistreatment of Jews in Germany were "outrageous atrocity reports." He maintained that "it is in fact correct that nearly all English correspondents have no understanding of the revolutionary movement of the last weeks and, with a kind of cold hostility, derisively criticize everything that suits them." He demanded that the ambassador immediately inform British leaders of the "scandalous behavior of the English correspondents."[23] Three days later, the anti-German opinion in the United States prompted a meeting of Dieckhoff, Prüfer, other members of the division, and Bülow-Schwante.

Although the reaction of the outside world and the intervention of Hindenburg through Neurath helped restrict the Nazi party's nationwide boycott of Jewish businesses to one day, 1 April, numerous beatings of Jews by Nazi mobs and the SA accompanied the event. Abteilung III nevertheless continued to ignore the violence; it collaborated with Hermann Goering, Hitler's brutal minister of the interior for Prussia, who ordered German Jewish groups to contact Jewish organizations abroad and deny the atrocity reports. Through its London embassy the division arranged for leaders of two of Germany's major Jewish agencies, the Central Association of German Citizens of the Jewish Religion (*Central-Verein*) and the Zionist Federation of Germany (*Zionistische Vereinigung für Deutschland*), to deliver a letter to Jewish groups in Britain, cautioning against "any exaggerated or false news spread about the happenings in Germany."[24]

Because of its key place in German foreign policy until mid-1935, improving the Reich's image in Britain preoccupied the division.[25] Prüfer arranged through Bülow and the Reich chancellery for Hitler to receive a pro-German and conservative member of Parliament, Col. Thomas Moore, during his visit to Berlin. But Prüfer and Dieckhoff refused, on the other hand, to forward to Hitler a letter protesting the "systematic brutality practised in the concentration camps," sent by prominent English leaders that included the archbishop of York, the bishop of Chichester, economist John Maynard Keynes, and historians George Trevelyan and G. P. Gooch. Dieckhoff sloughed off the affair by asserting that "such impertinent pieces of writing to the Reich chancellor cannot be considered."[26]

The protest against the Nazi regime did not limit itself to the Western countries. While the AA's gestures revealed a slight concern for opinion abroad on Hitler's part, he changed nothing in his domestic policy; hence the negative response from the world continued during 1933 and 1934. The barrage of foreign criticism and the boycotts of German exports intensified Prüfer's belief that an anti-German plot existed among the world's Jews. So did the stream of reports sent to Abteilung III by its mission leaders in the Middle East who, taking their cue from the division's leadership, carefully monitored Zionist and Jewish activities. An air of hysteria and a lack of sympathy for Jews dominated the cables. Information on the Zionists abroad also reached the division from the feared Nazi secret police (*Geheime Staatspolizei*, or Gestapo).[27]

A long and bitter protest against the anti-Jewish policies in the Reich developed in Egypt. The German minister in Cairo, Eberhard von Stohrer, one of the few Nazi party members in the AA and a virulent anti-Semite, repeatedly denounced the local Jewish colony's attacks against Nazism and its efforts to organize a boycott of German exports. Admitting that the "Jewish agitation" is "not solely comprised of Jewish elements, but also embraces other confessions," Stohrer demanded that the Egyptian government suppress the "anti-German movement" and urged that the AA take measures to halt it. In June 1933, Prüfer arranged with the Egyptian minister in Berlin, Hassan Nachat Pasha, for the Reich propaganda ministry to interview a prominent Egyptian journalist visiting Germany to counter, in Prüfer's words, "the especially active and poisonous Jewish agitation propaganda in Egypt." He suggested that the interview be published in Egyptian newspapers and used to explain "the attitude of the German government in the Jewish question," as well as how the German anti-Jewish "boycott was nothing other than a warning against the unscrupulous atrocity agitation."

During the fall, Prüfer received vulgar propaganda materials from Wolfgang Diewerge, a fanatical Nazi party leader in Berlin, emphasizing a familiar theme: an "international Jewish conspiracy against Germany in Egypt."[28] The AA official also attempted through Stohrer to persuade the Egyptian government to stop Leon Castro, a popular Jewish lawyer and defender of Egyptian Jews in a liberal trial against the German Association (*Deutscher Verein*) in Cairo, from speaking at public meetings. But Prüfer, despite his energetic measures to combat anti-German opinion in Egypt, stopped short of agreeing to Stohrer's suggestion that Germany boycott Egyptian cotton. Merely the threat of the boycott, however, Stohrer claimed three months later, "strongly disturbed Jewry" and persuaded the Egyptian government to silence the alleged enemies of Germany. Prüfer quickly exploited the situation by arranging for a radio broadcast by Nachat Pasha from Berlin to Egypt, praising the close tie of Berlin and Cairo, the music of Richard Wagner, and Hitler as "the hero of the new Germany and the pillar of its revolution."[29]

The Abteilung's attempts to conceal Germany's anti-Jewish policy from foreign opinion stretched into 1935. Prüfer, following his visit in the spring to the United States and Mexico, received a greater share of the division's daily work regarding the Americas.[30] Much of his attention focused on preventing an American rabbi, Ferdinand Isserman, from visiting Germany. Prüfer instructed the German missions in Europe not to issue Isserman a permit to return to the Reich because the rabbi, after a trip through Germany during the fall of 1934, had "given very hateful lectures" in America regarding "the German situation." Despite such efforts, a bureaucratic mistake allowed Isserman to procure a visa from the German embassy in Paris and travel in Germany for six weeks during August and September 1935. On his return to the United States, the rabbi did what the AA had tried to stop; he reported to the press that Nazism "has destroyed the universities, has exiled the great scholars, Jews and Christian alike, and has eliminated academic freedom."[31]

One of Prüfer's final actions in the Jewish question before his transfer to the personnel division reflected the conflict that characterized Nazi policy towards the Jews by 1935. In the spring, party radicals unchained a new wave of anti-Jewish terror, boycotts, and discrimination, sanctioned by the previous legislation that eliminated the Jews from government service and professional life. Such violence also expressed the arrogance and aggression resulting from Hitler's consolidation of his power and from his triumphs in re-arming Germany and regaining the Saar region, transferred from the Reich in 1919 to the administration of France and the League of Nations.

Although the records are unclear, the NSDAP soon called a halt to the outburst; apparently, some leaders considered the violence against Jewish businesses premature, and Hitler and other officials disliked spontaneous mob brutality, which was unpredictable and ungovernable. The regime, however, quickly channeled the violence into new legislation, resulting in Hitler's decreeing the Nuremberg laws, which banned marriage and sexual relations between Germans and Jews and stripped the latter of their German citizenship. With the Jews completely disenfranchised and defenseless before the law, influence in the Jewish question passed increasingly to the SS, which governed the police and concentration camps and began urging the forced emigration of the Jews.

What to do with the Jews had also concerned the AA and other government agencies. Beginning in 1933, apparently in keeping with Hitler's often repeated desire to make Germany "free of Jews" (*judenrein*), the regime had introduced measures that favored Zionism, aided the emigration of German Jews to Palestine, and permitted them to take a portion of their property with them. The Haavara (Hebrew for transfer) Company, in agreement with Berlin, received a monopoly on the shipping of goods to Palestine. The deal only made sense for the Jews, however, when contrasted with the confiscation of their property if they emigrated elsewhere; the arrangement with the Haavara Company reduced the proportion of a person's property stolen by the Nazi government.

The Nazis also employed Jewish migration to the British mandate as a device to expand German foreign trade and counter the threat of a worldwide Jewish boycott of German goods. Despite the Haavara agreement and the efforts of German Jewish groups to facilitate emigration, prejudices and economic fears in foreign countries led to significant restrictions on the number of German refugees they would accept. Although bitter divisions regarding the agreement with Haavara arose among the NSDAP, AA, and other groups during 1936 and 1937, at which time Britain began considering the partition of Palestine and the formation of a Jewish state there, at least one official in the AA disapproved of the ministry's pro-Zionist policy from its beginning.

Prüfer, fearing the impact of the policy on Germany's relations to the Arab world, differed with Referat Deutschland, which supported Haavara till 1936 in the belief that it would eliminate Jewry from Germany. Prüfer remained an ardent opponent of Zionism, promised his Arab friends that Germany did not intend to send its Jews to Palestine, and watched carefully the statistics of German Jews migrating there (Palestine accepted over one-third of those who left Germany between 1933 and 1937). Prüfer did favor Jews leaving the Reich for other countries, excluding the Arab lands.[32] But several of his colleagues, including Bülow and Dieckhoff, showed themselves less sympathetic to arrangements other than Haavara for Jewish emigration. On 18 April 1935, Max Warburg, the prominent Jewish banker from Hamburg and chairman of the Welfare Association of German Jews (*Hilfsverein der deutschen Juden*), which assisted Jewish migration both to Palestine and other countries, visited the AA and talked with Prüfer.

Warburg requested the ministry's help in stopping the Berlin police from changing the group's name to Welfare Association of Jews in Germany (*Hilfsverein der Juden in Deutschland*). According to the chairman, the association received "considerable amounts of foreign currency from abroad" for "easing the emigration of Jews from Germany," but the organization's members disapproved of the name change imposed by the Nazis and threatened to disband the group. Since 1933, Warburg told Prüfer, the association had acted "thoroughly in the sense of the new Germany" by assisting over 11,000 Jews to emigrate.

What upset Warburg and others in the Hilfsverein about the name change was what it symbolized: a further isolation of the Jews from the rest of German society and potentially greater obstacles to emigration. By 1935, culminating with the Nuremberg laws, the regime no longer allowed Jews to call themselves Germans. Hence, Jewish organizations had to alter their names so that they spoke for "Jews in Germany" rather than "German Jews." Prüfer, apparently believing that contributing to a "Jew-free" Germany took precedence over depriving the Jews of their German heritage, suggested that Bülow consider the complaint and sought backing for the Hilfsverein from the Referat Deutschland. Bülow, however, replied with a curt, "No thank you," and the Abteilung refused help by offering the simple bureaucratic notation "that it deals with a question for whose responsibility only the domestic authorities are competent."[33]

This and the other policies of Abteilung III already described show how old-line conservatives such as Prüfer, whose prejudice resulted mainly from political and economic resentments towards Jews, could easily accommodate the racial anti-Semitism of the Nazis and provide it with a cloak of respectability. Like many other fashionable and "intellectual" Jew-haters, Prüfer wished to dissociate himself publicly from the gutter-level anti-Semitism of Nazi leaders, which appeared too bloody for his aesthetic sensitivities. For instance, in a lecture on Middle Eastern affairs to a group of war veterans in Berlin on 28 November 1933, he gave no hint of his anti-Jewish views and made only slightly critical remarks about Zionism and the British presence in Palestine.[34] Nonetheless, he did not reject Nazism; to do so would have meant recognizing the criminality of Germany's actions and, therefore, betraying his long-held reverence for the Reich and its government.

While one must be careful not to conclude from the activities of Prüfer, Dieckhoff, and others in Abteilung III that the AA played a significant role in the Nazi seizure of power or that the German foreign service supported completely the events of 1933 and 1934, it is undeniable that the division's behavior illustrated its zealous acceptance of the Nazi regime's domestic policies. What the division did also raises further questions about the leaders of the AA, Neurath and Bülow. From the evidence of their actions during the early months of Hitler's government, during which they sought to defend Nazi policy against foreign criticism, it is clear that Abteilung III acted with their full approval.[35] The division provides another example of how narrow the dividing line was between the nationalism and pride of German conservatives like Neurath, Bülow, Prüfer, and Dieckhoff, and the intolerance and racism of Nazism. Prüfer and his superiors wasted little time in crossing that line.

eight

Executing Hitler's Foreign Policy, 1933-36

HISTORIANS of Nazi foreign policy have begun to challenge the traditional view that Hitler sought good relations with Britain and during World War II even hoped to ally with it.[1] Instead, according to recent evidence, the focus of German policy had shifted by 1935 and 1936 away from Britain and towards Italy and Japan. Even the Anglo-German naval agreement of 1935, traditionally hailed as Hitler's first accord with a major foreign power and the event that vaulted his principal adviser on England, Joachim von Ribbentrop, into prominence, was designed to mask his plans to build a huge navy that violated the treaty and could help him one day defeat the Anglo-Americans.[2]

The AA, whose goals in foreign policy often coincided with those of the dictator, took its cue from him regarding relations with Britain. It proceeded cautiously after 1933 and proclaimed Germany's desire for friendship with the British, all the while helping advance political and military preparations that could ultimately threaten England and world peace.[3] The role of Prüfer and Abteilung III in foreign policy between 1933 and 1936, particularly towards Britain, the Middle East, and Ethiopia reflected this two-sided nature.

Concealing Re-armament

Prüfer's involvement in the AA's efforts to deceive the British about German re-armament began with an incident late in October 1933, barely a week after Hitler had removed Germany from the Geneva disarmament conference and the League of Nations, actions that had led to negative foreign reaction but which presented little real danger for the Reich. Noel Panter, a British newspaper correspondent in Munich, published an article in the *London Daily Telegraph* describing Hitler's meeting with 20,000 SA in Bavaria and the efforts by Berlin to conceal the heavily "military character" of the gathering. The Bavarian police, on orders of its commander, SS leader Heinrich Himmler, immediately arrested and imprisoned Panter and a German journalist, Josef Ackermann, accusing them of espionage, based on their attempts to gather information regarding German violations of the disarmament clauses of the Versailles treaty.

The Reich's recent withdrawal from the Geneva conference meant that Panter's arrest occurred at a particularly sensitive moment for the Germans. The secret armaments program, till then in the planning and organizing stage, had just entered a new phase of acceleration; the Reich war ministry had also expanded the armed forces in July by ordering a build-up of special border formations and the training of 250,000 reservists in the SA. Radical Nazi party and police officials attempted to conceal the SA paramilitary activities from foreigners. The AA appeared to agree; as it told Himmler, it wished for nothing in the Panter incident that would encourage "English opinion to bother itself too much with the affair" and worsen Anglo-German relations.[4]

Tensions rose, however, as reports from Leopold Hoesch, the German ambassador in London, warned of serious repercussions within English opinion if Panter remained in custody, and as Sir Eric Phipps, the new British ambassador in Berlin, protested to Neurath. Prüfer, at the foreign minister's order, met on 31 October with Basil Newton, counselor of the British embassy, to inform him that "unfortunately it is still impossible to provide final information" regarding Panter's fate. The next day, Newton warned Prüfer "that the English press employs itself increasingly in unfriendly fashion with the incident" and that in the interest of both sides "the affair [should] be brought to a conclusion as quickly as possible."

Neurath, fearing that the episode could lead to further British and Western concern for Hitler's plans to re-arm, finally persuaded the chancellor to release Panter on 1 November 1933 and order him to leave Germany immediately. Even following Panter's return to England, however, Sir John Simon, the British foreign secretary, demanded an explanation from the Germans and mentioned the possibility of reprisals against the Reich. But Prüfer urged Bülow and Neurath to stand firm in the controversy, declaring that the Reich owed Britain nothing in the affair. He justified to his superiors Germany's removal of Panter and maintained that, while the journalist could not be charged formally with espionage and officially expelled, no one could be permitted "to damage Germany and prove that it violated the requirements of the Versailles treaty. This was especially the case with Panter's interest in information regarding the S.A. and S.S."[5]

Britain's reaction, like its response to Germany's withdrawal from the League and the Geneva meeting, was to do nothing, a response that would become familiar during the 1930s. Some leaders in London criticized war as a policy and Versailles as a peace settlement; Simon, despite warnings from Phipps of the dangers which the new Nazi regime posed for peace, insisted on following a policy of reconciliation with Germany. A few weeks after the Panter affair, British leaders held meetings in London with Ribbentrop, Hitler's "private diplomat," who emphasized his master's "peaceful views."[6] A deeply held pacifism among the British people and the failure of France to push for action against Germany fortified the English acceptance of the image of a pacific Hitler.

Following Hitler's purge of the SA in June 1934, which cleared a further path for the type of re-armament that the dictator and the Reichswehr demanded, the AA participated in other ways in the German policy of deception towards the Western powers. Prüfer, with the approval of Neurath and Bülow, organized a portion of the government's propaganda smokescreen, which disguised the real intentions of Hitler and Ribbentrop in concluding the Anglo-German naval accord of June 1935. Prüfer coordinated the heavily publicized exchange of visits by German and British war veterans' associations, which accompanied the agreement, with the objective of enhancing the impression of a Germany desiring peace. Not only did Prüfer make the AA's arrangements with other Reich ministries for the veterans' contacts, but he also collaborated in the project with Ribbentrop's special party office (*Dienststelle*), thereby aiding in a small way the success of the man whom Neurath and the Wilhelmstrasse already feared and despised as a rival in foreign policy.[7] It made no difference to Prüfer or his colleagues that at almost that same moment Hitler violated the Versailles treaty anew by announcing universal military conscription for Germany and by planning with his naval leadership the massive expansion of a German navy capable of defeating Britain and America in future wars.[8] In private meetings with Basil Newton, the British embassy counselor in Berlin, and English politicians visiting the Reich, Prüfer adamantly defended Germany's policies, including its rejection of an "Eastern Locarno pact" and other security accords proposed by Britain, France, and Russia.[9]

The Middle East: Between Disinterest and Stabilized Relations

Hitler's focus on political and military preparations in Europe as a means to establish global supremacy for Germany meant that after 1933 the Middle East remained, much as it had during the Weimar period, on the periphery of German foreign interests. Nevertheless, the Nazi regime held considerable appeal for the Arabs, who admired Berlin's rabid nationalism, anti-Jewish policies, and determination to revise the postwar peace agreement. Arab leaders viewed the Anglo-French mandate system in the Middle East and the Balfour declaration as parts of the injustice of that settlement.

Prüfer, who handled much of the AA's relations with the Orient till the beginning of 1936, emphasized the Reich's affinity with the Arabs. "Insofar as the actual forces exist for the emancipation of the Arab peoples from the influence of the great powers," he told an audience of war veterans in Berlin in November 1933, "we Germans observe them as ideally interested spectators, who see a parallel to our own past in the push of the Arab peoples for the formation of a national state."[10] His sympathy for a Pan-Arab state resulted partly from his belief in the propaganda value of the idea for Germany, particularly in recruiting Arab support for the Reich. However, it also stemmed from his deeply engrained hatred of England's domination of the Middle East and his view—apparently influenced by his experience with the Pan-Islamic movement in the world war—that the divine law of Islam would form the foundation of a future Pan-Arab nation.[11]

Although such ideas also attracted other Oriental experts in the AA, including Werner Otto von Hentig and Fritz Grobba, they contrasted sharply with Hitler's lack of concern for the Middle East. In fact, few Arab leaders realized that Nazi philosophy placed the Semitic Arabs at the bottom of its racial hierarchy.[12] They even failed to grasp how Germany's pro-Zionist policy and the Haavara agreement permitted Jewish migration to Palestine. Nor did the Arabs understand that Hitler, while not so worried about maintaining good relations and avoiding war with Britain as historians have traditionally argued, had little intention during the first years of his rule of raising Anglo-French suspicions by supporting the Arab side in Palestine and elsewhere in the Middle East. He also viewed the Mediterranean area—including its Arab portions—as belonging to the sphere of interest of his fellow fascist, the Italian dictator Mussolini.

The activities of Prüfer and Abteilung III demonstrated this clearly. Despite the interest of the division's deputy director in Pan Arabism, the AA's official policy reflected Hitler's idea and bordered on indifference towards the Arabs. Nevertheless, within that framework, Prüfer and others in Abteilung III experienced increasing contact, although carefully restrained, with leaders in the Arab East and slowly solidified Germany's relations with the non-Arab states.

During 1933 and 1934, numerous Arab officials, among them Haj

Amin al-Husayni, the Mufti (religious leader) of Jerusalem, and the Emir Abdullah of Transjordan, sought unsuccessfully to mobilize German diplomatic backing against the Western democracies by meeting with Heinrich Wolff, the German consul general in Jerusalem. Still other Arab pressure came to Kurt Ziemke, the German consul in Beirut; in August 1933 a Syrian nationalist and officer in the Syrian-French army, Hassan, approached the consul for money for a terrorist campaign to free Syria from France. Prüfer and Dieckhoff, however, quickly ordered Ziemke to avoid further contacts with Hassan. Several months later, another Syrian nationalist, Prüfer's friend and the editor of the Geneva-based journal, *La Nation arabe*, Shekib Arslan, requested a meeting with Hitler during a visit to Berlin. Arslan, whose ideas about a Pan-Arab state resembled Prüfer's, despised the French occupation of Syria and wished to exploit Franco-German and Franco-Italian friction to win both Germany and Italy for the Arab cause. But his visit to the Reich capital in the fall of 1934 only resulted in meetings with officials in Abteilung III who informed Arslan that Hitler could not receive him and that his suggestions were dangerous and unacceptable to Germany. Shortly after the Syrian returned to Switzerland, Prüfer concluded in a memorandum on 7 November 1934, which Hitler's chancellery approved three days later, that "Germany cannot support the Arabs with money or with arms."

The encounter did not end Arslan's efforts to recruit German aid, however; in April 1935, one of his nationalist followers in Syria approached the German consulate in Beirut with a similar plan and received the same answer.[13] The consul warned the AA that the political climate in Syria appeared ripe for a new round of anti-French violence and that French authorities in Syria suspected German intentions. Prüfer became concerned enough about France's possible hostility to investigate two Arab groups headquartered in Berlin, which allegedly served as anti-German front organizations for the French. In February 1935, a Pan Arab committee apparently associated with Arslan and his friend, Ihsan al-Jabiri, approached Fritz Grobba, the German minister to Iraq, with requests for propaganda, diplomatic, and "active" support from Germany for the committee's struggle against England and France. Not only did Grobba refuse, but Dieckhoff and Prüfer also ordered him to "avoid any connection with said group or its emissaries."[14]

On still other issues that could damage German and Anglo-French relations, the AA deferred completely to the Western powers. Shortly before Germany left the League of Nations in 1933, Prüfer cautioned that the Reich should remain neutral in the League's discussion of Iraq's persecution of its Assyrian minority. The director of the AA's section for affairs dealing with the League, Kurt von Kamphövener, and the ministry's official in charge of "minority questions," Conrad Rödiger, bitterly criticized England's refusal to support Berlin's demands, which had become increasingly belligerent since 1930, regarding the German minorities in Poland and Memelland. They urged that the Reich's delegation to the League support the Assyrians and be instructed to "say a few unpleasantries to the English in the debate." Prüfer disagreed, however, and maintained that Germany must not alienate England—despite its support of Iraq—over the affair; he refused to connect the minority issues in Europe with those in the Middle East and suggested that Germany remain neutral in the Iraq-Assyrian conflict. "Herein our wishes conform completely with those of the English," he told Kamphövener and Rödiger, "because we are interested in the recovery of peace and order in Iraq for economic reasons."[15]

Abteilung III also doggedly avoided conflicts with England regarding Germany's relations to Indian nationalists. During the 1920s, Berlin had provided a meeting place for a handful of Indian revolutionaries, including V. N. Chattopadhyaya and A. C. N. Nambiar, who viewed Bolshevism as a tool for overthrowing British imperial rule in India and who had founded in Germany the pro-Bolshevik League Against Imperialism. In 1929 Nambiar and Jawaharlal Nehru, a leader of the nationalist Congress party in India, established an Indian Information Bureau in Berlin, which sought to promote Indo-German relations. As the NSDAP rose to power in Germany, Hitler sought to placate England by praising its rule over India and characterizing the Indians as a "non-Aryan" subject race. His statements produced indignation among the Indian community in Germany; one Indian leader, Chempakaraman Pillai, had even sent a letter to Hitler in 1931, in which he complained about Nazi racism. When Pillai received a response from Hitler's secretary essentially upholding the Nazi leader's views, he sent the correspondence to the AA. Prüfer and others ·in Abteilung III had ignored the episode.[16]

Following Hitler's takeover, the SA implemented Nazi ideology by attacking and arresting numerous Indian students, raiding the Indian Information Bureau, and expelling Nambiar and several of his colleagues. Although Dieckhoff initially rejected the British protests against such treatment (by remarking sarcastically on a memorandum, "How do the English treat the Indians?"), Neurath and Prüfer appeared more concerned with its impact on German relations to India. An extensive anti-German campaign developed in the nationalist press in India, which even called for a boycott of German trade. Neurath complained to Goering, the Prussian interior minister who had encouraged SA and police violence, and Prüfer urged the Prussian ministry to free Nambiar and return his property. The police released Nambiar, who quickly fled to Czechoslovakia but returned to Germany in the fall of 1933, and the other Indians expelled were permitted to return to the Reich.

The AA went to great lengths, however, to avoid providing support for Indian nationalists in their struggle against Britain. The radical Congress party leader and former mayor of Calcutta, Subhas Chandra Bose, who had demanded that his movement follow a more aggressive anti-British tactic than Mohandas Gandhi's non-cooperation, visited Berlin in the summer of 1933 seeking European allies, but the AA refused to let him see Hitler. Instead, he met only Prüfer and Dieckhoff; although both treated Bose cordially and Prüfer told him that Germany did not "approve of everything that the British administration believes is good for India," they declared that Germany must remain neutral if a showdown developed between the Indian nationalists and Britain.

Prüfer also defended Hitler against Bose's criticism of the German chancellor's racism. In justifying the response of Hitler's secretary to Pillai's letter in 1931, Prüfer noted in a memorandum: "I explained to Herr Bose that this letter had already been written a few years before the National Socialists took over the government. Moreover, it did not come from Herr Hitler himself, but from his secretary. It was entirely possible that in the drafting of it, things were shaded so that they did not completely square with the opinion of the Reich chancellor."[17]

Disappointed, Bose went to Vienna during 1934 and 1935. In February 1935 he attempted unsuccessfully to persuade Prüfer to find a German publisher for his first book, *The Indian Struggle, 1920–1934,* which discussed the aims of the radical wing of the Congress party opposed to Gandhi. Bose failed to realize the depth of both Hitler's contempt for the "non-Aryan" Indians and the German commitment to doing nothing to alienate Britain and possibly jeopardize the dictator's immediate ambitions in Europe. The continued Nazi mistreatment of Indian students, Goering's vicious attacks on Gandhi, and derogatory articles in the Nazi press shocked Bose.

Prüfer remained unmoved by the Indian leader's protest against an especially vulgar discourse in the Nazi paper, the *Völkischer Beobachter,* proclaiming the supremacy of the Germanic race and its purity and referring to the degenerate "bastardized Indians." On the contrary, several months later, the deputy director of Abteilung III arranged for Goebbels, the fanatical Nazi propaganda minister, to give an interview to an Indian newspaper in which he declared, "Indeed, because we have such a high opinion of our race, we see the racial problems of other peoples much clearer with greater understanding and attention."[18]

His treatment by the Nazis notwithstanding, Bose may have refused to abandon efforts to enlist German support for his cause because of his connections to Prüfer and Dieckhoff. He met Dieckhoff and Prüfer again in January 1936, and shortly before returning to India, where he would serve briefly as president of the Congress party, he summarized his mixed feelings about Germany in a letter to Franz Thierfelder, general secretary of the German Academy in Munich: "I am extremely thankful to you for the efforts you made in arranging the meeting in January last. I had two long talks with Ministerialdirektor Dieckhoff and Gesandter Dr. Prüfer. Both of them were personally very cordial to me, as on former occasions. But the result of the interview was practically nil. I left them with the conviction that they attached very little importance to the Indian question."[19] When World War II began, Bose escaped India and returned to Germany, impressed with Hitler's early military successes and once again seeking support for the defeat and ousting of Britain from his country.

Egypt formed another part of the British empire which the Germans essentially ignored. Except for cultivating the trade with Egypt begun during the Weimar republic—a commerce that had declined with the depression—the Reich showed little overt concern for Egyptian affairs. A minor exception involved Prüfer's continued contacts after 1933 with the ex-Khedive of Egypt. Abbas Hilmi still resided in Switzerland and, although he had renounced his claim to the Egyptian throne, persisted in the hope that either he or his son might one day receive the crown. Despised and never forgiven by the British for his cooperation with the Central Powers in the war, bitterly resented by the Egyptian king and anti-British nationalists, and mistrusted by Turkey and France, the ex-Khedive's only encouragement lay with Germany.

Given Berlin's policy towards the Orient, however, Abbas Hilmi had little to hope for regarding his royal ambitions. Prüfer, by presenting to the Reich ministry of economics his traditional argument that the AA wished to keep the ex-Khedive from allying with the British, helped arrange the financing and construction of a new yacht for Abbas Hilmi during 1933 and 1934. However, when the political crisis of 1936, resulting from the death of King Fuad and his replacement by his sixteen-year-old son, Farouk, engulfed Egypt, the Germans made no effort to support the ex-Khedive's intrigue for the throne.[20]

This picture of general disinterest also held true for the AA's policy towards the non-Arab parts of the Orient, although between 1933 and 1936 the ministry nurtured the limited ties begun during the Weimar republic with the countries that lay along the northern frontier of the Arab states and bordered Russia: Turkey, Iran (which officially changed its name in 1935 from Persia), and Afghanistan.[21] These nations encouraged relations with Germany, seeking to lessen their traditional dependency on Russia and Britain; by 1936, they had established commercial agreements with the Reich in which Germany traded industrial goods for raw materials and agricultural products. In addition to offering potential economic opportunities for Germany, Turkey and its neighbors were less influenced by the British and French than were the Arab nations. By the late 1930s Turkey's control of the Black Sea straits and its significance as a source of chrome ore would make it the object of intense competition between Germany and the Western powers. Despite Prüfer's focus in the AA on political affairs and his opposition to Turkey's policy of maintaining its friendship with Russia and the Balkan states in order to prevent the penetration of other powers into the region, he accompanied a German trade delegation to Ankara in March 1934. A year later he participated in negotiations that led three German firms (Krupp, the Gutehoffnungshütte, and Nema) to sell armaments to Turkey and build a weapons factory there.[22]

Some historians have contended that the German interest in Turkey, Iran, and Afghanistan developed because the Nazis adjusted their racial theories to favor such states. Nazi ideologues proclaimed the Iranians and Afghans "Aryans" and the Turks a strong race that had allegedly adopted a government similar to the Nazi "leadership principle" (*Führerprinzip*).[23] The activities of Prüfer and Abteilung III confirm, however, that Nazi racism and persecution of the Jews damaged rather than fostered ties to the Middle East, even as they damaged German relations to the Western powers and the nationalists in India. Reports about German anti-Semitism in the Turkish press, inspired by the propaganda of the small NSDAP organization in Turkey, prompted the Abteilung to designate such articles as atrocity propaganda. The division asked the German minister in Ankara, Wilhelm Fabricius, to urge the Turkish government to halt the publications. A similar motive persuaded Prüfer and Dieckhoff to arrange a meeting between Hitler and Mahmud Bey, a Turkish editor and parliament member critical of Germany, during Bey's visit to Berlin in July 1933.[24] A year later, when riots against Jews broke out in Turkey, Prüfer cooperated with Martin Bormann in the Nazi party's main office to minimize publicity surrounding a visit to Germany by Cevat Rifat, Turkey's leading anti-Semitic journalist. Rifat planned to attend an anti-Semitic congress held in Nuremberg by the local Nazi leader, Julius Streicher. Both the Turkish government's wish to keep anti-Jewish incidents from appearing in the foreign press and Berlin's desire to protect its trade with Turkey prompted the AA to control reports of Rifat's activities.[25]

A more serious difficulty caused by Nazi racism, however, presented itself in Germany's relations to Iran. The Hitler government inherited the embittered feelings resulting from the anti-Shah activities of Iranian students in Germany and the scandal in the Iranian national bank involving

German officials, including the director, Kurt Lindenblatt. The SA launched brutal attacks on Iranian students in Germany in the spring of 1933, accusing them of being Communists and Jews, which heightened tensions even further and led to numerous protests to the AA by the Iranian legation. The Iranian press criticized Hitler's regime, and especially Nazi philosophy, which split mankind into higher and lower races and placed the Asian peoples in the latter category. Initially, the AA and the German press denied in astonishing fashion that Hitler had ever divided the races into such classes, but when the opposition between the two countries continued into 1934, the AA attempted to end the conflict and improve relations with Iran.[26]

Of greater significance in spurring the ministry to involve itself more in Iranian affairs, however, was the interest shown in Iran by a potential rival of the AA in German foreign affairs, the Nazi party's Foreign Policy Office (*Aussenpolitisches Amt,* or APA), headed by Alfred Rosenberg. The APA, by sending agents and propaganda to Iran, planned to dominate German policy there and include the country in an anti-Soviet bloc of Balkan and Asiatic states. Possibly because of Prüfer's connection to Bohle, one of Rosenberg's competitors in the NSDAP, and particularly because of his resentment towards the APA's attempted encroachment into the Wilhelmstrasse's coveted sphere of influence, Prüfer opposed the party office. When the APA and Reich propaganda ministry accused the AA of responsibility for Germany's poor relations with Iran and offered proposals for improved German propaganda and trade there, Prüfer promptly called them "useless propositions" and complained to the NSDAP leadership in Munich.[27] But more important in reducing the APA's influence among the German agencies competing in Iran was an agreement of the Reich economics ministry with Russia in September 1934, which favored the Soviet Union by enabling it to sell Iranian goods to Germany as Russian products.

To further undermine the APA and protect the AA's prerogative in handling German policy towards Iran, Prüfer encouraged his superiors to mend the Reich government's fences with Tehran. He reminded Dieckhoff and Bülow in July that "our relations to Persia, because of the Lindenblatt affair and the tension that has arisen from the foolish German press articles, have suffered badly."[28] At his direction, a subordinate in Abteilung III, Gottfried Aschmann, arranged for the editor of a German paper, the *Bayerische Staatszeitung,* to apologize to the Iranian minister in Berlin for the paper's anti-Iranian statements and to publish a retraction. Prüfer also issued instructions to the entire German press that "reporting on Persia should occur only with special caution." Finally, at the suggestion of the Iranian minister, with whom Prüfer had established a good rapport, he proposed that the Reich seek improved relations with Tehran by arranging for Germany to participate in the thousand-year anniversary of the birth of Firdusi, Iran's most famous ancient poet.

In keeping with these attempts at improved relations, the German government renamed a street in Berlin in honor of Iran and in September 1934 sent to Tehran a delegation of German scholars of the Orient, including Prüfer, to attend Iran's festivities honoring Firdusi and to carry gifts from Hitler to the Shah. On his return from Tehran in October, Prüfer proudly claimed to Dieckhoff and Bülow that such activities had flattered the Shah and improved German-Iranian relations. Wipert von Blücher, the German minister to Iran, confirmed the assessment.

Other factors influencing foreign policy were also responsible for the ministry's efforts at strengthening Germany's political and economic interests in Iran; the steadily growing anti-Bolshevism of the Nazi regime by 1935 and Berlin's search for a worldwide anti-Soviet coalition under Reich leadership helped dictate actions towards Tehran. In October 1935 and March 1936, despite continued friction between Iran and Germany over racial matters, the two countries signed trade agreements that opened the way for German economic penetration of Iran.[29] German firms received contracts for construction of the Trans-Iranian railroad (which the Shah viewed as his pet project) and, following further negotiations, the continuation of German air service across Iran to Afghanistan.

Although the Reich's relations to Afghanistan also remained of little consequence in German policy during the early years of the Hitler regime, closer economic ties between the two countries developed steadily, despite a series of incidents that threatened to destroy them.[30] The Afghan government and its monarch, Nadir, had received the new Hitler regime with mixed emotions. Although Kabul refused to permit the founding by the AO of a Nazi party group in the country in 1933, the government approved of the Reich's hostility towards Russia. The APA also spread propaganda and established agents in Afghanistan. The need to continue modernizing both the Afghan economy and its military spurred the signing of a credit agreement with Germany in March 1933.

The incidents that threatened relations involved several political murders in which persons with German connections were implicated; relations between the two countries were at a standstill for nearly two years. On 6 June 1933, Sayyid Kemal, a follower of Amanullah, the Afghan king ousted from power in 1929 and exiled in Italy, killed Sardar Muhammad Aziz, the Afghan minister to Germany and elder brother of King Nadir. The murder took place in Berlin. Afghan-German relations deteriorated immediately; Kabul accused the assassin of being associated with Ghulam Siddiq, Amanullah's former minister to Germany who had received asylum in the Reich in 1932. Siddiq still lived in Berlin, and Kabul alleged that he directed a campaign to destroy the family of Nadir.

The incident left Dieckhoff, Prüfer, and their superiors in the AA in a predicament. As Dieckhoff informed Neurath and Bülow, problems involving international law and in transporting the accused assassin prevented the ministry from extraditing him to Afghanistan.[31] Moreover, while the AA attempted to decide how to handle the affair, an Afghan teacher in the German school in Kabul murdered three persons at the British embassy; the killer admitted that he was a follower of Amanullah and he hoped to provoke a war between the present Afghan rulers and the British in India.

Kabul quickly executed the murderer along with other prominent leaders, including relatives of Siddiq. But the feud between the followers of Amanullah and King Nadir reached its peak with the king's murder on 8 November 1933, during a ceremony in the Afghan capital honoring the French and German schools. The assassin, a student from the German school, had no official tie to Germany, but sought blood revenge for the recent killings by the Afghan government. Kabul responded by executing several hundred more persons suspected of conspiring against Nadir.

Meanwhile, the AA's delay in deciding what to do with Muhammad Aziz's assassin led the Afghans to refuse to send a new minister to Germany, to cancel contracts with German firms, and to threaten severing diplomatic relations with Berlin. Not even Berlin's replacement of its minister in Kabul, Heribert Schwörbel, with Kurt Ziemke improved the situation. Finally, on 6 July 1934, more than a year after the murder of Muhammad Aziz, a Berlin court sentenced Sayyid Kemal to death. Nevertheless, a further delay ensued while a higher court heard the case in November; the court upheld the sentence. Prüfer, fearing irreparable harm to Germany's relations with Afghanistan if the Reich prolonged the affair further, recommended to Bülow that the punishment be carried out immediately and, "because the Afghans are very mistrustful" of Germany, that "a member of the Afghan legation be included as a witness to the execution."[32] The proposal illustrated anew Prüfer's lack of regard for others, particularly non-Germans; it provided a further example, moreover, of his idea that the interests of the German state held precedence over everything else, including legal considerations and principles of human dignity or morality.

The Germans executed Sayyid Kemal on 14 January 1935, despite an appeal from Amanullah that he be spared. The Afghan government, on the other hand, supported by the APA, demanded that Siddiq be expelled from Germany. But Siddiq had intimate ties to Prüfer, Dieckhoff, Hentig, and others in the AA, and the expulsion order never came. Although

Siddiq remained in Germany, Dieckhoff directed the Gestapo to warn him against future political activity. Rosenberg, the head of the APA, later maintained that his agency's work had led to a recovery in Afghan-German relations after 1935. Evidence shows that the execution of Sayyid Kemal produced the improved atmosphere, however; on 19 October 1935 the two countries signed a new credit agreement, and in the next two years the Germans delivered armaments to Afghanistan and negotiated the establishment of German airline service between Berlin and Kabul.[33]

While the activities of Prüfer, Dieckhoff, and Abteilung III illustrated Germany's general lack of interest in the Middle East after 1933, they also produced an element of success in achieving the Nazi government's objectives in the region. Although the AA went to great lengths not to alienate Britain or France, it nevertheless slowly stabilized Germany's relations and expanded its trade with several states, including Turkey, Iran, and Afghanistan, and established contacts with individual leaders such as the Mufti of Jerusalem and the radical Indian nationalist, Subhas Chandra Bose, who persisted in seeking the Reich's support during World War II. By 1935 and 1936, however, much of Prüfer's attention focused on two crises, one in Eastern Africa and the other inside the AA; the way each was handled played a role in strengthening the Nazi government and contributing to the disastrous course it had set for Germany.

The Ethiopian Crisis

Mussolini had decided in the spring of 1934 to push forward his plan to seize Ethiopia.[34] Even as the Fascist leader assured the Ethiopian emperor, Haile Selassie, of Italy's peaceful intentions, the Italians were fortifying their colony of Eritrea. Mussolini believed that the Western powers would not interfere with his plans because of their concern for the depression and the problem of Hitler's Germany. Fears that the Nazis intended to forge an Anschluss with Austria bothered Italy and France especially. Mussolini's negotiations with France in the fall appeared to bear these fears out, as Paris indicated its willingness to allow Italy an extension of influence in Ethiopia in return for Italian cooperation against Germany.

Haile Selassie tried to reach his own agreement with France, his traditional protector, but without result; his negotiations with Britain also produced little progress or protection. The most favorable European response came from Germany, with whose diplomats—including Prüfer, the AA's expert on Ethiopia—the emperor had been on good terms for many years. Haile Selassie hoped to exploit to Ethiopia's benefit the hostility that had developed between Germany and Italy over Nazi demands for the Anschluss of Austria to the Reich. Mussolini's anger was heightened by the coup attempted in July 1934 by the Austrian Nazis in Vienna.

On 28 October, Haile Selassie asked Wilhelm von Schoen, the German minister in Addis Ababa, if Ethiopians might be allowed to visit Germany to negotiate purchases of arms, including aircraft. The request, as Prüfer notified Schoen several days later, prompted immediate discussion among German leaders.[35] Neurath, apparently through reports from Schoen, the German missions in Rome and Naples, and Prüfer's contacts, had studied Italian military preparations in Eastern Africa and kept Hitler informed.

On 31 October 1934, the foreign minister, essentially repeating a memorandum he had received from Prüfer, sent a lengthy report to the Reich chancellor analyzing with remarkable perception Italy's general predicament. The memorandum noted that Mussolini could not safely proceed against Ethiopia without French support; England, it presumed, would remain neutral in return for territory from Ethiopia as provided for in a secret treaty from 1906. The Ethiopian army, Neurath told Hitler, "is hardly a serious opponent in an open campaign on the level of a European-armed troop," and the Italians would prevail in relatively easy fashion. The foreign minister, however, proposed that Germany, before defining its position in the affair, should remain neutral at least until Italy had struck an agreement with France.[36] Hitler apparently accepted Neurath's advice and adopted a wait-and-see attitude; he drafted a letter to Haile Selassie on 27 November, but it remained undelivered until an incident at Wal Wal raised tensions to the crisis level.

On 5–6 December, fighting occurred between Ethiopian and Italian forces on the border between Ethiopia and Italian Somaliland, near Wal Wal. Thirty Italians were killed. Mussolini charged Ethiopia with aggression and accelerated preparations for war; Haile Selassie took the issue to the League of Nations; and the French and Italians moved towards an agreement. Before the crisis reached a peak, however, the Ethiopians sought again to enlist German support. Prüfer, in a report for Dieckhoff and Bülow, correctly identified Italy as having attacked the Ethiopians inside the latters' territory at Wal Wal and hinted at his own anti-Italian feelings. "For Abyssinia," he told his superiors, "Italy is the archenemy, who continually threatens the freedom of the country and before whose aggression one always lives in fear. One cannot believe, as the Italians are presently asserting, that the Abyssinian shepherd attacked the Italian wolf."[37] Haile Selassie finally received Hitler's personal letter from the previous month, delivered by the German chargé d'affaires in Addis Ababa, Willy Unverfehrt. Although no copy of this letter survived and the chargé d'affaires insisted to the emperor that Germany had to remain strictly neutral in the conflict, Hitler must have given some encouragement to the ruler, because Haile Selassie provided Unverfehrt with a detailed list of Ethiopia's military needs.

Unofficially, however, the violently anti-Italian APA dispatched Steffen to Addis Ababa, apparently with the approval of Goering and Hess. A private arms dealer and honorary consul general of Ethiopia in Berlin, Hans Steffen was to promote a war in East Africa which the Nazis thought would relax the political pressure on Germany in Europe. Steffen advised Haile Selassie on 18 January 1935 to attack Italy before it could prepare itself and promised that Germany would supply Ethiopia with weapons. How many arms Steffen produced is unclear, but Berlin's wish not to antagonize Italy over issues so remote from Germany's concerns encouraged Hitler and Neurath to continue a neutral course. A memorandum by Prüfer of 10 January, changing his previous estimate on the length of the imminent conflict in Ethiopia and prophesying a longer war for Italy, may also have played a role in the decision.[38]

While Mussolini received a "free hand" in Ethiopia from France and while the Anglo-German naval agreement of June 1935 temporarily solidified the rapprochement between Rome and Paris, the Italians bitterly protested Steffen's arms shipments and other aid to Ethiopia allegedly offered by the new German minister there, Johannes Kirchholtes. Mussolini particularly feared having to defend Italy's northern border and neighboring Austria against a German attack. The Nazi press, hostile towards the Franco-Italian accords, fanned the controversy with anti-Italian propaganda.

Bülow, Dieckhoff, and Prüfer remained busy throughout the spring of 1935 denying Italy's allegations that Germany supported Ethiopia and assuring Rome of the Reich's neutrality. Prüfer, acting on orders from his superiors, reminded the German legation in Addis Ababa of the ban against military aid to Ethiopia.[39] He also carefully monitored the military situation in East Africa through Steffen, who had just returned from Ethiopia. Steffen informed him about Italy's build-up in Eritrea, the arrival of "very considerable sources of war material" in Ethiopia, and the "very confident" mood of the Ethiopians. At least some officials in the Reich were thinking of future political and economic advantages in Ethiopia for Germany: Prüfer talked with the NSDAP's Colonial Policy Office (*Kolonialpolitisches Amt*, or KPA) about potential mining concessions for the Reich in Ethiopia.[40]

By the summer of 1935, Britain's opposition to Italy had hardened in the League of Nations, yet London showed itself unwilling to risk a war over Ethiopia; the crisis also produced divisions between England and France. As Hitler, eager to separate Italy from the Western powers, exploited Mussolini's bitterness towards Britain and the League by relaxing tensions between Germany and Austria, the Italian dictator abruptly sought improved relations with Berlin. Despite Hitler's admiration for Mussolini and his interest in a rapprochement, the contempt in the Wilhelmstrasse for Italy and for German Ambassador Ulrich von Hassell, who encouraged rapprochement, led the AA to scorn such a proposal. The ministry, recognizing that Rome's concern regarding Ethiopia had prompted its sudden solicitation of Germany, preferred to continue playing the Reich's waiting game, confident that increasing isolation would make Italy more willing to make concessions to Germany.

By the beginning of July England had made it clear that it wished no military conflict with Italy; further, Britain and France sought to appease Mussolini by offering him territory and economic rights at Ethiopia's expense. Haile Selassie had no choice but to turn outside the League for help. On 10 July 1935, Kirchholtes informed the AA that a combination of Italian pressure and an empty Ethiopian treasury had stopped military deliveries to Ethiopia from Belgium; this action, said the German minister, posed an even greater threat to Haile Selassie's poorly equipped army.[41] After an unsuccessful request to the United States for aid, the emperor turned again to Germany.

One of the emperor's trusted advisers, David Hall, arrived incognito in Berlin and met with Prüfer, Hall's personal friend. Hall asked Prüfer whether Germany could provide Ethiopia with three million Reichsmarks for the purchase of machine guns and 30,000 rifles with ammunition. Hall reminded Prüfer of Haile Selassie's view, expressed to Prüfer in 1929, of the similarity in the international positions of Germany and Ethiopia. At present, Hall said, "the political interests of Germany and Ethiopia were identical in so far as a conflict with Italy over the Austrian question would some day probably be inevitable for [Germany] too." Thus, Hall continued, it was in the interest of both Germany and Ethiopia "to weaken the Italian enemy as far as we could. We now had an opportunity to do this by enabling the Negus to arm his troops to such an extent that they could offer the greatest possible resistance to the Italians."[42]

Prüfer informed Bülow of the visit, and Bülow discussed it with Neurath. While the state secretary feared that an accord with Ethiopia might have undesirable results if it became public, he opposed giving Hall a flat refusal. The extraordinary significance of the Ethiopian conflict for future German policy spurred Bülow to ask Neurath for a decision from Hitler himself. Apparently hoping to extend the Ethiopian war to divert Italy's attention from the Austrian question and German rearmament, Hitler agreed to meet Hall's request, thereby secretly reversing Berlin's policy of neutrality. The main condition was that the Ethiopians keep the transaction secret.

Through an arrangement with the Reich ministry of finance, Prüfer paid the Emperor's envoy in three installments on 23 August and 4 and 23 September 1935.[43] Kirchholtes sent a coded message of congratulations to Prüfer on 12 August; shortly thereafter Prüfer received a special decoration from Haile Selassie. Steffen immediately purchased weapons (including thirty anti-tank guns) and ammunition from Switzerland and the Rheinmetall-Borsig firm in Germany, changing the manufacturers' nameplates to ensure absolute secrecy. The Germans shipped the arms aboard a British freighter from Lübeck and Stettin to Berbera, a seaport in British Somaliland, from which the English allowed weapons from foreign firms into Ethiopia. In the autumn, Steffen sent another shipment of arms, apparently carried by the same freighter, through Belgium and Norway to Ethiopia.[44]

Italy invaded Ethiopia in October 1935. Inasmuch as the German supplies greatly assisted the Ethiopians in fighting the war and delaying an Italian triumph till May 1936, Prüfer made a significant contribution to the Reich's diplomacy in the affair. Hitler, responding to Mussolini's growing friendliness towards Germany and fearing that Italy could not simultaneously fight Ethiopia and the sanctions imposed on it by the League, shifted his policy at the end of September 1935 towards a more pro-Italian stance. Prüfer and his superiors in the AA persisted, however, in their hostility towards Rome. Despite the change in German policy, they once again aided Ethiopia by identifying and even helping remove a German officer and his Hungarian subordinates who worked as Italian agents in Addis Ababa. Prüfer had uncovered the spy network at the close of September while attending an international conference of scholars in Rome in his capacity as chairman of the German Oriental Society (*Deutsche Morgenländische Gesellschaft,* or DMG).[45] With Bülow's agreement, Prüfer not only notified the Ethiopians of the spies, which led to their flight from the country, but also called attention to the German officer's Muslim name and his previous activity in the Turkish army in order to deflect public attention from his connection to the Reich. Anti-Italian feelings among the diplomats did not stop there, however. Dieckhoff and Prüfer vented their anger by writing bitter and arrogant comments on Italian diplomatic notes protesting Germany's support of Ethiopia. Prüfer dispatched a memorandum to Dieckhoff, Bülow, and Neurath in December declaring the falsehood of Italian claims to using the war merely to "reconquer" portions of Ethiopia that once belonged to Italy.[46]

Hitler profited immensely from Italy's lengthy and costly adventure in Ethiopia. The public German policy of neutrality promoted the image of Hitler as a "peacemaker," an impression that he had carefully encouraged since 1933 while beginning re-armament. Furthermore, the diversion of Anglo-French attention to Italy permitted Germany to continue its re-armament undisturbed, to evade proposals from the Western powers for security accords, and to enhance its influence in the Balkans. But most important, the crisis over Ethiopia produced a rapprochement between Germany and Italy; the change in relations led to the Anti-Comintern pact between Berlin and Rome in 1937, to Germany's Anschluss with Austria, and to cooperation of the "Axis" in World War II.[47]

The failure of the Western democracies and the League of Nations to react to Mussolini's aggression also served to encourage Hitler to re-arm the Rhineland in March 1936.[48] In so doing Hitler violated the Locarno pact, shifted the balance of power in Germany's favor against France and its allies, and stimulated another step in Britain's disastrous policy of appeasement. As for Prüfer, his role in the Ethiopian affair may have contributed to his promotion, a month after German troops occupied the left bank of the Rhine, to director of the AA's personnel division. He soon found himself involved in a new crisis—the Nazi party's initial efforts to expand its influence in the ministry.

nine

Personnel Director in the Ministry, 1936-39

BY the spring of 1936, Hitler had consolidated his dictatorship at home and Germany's growing power had been demonstrated by its remilitarization of the Rhineland. Nazi pressure on the AA to replace its professionals with "politically reliable" National Socialists began to mount. A new wave of anti-Jewish laws at the end of 1935, which unleashed a campaign to remove those few "non-Aryans" in the civil service who had somehow survived the initial purge two years before, combined with the deaths of several leading careerists in the ministry to confront Constantin von Neurath with a crisis of morale and fear among the AA's officials. This situation coupled with a general reorganization of the AA in 1936 caused the minister to appoint Prüfer the new head of the ministry's personnel and budget division.

As previously discussed, the concern of the minister and his subordinates did not involve their disagreement with the main principles of Nazism, but rather their wish to preserve the elite membership of the AA—based on lengthy service, education, and entrance examinations—and its role in German foreign affairs against Nazi influence. Embracing what the regime stood for eventually proved incompatible with safeguarding the diplomats' position in the ministry, however. At least in Prüfer's case, Hitler's successes both at home and abroad intensified his nationalism and conservatism, his attraction to the Nazi leader, and his willingness to collaborate with those he despised as social and political inferiors—the very people he believed he could keep away from the Wilhelmstrasse.[1]

The Personnel Crisis and Prüfer's Appointment

By the summer of 1934, while Bohle and the AO lifted the ban on membership in the NSDAP in order to permit diplomats to join the party and contented themselves with such largely unsuccessful recruiting activities, some of the AO leaders began calling on Hitler to purge the agency.[2] But even after the death in August of Hindenburg, Hitler's only nominal superior, the Nazi leader refused, apparently still aware of his need for the peaceful image that Neurath and the diplomats were projecting abroad. Nevertheless, Hitler criticized several leading ambassadors, particularly Leopold Hoesch in London and Roland Köster in Paris, and such officials in Berlin as Bernhard Wilhelm von Bülow, Gerhard Köpke (director of the West European division), and Richard Meyer (head of the East European and Russian division).[3]

During the spring of 1935, however, a personnel crisis developed in the AA; the ministry found it increasingly difficult to gain Hitler's approval for even routine appointments and changes. Werner von Grünau, the personnel director, complained to Neurath and Bülow on 19 March 1935 about the party's "growing mistrust against the foreign ministry" and a decline in the AA's morale. Neurath, however, refused Grünau's suggestion that the minister talk with Hitler's deputy, Rudolf Hess, and make "a few small concessions in personnel affairs."

During the summer, Hess's subordinate, Bohle, began rejecting lists for appointments and promotions of diplomats; on 15 July Grünau informed the missions abroad that before an AA official could be promoted, his personnel file had to note whether or not he belonged to the NSDAP.[4] As delays occurred in the party's agreement to important appointments, Neurath complained to Hitler, who officially made them subject to approval by Hess. Late in 1935, the AA began a long-planned reorganization of its central office in Berlin, making personnel changes necessary, particularly in the highest ranks.

But Ribbentrop was rising in prominence following his triumph in the Anglo-German naval accord. As Hitler's personal adviser on foreign affairs, Ribbentrop rarely consulted the AA. He asked Hitler to name him state secretary in the AA and prepared his own plan to reorganize the ministry, in which he foresaw Prüfer handling affairs involving England and Western Europe.[5] Neurath refused to agree to the appointment, however, and promptly resigned in anger. Although Hitler rejected the resignation and did not place Ribbentrop in the AA, the Nazi leader attacked the ministry and even accused the foreign minister of protecting scoundrels and traitors in it.

With the Nuremberg laws of 15 September 1935 depriving Jews of

German citizenship and forbidding marriage and extramarital relations between Germans and Jews, the pressure intensified on Neurath to remove the Jewish officials he had succeeded in protecting. Though Neurath's treatment of such persons stood in contrast to his support of Nazi anti-Semitism to foreign governments, the minister seems to have acted exclusively from his desire to guard the AA against penetration by outside elements.[6] Meyer and Köpke, the former a Jew and the other having a Jewish grandmother, "retired" at the beginning of 1936. The "Aryan" officials in the ministry remained safe; Bohle, for example, to show the NSDAP's approval of Prüfer, invited him with forty-one other diplomats to the party's rally at Nuremberg in 1935, in which Hitler announced the new discriminatory legislation against the Jews.[7]

During the first half of 1936, the personnel problems in the AA reached a crescendo. The Nazi party leader in Switzerland, Wilhelm Gustloff, was assassinated in March; the slaying appeared to highlight the mounting opposition among foreigners to the small Nazi party organizations abroad operated by the AO. Hitler reacted by persuading Neurath to attach the foreign party leaders for their safety to Germany's diplomatic missions.[8] A far more significant problem ensued in the AA, however, when Bülow, Hoesch, and Köster suddenly died, and Grünau, seriously ill, retired, all within a few months of each other in 1936.

Neurath finally agreed to name Ribbentrop ambassador to London. Ribbentrop was bitterly disappointed because he wanted Bülow's position and consequently spent far less time in England than in Berlin, where he continued to curry Hitler's favor. To fill the other vacancies, the foreign minister inserted men whose skills were mediocre and courage lacking, including Ernst von Weizsäcker as head of the AA's new political division. Other officials held varying pro-Nazi sympathies: Hans Heinrich Dieckhoff (acting state secretary); Otto von Erdmannsdorff (extra-European section); and Prüfer (personnel and budget).[9]

Hess approved Prüfer's appointment on 8 April 1936. In the following months, the new personnel director received increasing attention from Bohle and the APA leader, Rosenberg; both Nazi leaders had visions of eventually heading the AA. They entertained Prüfer and his colleagues, Dieckhoff and Fritz Count von der Schulenburg, Germany's recently appointed ambassador to Russia, at the Nuremberg party rally in September. Prüfer appeared overwhelmed with the spectacle at which Hitler denounced communism and made references to his new Four-Year Plan, designed to prepare the German army and economy for war within four years. "Dearest," he wrote in a postcard to his wife, "there is great joy here everywhere."[10]

The Party's Initial Penetration of the AA

It is unclear how much the attitude of officials like Prüfer and Dieckhoff contributed to the AO's sharpening of its insistence during the remainder of 1936 that diplomats become party members or resign their offices. Mission leaders who entered the NSDAP included Herbert von Dirksen (Japan), Herbert von Richthofen (Belgium), Eugen Rümelin (Bulgaria), Hans Frohwein (Estonia), Johannes von Welczek (France), Hans Georg von Mackensen (Hungary, later state secretary in the AA), Victor von Heeren (Yugoslavia), Count Zech-Burkersroda (Holland), Heinrich Sahm (Norway), and Friedrich Werner von der Schulenburg. Bohle also placed Hans Schröder, a minor consular official and his former party leader in Egypt, in the AA's personnel division and successfully negotiated with Prüfer for his rapid promotion.[11]

Equally uncertain is the role played by Prüfer and Dieckhoff in the appointment of Bohle on 30 January 1937 to a special position in the AA as "chief of the Auslands-Organisation in the Auswärtiges Amt." The promotion resulted primarily from the bitter feud that had raged between the AO and AA since 1933, in which the AO and its several hundred party groups outside Germany had criticized the Reich's diplomats for their lack of party membership and alleged disloyalty to Nazism. Moreover, some party leaders abroad had attempted to usurp the official functions of the diplomats and claimed the authority to control the millions of Germans who lived outside the Reich, duties which the AA normally handled.

Hostility among the diplomats towards the AO's foreign groups had intensified because of its loud and boisterous propaganda activities. In addition, the AO often operated at cross-purposes to the AA, sometimes alienating the same foreign leaders whom the diplomatic corps was trying to woo. Not only did the party groups' blatant racism, anti-Semitism, and bombastic political agitation anger foreigners, but such activities also helped solidify opposition to Germany.[12] By the end of 1936, the role of the AO was developing rapidly in Austria and in Spain, where it participated in Germany's entry into the civil war. Serious difficulties for German diplomacy arose from the lack of coordination between the AO and AA in the United States, Switzerland, South Africa, the Netherlands, and other countries. A solution to the problem had become vital. Neurath hoped that by placing Bohle in the AA, the ministry would finally gain "a certain control over the Auslandsorganisation."[13]

Although the foreign press interpreted Bohle's promotion as meaning that the AO was being incorporated wholesale into the AA and thus hailed him as a potential successor to Neurath, the fact remained that only the AO leader—not the AO—joined the ministry, and Bohle found his authority there restricted significantly. He achieved solely minor changes in the AA's personnel and affected only the policy of the cultural-political division, which focused on the AO's capturing control over the German schools abroad. Hess, Bohle's boss, did not possess power like such Nazi leaders as Goering and Himmler, power which the AO chief could exploit.

While Bohle's influence in affairs regarding Germans abroad reached its peak in 1937, while he had access for a brief time to Hitler, he himself had been born outside Germany and possessed few close friends in the party.[14] When Ribbentrop, Bohle's archrival, became foreign minister in February 1938, Ribbentrop limited the authority of the AO and its leader even more. Nevertheless, Bohle and Prüfer worked closely together, often meeting personally, which stimulated a small, but steady, influx of party officials into the lower levels of the AA. Most entered at the rank of legation secretary, consul, and attaché.

The new German civil service law of 27 January 1937 also affected the relationship of the AA to Nazism. The decree restated many provisions from previous laws, emphasizing the importance of "Aryan" blood and party service in deciding bureaucratic appointments and promotions. Civil servants, according to the decree, owed personal fealty to Hitler, the leader (*Führer*) of the Reich and people (*Volk*). Civil servants' primary responsibility to the state was their commitment to the Führer, to whom they had to take an oath of loyalty unto death. The law, which was accompanied by a penal code detailing various punishments for disobedient civil servants ranging from a warning to dismissal and loss of pension, commanded the bureaucrats to defend the Nazi state, abstain from acts hostile or damaging to the regime, and promote the policies of the NSDAP and government.[15]

Hence, even a minor change in personnel required the AA and the party to follow extensive procedures. For an appointment or promotion, a candidate had to receive positive judgments regarding questions of rank and budget from the Reich ministries of interior and finance, the foreign minister, and the deputy Führer's office (Hess), which received information on the candidates' "political reliability" from the AO. The AO's estimate of the diplomats rested on reports Bohle received from his party leaders abroad; by 1937 he had compiled an extensive file on most of the foreign service. If a candidate received the party's blessing, the AA forwarded his name to Hitler's office for final approval.[16]

Bohle, Prüfer, and Prüfer's deputy, Carl Dienstmann, met frequently during 1937 to negotiate diplomatic rank for candidates whom the AO proposed for the ministry.[17] Several AO leaders received appointments to offices in the AA as assistants to Bohle or as bureaucrats in the cultural-political division. In addition, the AA commissioned a handful of party officials abroad as secondary diplomats and attached them to German missions in Salzburg, Rome, Milan, The Hague, Lima, Tokyo, Warsaw, Winnipeg, Davos, Capetown, and elsewhere. The AO's only significant appointment occurred in November 1937 when the AA named the founder of the NSDAP in Guatemala, Otto Langmann, minister to Uruguay. A large number of the AO leaders who entered the ministry belonged to the SS, including Bohle, whom Himmler promoted to SS Gruppenführer.[18]

Prüfer also collaborated with the AO in dismissing career diplomats from their posts for the slightest opposition to the NSDAP or because of hostile reports against them sent to Bohle by foreign party officials. In the fall of 1937, for example, Prüfer agreed to Bohle's demand for the recall of Walter von Falkenhausen, the consul in St. Gallen, because the diplomat had failed to attend a local party meeting and allegedly refused to cooperate with his party leader.[19] A similar fate befell Wilhelm Erythropel, the mission leader in Cuba. For equally dubious reasons, the AA removed mission officials in the Dutch East Indies, Ireland, England, and South Africa.[20]

The party, moreover, found Prüfer receptive to its racial attacks against mission officials. For example, when a Nazi leader in the Netherlands criticized Werner Otto von Hentig, the German consul general in Amsterdam and one of Prüfer's friends who had specialized in Middle Eastern affairs, for having arranged for a Jew to speak at a local German school, the AA ordered Hentig to return to Berlin. He later recalled his encounter with Prüfer, noting that the latter "thought that I had lost anything and everything to risk what I had done. . . . Prüfer asked me to represent my own case in the Brown House [Nazi party headquarters and Hess's office in Munich], because he could not do it."[21] Without the support of the AA, Hentig lost a scheduled promotion; a few months later, however, he received an appointment as head of the Middle Eastern desk in the political division.

On occasion, the AA cooperated with the AO in removing a diplomat for racial reasons. Wilhelm Haas, the chief of the trade department of the German embassy in Tokyo, was "retired" by the ministry because of the party's complaint that his wife was a Jewess and that he refused to offer his "wholehearted support of the National Socialist ideology." Prüfer, a few months later, issued a circular to AA personnel declaring that "many cases that have occurred" gave him occasion to note that any official wishing to marry must "prove the German ancestry of his future spouse before the marriage," or risk being "released."[22]

The fiercely anti-Semitic Prüfer was apparently irritated when Bohle asked him about his membership in the Pro-Palestine Committee, an association formed among German politicians in the summer of 1918 to foster Jewish settlement in Palestine and produce a change in German policy regarding Zionism. Bohle's inquiry possibly resulted from the AO's renewed interest in opposing the German government's agreement with the Haavara Transfer Company, which had aided the emigration of German Jews to Palestine and permitted them to take a portion of their property along. During the summer of 1937 the British government began considering the partition of Palestine and the formation of a Jewish state, and hostility to the plan from the AO intensified. In a testy letter to Bohle, the anti-Zionist Prüfer responded that he had belonged to the Pro-Palestine Committee in the 1920s, but only "at the wish of the Reichsminister at the time," who considered membership "automatic" for officials in the Oriental section of the AA. In defending himself, he claimed that similar groups had existed in France and England and included diplomats there. "My membership was a pure formality," he declared. "I have participated in none of the meetings of the society and have had no relations with its members, except for the specialists in the foreign ministry."[23]

His response apparently satisfied the party. Prüfer always proceeded cautiously in dealing with Bohle, and only rarely did he display his latent resentment at having to consult with the NSDAP. On one such occasion, Prüfer, who was fluent in eight foreign languages, insisted that a key requirement for being named to the ministry remain the candidate's passing of demanding language examinations. But Bohle and the party privately disagreed, admitting that "proficiency in languages is certainly very desirable" but that a foreign service candidate "has to understand clearly not only the nature of National Socialist philosophy and the tasks of the movement. . . , but [must have] already produced evidence of this in one way or another. Thus, the character of the candidate is most important, and a more or less basic knowledge of languages comes second." Who won or lost this disagreement is unclear; of the few new officials hired in the AA during 1936 and 1937, most had no university education or language training and belonged overwhelmingly to the NSDAP.[24]

The AO made little headway in the personnel and policy-making affairs in the AA during 1936 and 1937, enrolling only a third of the ministry's roughly 2,600 officials.[25] Probably its most serious threat to the AA was psychological in nature. With Bohle's presence in the Wilhelmstrasse, his frequent bombastic circulars to the diplomats, and the slow trickle of party officials into the AA, the diplomats ascribed to the AO an authority it never possessed. Evidence exists that the AO not only intensified its pressure on the ministry officials to enter the NSDAP, but also that the diplomats felt it increasingly necessary to join. Prüfer himself applied for admission to the party in May 1937 and received a membership card seven months later. Other careerists who joined included Ernst Woermann, Otto von Erdmannsdorff, Paul Barandon, Hans Borchers, and Herbert Siegfried.[26]

Bohle also concluded an agreement with Prüfer and Goebbels, the German propaganda minister and party leader in Berlin, whereby Nazi members working in Wilhelmstrasse 74 would belong to the AO's membership rolls instead of those of the Berlin party organization. The AO expanded the agreement at the end of 1937 when it created a local party group for the AA (*Ortsgruppe Auswärtiges Amt*), which administered party members in the foreign service who lived outside Germany.[27] Bohle, in a letter to Prüfer in December inflating the AO leader's accomplishments and thanking Prüfer for his friendship, declared: "I especially wish to tell you at the end of the first year of my activity in the foreign ministry, how much I value working with you. We are both agreed that 1937 signified a turning point in the cooperation between the foreign ministry and the party. It is thus a comradely duty for me to thank you for your substantial part in the realization of this good work together."[28]

The New Foreign Minister

The AA's general success in preserving itself against the party's ambitions probably contributed to the bitterness and hostility with which its professionals greeted Hitler's appointment on 4 February 1938 of Ribbentrop, the ministry's long-time rival in foreign affairs, to replace Neurath. The removal of Neurath and top military leaders occurred not because they opposed Hitler's plans for the annexation of Austria and destruction of Czechoslovakia, which the Führer had discussed with them on 5 November 1937, but because they raised objections about his calculations regarding the risks involved in such aggression. Ribbentrop's appointment was also related to Hitler's policy toward the nations of East Asia, and particularly his intention to align Germany with Japan and lessen its ties to China, a shift which the new foreign minister favored. The purge consolidated Hitler's power and surrounded him with wholly dependent tools who would blindly execute his policy of expansion.

In private Prüfer derisively referred to his new boss as "Ribbi" or the "champagne merchant" (*Sekthandler*). Prüfer despised Ribbentrop partly because he had replaced Neurath, one of Prüfer's own kind in the bureaucracy and a symbol of the AA's elitism, and partly because the new foreign minister had previously bypassed the diplomats in acquiring his influence in foreign policy directly through Hitler. Moreover, Ribbentrop was a social climber who exaggerated his personal role in German diplomacy and oversimplified complex political issues. He returned the diplomats' contempt, distrusted them, and essentially continued after 1938 to ignore them.[29]

Despite his enmity towards the Wilhelmstrasse, Ribbentrop initially aligned himself with the ministry and did not wish to feud openly with it. He took with him into the AA only a few of the aspiring and loyal party men from his Dienststelle and filled the highest positions with the ministry's own officials. Weizsäcker assumed the post of state secretary, Woermann became director of the political division, and Neurath's other division chiefs, including Prüfer, continued in their positions. The diplomats, on the other hand, apparently adjusted to their new leader by joining the party. Weizsäcker and Woermann entered the NSDAP and so did other mission leaders, among them Karl Ritter (Brazil), Franz von Papen (Austria/Turkey), Cecil von Renthe-Fink (Denmark), Hans Völckers (Cuba), and Eduard Hempel (Ireland).[30]

Despite Prüfer's party membership, however, a memorandum written for Ribbentrop a month later by one of his aides summarized the NSDAP's mixed view of him and suggested that the foreign minister would soon replace him. "The personnel division," observed the assistant, "has for years always been managed, but not directed. Prüfer has not distinguished himself substantially from his predecessors, although he has done much that is positive in other ways."[31] Still another strike against the personnel director, as viewed by Ribbentrop, was Prüfer's friendship with Bohle; the latter fancied himself a possible successor to Ribbentrop, which angered the foreign minister and led him to reduce the AO leader's already limited authority in the AA. Within three months, Ribbentrop persuaded Hitler to remove the party members in the AA from the jurisdiction of Bohle and Hess and to dissolve the Ortsgruppe Auswärtiges Amt.[32]

What scanty evidence survives suggests that another reason for Ribbentrop's eventual replacement of Prüfer involved Prüfer's continued efforts, with little apparent success, to influence promotions and appointments. On occasion, Prüfer did contribute to decisions about a fellow careerist. For example, as Hitler prepared to annex Austria and began looking for a loyal party man as ambassador there, he replaced Papen, the aristocratic and monarchist German representative in Vienna. Papen had narrowly escaped being shot during Hitler's purge of the SA in June 1934, and the dictator had sent him to Austria to get rid of him. Consequently, Papen eagerly sought another foreign post in 1938 that would both provide him with personal security away from his enemies inside Germany and satisfy his social tastes. He apparently wanted to live in Paris and thus pushed for the job of ambassador to France; as a part of his campaign, he intrigued against Count Johannes von Welczek, the Reich's ambassador in Paris. But Prüfer opposed the change, informed Welczek of Papen's scheme, and played a role in frustrating Papen's bid for an assignment to the French capital.[33]

Prüfer's efforts to block one of Ribbentrop's major appointments to the AA ended much differently for the personnel director, however, and undoubtedly hastened his removal from the post. Ribbentrop, especially after his embarrassment over not playing an active role in Germany's Anschluss with Austria through armed force on 13 March 1938, determined to increase his authority with Hitler against such other party leaders as Himmler, Goering, and Goebbels. That goal would necessitate his "nazifying" the AA by replacing the career diplomats in key positions with young and obedient officials from the Dienststelle Ribbentrop. One such opportunity occurred in the fall, when the foreign minister promoted Martin Luther to the AA. But Luther, who had risen with untiring zeal through minor party positions to become Ribbentrop's liaison for party affairs in the Dienststelle and had ingratiated himself with the minister's wife, was opposed by Prüfer's personnel division, which sought to stop the appointment.

Luther's difficulties did not stop with the NSDAP, however. He had recently been accused of embezzling money from his local party organization in Zehlendorf and faced a trial before one of the party's regional courts (*Kreisgericht*) in Berlin. Ribbentrop, however, asked Martin Bormann, Hess's deputy, to have the case suspended. Bormann intervened on Luther's behalf in August 1938 with the party's supreme court (*Oberstes Parteigericht,* or OPG), whose chief justice, Walter Buch, was Bormann's father-in-law. A few weeks later the OPG quashed the trial, and Luther entered the AA in November as a senior legation counselor and head of a new section in the ministry, *Referat Partei,* which handled liaison with the NSDAP.[34]

Although such evidence suggests that Prüfer attempted under the AA's new regime to affect personnel decisions, he accomplished little more than occasionally negotiating with Bohle regarding the appointment of AO leaders to low-level positions in the ministry. He also sent memorandums to the ministry regarding personnel regulations, which often reflected the steadily growing interference of the NSDAP into the diplomats' lives. He ordered them to report their membership in the party or its affiliated groups and to resign from non-National Socialist professional organizations, and he urged them to attend the AO's annual rally in

Stuttgart in August 1938.[35] Shorn of even the little influence he once possessed and detesting Ribbentrop's expanding authority over the AA, he privately compared his position to that of a "flea circus director" (*Flohzirkus Direktor*), whose job he described as hitching insects to tiny chariots at a carnival.[36]

It was not surprising that he was among the first division chiefs, along with the heads of Referat Deutschland (Bülow-Schwante) and the press division (Gottfried Aschmann), removed by Ribbentrop and replaced with the minister's party followers. Hermann Kriebel, a personal friend of Hitler, a party member since the 1920s, and for many years a consul general in China, took over the personnel division on 20 April 1939; his deputies included Schröder and a more ominous figure attached to Himmler, Heinz Bertling. Kriebel and his minions set forth with fanaticism to breed a younger group of activists in the AA, a "Ribbentrop generation," for supplanting the career diplomats. Although Bertling headed a new foreign ministry training school (*Nachwuchshaus des Auswärtigen Amtes*) established in Berlin, it had little success in producing the new Nazi diplomats.[37]

It appears, however, that Prüfer actually left the division at least six months before his official removal. Apparently ill from his tuberculosis and out of the office much of the time, he received occasional special assignments in Middle Eastern affairs. Already in August 1938, he participated in the efforts by the German minister in Cairo, Werner Freiherr von Ow-Wachendorf, to arrange for the sale of German armaments to Egypt. But such plans floundered from a lack of British approval. Although the Germans experienced more success in trade with Turkey and in selling arms to Afghanistan, Iran, and Iraq in return for strategic raw materials necessary to Hitler's plans for war, their concern for Britain's reaction dominated another venture in which Prüfer was involved: the Reich's interest in concluding an arms agreement with Saudi Arabia that would have provided weapons for the Arab cause in Palestine.[38]

To some Arabs, Germany looked like a promising ally against England, not to mention against the Jews; the ruler of Arabia, Ibn Saud, discussed reducing his dependence on England and purchasing German arms with Fritz Grobba, the German minister in Iraq, and with Rosenberg's APA. During the negotiations, when the Saudi deputy foreign minister, Fuad Hamza, visited Berlin in August, he met with Prüfer, Werner Otto von Hentig, and the head of the intelligence and counterintelligence office in the high command of the German armed forces (*Abwehr*), Admiral Wilhelm Canaris.

It was decided, however, that Fuad Hamza could not be trusted to keep the operation secret from Britain. This factor, along with the lack of economic benefit for Germany, the difficulty of shipping the arms to

Arabia, and the prospect that the weapons might fall into British hands for eventual use against Germany, led the AA and the Reich war ministry to oppose the arms deal. Only in the summer of 1939, when war with Britain appeared more likely, did Hitler and Ribbentrop reverse the policy; but even then, their sensitivity to the Middle East interests of their ally, Italy, delayed the negotiations with the Arabs.[39]

Despite Prüfer's insignificant role in such activities, the British embassy in Berlin observed his involvement and that of Hentig, recalling in a dispatch to London the anti-British activities of both men in World War I.[40] Among his other activities before his departure from the personnel division, Prüfer participated in the negotiations between Germany and Poland in October 1938 to settle their respective demands for territory in the Silesian area, where the projected annexations of the two countries, particularly the town of Oderberg (Bohumin), a major railroad center, might overlap as a consequence of the German takeover of the Sudetenland from Czechoslovakia.[41]

Ribbentrop, also apparently anticipating Prüfer's departure as personnel director, granted him a leave of absence from January through March 1939, which he used to vacation in China.[42] As Prüfer returned to Berlin, however, Hitler annexed the remainder of Czechoslovakia, and with England's and France's abandonment of attempts to appease the dictator's territorial claims in Central and Eastern Europe, the continent stood on the brink of another world war. German aggression in Europe, moreover, added to the problems that existed between the Reich and several non-European states, including Brazil, the largest country in Latin America. Such ramifications from German policies would eventually affect Prüfer's career.

Like other states in South America in 1937 and 1938, Brazil had reversed its previously friendly attitude towards Germany, banned the local Nazi party organization operated by the AO, and arrested many of its leaders. In addition, Brazil had declared the belligerent and pro-Nazi German ambassador, Karl Ritter, *persona non grata,* and demanded that Berlin replace him. The Germans, not to be outdone, recalled Ritter and ordered the Brazilian ambassador to leave the Reich. These events, followed in May 1939 by the outlawing of foreign political groups in Argentina, shocked the Germans, however. Germany had used the huge settlements of German farmers and merchants in the southern Brazilian states (Rio Grande do Sul, Santa Catarina, and Parana) to produce their largest foreign party group (nearly 3,000 members) as well as a noticeable penetration of the Brazilian government, the army, the native fascist movements (e.g., the Integralists, led by Plinio Salgado), and the economy.[43]

The Brazilians, however, indicated that they wanted cordial relations with Germany, as long as Berlin did not meddle in Brazil's internal affairs. President and dictator Getulio Vargas's regime especially valued its trade with the Reich, which provided Brazil with a market for its raw materials and a source for purchasing armaments and manufactured goods. Particularly the Brazilian military, which was fiercely nationalistic and anti-Communist, had urged the government to trade with Germany for weapons and equipment for the armed forces. In February 1937 and March 1938 the army had signed agreements with Krupp, the major German arms manufacturer.[44] Such ties also enabled Vargas to play the United States and Germany against one another, a policy that generally benefited the Brazilians.

During the first half of 1939, both countries worked toward a rapprochement; the chief of staff of the Brazilian army, General Pedro Góes Monteiro, accepted an invitation to attend army maneuvers in Germany. A Brazilian arms-purchasing commission established itself at Essen near the Krupp works, and a group of aviation officers inspected Germany's expanded air force facilities and laid wreaths at German war monuments. When Rio proposed a new exchange of ambassadors, Berlin agreed, and on 12 June 1939 Ribbentrop appointed Prüfer as the Reich's envoy to Brazil.

The announcement pleased the Brazilians. They considered the new appointee "completely the opposite" of the rude and unreasonable Ritter. Rio believed, moreover, that Prüfer's connections to the NSDAP, rather than being prejudicial, could facilitate "approximation between the two countries," and it considered his appointment an indication of Hitler's desire to improve German-Brazilian relations.[45]

Prüfer's arrival in Brazil was delayed for several months, however, by his attendance at the Ibero-American conference in Berlin during the summer. The meeting resulted from Ribbentrop's anger at the AO's injurious meddling into German affairs in Latin America, which had produced the worst attack abroad on the party's foreign groups in their brief history. In addition to their expulsion from Brazil and Argentina, the groups found themselves banned from Guatemala and Honduras and under pressure to disband in Costa Rica. The problems caused by the party in Latin America had also intensified the anti-German sentiment in the United States. German mission leaders from Latin America who attended the conference included Edmund von Thermann (Argentina), Wilhelm von Schoen (Chile), and Otto Langmann (Uruguay); they denounced the AO and Bohle and demanded that the party's officials abroad be totally subordinated to the diplomats. Although the meeting failed to solve the question of the NSDAP's interference in foreign policy, it represented a further curtailment of the influence of Bohle and the AO.

As Prüfer departed for Brazil, however, he seemed unconcerned about the important diplomatic issues that had prompted the conference, especially the disaster abroad generated by Nazi policy. Instead, he despised the way the meeting had provided Ribbentrop with an opportunity to snub the diplomats. The foreign minister had not attended the deliberations, but sent Weizsäcker as his representative; moreover, the minister had allegedly kept the diplomats in Berlin a few months longer without receiving them.[46] Prüfer also felt little remorse at the fate of Bohle and the AO's party groups abroad, not only because of his latent ill-feeling towards them, but also because they would be even less likely to cause him difficulties in his new post.

ten

Ambassador to Brazil: The Diplomacy of War, 1939-42

PRÜFER arrived in Rio de Janeiro with his wife and son on 17 September 1939, nearly three weeks after Hitler's attack on Poland had set off World War II. Although the Nazi dictator focused almost exclusively during the war on Europe and Russia and paid little attention to the Americas, Berlin directed its ambassador to preserve Brazilian neutrality and German-Brazilian trade, a task made significantly more difficult by the British blockade of the seas around Europe and the Americas.[1]

Brazil quickly became the most crucial element in the struggle between the Axis and the Allies for the support of Latin America. Germany and its cohorts, if they held the ports on the northeastern Brazilian coast (or Bulge) that lay a few hours' airplane flight from Africa and Europe, could close the South Atlantic to Anglo-American shipping, prevent the United States from supplying the beleaguered British in Egypt, and dominate North Africa and possibly the Middle East. Controlling that territory would provide Hitler with a position of immense power from which to attack the United States, which he considered Germany's ultimate enemy and which he envisioned would be conquered by the next generation of Nazis once he had established German rule over Europe and Russia.[2]

As in World War I, the conflict focused Prüfer's emotions against Germany's external enemies: the Western powers, including the United States, and world Jewry. His stabilization of German-Brazilian relations prompted Sir Geoffrey Knox, the British ambassador in Rio, to observe in August 1940 "that Herr Prüfer has shown in his dealings with the Brazilian Government more skill and circumspection than his predecessor.''³ Although Prüfer promoted relations with Brazilian officials, he lacked experience in Brazil's affairs and appeared unfamiliar with its culture and unable to deal effectively with the new diplomatic challenges which the country offered. He had difficulties in gauging the attitudes of its leaders and sensed that they were moving away from Germany, which indeed they were by the summer of 1941. Prüfer's bitter prejudices appear to have clouded his judgments. Occasional remarks in his diaries indicated that he did not respect the Brazilians, particularly because he believed they were dominated by the Jews and the United States. Yet while cautioning Berlin against measures that could worsen the situation between Germany and Brazil, he failed to report his doubts regarding Brazilian personalities and policies. Moreover, despite the Rio government's moderate treatment of the Germans in Brazil following its break of relations with Germany in January 1942, he refused to criticize Berlin's aggression at sea, which pushed Rio to declare war on the Reich seven months later.

For Prüfer's family the sojourn in Brazil produced little happiness. Possibly because of anxieties about relatives and friends back home, Anneliese Prüfer's health deteriorated. Already in ill health—tuberculosis had led to the removal of one of her kidneys in the 1920s, she was deaf in one ear, and doctors had forbidden her to have another pregnancy—in Brazil she suffered from incapacitating headaches, which may also have

Prüfer, his wife, and son arrive at the embassy in Rio de Janeiro, 1939.

resulted from the troubles which she and her husband experienced with their son, Olaf. The parents showed little sympathy for the child. For example, when the boy's tutor resigned, Prüfer blamed the youth without telling him the reason, punished him by giving his birthday presents to other children, and insisted that he learn not to "disgrace" his father's social position and family. Prüfer disciplined Olaf severely and, although he refused to lay a hand on him, often directed the boy's mother to beat him. While the father appeared unconcerned about what was happening, she worried about the son, informing her mother in a letter on 24 August 1941 that "he [Olaf] tries to console me by saying that I should not suffer from the harsh punishments that I am forced to submit him to."[4] Things would not improve for Prüfer or his family as their time in Brazil went on.

Preserving Brazilian Trade and Neutrality

Although the Germans desired reconciliation with Brazil, hoping to erase the unpleasant memory of the Reich's previous ambassador, the German embassy in the fall of 1939 arrogantly publicized Germany's triumph in Poland. Prüfer monitored the correspondence of the Nazi party's underground organization in Brazil with the AO, but he and the local party leader attached to the embassy, Hans-Henning von Cossel, worked

Prüfer's visit to São Paulo, 1940. He is seated at left in the back of the auto.

press. Woermann, the head of the AA's political section, directed Prüfer
to deny to the Brazilians that the Reich possessed political aspirations in
the Americas.[10] President Vargas, responding to the situation, designed
his speeches during June 1940 to appease both the United States and
Germany and appeal to the desire of the Brazilian public and leadership
for neutrality. Not only did he recognize his army leaders' enthusiasm for
the Nazi success, but he also realized the army's suspicions regarding
Brazilian-American military cooperation, which Washington's lack of armaments for Brazil had fueled.

Throughout 1940, the United States urged Brazil and other Latin
American states to allow American troops to occupy their naval and air
bases. The Vargas government, and particularly Góes Monteiro, refused,
emphasizing instead that the United States should send Brazil armaments
to equip its forces before it would allow the Americans on its soil. Although Prüfer and his subordinates in the embassy, such as Gen. Günter
Niedenführ, the military attaché, and Capt. Hermann Bohny, the assistant
naval attaché, apparently knew little of the negotiations on the arms deal,
the ambassador warned the AA on 8 June about the efforts of the United
States to place its troops in Brazil.[11] Ten days later, Prüfer made mention
to Berlin of "America's intensive economic offensive directed against
Germany" in Brazil, an effort which involved American loans and the
construction of a steel works there; Prüfer proposed that the Reich offer
Vargas a rival trade agreement.

Shortly after the reply from Emil Wiehl, the head of the AA's economic
policy division, permitting Prüfer to present the Brazilians with a similar
accord on the condition that Brazil remain neutral, Vargas asked the envoy to meet privately with him. The president assured him on 21 June that
Brazil wished to continue its trade with Germany. Vargas also requested
new agreements and appeared pleased with the diplomat's reply that his
country was prepared to sign contracts for the postwar purchase of Brazilian products, particularly coffee and cotton, and to build the steel mill
wanted by Brazilians. The Brazilian leader also downplayed the agitation
against Nazi fifth-column activities, reportedly telling Prüfer that it "was
due to foreign propaganda of lies which was carried on particularly by
Jewish emigrants . . . which he [Vargas] would not tolerate."[12]

Berlin directed the ambassador to begin immediate negotiations for an
agreement and pressed him to conclude it before the inter-American conference of foreign ministers, scheduled for the end of July 1940 in Havana. Knowledge soon spread of Prüfer's subsequent discussions with
Vargas and the Brazilian minister of finance, Artur de Souza Costa; for
example, the brother of the foreign minister, Olavo Aranha, who possessed ties to German commercial circles, approached the embassy and

offered to help the Germans in the negotiations. But Prüfer, who distrusted the foreign minister and his connections to the United States, considered his brother an opportunist, equally untrustworthy, and resisted Olavo's overture.[13]

Because the talks with Vargas and Souza Costa developed slowly, however, Prüfer soon agreed to hire Olavo as a middleman. Yet this, too, produced little, even though the Germans increased their offer to import millions of reichsmarks worth of Brazilian products yearly after the war. The discussion floundered with the changing fortunes in the fighting in Europe, the continued failure of German ships to get through the British blockade, and the success of Brazil's economic negotiations with the United States.[14] At the end of September 1940, Brazil concluded an accord with the United States in which the Americans agreed to help finance and construct the steel mill. Moreover, Brazil extended the rights of the United States-based Pan American airways to fly in the country, and on 1 October Rio suspended for several days the German-subsidized newspaper, *Meio Dia,* for having attacked a speech by Sumner Welles, the American under-secretary of state.

Prüfer reported to the Wilhelmstrasse on 17 October that recent events and the anticipation of Brazilians that the American President, Franklin Roosevelt, who had stood solidly behind England in the war, would soon be re-elected, had weakened the pro-German circle in the government around Dutra and Góes Monteiro. Another official friendly to the Germans, the police chief Filinto Müller, informed the embassy that he and the military leaders "could be saved only by a dazzling German victory over England and a consequent waning of Roosevelt's prospects." Two days later, Prüfer declared to the AA that Vargas was "the only reliable power factor in South America against the penetration of the U.S.A.," and he warned again of the danger of losing Brazilian neutrality if the Reich did not deliver the Krupp armaments to Brazil.[15]

Unknown to the ambassador, whom Aranha, the foreign minister, repeatedly assured that Brazil would resist American demands for bases in the northeast and that Uruguay would also oppose granting the United States the right to use its bases, the Vargas government was slowly committing itself to military collaboration with Washington. The U.S. agreed to supply armaments to Brazil, and Rio decided that in the event of an attack on any American nation (except Canada) by a non-American country, its resources should be placed on the side of the United States. On 25 October 1940 Prüfer reported increased activity in the capital's harbor and along the Brazilian coast by warships from the United States, some with planes that flew reconnaissance missions into the country.[16] Nevertheless, because of the United States' inability to supply Brazil with arms and the Brazilian military leaders' unwillingness to allow American troops on their soil until the weapons arrived, intimate military collaboration eluded the two countries.

Prüfer's information about the presence of the American ships and planes came from his cooperation in a new and extensive intelligence organization established in Brazil during the fall of 1940 by the Abwehr; the network was also designed to observe ships traveling around South Africa destined for England. The head of the network, Albrecht Engels, a German businessman in Rio, established contacts with agents in other Latin American countries, including the German military attaché in Buenos Aires, Captain Dietrich Niebuhr, and an agent of the German security service (*Sicherheitsdienst,* or SD), Johann Siegfried Becker.

Using a system of code names, Engels and his spy ring sent reports to Germany through the mail, using secret ink or microdots as well as clandestine radio transmitters. Engels frequently dispatched his more urgent messages, however, by diplomatic cable through Prüfer and others in the embassy, notably Hermann Bohny and a staff member, Gustav Glock. Engels also funneled bribery money through the embassy to informants, and Prüfer contributed to the operation by forcing the recall to Germany of agents whom he described as "imprudent and frivolous."[17]

Such activities also provided the Germans with information on the movement of American ships through Brazilian ports and into the South Atlantic. An incident at the end of November 1940 was even more important in affecting Washington's relations with Brazil, however. The British seized the *Siqueira Campos,* a Brazilian freighter loaded with German arms, off the coast of Portugal. Because of Washington's support of England in the war, Brazilian antagonism towards Britain threatened to spill over against the United States. But when the Brazilians persuaded the United States to pressure the British into releasing the *Siqueira Campos* on 18 December, the tensions eased and relations improved dramatically.

Throughout the crisis, Prüfer judged correctly the severe blow it dealt to Brazil's relations to Britain, and he cautioned Berlin to act with reserve in the affair.[18] The incident also prevented the ambassador from attending a meeting in Buenos Aires among the German ministers from Argentina, Chile, and Uruguay to discuss the increasing anti-German activity of the United States in their countries.[19] The role of Washington in the *Siqueira Campos* affair and other events in Brazil during the latter half of 1940 supported the diplomats' view that that the United States had become Germany's greatest rival in Latin America.

With the seizure of the *Siqueira Campos,* moreover, the British appeared to have provided the Axis with an opportunity for further diminishing England's influence, at least in Brazil. In one of his final notes to the AA in 1940, Prüfer asked for a large shipment of copies of Hitler's address to Berlin armaments workers on 10 December, in which the dictator lashed out at the British by promising them further war and declaring: "Only a madman can say that I ever had a complex of inferiority vis-à-vis the English!" The speech, Prüfer believed, would be excellent propaganda. It had made an "extraordinarily strong impression" on the "man in the street" in Brazil, he reported, who discussed it "passionately" and found himself "mostly in agreement."[20]

1941: Rio's "Twilight Policy Between Day and Night"

Much to the disappointment of Prüfer and the embassy, neither the *Siqueira Campos* incident nor Vargas's New Year's speech to Brazilians, which appeared to condemn the British, produced a change in Brazil's relations with Germany and the United States. Although Prüfer learned of bitter disagreements within the Rio government between Dutra and the foreign minister, Aranha, over Brazilian policy towards Britain, Vargas settled the conflict by lessening the influence of the army and successfully concealing what he had done from the Germans.[21]

As the United States made further gains against the Axis in Brazil during the first half of 1941 and Germany's inability to counter the trend became evident, Prüfer urged Berlin to follow a policy of restraint, lest the Reich drive Brazil into the arms of the Anglo-Americans. During January the Brazilian government ordered newspapers not to criticize the United States and directed that exports of Brazilian raw materials used for war could only leave with the government's consent, except for those going to the United States.

A few months later, Brazil agreed that only the United States would be permitted to obtain strategic Brazilian minerals (such as rubber, rock quartz, manganese, and mica). Washington also waged a propaganda campaign on a grand scale; numerous "goodwill ambassadors" poured into Brazil, extolling the virtues of the United States and Britain.[22] Soon Aranha and the Japanese ambassador to Rio, Itaro Ishii, intimated to Prüfer for the first time their belief that the United States would enter the war.

While the German official reported the declining situation to his government without explaining who he thought was responsible, he privately accused the Jews who, he claimed, controlled the United States.[23] On one occasion, Prüfer recorded in his diary that an American doctor had told him about "hair-raising things regarding the hatred towards Germans and hate-mongering by Jews in New York." On 12 January 1941 he attributed the visit to Brazil of Stefan Zweig, the German writer forced into exile by the Nazis, to the "growth of Jewish-American propaganda in the cultural area." He complained at still another point: "American propaganda becomes forever stronger and louder, thus it is not very clever. Indiscriminantly, some people, journalists, professors, economists, blue stockings, Jews, and clerics have been unleashed on South America, who clatter as clumsily and aimlessly as possible. . . ."[24]

Prüfer also maintained that Brazilian leaders who negotiated economic agreements with the United States, like industrialist Guilherme Guinle, did so because they were Jewish. Prüfer's anti-Jewish attitudes and diplomatic status, moreover, could produce vicious results; he supplied legal support through the embassy for Alfred Engling, an official of the Hermann Goering mining company in Germany, who arrived in Rio to remove the Jewish and Czech employees from a subsidiary, the Skoda works, and replace them with Germans. Through the embassy's influence on officials in the Brazilian ministry of justice, Engling received a power of attorney to manage both Skoda's personnel and financial affairs.[25]

While Prüfer expressed his bitterness in private towards those nations and peoples he despised as Germany's enemies, the more important and secret military inroads made by the United States into Brazil repeatedly eluded him and illustrated that he was removed from the mainstream of diplomacy in Rio. Such problems also resulted in his committing occasional blunders that undermined relations between the Reich and Brazil. The American successes emphasized the failure of the Germans to affect Brazilian politics and illustrated Hitler's disinterest in Latin America.[26] America's increased pressure on Brazil coincided with the worsening of relations between the Reich and the United States in the spring of 1941, particularly following Washington's Lend-Lease agreement with Britain. This accord embodied America's "undeclared war" on Germany, which developed during the year and in which the United States provided all aid to the British, short of declaring war.

The United States, as in its policy in other Latin American countries, persuaded the Vargas government to begin removing the Axis from the airlines in Brazil. Although the war had forced the German-owned Lufthansa airline to discontinue it trans-Atlantic flights to Brazil, the Italian Lati line and the German-controlled Condor, Vasp, and Varig airways continued their flights, frequently carrying Axis agents and flying reconnaissance missions. Prüfer's numerous suggestions for how Berlin might protect the Axis airlines went unheeded. When the United States developed the policy of offering aircraft, financial credits, and technical aid in return for "de-Germanization," Brazil slowly removed the German personnel in Vasp and Varig at the beginning of 1941 and reorganized Condor.[27] Jefferson Caffery, the United States ambassador to Rio, who was particularly close to Aranha and enjoyed easy access to Vargas, played a significant role in this and other agreements. Prüfer, who envied Caffery's influence, accused him of homosexuality and of being "brutal and addicted to drink," and called him "the gangster."[28]

What apparently eluded Prüfer and the embassy completely, however, was the United States' expansion in March 1941 of financial credits to Brazil for the purchase of more military equipment.[29] Nor did the embassy learn until late about the lengthy negotiations among the Brazilians and the United States-based Pan American Airways, which acted secretly on behalf of the American government, for the airline's Brazilian subsidiary, Panair do Brasil, to construct and expand the air facilities around Natal in northeastern Brazil. With the German desert units under General Erwin Rommel sweeping through North Africa, Natal provided the main link across the South Atlantic for supplies from the United States to reach the hard-pressed British forces.

Concern in the United States for securing its use of northeastern Brazil flared in May 1941, when the Vichy government of France concluded a tentative agreement with Germany permitting Berlin to employ Dakar as a submarine base. Although Pan American surveyed the Natal region at the end of April and began ferrying aircraft through it to the British in Africa a month later, Prüfer first learned of the operation from an official "friendly to Germany" in the Brazilian foreign office (*Itamaraty*), possibly Fernando Nilo Alvarenga, a diplomat and member of Vargas's staff, and reported it to the AA on 18 June.[30] As the ambassador learned more about such activities, which involved the expansion of American influence into both Brazil and other Latin American countries, acquiring intelligence information became even more significant.

The increasing role of intelligence operations may have been responsible for an incident a week later in which a radio transmitter, sent by Prüfer through diplomatic pouch to Peru to increase communication between the German legation in Lima and the AA, was seized by the authorities and returned to Rio through Buenos Aires. A committee in the Argentine parliament investigating pro-Nazi activities confiscated the transmitter and proclaimed it as evidence of German subversion. The affair, along with several other incidents involving Reich diplomats in Latin America, including Bolivia's expulsion of the German minister in La Paz, Ernst Wendler, for allegedly plotting with the Bolivian military to overthrow the government, increased the popular belief in the existence of a vast Nazi fifth column subverting the Americas.[31]

Although such views were exaggerated, they possessed some foundation with respect to Brazil. At the beginning of July, the Abwehr agent, Engels, expanded his intelligence network to Recife to keep tabs on the

Pan American activity, the passage of military aircraft through the region, and the increasing American naval patrols operating from ports along the coast. This increasing pressure may have been the source for Prüfer's gloomy observation in his diary on 1 July 1941: "Brazil has practically placed its air bases in the north at the disposal of the Americans. In the past weeks, 15 to 20 American airplanes flew from Natal to Bathurst."[32]

Such reports resulted in a flurry of receptions for Brazilian officials at the embassy in the hope that the festivities would produce more information. In preparing for them, however, Prüfer noted the "first signs of an ever stronger tightening of the attitude by official Brazil against us." Three members of the government who had previously expressed the wish to be invited to the embassy suddenly "declined at the last moment." Nevertheless, Prüfer entertained Lourival Fontes, the director of the government's press and propaganda department, and other dignitaries, and on 3 July Niedenführ received eight generals, including Dutra. Although the guests proclaimed Brazil's continued commitment to neutrality, the military leaders informed the attaché of the large American loans to Brazil for military equipment.[33]

News continued to arrive at the embassy that American planes flew through northeast Brazil on their way to West Africa. The Cuban minister warned Prüfer "about underestimating America" and advised the Germans to "avoid war for as long as possible. Should American industry operate with 'full speed,' it will mobilize unlimited forces. If one could only keep Roosevelt out of the war, the parent ship 'England' would be destroyed."[34] Prüfer appeared impressed with the argument, although not enough so to pass it along to the AA. Instead, despite his reservations about the sympathies of important Brazilian leaders, he informed the ministry on 11 July that "responsible personalities of the Brazilian government" continued to place "great value on close economic cooperation with us" and that they felt "with bitterness the weakness of Brazil's economic and political position, which led to its increasing dependence on the U.S.A." He cautioned, moreover, against "economic countermeasures" that "would affect the local mentality in a provocative way and push Brazil only further into the clutches of our enemies."[35]

What role Germany's massive invasion of Russia, which had begun three weeks earlier and which seemed to lessen the Axis threat to the Americas, played in Prüfer's advice is unclear. From the few brief comments about the Russian campaign in his diaries, it appears that Prüfer possessed little initial interest in the attack. But six weeks later, the continued rapid movement of the German forces into the Soviet Union prompted greater enthusiasm. "In Germany," he declared, "one believes that the following will occur: Russia will still be defeated before this year is out, whereupon its resources will be at our disposal. America shall no longer risk entering the war, and England will have to face our entire combat strength." What would remain for Britain, he concluded, "is only surrender or resistance until its annihilation."[36]

Complicating his task in advising the AA on the course to follow towards Brazil, however, was Prüfer's increasing difficulty in judging the attitudes of Brazilian leaders. He met often with Aranha, who nearly always proclaimed Brazil's resolve to remain neutral, even if the United States should enter the war. The ambassador's dislike of the minister seemed to wane at times, and Prüfer appreciated the Brazilian dilemma that Aranha represented. "This twilight policy between day and night," Prüfer wrote in his diary, "may not be very heroic, but it is useful for the weak Brazil." On another occasion, he remarked about Aranha: "I have the impression that he is concerned about being fair with us."[37] Prüfer still counted Dutra, the war minister, and the police chief, Müller, as pro-German. Relations between the Germans and Góes Monteiro, the army chief of staff, had apparently cooled, however. On one occasion at the beginning of the year, Müller had told Prüfer that while Góes Monteiro favored the Germans, the army leader believed that if the United States entered the war, Brazil must "go along" because "the peoples of the continents represented a community of fate that must cooperate in everything." Prüfer continued to meet with Góes Monteiro during 1941, but much of the army leader's time was spent helping negotiate the military agreements with the United States. Moreover, Góes Monteiro may have been one of the pro-German officers who now harbored doubts about an Axis victory.[38]

Prüfer placed his greatest trust in the Brazilian president, Vargas, who carefully cultivated the German envoy's friendship and balanced the factions in the military and diplomatic corps in his government. Called "the boss" by Prüfer, Vargas continued the policy he had developed in 1940: he kept himself and Brazil from the inescapable position of casting their fortunes with the United States by secretly assuring the Reich ambassador of Brazil's friendship and commitment to neutrality. It is difficult to judge Vargas's motives; Prüfer's dispatches and diaries substantiate the picture of the president, fashioned by most historians, of an opportunistic and deceptive politician who convinced the Germans of his difficult position in the war, his dislike of American pressure, and his sympathy for the Reich.[39] On the other hand, Caffery, Prüfer's American counterpart in Rio, was persuaded by June 1941 that Vargas, as the ambassador informed Washington, "has been leaning more and more in our direction during the past few months" and "is definitely on our side."[40]

Vargas possessed several capable subordinates, including his secretary, Luiz Vergara, to help him play his political game. Vergara relayed messages from the president to Prüfer, won the German's confidence, and persuaded Prüfer that he was genuinely "friendly to Germany." But a member of Vargas's staff far more pro-German was the diplomat, Alvarenga. He, too, emphasized to Prüfer the sincerity of the president's "attitudes" towards the Reich.[41] Alvarenga was present on at least one occasion when Vargas's brother, Benjamin, both denounced to Prüfer the president's enemies in the business community favoring trade with the United States and proclaimed his ideological affinity with Nazism.

Although it is impossible to judge whether the brother genuinely held such views, Prüfer was impressed enough with Benjamin Vargas to describe him as a "friend of the authoritarian state and anti-Semitism" who demanded the elimination "of the false Pan Americanism, which serves only the hegemony of the Jewish clique around Roosevelt and which has networks in all Latin American countries." In place of Pan Americanism, the brother allegedly told Prüfer, Brazil should form a "federation" with neighboring Argentina and Chile based on "a common Latin culture and Catholic faith against the Anglo-Saxons and Jews, who are foreign in race and belief and crave power."[42]

During the crucial days in June 1941, as the Brazilian government put the final touches on the agreement permitting Pan American airways to construct and lease the air facilities in the northeast, Vargas asked Müller to invite Prüfer to a secret meeting, where Vargas discussed "the increasing American pressure" which, he said, was illustrated by Roosevelt's request that he visit Washington. Vargas offered to approach the United States "with a proposal for mediation" in the war "instead of as an ally" and asked for Berlin's opinion. When Ribbentrop rejected the idea, Prüfer arranged through Benjamin Vargas for a secret meeting with the Brazilian president to communicate the German reply; during that meeting President Vargas agreed, as Prüfer later reported, "that considering the increased tension between the U.S.A. and the Axis Powers he, too, no longer considered the mediation he had proposed to be opportune." Prüfer appeared persuaded of Vargas's sincerity.[43]

Ribbentrop and the AA, however, failed to respond to Prüfer's renewed warning on 23 April 1941 that the positions of Vargas and Dutra, "the bulwark against the inclusion of South America in Roosevelt's anti-German policy," would be seriously weakened and the United States would gain considerable advantages if the deliveries of the Krupp armaments were suspended. Since the *Siqueira Campos* incident five months before, England was no longer permitting shipments of the materials on Brazilian vessels, and a temporary agreement between Berlin and Rio had resulted in storage of the remainder of the arms in Lisbon and Germany. But when the German army confiscated a portion of the weapons scheduled for delivery and used them in Russia and North Africa, Ribbentrop, whose initial opposition to the invasion of the Soviet Union had caused momentary tensions with Hitler, did not urge either the dictator or Wilhelm Keitel, the chief of the high command of the military (*Oberkommando der Wehrmacht*, or OKW), to resume the shipments.[44]

The AA cooperated more closely with Prüfer's proposals for freeing those German commercial ships anchored in Brazilian harbors and unable to return to Europe because of the British blockade, a lack of fuel, and the Brazilian interest in acquiring the vessels for its merchant marine. Prüfer insisted that selling the ships would strengthen Dutra and Vargas and preserve Brazilian neutrality. The German navy and Abwehr, however, opposed the transaction because they intended to use several of the freighters as V-Schiffe to provision German warships and submarines.

The AA, moreover, wished to keep the ships for German trade and to make certain that they did not fall into enemy hands; initially, therefore, the ministry offered only one boat (the *Bollwerk*) for sale. But at Prüfer's request, the ministry agreed on 23 June 1941 to permit him to negotiate for the sale of three ships (the *Maceio*, the *Bollwerk*, and the *Montevideo*) in return for Brazilian permission for the remaining five, which the Reich government had designated as "blockade runners" (*Blockadebrecher*), to leave for Europe. Four of the latter soon left Brazil, but only one reached France; the last one, the *Windhuk*, remained anchored in Santos.[45]

Still other problems in the fall of 1941 signified a decline in Germany's position in Brazil. The threat of war between the Reich and the United States increased when Roosevelt and Churchill signed the Atlantic Charter and when an undeclared naval war developed between Germany and America.[46] Although the Brazilians still refused to allow troops from the United States into the northeast until the Americans delivered the promised armaments to Brazil, Pan American began construction on the air facilities in the region. The United States also signed a Lend-Lease agreement with Brazil, and the two countries agreed to establish joint military commissions to discuss future collaboration between their armies.[47]

Although Dutra complained on 6 November through Müller to Prüfer and Niedenführ about the alleged bullying tactics of the United States, and particularly about the chief of the American military mission in Rio, General Lehman Miller, an incident four days later illustrated anew the confusion among Prüfer and the embassy about the attitudes of the Rio government.[48] Vargas gave a speech commemorating the fourth anniversary of the Brazilian constitution at a celebration in the war ministry, and Dutra joined other military leaders in declaring his loyalty to the president. Vargas maintained that Brazil was committed to continental solidarity and would take part in the common defense of the Americas. Although the Brazilian press and leaders in the United States, including Roosevelt, praised the speech—and one had to look at it carefully to discover much of benefit for the Axis—Prüfer claimed to the AA that the Brazilians had issued an "exhortation to Washington's war agitators not to go too far."[49]

Throughout November, amid rumors that Brazil would join the United States in occupying Dutch Guiana and the Azores, Prüfer continued to receive mixed signals from the government. When Aranha proclaimed that Brazil would not remain neutral if another American nation entered the war and Prüfer questioned Vargas about the remark, the president responded through a confidant and Benjamin Vargas that the foreign minister had erred in his statement.[50] A few weeks later, however, this issue suddenly leaped to the forefront when Japanese aircraft attacked and crippled the United States Pacific fleet at Pearl Harbor. The United States declared war on Japan, Germany's ally in the recently signed Tripartite pact that included Italy.

On 11 December 1941, Hitler, for reasons that remain an endless source of debate and that related significantly to his racist ideology and hatred that resulted from it, joined Italy in going to war against America.[51] Vargas immediately declared Brazil's solidarity with Washington. Aranha maintained to the Latin American diplomats accredited to Rio that the attack on the United States represented an assault on all of the Americas, and he urged their countries to respond by supporting the United States unanimously. On 12 December, the Central American and Caribbean states joined the war on Germany; Mexico, Colombia, and Venezuela soon severed diplomatic relations with the Reich. Even Dutra expressed to Aranha his "pro-United States attitude."[52]

In the weeks that followed, the American republics organized a conference of their foreign ministers, scheduled for Rio in mid-January 1942 and, at the United States' insistence, presided over by Aranha, the leader of the pro-Allied faction in the Brazilian government. While the German ambassadors in Argentina and Chile received assurances from those countries' governments that they would remain neutral, several emissaries from the Brazilian government, including Vergara, Nabuco, Müller, and the pro-Axis Portuguese ambassador, Martinho Nobre de Mello, maintained to Prüfer that the most recent crisis would not change Brazil's policy.

Simultaneously, however, the Brazilian government froze the assets of Axis nationals in the country, banned telegraph communication between the German embassy and consulates, forced the German-controlled Condor airways to suspend some of its flights, and closed the last trans-Atlantic Axis airline, the Italian Lati.[53] Germans were also imprisoned in Petropolis, the site of Vargas's summer residence, and the Americans and British pressed Brazil to close the numerous secret radio transmitters operated by the Abwehr. One of the small spy groups was hurt when the Allies blacklisted Marathon Oil, the business firm from which it drew its agents, and when the police temporarily arrested a key operative in Recife. "The protectorate," Prüfer lamented on 16 December using code names in his diary, "was devastated the night before last."

Prüfer attempted not to antagonize the Brazilians further. He advised the AA not to retaliate.[54] Prüfer persuaded the AA not to order the *Windhuk,* the German ship in Santos that had been the object of intense German-Brazilian negotiations, to risk sailing for Europe, thus providing Brazil with a reason to sever relations with the Reich. Several weeks later, after their crews had secretly destroyed their engine rooms, the *Windhuk* and *Montevideo* were sold to the Rio government.[55]

During the month before the Rio conference, the AA directed the ambassador and other German mission leaders in Latin America to use propaganda and every other means to influence the diplomats attending the meeting favorably towards Germany. The ministry was particularly conscious of the impact that Brazil could have on the other Latin American countries; consequently, it urged Portugal and Spain, both neutral but friendly to the Axis, to place pressure on Rio. It also directed the embassy to intensify propaganda against the United States. But the Brazilian government's press and propaganda department banned criticism of the U.S. Prüfer complained about such censorship and recommended that the Germans beam short wave radio broadcasts to Brazil in Portuguese, attacking Washington and including "continual references to the Jewish influence on Roosevelt."[56]

Although Prüfer told Berlin that a reasonable possibility existed of Brazil's remaining neutral after the Rio conference—particularly if Argentina and Chile did so—he had his doubts in private. He called Nabuco's intimations of continued Brazilian neutrality "optimistic chatter."[57] In his diary Prüfer recorded with apparent agreement the racial and political views of a friend from Belo Horizonte, a professor, who felt "fairly pessimistic" about the future, claiming that there was "neither patriotism nor a sense of community" among Brazilians. "The racial mixture prevents any healthy development," the professor continued, according to Prüfer, "all the more since the population is thoroughly infected." Of Vargas, the friend "talked very unfavorably," believing the president was "indeed clever, but without character and therefore unreliable."[58]

The observer's skepticism proved well-founded. The United States hoped that the Rio conference would produce a declaration by all the American republics severing diplomatic relations with the Axis. On 31 December Vargas and Aranha secretly expressed their approval of the American position. Two days later, Prüfer, even without the knowledge of the Brazilian leaders' decision, greeted the new year by again expressing his dubious view towards Germany's situation. "We are stuck in a thick fog," he observed, "from which one cannot see a way out."[59]

From the Rio Conference to a Declaration of War

As the meeting of foreign ministers opened in Rio on 15 January 1942, the Germans redoubled their efforts to persuade the participants to remain neutral. The next day, Prüfer and his fellow Italian and Japanese ambassadors sent notes to Aranha, warning that a break in diplomatic relations would inevitably lead to war.[60] Prüfer also dispatched messages to Vargas and Dutra, advising them of the same and, in what could only be regarded as a threat, adding that war would have "severe consequences for Brazil, because the very long coastline could not be protected effectively either by its own forces or by the American fleet."[61]

Vargas, meanwhile, negotiated with Sumner Welles, the leader of the American delegation. They produced a compromise statement that Argentina could support at the conference, thereby helping allay the fears of Dutra and Góes Monteiro about the lack of Argentine help in protecting Brazil's southern frontiers in the event of a war with the Axis.[62] The president, in his customary fashion, also sought to protect himself with the Germans by sending Vergara to tell Prüfer (erroneously) that Washington was using "the strongest pressure," including the threat of a boycott, to force Brazil to a rupture with Germany and its allies.

Müller gave a similar story to Niedenführ and predicted that Brazil would break relations with the Axis. The gloomy estimates even existed in Berlin, where Cyro Freitas Valle, the Brazilian ambassador there, forecast doom to Weizsäcker. On 21 January 1942 Prüfer advised the AA that he and the Spanish ambassador, Raimundo Fernández-Cuesta y Merelo, had found it difficult to contact Brazilian officials. A few hours later, he concluded that "no one any longer doubts that Brazil has yielded to American will," and he predicted that the meeting would end soon.[63]

The following day, however, the picture seemed less clear. As Prüfer and the embassy learned through Niedenführ's contacts in the army, Vargas was torn between the factions in his government—one around Aranha that urged joining the United States, and an opposing one around Dutra; Vargas did not wish to make a final decision until he possessed a consensus. Prüfer called the followers of Aranha "Jewish and Freemasonry forces."[64] When the president agreed with Aranha after acquiring assurances from Welles that the United States would ship armaments to Brazil, Prüfer, extremely disappointed, attacked Dutra and the military privately for not having "brought their influence to bear" on Vargas.

The Rio conference ended on 28 January 1942 with the American republics approving a resolution that only recommended a break with the Axis. Each did so immediately, except for Chile (which severed relations in January 1943) and Argentina (January 1944). With Mexico leading the way on 22 May 1942, the remaining Latin American countries eventually declared war against one or more of the Axis by the end of hostilities in 1945, although Argentina only joined the war during the last month because of Allied pressure.[65]

Brazil's break of relations with Germany on the evening of 28 January 1942 changed the situation quickly for Prüfer and the other German diplomats in the country. Their return to the Reich would be delayed for several months, as Germany initiated increasingly warlike policies against Brazil and as Berlin and Rio negotiated through their intermediaries, Spain and Portugal, an exchange of each other's diplomats and settled other issues between them. Aranha, apparently not wishing to alienate the Germans completely and still hoping for a way to keep Brazil out of the war, assured Prüfer that the German officials would be well-treated and that he wished to make their "remaining stay and departure as easy as possible." The Brazilians closed the German embassy and placed its personnel under surveillance.

Not even the police's discovery of the remnants of a powerful radio receiver in the former embassy building, in clear violation of Brazilian law, affected the treatment of the diplomats. On 10 February 1942, Aranha, apparently wishing to impress Brazil's moderation on Prüfer, visited with the ambassador and emphasized Rio's wish to return the Germans safely home. On the other hand, reports also reached Prüfer that emphasized Vargas's pleasure with the decision at the Rio meeting. "What was told us," the ambassador commented, possibly indicating the extent to which he had believed the president's repeated professions of friendship for Germany, "was noise and smoke."[66]

While Brazil treated the several hundred German officials in the country well, Prüfer mentioned nothing of it to Berlin. Whether Brazil's handling of the diplomats would have affected German policy is doubtful; during the ensuing weeks, the Reich's submarines sank four Brazilian steamers off the coast of the United States, causing anger in both Brazil and America and speeding the latter's delivery of naval equipment to Rio. Retaliating, the Itamaraty restricted Prüfer and members of the embassy to their homes at night and increased the surveillance and arrest of German spies in Brazil and the search for their clandestine radios.[67] With less success, the Abwehr network around Engels kept Germany informed of the rising anti-Axis sentiment in Brazil, the movement of ships through Brazilian ports, and the expanding coastal patrol activities of the American and Brazilian military.

Following the Rio meeting, Engels and his radio became the official channels of communication between the embassy officers and Berlin. Prüfer sent messages to the Wilhelmstrasse describing the fortunes of the Germans in Brazil; except for temporary detentions and house searches, he reported, those in Rio were not unduly harassed and possessed unlimited use of the mails and hospitals. The Brazilians had mainly arrested Germans in the southern states. Movements of his staff, Prüfer said, remained "completely unhindered." However, as British intelligence and the American FBI closed in on the German radios and agents, the security of the Engels network became a matter of great concern to the Abwehr, which urged caution and admonished Prüfer to use Engels's transmitter sparingly and to convey his messages in "short catch words."[68]

Continued attacks on Brazilian ships by German submarines during March incensed public opinion, however; crowds rioted against Axis stores in Rio, and the newspapers called for vigorous measures against the "fifth column." On 11 March 1942 Vargas made Axis firms and persons financially responsible for damages to Brazilian persons and property from "acts of aggression" by Axis countries. Prüfer, ignoring the ships sunk by the Germans and the resulting loss of Brazilian lives, angrily blamed others, including the supposed "Jewish press," for what was happening.[69] Events now forced the Brazilian police, aided by German radio messages intercepted by the American embassy, to act against the Abwehr; on 18 March the Brazilians began rounding up suspects, which included Engels himself. The resulting wave of arrests netted by the end of the month nearly 200 Axis agents who belonged to four espionage rings.[70]

While Prüfer, with the Spanish ambassador Cuesta y Merelo visiting the interned Germans on his behalf, bitterly protested the maltreatment of some of the prisoners, he and Bohny recruited a new spy cell from among Brazilians of non-German descent. Its members belonged to the Brazilian fascist movement, Integralism, headed by the nationalist, Plinio Salgado, who since 1939 had lived in exile in Lisbon, where he maintained connections to German diplomatic circles and the SS. Tulio Regis do Nascimento, a Brazilian army captain and reputed drug addict, organized a small network of informers and couriers; they reported on ship movements to Bohny and Niedenführ and, because most of the Abwehr's radios had been seized or destroyed, traveled to Buenos Aires, where they relayed messages for transmission to Berlin.[71]

Prüfer continued, meanwhile, to negotiate through Cuesta y Merelo with the Itamaraty regarding the exchange of the German and Brazilian diplomats. By the beginning of May, the Brazilians had approved the departure of 300 German officials and their families from the country;

the first shiploads left Rio for Europe on 7 May.[72] Two weeks later, however, as Germany intensified its aggressive policy on the high seas, the situation worsened dramatically for the Germans remaining in Brazil. Mexico declared war on the Axis powers after their submarines torpedoed two of its ships. By then Brazil had lost eight vessels, and on 2 and 26 June 1942 torpedoes claimed two more. Although Prüfer appeared to recognize that the Reich had made Brazil increasingly dependent on America, he failed to express his feelings to the AA, noting only in his diary that "the totally helpless Brazilian government has yielded to American pressure and will be pulled into the war."[73]

Word about the mistreatment of the imprisoned Abwehr agents again reached Prüfer during May and June.[74] He protested to the Itamaraty through the Spanish ambassador, and when the complaints from the prisoners persisted and one group smuggled a note to him about their conditions, he launched another protest through Cuesta y Merelo. Although Aranha rejected a warning from Berlin delivered by Spain on 22 June, the foreign minister investigated the situation; after receiving an admission from Müller, the police chief, that some beatings had occurred, he transferred part of the prisoners to a new location, where they received better treatment. Prüfer believed that Rommel's success in North Africa might also improve the plight of the prisoners.[75]

Prüfer once again failed to inform the Wilhelmstrasse of Aranha's efforts, however. Thus even after all the evidence to the contrary, Berlin remained convinced that Vargas was a victim of American pressure and friendly to Germany while his minister, in the words of Goebbels, Hitler's propaganda leader, "is evidently a character bought by Roosevelt and is apparently doing everything possible to provoke a conflict with the Reich and Axis Powers."[76] Hence, when German radio singled out Aranha as responsible for the alleged abuses against Germans in Brazil, Prüfer in his diary called it "a factually incorrect and accordingly imprudent attack." Furthermore, he was aware that Niedenführ had contacted German naval intelligence and Abwehr and had denounced Aranha, which had contributed to the radio's attacks on the minister.

Nevertheless, Prüfer mentioned nothing to Cuesta y Merelo for transmission to the AA and, following his usual blind obedience of the Berlin government, refused to criticize German policy, which continued to force Brazil towards war.[77] Brazilian and American air patrols, responding to the German submarine attacks and operating from bases in the northeast, began sinking U-boats in the South Atlantic. Hitler retaliated in mid-June by sending ten submarines to ravage Brazilian shipping, thereby escalating the "undeclared war" on the high seas.

Meanwhile, after the notoriously pro-Axis Müller was removed at the end of July 1942 and the arrangements for Prüfer to depart from Rio with the remainder of the German diplomats were nearly completed, Aranha visited with him a final time. At the foreign minister's request, they met secretly for two hours on the night of 3 August. The minister began by saying that the heavy hand from the United States had provided Brazil with no alternative but to break relations with Germany. Neither he nor Vargas wanted war, the minister continued, and they hoped for the redevelopment of German-Brazilian trade. He concluded by emphasizing that Brazil could not tolerate the sinking of its ships off its own coasts and that this practice had contributed to Brazil's imprisonment of the Germans suspected of sabotage.

Prüfer, refusing to acknowledge that the German submarine attacks had begun before the mass of arrests of the Abwehr agents during the spring, replied that the Reich's measures had resulted from "the colossal atrocities against the German prisoners." As the two men ended their discussion, the minister appeared to surprise Prüfer when he informed him that the Brazilians had intercepted secret radio messages sent by the German agents to the Reich and Argentina, including two by the ambassador himself.[78]

After the war, Prüfer maintained that his discussion with Aranha persuaded him to telegraph Berlin immediately (apparently through Cuesta y Merelo) to warn it that attacking Brazilian ships along its own coast would prompt Brazil's declaration of war on the Reich. It is difficult to accept his claim because of his previous refusal to send such a dispatch and because a copy of such a message has never been found in the captured AA files. Moreover, if Prüfer sent the communication, he did so much too late to have an impact on German policy. Not only did Hitler have little interest in Latin American affairs, rarely viewing the AA's correspondence, but also the submarines he had sent to Brazil arrived in the latter's waters on 15 August.[79]

With Aranha's agreement, Prüfer and the last German officials left on a Brazilian steamer on 17 August. He was satisfied that, under difficult circumstances, he had done his best for his nation's cause while in Brazil; he had left Nascimento and the Integralist intelligence network in operation and was confident about the outcome of the war. Despite the United States' massive expansion of its influence in Latin America and the disaster caused for Germany by Berlin's aggressive policies, Prüfer appeared impressed with the claim by an informant that the United States had "turned out to be generally a big humbug" in Brazil and that the country felt "a severe disillusionment" with America.

Prüfer was also apparently unaware of the realities of the war in Russia and the Far East, particularly America's defeat of the Japanese near Midway and the first successful landing on Guadalcanal; he recorded in his diary that "no one any longer doubts in the victory of the Axis."[80] As his ship left Rio harbor and moved into the Atlantic, the German submarines prowling Brazil's waters sank five of its ships, killing over 600 persons in three days. On 22 August the country declared war on Germany.

eleven

The Return to Germany, 1942-43

PRÜFER'S arrival in Berlin in the autumn of 1942 abruptly ended his faith in an Axis victory. The AA's impotence in determining Germany's policies particularly shocked and angered him. The defeats suffered by German forces at Stalingrad and in North Africa and the increasingly effective bombing of the Reich by the Anglo-Americans, caused him to sense the nation's impending doom. Yet, while complaining privately to his closest and most trusted associates about Nazi party "outsiders" ruining the AA and undermining Germany, he never criticized Hitler or Ribbentrop and continued to serve the regime for another year.

Word that the Nazis were exterminating Jews in the East, however, did not bother him; he remained a rabid anti-Semite, persuaded that the Jews both manipulated the Allies and selfishly sought Germany's destruction. His only concern was for the health of himself and his wife, Anneliese. During the summer of 1943, at age sixty-two, plagued by poor health, disillusioned and bitter about what he believed was Germany's imminent defeat, and obsessed with saving himself and his family from sharing further in the Nazi catastrophe, he arranged for a leave from the AA and moved to Switzerland for the remainder of the war.

Final Demise: The AA and the Old Guard

The Brazilian freighter with Prüfer, his wife and son, and the other Germans arrived safely in Lisbon, and from there a train carried them to Frankfurt, where Ernst von Weizsäcker, the state secretary in the AA, greeted them as heroes on 16 October 1942.[1] A week later, following a brief visit to Berlin and the AA, where he received a special assignment in the section for Middle Eastern affairs, Prüfer reported to Ribbentrop at the latter's field headquarters near Berdichev in the Ukraine and discussed with him Brazil's declaration of war. The spirit among the minister's immediate staff, Prüfer recalled later, was low and could hardly "suggest victory. All are overworked, tired, and worried."

He noted, furthermore, that Ribbentrop was being treated by a doctor, looked "very tired," and "had little to say about my report concerning the situation and my activities in Brazil." Neither the minister nor his special ambassador for military-economic affairs, Ritter (the man whose offensive behavior in Brazil resulted in his being sent home in 1938, thus opening the assignment there for Prüfer), recalled seeing the telegram that Prüfer claimed he had sent from Brazil, warning the AA about Rio's certain declaration of war if German submarines attacked its ships along the Brazilian coast.[2] As their meeting ended, Ribbentrop granted Prüfer's request for a leave of several weeks; the Prüfers retired to a residence they owned in Baden-Baden.

As Prüfer soon learned, the Reich to which he and his family returned had changed significantly from the one they had left in 1939. Despite the relatively comfortable life which he continued to lead as a high-level official—the Prüfers ate well, met frequently with friends, were entertained in movie theaters—three years of war had begun to take their toll on most of the nation and its people. That optimism regarding the war's outcome which had dominated the Germans in Brazil contrasted with the mounting pessimism, resignation, and war weariness that suddenly confronted Prüfer in Germany. The mood reflected the growing problems with food supplies and the black market, three years of restrictions in all areas of public life, the increasing intensity and scope of daily enemy air attacks, and the concern for the lives of family members at the front and civilians at home who fell victim to the air raids. Although the bombings fostered increasing hate and stubborn resistance towards the enemy—to the benefit of the Nazi regime—they produced fear in the people and the desire for an early end to the war.[3]

News of the American landings in Morocco and Algeria, of the retreat by Rommel's exhausted and poorly equipped forces before the British in Libya, and of the developing battle around Stalingrad, clouded Prüfer's spirits as he arrived in Berlin on 11 November to begin work at the AA. His wife and son remained in Baden-Baden. "The mood here in Berlin appears to be even a shade worse than in Baden," he recorded in his diary, "although this is not meant to imply that it is very good there either." About the events in North Africa, he declared that the Allies "have had their first great success, and the Jews are rejoicing."[4]

More immediate problems, however, attracted his concern. The organization and functioning of the Wilhelmstrasse had changed markedly from when he had left for Brazil. On the one hand, Ribbentrop's creation of his personal secretariat (*Büro RAM*), which he staffed with his party minions and which acted as a traveling field headquarters (on a special train, the *Westfalen*) accompanying the minister as he followed Hitler across Europe, stripped the career diplomats who remained in the AA's headquarters in Berlin of their last threads of power. New massive information and radio divisions concerned with propaganda and controlled by party men had also changed the texture of the organization, and the emergence of *Abteilung Deutschland,* which acted as the AA's liaison to the NSDAP and SS, contributed to the demise of the professionals' authority.

Ribbentrop's establishment of eleven interdivisional regional committees (*Länderkomitees*) in the AA composed of idle repatriated ambassadors and ministers and devoted to propaganda matters, added to the confusion. Since Ribbentrop's appointment as foreign minister, the total staff of the AA had expanded by 143 percent, from 2,665 employees in 1938 to 6,458 by 1943. The mushrooming of agencies and personnel and the rift between the minister, who visited Berlin only occasionally, and the AA's massive apparatus in the capital, duplicated administrative functions and produced clashes of jurisdiction that paralyzed the ministry. Consequently, Prüfer and his colleagues were left to bicker and complain among themselves and discuss matters of little importance.[5] Since 1933 their negotiations and compromises with the Nazis, which Prüfer's career illustrated with such clarity, had preserved the facade and arrogance of the ministry, but had destroyed its substance.

Prüfer's reactions to his first meetings in the AA illustrated his unhappiness. "A pretty picture of German unity!" he exclaimed in his diary, describing a conference in Ernst Woermann's office to discuss the deployment of a military unit called the German-Arab training division (*Deutsch-Arabische Lehrabteilung,* DAL), which was the center of a factional conflict in the ministry's Oriental section.[6] Also apparent to Prüfer and the other careerists was how the expansion of the war, particularly the advance of German armies into Eastern Europe and Russia and the rupture of diplomatic relations between the Reich and many other countries, had reduced the AA's influence in major policy matters.

Ribbentrop's position with Hitler had also declined, partly because of his differences with the Führer over the invasion of the Soviet Union. More significant in his loss of influence, however, were the minister's jurisdictional quarrels with more powerful rivals such as Himmler, Goebbels, and Alfred Rosenberg, since 1941 head of the vast ministry for the occupied Eastern territories. By the end of 1942 the AA had become a subsidiary to other Nazi agencies, especially the SS. Through Martin

Luther's *Abteilung Deutschland,* the ministry conducted negotiations that led to the SS's mass deportations of Jews from Germany's satellite countries in Eastern, Western, and Northern Europe to their destruction in the Nazi death camps in Poland. The AA also facilitated the importing of slave labor for Germany from France, Eastern Europe, and Russia and the recruiting of SS troops in the satellite countries.[7]

Despite his previous antagonism towards Ribbentrop and the gossip among the careerists in the AA about the minister's sagging influence with Hitler, Prüfer dived into his new duties with enthusiasm and defended the minister against the criticisms of others.[8] Although he rarely saw Ribbentrop during the latter's visits to Berlin, he prepared numerous reports for the minister regarding Oriental affairs. The Middle Eastern section provided an example of how drastically the ministry's position and that of the careerists had deteriorated.

From the beginning of the war, confusion and neglect dominated German policy towards the Middle East. The AA had joined the Abwehr, as well as naval and other military officials, in urging Hitler to concentrate on defeating England in the Mediterranean and Middle East, thereby seizing valuable oil supplies for Germany, destroying Britain's communications with Asia, and permitting the Nazis to threaten Russia from the south and west. Moreover, it was argued, Germany could claim the support of the Arabs, whose hostility to Britain and the Jews attracted them to Germany. During 1939 and 1940, the Mufti of Jerusalem, Haj Amin al-Husayni, and his pro-German followers who fled from Palestine to Iraq, declared their sympathy for the Axis in the hope of obtaining from Berlin a promise of military support and a declaration guaranteeing Arab independence in the Middle East. But Hitler, obsessed with conquering Europe and Russia, afraid of alienating Italy, Vichy France, and Turkey, and guided by a racial ideology that saw Arabs as inferiors, refused to support their demands for independence from the Western powers. During 1941 Germany tried and failed to stop Britain's defeat of a revolt in Iraq led by Rashid Ali al-Gailani, the pro-German Iraqi prime minister; the Reich offered less help to the Vichy forces in Syria, who were also defeated by the British. Axis troops under Rommel, moreover, were unable to conquer Egypt. The Arab leaders, the Mufti and Rashid Ali, fled for safety to Berlin, where Husayni continued to link his offers of collaboration with the Axis to promises from Germany and Italy that would guarantee the autonomy of the Arab states and recognize his leadership of the Arab world. Except for a letter in April 1942 from Ribbentrop to the Mufti and Rashid Ali recognizing the goal of Arab independence, Germany's support for the Arab cause, and German cooperation in eliminating the Jewish national home in Palestine, the Nazis carefully avoided committing themselves to the political merger of the Arab lands in the Middle East, thereby maintaining the Italian alliance.

Intrigue and Factionalism in the Oriental Section

By the fall of 1942, with the war in Russia and the battle in North Africa turning against the Axis, the AA's role in Middle Eastern affairs had been relegated to mediating a bitter conflict between the Mufti and Rashid Ali over leadership of the Arab independence movement.[9] The dispute also led to a personality struggle and factional quarrel in the AA. The administrative clash was between Nazi party official Erwin Ettel, former Reich envoy to Iran who now was assigned to deal with Husayni and Gailani, and Fritz Grobba, the special "commissioner for Arab affairs" in the AA and former minister to Iraq.

Prüfer, on his return to Berlin, became embroiled in the squabble. Ettel supported Husayni, calling him an "old fighter" who had won the respect of the vast majority of Arabs in the Near and Middle East and a "fanatical idealist" who had led an uncompromising struggle against the supposed deadly enemies of Nazi Germany: the English, Jews, and Freemasons. To enhance his claims to Arab leadership, Husayni boasted of heading an alleged secret Arab organization to which Rashid Ali was subordinate, and styled himself the Grand Mufti (*Grossmufti*), dropping altogether the territorial qualification "of Jerusalem" and showing that his ambitions extended beyond Palestine. Grobba, aided by his deputy, Ulrich Granow, backed Rashid Ali, proclaiming that while the Mufti was the "spiritual leader" of the Arab independence movement, Gailani provided Germany with conventional political experience and would be of greater military use to the German army once it conquered Russia and crossed the Iraqi frontier to invade the Middle East.

Although AA leaders Ribbentrop, Weizsäcker, and Woermann tried to avoid involvement in the dispute in the hope of using both Arab leaders for Nazi propaganda, Ettel persuaded Ribbentrop in October 1942 to replace Grobba with Prüfer. The AA had received word from the German embassy in Ankara that Arab nationalists in neutral Turkey were pleased with Prüfer's return to Germany. Discontent existed among the nationalists, who believed that the Axis had diverted the Mufti and Rashid Ali from their mission of unifying the Arab peoples; the nationalists sought to advance Rashid Ali's ambition to lead a combined German-Arab attack on Iraq following the Reich's expected defeat of the Soviet Union.[10] The Mufti and Ettel also enlisted the support of Hans Georg von Mackensen in their campaign to eliminate Grobba's influence in Arab affairs; von Mackensen, the German ambassador to Rome, urged the AA to end Grobba's intrigue.

As Prüfer soon discovered, one of the main issues in the clash involved the composition, deployment, and control of the German-Arab training division (DAL), a small military unit comprising Arab followers of both Husayni and Rashid Ali, which trained at Cape Sounion and was commanded by the German general and Grobba's cousin, Helmuth Felmy. At a meeting on 19 November with Karl Schnurre of the AA, representatives from the high command of the Wehrmacht (OKW) confirmed to Prüfer that it had sent the unit to the Russian front.

Prüfer informed the OKW that the transfer had occurred "without the knowledge and against the will" of Husayni, who demanded that the DAL be used to fight the British "under an Arab command and under an Arab flag" in Egypt, Palestine, or Syria, where the Arabs would join it, fighting for a common cause and forming a Pan-Arab empire. When the OKW refused to agree with the Mufti's wish, Prüfer and Schnurre urged its representatives to meet with Husayni to avoid "a break with the Grand Mufti under all circumstances." Shortly thereafter, Prüfer attempted to persuade Grobba to be more cooperative with Husayni and Ettel. When Grobba refused, Prüfer denounced him privately as "absolutely unreasonable" and "blinded by vanity and ambition."[11]

With Germany's declining fortunes in North Africa, however, its interest in the Mufti grew. As Anglo-American troops occupied the former Vichy territories of Morocco and Algeria, the German army rushed forces into Tunisia in an attempt to shore up sagging Axis units. The AA sent Rudolf Rahn, a civilian administrator, to Tunisia to spread Axis propaganda against the Anglo-Americans, acquire the support of local Vichy officials and Arabs (Maghrebians), and retain the friendship of Germany's Italian allies, who hoped eventually to receive Tunisia for themselves. Husayni, while visiting Rome, warned Arabs in radio addresses beamed to North Africa not to cooperate with the Anglo-Americans. Possibly sensing the Axis defeat in the war and hoping to enhance his prestige and influence in postwar negotiations with the Allies, Husayni also proposed to the Germans that they promise independence to the Maghreb Arabs, led by the Bey of Tunisia and the Neo-Destour, a local nationalist party, in return for creating an Arab "liberation army" to help the Axis fight the enemy. The Mufti offered, moreover, to travel personally to Tunisia to organize the Arab revolt.

Because of the Reich's serious shortage of manpower from struggles in North Africa and Russia, the Mufti's idea fell on fertile soil. Both the Abwehr and the AA accepted it. Prüfer and Wilhelm Melchers, the head of the AA's Middle Eastern section, approved the inciting of such nationalist revolts but opposed support of Pan-Arab proposals for fear of alienating the Italians and neutral Turkey. Prüfer, on the basis of information from intelligence sources in Turkey, especially feared that Germany's recent setbacks in North Africa and the Soviet Union would lead Turkey to succumb to Allied pressure, give up its neutrality, and provide the center for an Allied thrust into the German-controlled Balkans.[12] Shortly after Husayni's return from Rome, a meeting on 9 December 1942 among Weizsäcker, Woermann, Abwehr officials, and Prüfer produced the decision to recommend the Mufti's plan to Ribbentrop and Hitler.

Only Rahn, who argued that the Arabs had "no fighting value" and posed dangers to local Italian and French settlers, opposed it. Hitler, however, also rejected the scheme, fearing it would bring the wrath of those powers who were either neutral towards or allied with the Reich and who hoped to acquire new colonies in North Africa from the war: Spain, Italy, and Vichy and its chief of state, Marshal Philippe Pétain. The decision frustrated Prüfer, who denounced the Vichy French for having offered little resistance to the Anglo-American landings in North Africa and for having "played a double game with us."[13] Despite Hitler's decision and the fact that Rahn was correct when he claimed that the Mufti could not provide much help for the Axis in North Africa, Weizsäcker and Ribbentrop continued entertaining thoughts of sending Husayni to Tunisia. Moreover, the Abwehr informed the Mufti that the DAL would be transferred from the Caucasus to North Africa.[14]

Although the Mufti failed on his return to Berlin to receive a commitment from the Reich government for his Pan-Arab ambitions, he moved closer to eliminating his rivals, Rashid Ali and Grobba. In a 14 December meeting with Woermann, Husayni bitterly criticized Grobba, and requested the latter's removal from Arab affairs. Grobba, declared the Mufti, had opposed the Arab holy man's leadership of the forthcoming opening of the Central Islamic Institute in Berlin and the celebration of the Muslim festival of Bairam. Woermann, apparently because of the recent upsurge in German attention regarding Husayni, asked Prüfer to "find a solution to the matter."[15] Complaining in private about the petty bickering and how it illustrated the bankruptcy of German policy in the Arab East, Prüfer supported the Mufti in this latest squabble. He enlisted the help of Melchers and Hans Schlobies, another member of the Middle Eastern section, and met with Ribbentrop on the matter. The minister ordered Grobba transferred from the section to a remote position in the German embassy in Paris and replaced him as head of the Arab regional committee (Länderkomitee) for propaganda with Melchers. Prüfer informed Grobba of the decision on 18 December 1942, noting to himself:

"I gave Gr. the bad news, which he appears to have accepted quietly. I
fear that he will continue to intrigue." Barely a week later, the demoted
official fulfilled the prophecy by angrily attacking the Mufti and Ettel
before Prüfer and opposing the assignment of his former assistant,
Granow, to the Latin American section.[16]

While this affair smoldered on, however, Prüfer received another task
shortly before he left Berlin for Baden-Baden and the Christmas holiday.
Ribbentrop, apparently sensing Prüfer's continued loyalty to the minister
and the AA, asked him to investigate the financial and propaganda activities of Luther, the minister's protégé and head of Abteilung Deutschland.
"Something seems to be rotten," Prüfer mused about Luther following
the meeting.[17] Because Prüfer had opposed Luther's entry into the AA in
1938 and because research has shown that Ribbentrop intended to remove
his division chief for disloyalty, one suspects that the minister placed
significant trust in Prüfer's ability to conduct an investigation that would
provide additional reasons (e.g. financial corruption) for eliminating
Luther.[18] Prüfer, moreover, represented much of the old corps in the AA
who despised Luther as the embodiment of the Nazi party's influence and
that of unwanted "outsiders" in the AA, whom the careerists blamed for
their decline.

With the surrender on 2 February 1943 of the German 6th army at
Stalingrad and the defeat of the Germans and Italians in North Africa
during the spring, the new year brought dramatic changes for Prüfer. The
events of the ensuing months persuaded him of the Reich's imminent
collapse, completed his disillusionment with the AA, and encouraged him
to leave the country. The nagging problems he had encountered in the
ministry worsened. Grobba, for example, successfully delayed moving to
Paris and attempted with Granow to undermine Prüfer's efforts at unifying the Mufti and Rashid Ali. Grobba's contacts with Rashid Ali, which
included giving him a private reception and a tour of the Berlin radio
station, the *Grossdeutsche Rundfunk,* prompted Prüfer and Ettel to gather
further evidence against their nemesis. They accused Grobba of using
"Freemason methods," of agreeing to a military pact between Rashid Ali
and Felmy without the AA's knowledge, and of sending a report to
Himmler criticizing the AA. Much to Prüfer's despair, the charges,
which Grobba denied, backfired; Grobba finally departed for Paris, while
Prüfer's activities elicited disapproval from Woermann, whose patience
with the persistent bickering was apparently wearing thin.[19] Possibly to
show progress in the affair, Prüfer informed Weizsäcker and Ribbentrop
on 25 January 1943 that "unity among the Arab leaders presently in
Germany" had "at least been recovered superficially."[20]

But the sources of Prüfer's frustration multiplied. He supported the
Mufti's repeated demand that the Axis issue a declaration to the Arab

world, particularly to the Bey of Tunis, guaranteeing them autonomy if they joined the war in North Africa against the Anglo-Americans; Prüfer had no influence in such policymaking, however, and was forced to advise Husayni that he should undertake nothing without the Italians. Prüfer did show Woermann and Weizsäcker a letter to the Mufti from Shekib Arslan, the Syrian nationalist exiled in Switzerland, urging that Germany conclude an anti-Allied agreement with the dominant nationalist movement in Tunisia, the neo-Destour party and its leader, Habib Abu Raqiba (Bourguiba); Prüfer's procurement of the incriminating document contributed slightly to Axis policy. Following Italy's indecision and Rahn's opposition to the plan for fear of losing French cooperation in Tunis, the Axis released Bourguiba and other neo-Destour leaders from French prisons and returned them to Tunisia, but they generated little nationalist support for the Axis cause.[21]

Prüfer, moreover, found his investigation of Luther and his propaganda agencies, the German information office (*Deutsche Informationsstelle,* DIS) and the Mundus corporation, blocked at every turn. Luther had not cooperated in interrogations, yet by interviewing his subordinates and receiving aid from Gustav Adolf Steengracht von Moyland, a Luther enemy on Ribbentrop's personal staff, Prüfer had concluded that the DIS and Mundus were a "most highly objectionable conglomerate of profiteering, careerism, and terror."[22] He reported the results of his investigation to Ribbentrop on 6 February, but only when Luther was arrested four days later and sentenced to a concentration camp did Prüfer learn the reason for what had happened. Luther had conspired unsuccessfully with Walter Schellenberg, the head of foreign intelligence in the SS, to persuade Himmler to overthrow Ribbentrop, who, Luther believed, had failed with the careerists in the AA to stop the encroachments on the ministry by the SS and the party.[23]

Ribbentrop also called on Prüfer to investigate an attack on the minister by one of his colleagues, Goebbels. Hitler's propaganda chief, who was about to proclaim "total war" in Germany and to pursue that policy of frenzy, had denounced Ribbentrop for repairing the damage from an air raid to his villa in the Berlin suburb of Dahlem. Such selfishness, Goebbels told the Führer, could not be tolerated because it took laborers away from more vital wartime tasks. Prüfer, however, much to his distaste, spent one entire evening interrogating the workmen at the villa and concluded that Ribbentrop "had nothing to do with it. It concerned his overzealous house manager, who wanted to make himself popular." Although Hitler let the matter drop, Goebbels still fumed two months later about how his rival had "acted disgracefully during the last air raid."[24]

When not involved in the factionalism and strife, Prüfer spent much of his time grumbling privately with other old careerists, such as Dieckhoff,

Schulenburg, and the personnel director, Schröder, about their inactivity and lack of influence, and the proliferation in the AA of meaningless committees and meetings. "If only there were someone who would quite openly tell the Führer about all these loathsome things," he declared on 21 January 1943, revealing how thoroughly the diplomat had fallen under the spell that had bound most Germans to Hitler since 1933.[25] Two days later, full of self-pity about his age and declining health, Prüfer approached Weizsäcker about receiving a discharge from the ministry, but the state secretary refused. Because of manpower shortages in the AA caused by the war, the agency was thrown back increasingly on its careerists; Ribbentrop insisted on no wartime resignations, labeling such requests "desertion."[26]

Leaving the Sinking Ship

In addition to Prüfer's disillusionment with the AA, however, his interest in retirement was compounded by his inability to deal with mounting family problems and his fear that Germany would lose the war. The sudden news of the defeat of German forces at Stalingrad depressed him, and shortly after he moved from the Hotel Adlon to a house in Dahlem owned by Werner Best, a senior SS police official, Prüfer experienced firsthand the increased British air raids on Reich cities in January and February 1943. During one of the attacks, a fire bomb struck his residence, destroying the property he had there.

But even more unsettling to him was the tense relationship that had developed with his wife, Anneliese. The two quarreled often; she criticized his heavy drinking and repeated infidelity, and in the spring of 1943 she briefly entered a hospital, suffering from physical exhaustion and nervous tension. Her health, which had declined in Brazil, worsened. Evidence indicates that she also worried about the safety of her mother and sisters, who still lived in Berlin.[27] Prüfer, on the recommendation of a doctor who testified to the AA that the elderly diplomat suffered from liver, kidney, and heart problems, was eventually granted a leave that lasted throughout March.

While Prüfer fretted about himself and his family, however, he exhibited no concern about the fate of others in the war, despite the knowledge he had regarding the Nazi extermination of the Jews in death camps in Poland and other execution sites in the East.[28] Even in Brazil, he recalled after the war, he and his wife had heard "rumors" from German and enemy sources about the "mass deportation of Jews" to the East; while traveling through Spain on the return in October 1942 to Germany, he had received further information from an SS official. Such reports, he claimed later, "seemed to us to be so dreadful that we held them to be 'atrocity stories,' or at the very least exaggerated, like so many other reports of enemy propaganda that had proved to be incorrect."[29] But shortly after he arrived back home, he had learned the truth about the deportations and what they meant. Except for the hatred he believed the Holocaust could inspire against Germany, he responded to the news with a combination of apathy and opportunism. A brief passage in French in his diary on 22 November 1942 illustrated his response: "This morning they told me horrible stories concerning the treatment of the Persians [an expression for Jews on Berlin's Kurfürstendamm]. Men, women, and children have been slaughtered in large numbers by poison-gas or by machine guns. The hatred which inevitably must arise from that will never be appeased. Today every child knows this in the smallest detail."[30] As evidence that he possessed little conscience about the atrocities, he knowingly purchased land in Baden-Baden confiscated by the German government from Jews.[31]

One can only conclude that such behavior, which ranged from indifference towards the fate of the Jews to exploiting their misfortune for his own benefit, resulted from Prüfer's old-fashioned anti-Semitism and enthusiastic support for Nazi measures against the Jews.[32] In fact, the war's end and Germany's defeat heightened his hatred of the Jews.[33] That he remained a cooperative, though minor, tool in the Nazi policy became evident in the spring of 1943 with his knowledge and implicit approval of the Mufti's growing involvement with the SS and its destruction of the East European Jews. In collaboration with Himmler, whose need for troops had reduced the SS's racial requirements and led to the creation of "non-Aryan" units, Husayni visited Germany's puppet country of Croatia in March and April, supervising the formation of Muslim SS units in Croatian-dominated Bosnia and Herzegovina. These units skirmished for a time with Marshal Tito's Communist partisans, composed primarily of Christian Serbs, and distinguished themselves largely by committing a number of atrocities.[34]

Prüfer also had received knowledge of the Mufti's opposition against the emigration of Bulgarian Jews to Palestine. Husayni had sent a personal note to Ribbentrop through the Italians asking the minister not to permit Jews to leave the Balkans. Despite the success of the Germans in stopping any attempt at large-scale emigration from southeastern Europe, thereby condemning most of the Jews of the region to deportation and death in Poland, rumors regarding their movement from Bulgaria during the spring and summer of 1943 reached the Mufti. Husayni, who suggested that the Jews be sent to Poland "under strong and energetic guard," followed his request to Ribbentrop with a number of messages of concern, also sent through the Italians, to the AA. Prüfer received a copy of one of the notes on 12 May, and the AA believed that the Mufti would discuss it with him during their meeting the next day.[35] It is unclear whether they touched on the subject, but evidence shows that Prüfer only disapproved of Husayni's increasing association with the Italians. He declared after their meeting: "I no longer quite trust the Mufti. He has been thinking about postwar development without us. . . . I fear that he could turn out to be one of the notorious ship rats. Perhaps this is the reason why he assiduously courts Italy."[36]

Ironically, however, Prüfer was even then attempting to abandon the ship himself. Experiencing firsthand the frightening air raid alarms and the destruction wrought by Allied bombers on Berlin and the Reich, there mushroomed inside him the dual emotions of hatred for the enemy and hope that the rumors of German-Soviet peace discussions would be verified. Conclusion of such an agreement, he believed with some AA colleagues, represented the only alternative for Germany against the Anglo-Americans and their allies. "The U.S.A. with its Jews," he declared, "are sterile soil for the seeds of peace." Moreover, he was devastated at the news of the Axis' loss of Tunis, which he believed was more critical than the struggle in Russia and which he prophesied "can cost us the entire war."[37] With his world—i.e., the German state, which had served as a surrogate family providing him with status, security, and identity—collapsing around him, he intensified his efforts to acquire an extended leave from the AA. He hoped that the request would not only lead to retirement from the ministry but also, in keeping with his characteristic self-centeredness, to his removal with his wife and son to safety in neutral Switzerland.

Prüfer's chance for success increased following the shake-up in the AA in the wake of the Luther scandal, during which Ribbentrop had dismantled Abteilung Deutschland in favor of new agencies and replaced Weizsäcker and Woermann with Steengracht and a loyal career diplomat, Andor Hencke. From Steengracht, with whom Prüfer had cooperated in the investigation of Luther, and from Schröder, he sought permission to visit Switzerland, ostensibly to gather information on the Middle East from Arab exiles living there. Prüfer hoped, however, to parlay his mission and declining health into retirement across the border. Steengracht approved his proposal to spend three weeks there; the diplomat arrived in Davos with his wife on 21 May 1943. During the visit, he met several contacts from the Mideast: Shekib Arslan; Aziz Izzet Pasha, an Egyptian politician close to the royal family in Cairo; and the aging ex-Khedive, Abbas Hilmi, whose offer to help the Germans in the Egyptian campaign in 1941 had represented his final, illusory hope that he might return to the throne.

Prüfer could not stay in Switzerland on this trip, however, and his report upon returning to the Reich on 17 June reflected Germany's changed position in the Arab world since the loss of Tunis. With the expulsion of the Germans from the Arab East, Arab politicians had cast their lot with the Allies; even in Palestine, moderate Arabs organized their forces against the Husayni clan, and in Syria and Lebanon, the British supported anti-French forces that ended French rule in both areas. Relations had also cooled between exiled Arab officials and the Germans. Prüfer reported a state of depression among the Orientals living in Switzerland over the Axis defeat in North Africa. The ex-Khedive criticized Germany's Arab policy, and the others allegedly claimed that only a German-Soviet alliance against the Anglo-Americans could improve the Reich's situation.[38]

Despite the collapse of Germany in the Arab world and the insignificance of Prüfer's information from the exiles, Ribbentrop approved his proposal for an indefinite leave to Switzerland for "the preservation of a continuous contact with the Orientals living there, who have been till now valuable sources of information for us because of their country and [relationship to] enemy circles." To conceal the nature of Prüfer's mission, which received the code name "Rosita," he was not attached to the German legation in Switzerland, but acted instead as a private citizen residing in the country for a more "favorable climate" for his "weakened health."[39]

As Prüfer prepared amid the enemy air raids and news of continuous military defeats to leave the nation he had served so obediently for nearly four decades, he sensed a calamitous ending for the Reich and its government and he attempted to analyze what had gone wrong. Blinded by his nationalism, xenophobia, and anti-Semitism, which had contributed to his support of Nazism, he refused to blame Hitler.[40] "The Führer is a great, a very great man," he declared, "who made our nation—at that time facing ruin—into the most powerful country on earth; and this in an incredibly brief and victorious period of time from 1933 to 1941." Nor did Prüfer find fault with the ideals of Nazism. "All this is terrible for me to see," he admitted to himself, "not only because I have always been a person who is very attached to his homeland and always will be, but also because I was sincerely converted to some of the beautiful ideas of National Socialism."

What, he asked, had produced the rapid change after 1941, "bringing us one defeat after another?" He concluded that it was the "camarilla" of ambitious, but uneducated, party men and outsiders in the govern-

ment who had failed Hitler and Germany, "the vortex around the center."[41] Although he did not know it, the catastrophe which the Reich
experienced would be far worse than he suspected, and he would have
many years to agonize over it. With his wife and son, who was now
thirteen, he crossed by train into Switzerland on 7 September 1943,
where the three would remain until after the Reich's final, devastating
collapse.

twelve

Epilogue: The War's End and Aftermath

FROM across the border, Prüfer witnessed the final defeat, destruction, and division of that which he had worshiped and served for nearly four decades—the German state and its power. His escape to Switzerland and his attitudes during the remainder of the war provided further evidence that the conflict, instead of provoking the Germanic heroism of the Niebelungen type that Goebbels demanded in his call for "total war" in February 1943, produced a growing concern by Germans for their own personal interests and "survival."[1] Much of his attention focused on his wife's continued illness; his poor health and that of his son; worries about being recalled to Germany; and the gradual cutback of his salary as the Reich government collapsed in 1944 and 1945 and officials in the German legation in Bern, apparently including Otto Köcher, the minister, sabotaged payments to him. On 25 November 1944, Prüfer received his retirement from the AA, which became official on 1 April 1945.[2]

Except for maintaining a meaningless contact for Berlin with the ex-Khedive and other Arabs, and providing occasional advice to the AA on mediating the strife between the Mufti and Rashid Ali, Prüfer spent much of his time following the disastrous course of the war in Swiss newspapers, over short-wave radio, and through information from German diplomatic couriers sent to the legation. As the bombings of the Reich increased, leveling Germany's cities, and as German forces retreated in Italy, in Russia and Eastern Europe, and in the West following the Anglo-American landings in France in June 1944, his criticism mounted against both the Nazi regime and the enemy.

Once during November 1943, shortly after his arrival in Switzerland, Prüfer discussed in his diary "an idea [about] how Germany could still be saved." Like certain factions in the secret nationalist and conservative German resistance against Hitler, he believed that the "current regime must disappear and a decidedly democratic one take its place." Prüfer was also uncompromising in his opposition to a German surrender, adding that the new German government should "not grovel for peace but decide to continue the war" to lay claim "to what legitimately" belonged to the Reich and "what the German people want, thus what the Austrian branch also demands—the right of unity." Prüfer rejected both German responsibility for the war and payment of compensation to the Allies, demanding instead "full equality" for Germany in a "democratic, well-ordered postwar life." He also thought that Franz von Papen would be Hitler's successor.[3]

The destruction wrought on Germany by enemy bombers, however, concerned him much more. Responding on 18 February 1944 to further heavy air raids on Berlin and to the Allied shelling of the abbey atop Monte Cassino in Italy—President Roosevelt had proclaimed that such monuments could not be spared when American lives were at stake—Prüfer raged against the Western Allies. His attack illustrated a continued arrogance towards them and a racism that had been implicit in his insolence and hostility towards non-Germans throughout his life, but which appeared for the first time in his diaries during the war. Prüfer called the Anglo-Americans "barbarians, worse than all Huns" and "vengeful destroyers" of European culture, who supposedly wished "to set Niggers and other scum, belly-dancing, and jazz in its place." The bombings of the Reich, he maintained, would reduce the Germans to "proletarians" and destroy "class distinctions." The "pilots of the R.A.F. are paving the way for Communism in Germany," he alleged. He ranted further: "Out of hatred from wounded vanity and inspired by the Jews, Churchill and Roosevelt will watch the *danse macabre* until the red tide will also wash them away."[4]

The impending disaster enflamed his hatred of the Jews and his belief that they conspired with the Allies to destroy Germany. On one occasion, he blamed the Western powers for the Holocaust; pretending that he was talking to the Allies in his diary, he asked: "how are you able to rebuke us when our government found no serious resistance along the path that led to the annihilation (which is still very much disputed by you) of the Jews?"[5] Noting the continued refusal to allow Jews from Southeastern Europe to emigrate to Palestine, he ignored Germany's role in the policy and observed that "only" the opposition of the Rumanian and Bulgarian governments had prevented the emigration. Of the deportation of Jews from Hungary to Poland in 1944, he worried about the effect on Germany. "Sending the Hungarian Jews caused a sensation," he declared in language in his diary that hid the true meaning of what he was discussing, "and will be exploited significantly in propaganda against the Germans. Protests hail from all sides."[6]

As the Soviet and Allied armies liberated the Nazi death camps, revealing officially for the world the horror that had occurred in them, he showed a mixture of surprise and disbelief, but then shifted the responsibility from Germany to the enemy. "The Russians publish gruesome portrayals of the discovery in the concentration camp at Lublin," he noted on 31 August 1944, and added that this appeared to make the earlier massacre of Polish officers in the Russian forest at Katyn (for which he held the Soviets responsible) "no longer so hideous."[7] At the news a few months later that the Soviets had tried and executed SS officials from the camp at Maidanek for having contributed to the murder of nearly a million and a half Jews, he observed in his diary only that the SS "apparently are supposed to be responsible for the gassing of a number of Jews and other people unpopular" with the Nazis. "It should not be denied that the S.S. have been guilty many times of severe atrocities," he continued. "But it is simply disgusting that Soviet Russia, to say nothing of the Bolshevists, could set itself up as judges over the S.S. with the applause of their French, British and American friends."[8]

Amid further revelations of the Nazi genocide, he exonerated the German people and placed the blame on the SS, which he apparently considered a troop of youthful idealists. Reacting to the account in April 1945 by the Allies of the death and suffering at Buchenwald, he proclaimed that it was "simply dreadful that the Nazis should have succeeded in brutalizing our youth so much that they were capable of such crimes." However, when the Soviet writer, Ilya Ehrenburg, called for the total destruction of Germany in the spring of 1945, he fumed: "Not a single person abroad responded in a Christian sense to this paroxysm of Jewish hatred. This Jew nearly justified the persecution of his people by Hitler."[9]

On the other hand, the reduction of German cities to rubble, the devastation suffered by the population, and the discouraging news from the battlefronts demoralized Prüfer, increasing his longing for "an immediate end to this insane war."[10] His support for the Nazi regime continued to dwindle as Germany's fate became clearer; he steadfastly blamed the defeat on the Nazi leadership around Hitler and, frequently indulging in self-pity, viewed the German people and leaders like himself as victims, both of their rulers and of Allied air raids. At news that bombings of Berlin at the end of November 1943 had destroyed much of the AA, he denounced the head of the ministry's press division, who had proclaimed in a propaganda release the capital's pride in participating in "the common front" against the enemy: "Is the man really so stupid as to believe that he is making an impression on the foreign correspondents with that? . . . The second and even third-class vermin, to which this youthful, black marketeer Schmidt belongs, simply should be spat upon. Those are Ribbentrop's men."[11]

In contrast, he only reluctantly abandoned Hitler, in whom he had placed his hopes and expectations for rebuilding Germany into a world power. "The Führer is a heroic figure because of his leadership," he declared while condemning the dictator's subordinates, "whatever else one may say and whatever disasters may have come to the German people." Six months later, however, under the shadow of the huge Soviet offensives in the summer of 1944 that brought the enemy near to East Prussia, Prüfer appeared less enthusiastic about Hitler. His main concern at the news of the attempted assassination of the Nazi leader on 20 July by a handful of military officials was not so much for Hitler's welfare, but for saving the reputation of the upper classes from which the military leadership was drawn and to which Prüfer belonged.[12] By mid-April 1945, as the Soviet armies began their assault on Berlin and the Anglo-Americans advanced into central and southern Germany, Prüfer's despair and desire for an end to his nation's debacle prompted him to ask: "When will Hitler's demise come?" Nevertheless, he refused to renounce the Nazi chief; on 20 April he celebrated Hitler's birthday.[13]

His attitude hardened with the war's close in Europe two weeks later, with Germany's surrender, and with the country's division among the victors, including France. Although he wrote a letter to the Vatican on 10 October 1945 claiming to be an apostle of Christian love and urging the Pope to outlaw war, establish a unified "world state," and prevent a future war with the "forces of nihilism" in the Soviet Union, his diaries betrayed his true feelings. He filled them with the wildest tirades of hate against the Allied occupation of Germany, the war crimes trial in Nuremberg, and the expulsion of the German minorities from Eastern Europe. Despite the efforts of Anglo-American officials to clothe and feed the Germans in their zones, he proclaimed that the de-Nazification proceedings were "worse than the Jewish persecution by the Nazis and can only have similar terrible results."[14]

The persistence and, indeed, intensification of his anti-Semitism after the war was not altogether unusual. Although the findings of postwar public opinion surveys suggested that an overwhelming majority of Germans disapproved of the "actions against the Jews," recent research has shown that the Holocaust did not prevent the continuation of anti-Semitic stereotypes and activities in the Federal Republic.[15] Prüfer, revealing the depth of his irrationality and possibly even his own feelings of guilt, attempted to deny having knowledge during the war of the Nazi extermination of the Jews, declaring that he "had no idea of the horrifying atrocities that occurred in the concentration camps. We heard of the outrages in specific cases, also of certain camps like Dachau and Oranienburg, in which the inmates were badly treated, also of the deportation of the Jews to the East, but never of wholesale murder and conscious extermination."[16] He mentioned nothing of his views regarding such war crimes, however, while giving affidavits at the American consulate in Geneva in defense of Neurath and Bohle, who were being tried at Nuremberg. Instead, ignoring the massive evidence produced at the trials that documented the Holocaust, he remarked in his diary: "What Goebbels and Streicher did not do to make the German people really anti-Semitic, the fools at Nuremberg will achieve."[17]

Part of this crescendo of hatred and self-pity resulted from the loss of Prüfer's pension, which soon left him near poverty. Because the Swiss government considered him something between a refugee and an émigré, Bern kept him under surveillance and prohibited him from taking a job. Nevertheless, the government did not expel him as it did numerous NSDAP leaders who had organized party groups, spread propaganda, and spied on local Germans. The Swiss resisted pressure from the Western Allies to return to Germany all Reich officials who had escaped to Switzerland and chose to decide on the merits of each case who was entitled to asylum. To add to Prüfer's woes, the French confiscated his property in Baden-Baden. Jeanne Kleinmann, a Jewish heir to the land, which Prüfer had purchased from Jewish property expropriated by the Nazi government, arrived in Geneva and, following lengthy negotiations between them, she received the property in exchange for a monetary settlement.[18]

Prüfer's dire condition by the spring of 1946 was reminiscent of his troubles in 1919, following World War I. He proclaimed in his diaries the wish to return to imperial Germany, observing that "I am much closer to this era of my father's than today's. It was really 'the good old time.' "[19] Reality, however, found him begging for money from persons he had always considered of less stature. These included Fraulein Martha Rohde, his one-time secretary and mistress, and even a Jewish colleague in the AA, Paul Schwarz, who had resigned in 1933 in protest against the Nazi regime and had moved to New York. As the summer wore on, Prüfer's search became more desperate; he attempted to write a book, an autobiography that "should support the thesis that the German people were not to be blamed for the outbreak of the war," but it was never published.[20] In July 1946 he wrote to David Hall, the adviser to Haile Selassie, who had returned to power in Ethiopia in 1941, requesting that Hall deliver a letter to the Emperor asking him for money and reminding him of Prüfer's help in 1935 in procuring a German loan for the ruler in his war against Italy. After numerous delays, Hall arrived in Geneva in June 1947 with the badly needed funds.

Six months later, however, Prüfer's financial plight had worsened again, prompting him to search for employment outside Switzerland.[21] He negotiated with Balabhai Desai, the Indian minister in Switzerland, and his adviser, A.C.N. Nambiar, about an appointment to the new government in Delhi, which had just won its freedom from England. Desai and Nambiar had been followers of Subhas Chandra Bose, the radical Indian nationalist who had known Prüfer during the 1930s, had opposed the moderate anti-British Congress party of Gandhi and Nehru, and had collaborated in the war with the Axis against Britain; Prüfer had also known Nambiar and helped free the Indian from imprisonment by the SA in 1933.[22] Although Bose had died in a plane crash in August 1945, his followers still believed him to be alive and destined to return to India to lead its liberation. As the Delhi government and Bose's rival, Nehru, sought to consolidate their power in India and define their relationship to Britain, Desai, Nambiar, and other followers of Bose in the newly created Indian foreign ministry, which included K.P.S. Menon, arranged for Prüfer's appointment as a professor of international studies at Delhi University. The job, according to Desai, would be a cover for Prüfer's real position of training diplomats for the fledgling ministry.

Prüfer and his family arrived in Delhi on 25 October 1948.[23] When the Nehru government elected to retain strong ties to Britain, partly through the efforts of the latter's governor-general, Lord Louis Mountbatten, and decided in May 1949 to remain in the British Commonwealth, Bose's followers lost the remnants of their influence in the Delhi government. Opposition to Prüfer emerged in London and among the dominant pro-British faction around Nehru. Although Prüfer delivered several lectures to small groups of Indian diplomats, he never taught at the University and spent three years sitting idly in India. Of the faculty at the University, which ignored him, he complained later: "As Englishmen, they despised me as much as they did all foreigners." Much of his time was spent attending movies, such as *Oliver Twist,* which he described as a good film "strongly anti-Jewish." His independent son, Olaf, added to his worries; they quarreled bitterly, particularly as the young man befriended Jews and pro-British elements and received jobs at All India radio and in the Indian government's department of archaeology. When Prüfer left India in February 1951, bored and disappointed, his son remained.[24]

On arriving in Europe, Prüfer returned to Germany for the first time since the war and settled in Baden-Baden. He noted the economic recovery of the Germans, but declared that the "immense reawakening of forces" in the new Federal Republic was "directed towards the evils of radicalism and nihilism."[25] The Korean War had heightened his obsession with the alleged threat to Western Europe from the Soviet Union and Communism. "There is only one way out for the U.S.A.," he believed, "an immediate, surprise (?) attack on Russia." Prüfer attributed America's refusal to use the atomic bomb in the Korean War to the Jews, whose actions he alleged would lead "to the Bolshevization of the world." His increasingly pronounced racism expressed itself when he declared: "The colored Asians and their followers, the African Negroes, will rule the world with all of their Semitic associates in the East and West. The revolt of the slaves leads to triumph. The previous 'rulers' will be coordinated by the 'slaves.' The world is open to Jehovah's empire and His chosen people."[26]

Prüfer traveled often to the nearby German capital, Bonn, visiting the republic's foreign ministry, which had hired many of his associates in the AA prior to 1945, including Wilhelm Melchers and Kurt Munzel. The ministry began to pay a portion of Prüfer's pension, thereby solving his financial problems, and consulted him periodically on Arab affairs.[27] Despite his disapproval of the Bonn regime, he nevertheless continued to seek his identity in service (although not official) to it. The remainder of his time he spent attending meetings of the DMG, traveling (e.g., to Spain in 1952), and visiting such friends as Hans Schröder, Hans-Henning von Cossel, Carl Dienstmann, Helmut von Langenn-Steinkeller, Erich Heiden, and Karl Ritter. In the summer of 1953 Prüfer suffered a stroke; he recovered enough, however, for Haile Selassie to receive him in the fall of 1954, during the emperor's visit to Europe.

Despite Prüfer's wasted appearance and inability to hear, the AA invited him to Bonn to attend a reception for a delegation visiting from the Arab League. The ministry apparently hoped to impress its visitors with his pro-Arab views and lengthy involvement in Oriental affairs. An Egyptian official, Kamal al-Din Galal, testifying later at a trial of foreign ministry officials accused of accepting bribes from the Arabs, described the aged Prüfer: "As I arrived [at Munzel's] . . . I found Ambassador Prüfer there, with whom I had been acquainted for at least 30 years. Everyone knew that Herr Prüfer was as deaf as a post. He sat there. I knew him, I revered him: he was a great Orientalist. . . ."[28]

Death finally ended Prüfer's long service on 30 January 1959.[29] His career, though distinguished, was most noteworthy for the failure it reflected. He was not unique. For nearly a half century, a generation of German officials whose lives began during the era of the Kaiser and whose careers ended with Hitler, followed the same path. They did not succeed in placing Germany peacefully into the community of nations;

Prüfer at Baden-Baden, 1957

instead they contributed to a regime that committed unprecedented political crimes. Prüfer's example shows that at least one official, despite the catastrophes in 1918 and 1945, was unable to learn much from what had happened to himself and the nation he idolized. His narrow political and cultural attitudes never changed, and he refused to the end to admit that the ruling classes in the Reich, to which he had proudly belonged, shared significant responsibility for the country's demise and ruin and the world's suffering.

What also makes Prüfer worthy of study is that this problem may not have been confined to German functionaries who supported Nazism. A kind of inability or refusal like Prüfer's to grasp what had happened even extended to some German officials who opposed National Socialism. When the conservative and nationalist resistance attempted to topple Hitler in the July plot of 1944, thereby taking what it believed would be a first step toward peace with the Allies and a new morality for Germany, its leaders nevertheless hoped to retain for the Reich the territories demanded by nationalist and conservative circles since World War I. In addition, as recent evidence has shown, while most of this part of the resistance may have been disgusted by the mass murder of the Jews, few of its members were even then willing to contemplate the restoration of full citizenship in the Jews who survived.[30] The Nazi regime illustrated not only the awful destructiveness that can result from prejudice, nationalism, and mindless obedience, but also just how deeply such qualities can infect a society, even its most educated sociopolitical elite.

Abbreviations

The following acronyms and abbreviations are used in the notes and text:

AA	*Auswärtiges Amt;* German foreign ministry with headquarters in the Wilhelmstrasse in Berlin
Abt.	*Abteilung;* a division or department in the AA
ADAP	*Akten zur Deutschen Auswärtigen Politik,* 1918–45 (Göttingen: Vandenhoeck und Ruprecht, 1966–81), Series B
AO	*Auslands-Organisation;* foreign organization of the NSDAP
APA	*Aussenpolitisches Amt;* foreign policy office of the NSDAP
BA	*Bundesarchiv,* Koblenz
BDC	Berlin Document Center, Berlin
Chef AO	*Büro des Chefs der Auslands-Organisation im Auswärtigen Amt;* office of chief of the AO in the AA (1937–41)
DAL	*Deutsch-Arabische Lehrabteilung;* German-Arab training division
Diplogerma	German diplomatic mission
DIS	*Deutsche Informationsstelle;* German information office in the AA's Abt. *Deutschland*
DGFP	*Documents on German Foreign Policy, 1918–1945,* (Washington, D.C.: U.S. Government Printing Office, 1949–), Series C and D
DMG	*Deutsche Morgenländische Gesellschaft;* German Oriental Society

FO	Foreign Office, London
FRUS	*Foreign Relations of the United States* (Washington, D.C.: U.S. Government Printing Office, 1951–)
Gestapo	*Geheime Staatspolizei;* secret state police
GFMA-UC	German Foreign Ministry Archives-University of California, microfilm
GFMA-UM	German Foreign Ministry Archives-University of Michigan, microfilm
IMG	*Der Prozess gegen die Hauptkriegsverbrecher vor dem Internationalen Militärgerichtshof Nürnberg 14. November 1945–1. Oktober 1946* (42 vols.; Nuremberg, 1948)
KPA	*Kolonialpolitisches Amt;* colonial policy office of the NSDAP
NARA	National Archives and Records Administration, Washington, D.C.
NG	Nazi Government Ministries Series (Nuremberg documents)
NSDAP	*Nationalsozialistische Deutsche Arbeiterpartei;* National Socialist German Workers' party, or Nazi party
OKW	*Oberkommando der Wehrmacht;* high command of the German armed forces
OMGUS	Office of Military Government for Germany, United States
OPC/KO	Olaf Prufer Collection/Kent, Ohio
OPG	*Oberstes Parteigericht;* supreme court of the NSDAP
PA	*Politisches Archiv des Auswärtigen Amts,* Bonn
PRO	Public Record Office, London
RG	Record Group; collections of documents in the NARA
SA	*Sturmabteilung;* storm troopers of the NSDAP
SD	*Sicherheitsdienst;* security service
SIS	Secret Intelligence Service, Great Britain
SPD	*Sozialdemokratische Partei Deutschlands;* Social Democratic party of Germany
SS	*Schutzstaffeln;* elite guards of the NSDAP
USPD	*Unabhängige Sozialdemokratische Partei Deutschlands;* Independent Social Democratic party of Germany
UStS	*Unterstaatssekretär;* under-secretary of state in the AA
VB	*Völkische Beobachter;* national newspaper and major propaganda organ of the NSDAP
WO	War Office, London
Zsg.	*Zeitgeschichtliche;* contemporary (used in identifying a collection of Nazi records in the BA)

Notes

For further information regarding the original records that appear in the notes, the reader's attention is called to "A Comment on Archival Sources" in the bibliography (p. 243).

Preface

1. New studies have undermined the engrained notion that the *petit bourgeoisie* formed the Nazis' major support, showing instead that Hitler was acclaimed by elements of many different social groups, especially the higher circles of German society. See Richard F. Hamilton, *Who Voted for Hitler?* (Princeton: Princeton University Press, 1982), 77–90, 118–21, 136–38, 152, 197–98, 219, 323–40; Thomas Childers, *The Nazi Voter: The Social Foundations of Fascism in Germany, 1919–1933* (Chapel Hill: University of North Carolina Press, 1983), passim, which focuses on the different groups in the middle class; and Michael H. Kater, *The Nazi Party: A Social Profile of Members and Leaders, 1919–1945* (Cambridge, Mass.: Harvard University Press, 1983), 27–31, 62–71. The cooperation of the most notorious members of the sociopolitical elite with Hitler, such as Franz von Papen and Alfred Hugenberg, despite their denials, has been documented for a long time.

2. Hitler's contempt for the diplomats notwithstanding, the AA's staff remained largely intact after his appointment as chancellor. Note the extensive literature that includes Hans-Adolf Jacobsen, *Nationalsozialistische Aussenpolitik 1933–1938* (Frankfurt/Main: Alfred Metzner Verlag, 1968), 25–26, 623–32; Gerhard L. Weinberg, *The Foreign Policy of Hitler's Germany*, vol. 1, *Diplomatic Revolution in Europe, 1933–36* (Chicago: University of Chicago Press, 1970), 8–12; Fritz Fischer, *Bündnis der Eliten. Zur Kontinuität der Machtstrukturen in Deutschland 1871–1945* (Düsseldorf: Droste, 1979), 75–82; Paul Seabury, *The Wilhelmstrasse: A Study of German Diplomats under the Nazi Regime* (Berkeley and Los Angeles: University of California Press, 1954), 26–30; Konrad Jarausch, "From Second to Third Reich: The Problem of Continuity in German Foreign Policy," *Central Euro-*

pean History 12 (1979): 72–73; David Schoenbaum, *Hitler's Social Revolution: Class and Status in Nazi Germany, 1933–1939* (New York: Norton, 1980; first pub. 1966), 200–203; and Elke Frank, "The Wilhelmstrasse During the Third Reich: Changes in Its Organizational Structure and Personnel Policies," unpublished Ph.D. dissertation, Harvard University (1963), 184.

3. Like Prüfer, 65 percent (215) were born before 1900. Of that number, 74 percent (160) were Protestant; 74 percent (160) came from the *Mittelstand* (their fathers were mainly in the civil service, other professions, and the military); 60 percent (128) held a university degree; 37 percent (80) had entered the AA during Imperial Germany (another 43 percent [93] had entered during the Weimar republic); 55 percent (118) joined the Nazi party after 1933; and 86 percent (185) fought in World War I. See the "Personalbogen" completed in the summer and fall of 1944, National Archives and Records Administration, Washington, D.C. (hereafter NARA), Microcopy T-120 (Records of the German Foreign Ministry Received by the Department of State)/Rolls 2537–2540.

4. To my knowledge, despite the many fine histories of various aspects of Nazi foreign policy, only two detailed studies exist of career German diplomats. See John L. Heineman, *Hitler's First Foreign Minister: Constantin von Neurath, Diplomat and Statesman* (Berkeley: University of California Press, 1979), which focuses almost exclusively on the period after 1932; and Christopher Sykes, *Troubled Loyalty: A Biography of Adam von Trott zu Solz* (London: Collins, 1968). A brief biographical sketch of Ernst von Weizsäcker, the Nazi state secretary in the AA from 1939 to 1943, is in Leonidas E. Hill, ed., *Die Weizsäcker Papiere 1933–1950* (Berlin: Propyläen Verlag, 1974), 26–59. For books that examine the main Nazi ministers, consult Helen Kehr and Janet Langmaid, eds., *The Nazi Era, 1919–1945: A Select Bibliography of Published Works from the Early Roots to 1980* (London: Mansell, 1982), 63–68.

5. Such issues remain important subjects of debate, despite the view, which has some merit, of Pierre Aycoberry, *The Nazi Question: An Essay on the Interpretations of National Socialism (1922–1975)*, trans. Robert Hurley (New York: Pantheon, 1981), 226, that "the main questions were raised between 1960 and 1970" regarding German history and that "for the time being historical work consists in amplifying or refuting the dozen or so important works that appeared in that decade." However, to dismiss the importance of Nazism in modern history, as David Calleo, *The German Problem Reconsidered: Germany and the World Order, 1870 to the Present* (Cambridge and London: Cambridge University Press, 1978), 206, appears to do when he declares that "whatever faults and ambitions the Germans had were amply shared by the other major nations of the modern era" and to assume that the "Germans, in fact, were not so different from their British, French, and Russian neighbors," is to ignore the issues, which were so terribly unique to Germany, summarized by Istvan Deak, "How Guilty Were the Germans?" *The New York Times Review of Books* (31 May 1984), 37–42.

6. According to Aycoberry, *Nazi Question,* 225, "This doubt leads to another: one cannot say for certain whether the Third Reich was a radical departure from, or a continuation of the preceding regimes. The question remains open, like a gaping hole in the historical consciousness. We still have not settled with the past."

7. Examples are Ian Kershaw, *Popular Opinion and Political Dissent in the Third Reich: Bavaria, 1933–1945* (New York: Clarendon Press-Oxford, 1983), 246–57, which notes the influence of the Catholic Church in tempering the old-fashioned anti-Semites; Deak, 39; Karl A. Schluenes, *The Twisted Road to Auschwitz: Nazi Policy Toward German Jews, 1933–1939* (Urbana: University of Illinois Press, 1970), 57–58; and Otto Dov Kulka, "Die Nürnberger Rassengesetze und die Deutsche Bevölkerung im Lichte geheimer NS-Lage- und Stimmungsberichte," *Vierteljahrshefte für Zeitgeschichte,* 32 (1984): 606–8, which

distinguishes between the reaction of the "radicals" and the moderates to the laws. For extensive discussions of the different categories of German anti-Semite, see Kershaw, 231–45; and Sarah Gordon, *Hitler, Germans and the "Jewish Question"* (Princeton: Princeton University Press, 1984), 166–97.

8. For example, see Herbert A. Strauss and Norbert Kampe, eds., *Von der Judenfeindschaft zum Holocaust* (Frankfurt: Campus Verlag, 1985), especially the essays by Walther Hofer, "Stufen der Judenverfolgung im Dritten Reich 1933-1939," 172–85; Wolfgang Scheffler, "Wege zur 'Endlösung,' " 186–214; and Herbert A. Strauss, "Der Holocaust: Reflexion über die Möglichkeiten einer wissenschaftlichen und menschlichen Annäherung," 215–33. Other sources include Kater, 28, 30, 56, 102, 107, 110–14; Johnpeter Horst Grill, *The Nazi Movement in Baden, 1920–1945* (Chapel Hill: University of North Carolina Press, 1983), 355–56; Weinberg, *Foreign Policy,* I:23–24; and Eberhard Jäckel, *Hitler in History* (Hanover, N.H.: University Press of New England, 1984), 91. For the prominence of anti-Semitism in the Nazi appeal before 1933, see the extensive index entry on the subject in Eberhard Jäckel and Axel Kuhn, eds., *Hitler. Sämtliche Aufzeichnungen 1905-1924* (Stuttgart: Deutsche Verlags-Anstalt, 1980), 1294. Another example of how the old-style anti-Semitism enabled a German conservative and nationalist to collaborate in Nazi racial policies is in John A. Leopold, *Alfred Hugenberg: The Radical Nationalist Campaign Against the Weimar Republic* (New Haven: Yale University Press, 1977), 146, 196 n.101, 254 n.47.

Chapter One

1. Curt Prüfer, "Schweizer und Indisches Tagebuch vom 13.III.46–2.2.51," entry for 27 Jan. 1947, Olaf Prufer Collection/Kent, Ohio (hereafter OPC/KO). In addition to this diary, Prüfer left four other volumes of diaries from the latter part of World War II and the postwar period: I ("Tägliche Notizen 11.11.42 bis 7.1.44"); II ("Tägliche Notizen 10.1.44 bis 6.9.44"); III ("Tägliche Notizen 7.9.44 bis 21.4.46") and IV ("Tägliche Notizen 22.4.46 bis 17.4.49 Genf-New Delhi"), which are also in OPC/KO. These particular diaries will be cited hereafter as "Notizen," vol. number, and entry. In the same collection is a similar diary without a volume number, titled "Tägliche Notizen New Delhi 12.4.49." Other more extended, but non-daily, entries on various subjects after 1944 are in three volumes: "Schweizer Tagebuch;" "Schweizer und Indisches Tagebuch vom 13.III.46–2.2.51," which actually contains material through October 1954; and "Tagebuch. Indien/Heimreise Februar 1951." Each is cited hereafter by abbreviated titles and entry.

2. From the "Ahnenpass" for Prüfer's son, Olaf Herbert Hermann Carl Prüfer (spelled Prufer today), OPC/KO; and interview, O. Prufer with the author, 27 June 1982.

3. Prüfer, "Schweizer Tagebuch," entry for 2 Feb. 1944, OPC/KO; interview, O. Prufer, 27 June 1982; Prüfer, "Personalbogen," 24 Oct. 1944, T-120/2539/E309772-773; and James C. Albisetti, *Secondary School Reform in Imperial Germany* (Princeton: Princeton University Press, 1983), 171–241.

4. The general behavior patterns that frequently result from a childhood and family life such as his are discussed in Robert F. Massey, *Personality Theories: Comparisons and Syntheses* (New York: D. Van Nostrand Co., 1981), 60–66; and Duane Schultz, *Theories of Personality,* 2d ed. (Monterey, Calif.: Brooks/Cole, 1981), 79–82; interviews, O. Prufer, 27 June 1982 and 5 Apr. 1986.

5. The British, he once asserted, were homosexuals because they attended private schools. He also occasionally accused his son, Olaf, with whom he did not have a happy relationship (see herein, for example, 81-83, 144, 184), of being homosexual; interviews,

O. Prufer, 27 June 1982 and 5 Apr. 1986. Other instances and evidence of this trait in Prüfer's character are discussed herein, 233 n.28.

6. Prüfer, "Personalbogen," 24 Oct. 1944, T-120/2539/E309772–773; and interview, O. Prufer, 27 June 1982.

7. Standard works include Hans-Ulrich Wehler, *Das Deutsche Kaiserreich 1871–1918,* 5th ed. (Göttingen: Vandenhoeck & Ruprecht, 1983), 19–141; Geoff Eley, "The Wilhelmine Right: How It Changed," in Richard J. Evans, ed., *Society and Politics in Wilhelmine Germany* (London: Croom Helm, 1978), 112–35; Hartmut Kaelble, "Social Mobility in Germany, 1900–1960," *Journal of Modern History,* 50 (1978): 439–61; James J. Sheehan, ed., *Imperial Germany* (New York: Franklin Watts, 1976), especially 61–152 on "Elites and Institutions"; and John C. G. Röhl, "Beamtenpolitik im Wilhelminischen Deutschland," in Michael Stürmer, ed., *Das kaiserliche Deutschland. Politik und Gesellschaft 1870–1918* (Düsseldorf: Droste, 1970), 287–312.

8. Interview, O. Prufer, 27 June 1982; and Anneliese Prüfer, "Curt Prüfer," 23 Mar. 1959, OPC/KO. Moreover, see herein 58–59, 81.

9. A brief survey is Thomas W. Kramer, *Deutsch-ägyptische Beziehungen in Vergangenheit und Gegenwart* (Tübingen and Basel: Horst Erdmann Verlag, 1974), 192–213.

10. A. Prüfer, "Curt Prüfer," 23 Mar. 1959; Curt Prüfer, "Ein ägyptisches Schattenspiel, Li'b ed-der," Ph.D. dissertation, University of Erlangen (1906), both in OPC/KO; interview, O. Prufer, 27 June 1982; and Prüfer, "Personalbogen," 24 Oct. 1944, T-120/2539/E309773. Charles E. McClelland, *State, Society, and University in Germany, 1700–1914* (Cambridge: Cambridge University Press, 1980), 235–36, 240, 333, discusses the background and status of the University of Erlangen.

11. See, for example, "Eine Nacht bei den Derwischen," *Berliner Lokal Anzeiger,* 4 Nov. 1906, in OPC/KO, which mentioned Zechlin. On the latter, note Walter Zechlin, *Pressechef bei Ebert, Hindenburg und Kopf: Erlebnisse eines Pressechefs und Diplomaten* (Hannover: Schlütersche Verlagsanstalt und Buchdrückerei, 1956).

12. It is also probable that Prüfer knew ancient Egyptian hieroglyphics. See Paul Kahle, "Curt Prüfer (26.7.1881–30.1.1959)," *Zeitschrift der Deutschen Morgenländischen Gesellschaft,* 111 (1961): 2; and Prüfer, "Personalbogen," 24 Oct. 1944, T-120/2539/E309775.

13. Such themes are in Konrad H. Jarausch, *Students, Society and Politics in Imperial Germany: The Rise of Academic Illiberalism* (Princeton: Princeton University Press, 1982); his article, "Liberal Education as Illiberal Socialization: The Case of Students in Imperial Germany," *Journal of Modern History,* 50 (1978): 609–30; and McClelland, 314–21.

14. Dragomen were translators chiefly of Arabic, Turkish, or Persian. Regarding their other official duties and the relationship of the consular and diplomatic services in the German and British governments, see Lamar Cecil, *The German Diplomatic Service, 1871–1914* (Princeton: Princeton University Press, 1976), 5–19, 42–43, 59, 66, 79; and Zara S. Steiner, *The Foreign Office and Foreign Policy, 1898–1914* (Cambridge: Cambridge University Press, 1969), 184. For example, the German ambassador to Turkey, Freiherr Hans von Wangenheim, accused Gerald Henry Fitzmaurice, the Dragoman at the British embassy in Constantinople, of forming a conspiracy in 1913 to remove pro-German ministers from the Turkish government. See Wangenheim to the German chancellor, Theobald von Bethmann Hollweg, 24 Apr. 1913, *Die Grosse Politik der Europäischen Kabinette 1871–1914. Sammlung der Diplomatischen Akten des Auswärtigen Amtes,* ed. Johannes Lepsius, Albrecht Mendelssohn Bartholdy, and Friedrich Thimme, 40 vols. (Berlin: Deutsche Verlagsgesellschaft für Politik und Geschichte, 1925–26), XXXVII:163–64

(hereafter *Grosse Politik*). See, too, interview, O. Prufer, 27, 29 June 1982; and Curt Prüfer's sworn affidavit, 16 Apr. 1946, Document Neurath-4, *Der Prozess gegen die Hauptkriegsverbrecher vor dem Internationalen Militärgerichtshof Nürnberg 14. November 1945–1. Oktober 1946*, 42 vols. (Nuremberg, 1948), XL:453 (hereafter *IMG*).

15. Interview, O. Prufer, 27, 29 June 1982; and Cecil, 42–43.

16. Curt Prüfer, "Ägypten," *Süddeutsche Monatshefte* (July 1918), 271–72, copy in OPC/KO.

17. Ronald Robinson and John Gallagher, *Africa and the Victorians: The Official Mind of Imperialism* (London: Macmillan, 1974; first pub. 1961), 84–87; 462–67.

18. Robert L. Tignor, *Modernization and British Colonial Rule in Egypt, 1882–1914* (Princeton: Princeton University Press, 1966), 48–59; David S. Landes, *Bankers and Pashas: International Finance and Economic Imperialism in Egypt* (Cambridge, Mass.: Harvard University Press, 1958); and Robinson and Gallagher, 85–87.

19. Tignor, 50. Also on the first British commissioner, Lord Cromer, and his status, see Steiner, 237–38.

20. Wehler, 172–75; Paul M. Kennedy, *The Rise of the Anglo-German Antagonism, 1860–1914* (London: Allen and Unwin, 1980), 161, 167–75; and A. J. P. Taylor, *Germany's First Bid for Colonies: A Move in Bismarck's European Policy* (New York: Norton, 1970), 4–6.

21. Kennedy, *Anglo-German Antagonism*, 175–82; Raymond James Sontag, *Germany and England: Background of Conflict, 1848–1894* (New York: Norton, 1969; first pub. 1938), 186, 196–99, 201, 218–19; Taylor; and Wehler, 175–76.

22. Wehler, 165–92; Andreas Hillgruber, *Germany and the Two World Wars*, trans. William C. Kirby (Cambridge, Mass.: Harvard University Press, 1981), chap. 1; Imanuel Geiss, *Das Deutsche Reich und die Vorgeschichte des Ersten Weltkriegs* (Munich: Carl Hanser Verlag, 1978), 28–53; and William L. Langer, *The Franco-Russian Alliance, 1890–1894* (New York: Octagon, 1967; first pub. 1929).

23. Fischer, *Bündnis der Eliten*, 18; Wehler, 187–89; William L. Langer, *The Diplomacy of Imperialism, 1890–1902*, 2d ed. (New York: Knopf, 1951), 213–58; Sontag, 266–342; and Paul M. Kennedy, *The Samoan Triangle: A Study in Anglo-German-American Relations* (New York: Barnes & Noble, 1974), especially 25–51, 76–87, 108–45, 178–98.

24. The standard account of German policy in the Middle East is Ulrich Tumpener, *Germany and the Ottoman Empire, 1914–1918* (Princeton: Princeton University Press, 1968), chap. 1. Despite its polemics, Lothar Rathmann, *Berlin-Baghdad. Die imperialistische Nahostpolitik des kaiserlichen Deutschlands* ([East] Berlin: Dietz Verlag, 1962), 12–62, is useful. On William's activities during the Fashoda crisis, see Kennedy, *Anglo-German Antagonism*, 237, 250; and Jamie Cockfield, "Germany and the Fashoda Crisis, 1898–99," *Central European History*, 16 (1983): 256–75.

25. Prüfer's views, are in interview, O. Prufer, 27 June 1982; and pp. 9–10 herein. Further, note Eckart Kehr, *Schlachtflottenbau und Parteipolitik 1894–1901* (Berlin, 1930), 93–120, 305–31, 343–65; Holger H. Herwig, *Luxury Fleet: The Imperial German Navy, 1888–1918* (Winchester, Mass.: Allen & Unwin, 1980); Wehler, 165–71; and Jonathan Steinberg, *Yesterday's Deterrent: Tirpitz and the Birth of the German Battle Fleet* (London: MacDonald, 1965), especially chap. 4. A good summary of the German government's orchestration of nationalism through the press and patriotic leagues is Kennedy, *Anglo-German Antagonism*, 365–82.

26. Wolfgang Petter, " 'Enemies' and 'Reich Enemies:' An Analysis of Threat Perceptions and Political Strategy in Imperial Germany, 1871–1914," in Wilhelm Deist, ed., *The German Military in the Age of Total War* (Warwickshire, U.K.: Berg, 1985), 22–40. The

best recent treatment of Pan German ideology and the "world of enemies" it conjured up for the Reich is Roger Chickering, *We Men Who Feel Most German: A Cultural Study of the Pan German League, 1886–1914* (Boston: Allen and Unwin, 1984), 74–125.

27. For the German-Egyptian agreement, see Kramer, 55–56. The general nature of the entente is discussed in Pierre Guillen, "The Entente of 1904 as a Colonial Settlement," in Prosser Gifford and William Roger Louis, eds., *France and Britain in Africa: Imperial Rivalry and Colonial Rule* (New Haven: Yale University Press, 1971), 358–66; Kennedy, *Anglo-German Antagonism,* 268–69; and Tignor, 214–15.

Chapter Two

1. "German Intrigue in Egypt," *The Times* (London), 6 Jan. 1915.

2. For instance, AA to Bernstorff, 25 Mar. 1907, microfilm, "German Foreign Ministry Archives, 1867–1920," University of Michigan (hereafter GFMA-UM) reel 31/frame 0753. Fritz Fischer, *Germany's Aims in the First World War* (New York: Norton, 1967), 123, discusses Oppenheim's effect on the Kaiser.

3. The literature here is vast and includes Wehler, 196; Geiss, *Das Deutsche Reich,* 121; Norman Rich, *Friedrich von Holstein: Politics and Diplomacy in the Era of Bismarck and William II,* 2 vols. (Cambridge: Cambridge University Press, 1965), II:488–90; Gordon A. Craig, *Politics of the Prussian Army, 1640–1945* (New York: Oxford University Press, 1964), 290, 295n; Andreas Hillgruber, *Germany and the Two World Wars,* 18; and Konrad H. Jarausch, *The Enigmatic Chancellor: Bethmann Hollweg and the Hubris of Imperial Germany* (New Haven: Yale University Press, 1973), 148–84.

4. Such aspects of the Dragoman's official duties are in Cecil, 17–18.

5. For example, Kramer, 189–90, who overestimates German economic influence in prewar Egypt; more accurate is Kurt Grunwald, "Penetration Pacifique—The Financial Vehicles of Germany's 'Drang nach dem Osten,' " in Jehuda L. Wallach, ed., *Germany and the Middle East, 1835–1939* (Tel-Aviv: Israel Press, 1975), 96–97.

6. "Arabische Hochzeitsgebräuche," *Der Tag,* 4 Aug. 1907; "Haremsleben in Ägypten," *Berliner Lokal-Anzeiger,* 31 July 1908; and "Ägyptischer Aberglaube," *Berliner Lokal-Anzeiger,* 31 Aug. 1908, each in OPC/KO.

7. The Akaba affair was a conflict between Egypt and Turkey over their boundary in the Sinai peninsula in which Britain forced the Sultan not to occupy land near the Suez Canal; the Egyptian nationalists supported Turkey. In the Dinshawai incident of June 1906, Cromer brutally executed or imprisoned twenty Egyptian peasants for shooting a British soldier. A summary of the relationship among the various factions of nationalists, the Khedive Abbas Hilmi II, and Cromer is Tignor, chaps. 5 and 8. Kramer, 57–62, 67–69, is especially anti-British.

8. Bernstorff to Bülow ("Inhalt: Unterredung mit Lord Cromer"), 7 Apr. 1907, GFMA-UM/31/0771.

9. Frank C. Lascelles to Sir Edward Grey, 11 Apr. 1907, Public Record Office, London (hereafter PRO), Foreign Office Series (hereafter FO), 371/File 248/Papers 11874. Prüfer may have written some of the articles, inasmuch as he produced a number of the Cairo agency's pieces for the German press; see the clippings he saved in OPC/KO, some of which are cited later in this chapter.

10. The British were closely informed on Oppenheim's ambitions; see J. Ramsay (British resident in Baghdad) to the government of India, 19 Nov. 1906, FO 371/245/1150. On the prejudice against Jews in German society, which made it nearly impossible for them to acquire the prerequisites necessary for a diplomatic career, and on Oppenheim's lack of success in persuading the anti-Semitic AA officials, Herbert von Bismarck and later Fried-

rich von Holstein, to promote him, see Cecil, 95–102. Not very informative on Oppenheim's career before World War I is R. L. Melka, "Max Freiherr von Oppenheim: Sixty Years of Scholarship and Political Intrigue in the Middle East," *Middle Eastern Studies*, 9 (1973): 81. Oppenheim's influence on Prüfer is from O. Prufer to author, 20 Sept. 1982. Finally, see the memoirs of the Oriental secretary at the British residency, Ronald Storrs, *Orientations* (London: Nicholson & Watson, 1943), 121.

11. On Prüfer's accompanying Oppenheim, see the Egyptian government memo, "Note confidentielle a Son Excellence le President du Conseil des Ministres," 11 Nov. 1911, FO 371/1114/44628.

12. Oppenheim to Bülow, 31 July 1906, GFMA-UM/31/0661; and Oppenheim to Bülow of 26 May 1908, GFMA-UM/32/0100. The Baron was also accused by the French of inciting rebellion among the French Legion and Arab population in Algiers; "The Foreign Legion in Algeria," *The Times* (London), 17 Dec. 1908.

13. Storrs, 121; Oppenheim to AA, 19 Dec. 1908; and Oppenheim to Bülow, 29 May 1909, GFMA-UM/28/0306–07, 0367–70.

14. Oppenheim to Bülow, 28 May 1909, GFMA-UM/28/0365–66; and Kramer, 60–61.

15. Storrs, 121; and John de Salis (counselor at the British embassy in Berlin) to Grey, 8 July 1908, FO 371/452/24070.

16. Bernstorff to Bülow, 7 Apr. 1907, GFMA-UM/31/0773–74; and Tignor, 296.

17. For example, Bernstorff to Bülow, 26 Apr. 1907, GFMA-UM/28/0213–14; and 11 Feb., 30 May, 1 July, and 17 Nov. 1908, 32/0069, 0102–04, 0110–12, 0138–0140. In his letter of 5 Apr. 1907, GFMA-UM/31/0766–70, the consul general even noted his discouragement of the recently established German Orientbank's effort to help the Khedive protect part of his property from potential British confiscation by transferring his holdings in the Egyptian state railroad to a German company. Such German activity, Bernstorff believed, might anger the British.

18. Alfred von Kiderlen-Wächter (state secretary in the AA) to William II, 24 Sept. 1911, which includes the Kaiser's marginalia on Oppenheim, *Grosse Politik*, XXX:49–50; and Melka, 81.

19. See the British surveillance records on the German agents, Gerard Lowther (ambassador to Turkey) to Grey, 8 Aug. 1911, FO 371/1261/31881; and report of the British consulate general Baghdad, 4 Dec. 1911, FO 371/1490/3025.

20. For example, his criticism of the *Egyptian Daily Post*'s attack on Gorst and the Khedive, Hatzfeldt to AA, 5 May 1910, GFMA-UM/32/0212; and his comments against the *Kölnische Zeitung*'s claim "that Egypt stands on the brink of revolution," Hatzfeldt to Bethmann Hollweg, 16 July 1910, GFMA-UM/32/0273.

21. "Brief aus Ägypten," *Hamburger Fremdenblatt*, 2 Nov. 1910; and "Suez," *Berliner Lokal-Anzeiger*, 12 July 1910, in OPC/KO. Prüfer also bitterly denounced the British conquest of the Sudan, "Die Ausbeutung des Sudans," *Hamburger Fremdenblatt*, 16 September 1911.

22. "Die nationale Bewegung in Ägypten," *Hamburger Fremdenblatt*, 17 Jan. 1911, OPC/KO.

23. Lord Kitchener to Grey, 30 Sept. 1911, FO 371/1114/39288; and the memo enclosed in British agency Cairo to FO, 19 Nov. 1911, FO 371/1114/47430. Regarding the German policy of economic and political penetration of Turkey, see p. 11 herein.

24. Note German embassy Pera (Hans von Miquel) to Bethmann Hollweg ("Vertraulich. Inhalt: Stellung des Khedive zu England."), 12 June 1911, identifying ministers in the Ottoman government that were pro-British; Zeine N. Zeine, *The Emergence of Arab Nationalism: With a Background Study of Arab-Turkish Relations in the Near East*, 3d ed. (Delmar, N.Y.: Caravan Books, 1976), 50–51, 65–72; and M. S. Anderson, *The Eastern*

Question, 1774–1923: A Study in International Relations (New York: Macmillan, 1966), 275–76.

25. Quoted in British agency Cairo to FO, 19 Nov. 1911, FO 371/1114/47430.

26. An accusation by William II in his marginalia on the letter to him from Kiderlen-Wächter, 24 Sept. 1911, *Grosse Politik,* XXX:49–50. On German policy in the war, in which Kiderlen, the AA's secretary of state, supported Italy, and Adolf Marschall von Bieberstein, the German ambassador to Turkey, backed the latter, note W. David Wrigley, "Germany and the Turco-Italian War, 1911–1912," *International Journal of Middle East Studies,* 11 (1980): 313–38.

27. Only a few hundred Egyptians volunteered and roughly a third of the planned money was collected; Hatzfeldt to Bethmann Hollweg, 15 Nov. 1911, GFMA-UM/28/0456–57; and Kitchener to Grey, 30 Sept. 1911, FO 371/1114/39288.

28. See p. 11 herein.

29. Tignor, 307–15; and Kramer, 68–70.

30. Note p. 17 herein.

31. See p. 12 herein.

32. Kitchener to Grey, 30 Sept. 1911, and the accompanying FO minute, FO 371/1114/39288.

33. Grey to Sir Edward Goschen (ambassador in Berlin), 31 Oct. 1911, FO 371/1114/43304; and Kitchener to Grey, 28 Oct. 1911, FO 371/1114/42615.

34. Vansittart, "Minute," 11 Nov. 1911; and Hatzfeldt to Kitchener, 3 Nov. 1911, in FO 371/1114/44628.

35. Storrs, 122.

36. Kitchener to Hatzfeldt, 4 Nov. 1911, and the accompanying Egyptian report, "Note Confidentielle . . . ," 3 Nov. 1911, FO 371/1114/44628.

37. See the various FO minutes and Kitchener to Grey, 27 Jan. 1912, FO 371/1361/4779.

38. According to Nadav Safran, *Egypt in Search of Political Community: An Analysis of the Intellectual and Political Evolution of Egypt, 1804–1952* (Cambridge, Mass.: Harvard University Press, 1961), 92, 95, Lutfi constructed "a nationalist doctrine within the framework of a comprehensive socio-political philosophy inspired by Aristotle, Rousseau, Locke, Bentham, and Spencer." Because he believed that history had produced a "pharaonic core" and "distinct Egyptian personality," the philosopher "was not afraid that Egypt might lose her personality through wholesale borrowing from the West. Time and the Egyptian core would synthesize the borrowings into something distinctly Egyptian." See, moreover, Storrs, 122.

39. Hans von Miquel to Bethmann Hollweg, 28 Nov. 1913, GFMA-UM/138/0028.

40. Miquel's reports regarding the Khedive included those of 15 Aug. 1912, 14 Oct. and 28 Nov. 1913, and 17 Jan. and 15 Feb. 1914, GFMA-UM/138/0003, 0022, 0028, 0031, and 0032; and 4 and 19 Dec. 1912, GFMA-UM/32/0369–70, 0372–73. Note, in addition, Storrs, 118.

41. The high point of such a policy was the mission in 1912 of the British envoy, Lord Haldane, to Berlin. The German chancellor, Bethmann Hollweg, pursued British neutrality until the end of the July crisis of 1914 that produced World War I; Geiss, *Das Deutsche Reich,* 71–74; and Wehler, 194–95.

42. AA to Miquel, 12 Nov. 1913, OPC/KO.

43. See the publisher's certification of Prüfer's authorship of the translations, "Herrn Dr. C. Prüfer, Berlin-Tempelhof," 15 Mar. 1921, on the inside front cover of the book of etchings, *Abu'l-'Ala. Arabische Gedichte aus dem zehnten Jahrhundert. Radierungen von*

Richard von Below (Munich: F. Bruckmann, 1920), in OPC/KO. Kahle notes the fine quality of the translations, p. 1.

44. A. Prüfer, "Curt Prüfer," 23 Mar. 1959; Curt Prüfer, "Der arabische Dialekt von Ägypten," *Bädekers Ägypten* (Leipzig: Verlag von Karl Baedeker, 1913), xxviii–xlv; "Studienfahrt nach Oberägypten," *Ägyptische Nachrichten*, 5 Dec. 1913; and several more articles by him in *Beilage zur Vossische Zeitung*, all in OPC/KO.

Chapter Three

1. See his memo, "Erregung von Unruhen in Ägypten," n.d. (but can be dated at the beginning of August 1914); and accompanying letter, *Politisches Archiv des Auswärtigen Amts,* Bonn (hereafter PA), *Nachlass* Prüfer/*Politische Aufsätze.*

2. Note particularly Jarausch, *Enigmatic Chancellor,* 196, 269; and Wehler, 207–12. The subject of German war aims, following Fritz Fischer's controversial studies of the 1960s, has produced a literature too vast to cite here; summaries include Imanuel Geiss, ed., *July 1914, The Outbreak of the First World War: Selected Documents* (New York: Charles Scribner's Sons, 1967); Jarausch, especially 189–228, 259, 291, 294, 312, 401–2, 407–23; Hans Herzfeld, *Der Erste Weltkrieg,* 6th ed. (Munich: Deutscher Taschenbuch Verlag, 1982), 29–46, 284–87, 292, 301, 306, 315, 317–23; and Hillgruber, *Germany and the Two World Wars,* chaps. 3–4.

3. Ulrich Trumpener, *Germany and the Ottoman Empire,* 16–20; Herzfeld, 116; and Fischer, *Germany's Aims,* 121–22.

4. Fischer, *Germany's Aims,* 126.

5. Ibid., 124. See, moreover, German embassy Therapia to AA, 22 Aug. 1914; and Zimmermann to the embassy, 25 Aug. 1914, PA/*Aktengruppe Weltkrieg*/Serial L1405 (*Unternehmungen und Aufwiegelungen gegen unsere Feinde—Ägypten, Syrien und Arabien*).

6. Fischer, 126–31; Renate Vogel, *Die Persien- und Afghanistanexpedition Oskar Ritter v. Niedermayers 1915–1916* (Osnabrück: Biblio-Verlag, 1976); Carl Mühlmann, *Das Deutsch-Türkische Waffenbündnis im Weltkriege* (Leipzig: Verlag Köhler und Amelang, 1940), 70–76, 85; and Ulrich Gehrke, "Germany and Persia up to 1919," in Jehuda L. Wallach, ed., *Germany and the Middle East, 1835–1939* (Tel-Aviv: Israel Press, 1975), 112–14.

7. In particular, Christopher Sykes, *Wassmuss: "The German Lawrence"* (London/New York: Longmans, Green & Co., 1936); Hans Lührs, *Gegenspieler des Obersten Lawrence,* 9th ed. (Berlin: Vorhut-Verlag Otto Schlegel, 1936), p. 7; Dagobert von Mikusch, *Wassmuss: Der Deutsche Lawrence* (Berlin: Büchergilde Gutenberg, 1939); and the memoirs by Oskar von Niedermayer, *Im Weltkrieg vor Indiens Tor: Der Wüstenzug der deutschen Expedition nach Persien und Afghanistan,* 2d ed. (Hamburg: Hanseatische Verlagsanstalt, 1936), and Werner Otto von Hentig, *Mein Leben—Eine Dienstreise,* 2d ed. (Göttingen: Vandenhoeck & Ruprecht, 1963), 91–200.

8. Ferdinand Tuohy, *The Secret Corps: A Tale of 'Intelligence' on All Fronts* (New York: Thomas Seltzer, 1920), 176–77. Good for contrasting Lawrence's education and career with Prüfer's are Konrad Morsey, *T. E. Lawrence und der arabische Aufstand 1916/18* (Osnabrück: Biblio-Verlag, 1976), 9–52, 274–80; and Uriel Dann, "Lawrence 'of Arabia'—One More Appraisal," *Middle Eastern Studies,* 15 (1979): 154–62.

9. Ulrich Trumpener, "German Officers in the Ottoman Empire, 1880–1918: Some Comments on their Backgrounds, Functions, and Accomplishments," Wallach, ed., *Germany and the Middle East,* 43; and Friedrich Freiherr Kress von Kressenstein, *Mit den Türken zum Suezkanal* (Berlin: Vorhut-Verlag, 1938), 29.

10. See AA (Zimmermann) to German embassy Constantinople, 25 Aug. 1914; AA to the embassy, 28 Aug. 1914; the head of the administrative district (*Landkreis*) Göttingen to the foreign minister, 12 Aug. 1914 ("Betrifft: Reisepass für den Preussischen Staatsange-höriger Dr. phil. Curt Max Prüfer."), PA/*Weltkrieg*/L1405; and Prüfer's war diary, "Krieg, 1914–1918," entry for 28 Aug. 1914, OPC/KO. Kramer, 181–83, contains little on German-Egyptian relations during the war.

11. Prüfer, "Krieg," entries for 29–30 Aug. 1914, OPC/KO.

12. Ibid., entry for 4 Sept. 1914. Many of the divisions, rivalries, and fears that Prüfer observed and that subsequently characterized the German alliance with Turkey and war effort in the Middle East are chronicled in Trumpener, *Germany and the Ottoman Empire*, 22–37 (and especially between Wangenheim and Liman, 73–79).

13. Details of the meetings are in Prüfer, "Krieg," entries for 5–6 Sept. 1914, OPC/KO; and "Further Interrogation of Lieutenant Mors," n.d., Great Britain, FO, *Correspondence Respecting Events Leading to the Rupture of Relations with Turkey, November 1914* (London: His Majesty's Stationery Office, 1914), 73–74 (doc. no. 181).

14. The standard works include Zeine and George Antonius, *The Arab Awakening: The Story of the Arab National Movement* (Philadelphia: Lippincott, 1939).

15. See pp. 44, 52–53 herein. Enver's accusations against the Khedive and his refusal to involve him in the later German-Turkish military operation against Egypt are in Wangenheim to AA, 29 Aug. 1914; and German embassy Rome to AA, 29 Nov. 1914, PA/*Weltkrieg*/L1405. See also Fischer, *Germany's Aims*, 128.

16. Prüfer, "Krieg," entry for 6 Sept. 1914, OPC/KO.

17. Ibid., entry for 7 Sept. 1914; Prüfer's report, German embassy Therapia to AA, 7 Sept. 1914, PA/*Weltkrieg*/L1405; and Fischer, *Germany's Aims*, 128.

18. Bethmann to AA, 7 Sept. 1914, GFMA-UM/22/0745.

19. Prüfer, "Krieg," entry for 9 Sept. 1914, OPC/KO.

20. Wangenheim to AA, 9 Sept. 1914, GFMA-UM/136/0403; and Trumpener, *Germany and the Ottoman Empire*, 37–38.

21. Prüfer, "Krieg," entry for 8 Sept. 1914, OPC/KO; and "Further Interrogation of Lieutenant Mors," n.d., FO, *Correspondence*, 73 (doc. no. 181).

22. Prüfer mentions the report in "Krieg," entry for 12 Sept. 1914, OPC/KO; see also A. P. Wavell, *The Palestine Campaigns*, 2d ed. (London: Constable, 1929), 24–25.

23. Wangenheim to AA, 20 Sept. 1914, PA/*Weltkrieg*/L1405; Kress, 28; Trumpener, *Germany and the Ottoman Empire*, 39; and Bethmann to AA, 14 Sept. 1914, GFMA-UM/136/0413. One officer accompanying Kress and Prüfer was lieutenant Erich Heiden, who remained a close friend of Prüfer's long after the war; see Heiden to Karl Kettenbeil, 19 Sept. 1962, OPC/KO.

24. See Prüfer, "Krieg," entries for 20 Sept.–19 Oct. 1914, OPC/KO; and Djemal Pasha, *Memories of a Turkish Statesman, 1913–1919* (London: Hutchinson, n.d.), 137–49, who mentions many of Prüfer's contacts.

25. Prüfer, "Krieg," entries for 8, 15, 23, 26–27, 29 Oct. and 1 Nov. 1914, OPC/KO.

26. AA to Wangenheim, 14 Oct. 1914, GFMA-UM/23/0054.

27. Quoted in George Macmunn and Cyril Falls, *The History of the Great War*, 4 vols. (London: His Majesty's Stationery Office, 1928), I:15.

28. See FO, *Correspondence*, 43–45, 73–74, (doc. nos. 125, 181); and ibid. Mors received the unusual sentence of life imprisonment; most such prisoners were executed, particularly by the Germans.

29. Kress, 53, noted: "In the broader perspective, as long as we controlled the desert . . . we held the loyalty of the Bedouins completely. It also deserves mention that not a single Bedouin had tried to earn part of the very high reward which the British had placed on the heads of us German officers and of Dr. Prüfer before Turkey entered the war."

30. Grey to Louis Mallet (British ambassador in Constantinople), 24 Oct. 1914; and Mallet to Grey, 29 Oct. 1914, FO, *Correspondence,* 69, 71 (doc. nos. 166, 176).

31. Many suspected troublemakers were deported to the British prison on Malta; Egyptian ministry of interior, "General Situation in Egypt," 27 Dec. 1914, FO 371/2355/4307. On the events leading to Turkey's entry into the war, see Herzfeld, 116–17; and Trumpener, *Germany and the Ottoman Empire,* 49–62.

32. Prüfer to Oppenheim, 31 Dec. 1914, GFMA-UM/23/0639; and Prüfer, "Krieg," entries for 5, 10–11 Nov. 1914, OPC/KO.

33. Prüfer, "Krieg," entries for 26, 28 Nov. and 6 Dec. 1914, OPC/KO.

34. Except for Prüfer's report to Oppenheim, 31 Dec. 1914, GFMA-UM/23/0640, describing Muntaz Bey's raid on the canal as "a pitiful fiasco," the details of these operations are sketchy. Prüfer and several others on Kress's staff constructed a bomb destined to be carried into Egypt by Escref Bey and his band of "volunteers"; see Prüfer, "Krieg," entries for 12, 19 Nov. 1914, OPC/KO. Prüfer discussed mining and dynamiting the Suez Canal in the entries for 10, 15, 16, and 25 Oct. 1914. Kress, according to the entry for 20 Oct., approved the mining project, but then had doubts because of the unreliability of the Bedouins and the possibility of alerting the English to the other efforts under way to attack the canal; Kress to the chief of the German military mission in Turkey, 25 Oct. 1914, GFMA-UM/23/0157–58. The British discovery of the mine in the gulf of Suez is in Macmunn and Falls, I:212 n. 1. Also on Muntaz Bey and Escref Bey, note Djemal Pasha, 148.

35. Prüfer to Oppenheim, 31 Dec. 1914, GFMA-UM/23/0637–38.

36. W. W. Gottlieb, *Studies in Secret Diplomacy* (London: Allen and Unwin, 1957), 49–52; Zeine, 104–10; Antonius, 126–34; and Elie Kedourie, *England and the Middle East: The Destruction of the Ottoman Empire, 1914–1921* (London: Bowes and Bowes, 1956), 48–55. Regarding Prüfer's views, note his "Krieg," entries for 30 Oct. and 6 Nov. 1914, OPC/KO.

37. For Prüfer's warnings and misjudgments, see his reports to Oppenheim of 3 Nov. 1914 and 31 Dec. 1914, GFMA-UM/23/0213–14, 0635.

38. Note, for instance, Oppenheim, "Vorschläge wegen Besetzung der in meiner Denkschrift erwähnten neuen oder neu zu besetzenden Posten für den Nachrichtendienst etc.," 20 Nov. 1914; and Oppenheim to Zimmermann, 13 Nov. 1914, GFMA-UM/23/0270, 0165–66.

39. Herzfeld, 118; Wavell, 23, 27; and Prüfer, "Krieg," entries for 27, 30 Oct. 1914, OPC/KO. Moreover, none of the reports I have seen sent by Kress's staff to Constantinople or Berlin mentioned figures. Given the low estimates the Germans seemed to receive, one might question the assertion of Djemal Pasha in his memoirs, 155, that the Turks believed the British had 35,000 troops along the canal and 150,000 in the interior.

40. Kress, 67, 74: "We were only very badly instructed on the situation of the enemy." On the other hand, British intelligence reports on the Turkish expedition in Syria and Palestine, while more detailed than the German, were only partially accurate; for example, see the general commanding officer in Egypt to the War Office (hereafter WO), 6 Jan. 1915, PRO/WO 106/File 1568.

41. Prüfer to Oppenheim, 31 Dec. 1914, GFMA-UM/23/0641–42; and Mühlmann, 89–90.

42. There was much irony in the last statement, given Abdullah's secret contacts with Kitchener about his father and family supporting the British. Note Prüfer, "Krieg," entry for 11 Jan. 1915, OPC/KO.

43. For the German view, see Mühlmann, 89–91; and Kress, 45–46, 85–90. Regarding the British side, note Macmunn and Falls, I:25–36; and Wavell, 26–30.

44. Prüfer, "Krieg," entry for 20 Jan. 1915, OPC/KO; and Kress's problems with Djemal, 71–74. In his entry for 22 Jan., Prüfer remarked: "Kress called us together and

developed the plan of attack, which will also be his justification in the event that Djemal I arranges something else." Such examples appear to support the conclusion of Trumpener, *Germany and the Ottoman Empire,* 69–70, that the influence of the Germans and Austrians on Ottoman military operations was limited.

45. Prüfer, "Krieg," entry for 18 Jan. 1915, OPC/KO.

46. Ibid., entries for 25–26 Jan. 1915. Because the bombs exploded in the sand, they were less destructive than they might have been.

47. Ibid., entries for 28–30 Jan. 1915.

48. Ibid., entry for 2 Feb. 1915.

49. See his description of the struggle in ibid., entry for 3 Feb. 1915. The standard histories of the battle are those mentioned in n.43 above.

50. Ibid., entry for 4 Feb. 1915.

51. Prüfer to Wangenheim, 9 Feb. 1915, GFMA-UM/23/0866.

52. Prüfer to Oppenheim, 9 Feb. 1915, ibid., 0868.

53. Ibid., 0868–69.

54. Prüfer to Oppenheim, 24 Feb. 1915, GFMA-UM/24/0276–77.

55. Kress, 98–99; Djemal Pasha, 158–59; Herzfeld, 118; Mühlmann, 91; and Trumpener, *Germany and the Ottoman Empire,* 121–22. Even the British learned three weeks after the battle that this was the new German-Turkish strategy; note the British minister in Athens, F. Elliot, to FO, 27 Feb. 1915, FO 371/2483/23234.

Chapter Four

1. Oppenheim, memo, 22 Jan. 1915, GFMA-UM/136/00584.

2. Trumpener, *Germany and the Ottoman Empire,* especially chaps. 3, 7–10; Mühlmann, 29–37; Herzfeld, 83–87, 118; Antonius, 186–88; and Zeine, 110–13.

3. Wangenheim to Bethmann, 2 Apr. 1915, GFMA-UM/24/0160–61.

4. Captain Humann (German military attaché in Constantinople), "Besprechung mit Enver Pascha am 11. April 1915. Vertraulich.," ibid., frames 0232–34; Mühlmann, 27–28; and Fischer, *Germany's Aims,* 128–29.

5. Prüfer, "Propositions concernant l'organisation du service des renseignements sur l'Egypte," 1 Mar. 1915, ibid., frames 0271–72.

6. David Yisraeli, "Germany and Zionism," in Jehuda L. Wallach, ed., *Germany and the Middle East, 1835–1939* (Tel-Aviv: Israel Press, 1975), 142–43; and N. Gordon Levin, ed., *The Zionist Movement in Palestine and World Politics 1880–1918* (Lexington, Mass.: D.C. Heath, 1974), xiii–xiv.

7. Most Zionist leaders hoped to establish equality of rights and an independent Jewish community in Palestine, but within the Ottoman empire. Detailed discussions are Egmont Zechlin, *Die Deutsche Politik und die Juden im Ersten Weltkrieg* (Göttingen: Vandenhoeck und Ruprecht, 1969), 288–309; and Walter Laqueur, *A History of Zionism* (New York: Holt, Rinehart, and Winston, 1972), 108–12.

8. Zechlin, *Deutsche Politik und die Juden,* chap. 18; Laqueur, 176–77; and Yisraeli, "Germany and Zionism," 144.

9. Zechlin, *Deutsche Politik und die Juden,* 317–25; and Yisraeli, "Germany and Zionism," 144–45.

10. Zechlin, *Deutsche Politik und die Juden,* 327, which also contains a brief summary of anti-Semitism in Germany and the reaction of German Jews to it (chap. 2). Other basic histories of the nationalist and anti-Semitic movement include George L. Mosse, *Crisis of German Ideology: Intellectual Origins of the Third Reich* (New York: Grosset & Dunlap, 1964); Hermann Glaser, *The Cultural Roots of National Socialism,* trans. Ernest A. Menze

(Austin: University of Texas Press, 1978), 220–28; Fritz Stern, *The Politics of Cultural Despair: A Study in the Rise of the Germanic Ideology* (New York: Anchor Doubleday, 1965); Peter G. J. Pulzer, *The Rise of Political Anti-Semitism in Germany and Austria: 1867–1918* (New York: John Wiley, 1964); and Paul W. Massing, *Rehearsal for Destruction: A Study of Political Antisemitism in Imperial Germany* (New York: Harper, 1949).

11. Wangenheim to Bethmann, 3 Feb. 1915, esp. enclosing the letter from the German consul in Jaffa (Brode) to the consul in Jerusalem (Schmidt), 11 Dec. 1914, GFMA-UM/23/0657, 0681–84.

12. Prüfer, "Krieg," entry for 25 Dec. 1914, OPC/KO; and interview, O. Prufer, 27 June 1982. Regarding the increase of anti-Semitism in Germany during the war, see Zechlin, *Deutsche Politik und die Juden*, 516–65.

13. Prüfer to Oppenheim, 31 Dec. 1914, GFMA-UM/23/0635–36.

14. Loytved Hardegg to Bethmann, 26 Nov. 1914, ibid., frame 0371; and Prüfer's meeting with the director, Finkelstein, and Loytved, in "Krieg," entry for 16 Oct. 1914, OPC/KO.

15. Wangenheim to AA, 12 Apr. 1915, GFMA-UM/136/00614.

16. For instance, Neurath to AA, 2 Nov. 1915; and Wangenheim to AA, 21 Oct. 1915, GFMA-UM/25/0052, 0029; Bülow (German military attaché at the embassy in Rome) to AA, 15 Apr. 1915; Wangenheim to AA, 21 June 1915; and "Aussage des Agenten Rothschild," n.d., GFMA-UM/24/0218, 1634, 0645–49.

17. Note the British intelligence memo, "From the G.O.C. in C. Egypt to C.I.G.S.," 13 June 1916, FO 371/2672/115450; Tuohy, 176; and on Aaronsohn, Isaiah Friedman, *The Question of Palestine, 1914–1918: British-Jewish-Arab Relations* (New York: Shocken, 1973), 120–22.

18. Prüfer, "Krieg," entry for 9 Jan. 1915, OPC/KO. O. Prufer, interview with the author, 27 June 1982, maintains that his father had a sexual relationship with her. Not much biographical information exists on Minna Weizmann, except for a brief note about her in Chaim Weizmann, *The Letters and Papers of Chaim Weizmann,* ed. Meyer W. Weisgal, Gedalia Yogev, and Barnett Litvinov, et al., Series A, 3 vols. (London: Oxford University Press, 1971), II:468. Some information is in the letter of the Weizmann biographer, Yehuda Reinharz, to the author, 4 Mar. 1983. Confirming that the Weizmann who spied for Prüfer was a young physician from Russia is H. Steinbach-Schuh to Dr. Ziemke, 2 Aug. 1915 ("Betrifft ägyptische Agentin Minna Weizmann."), GFMA-UM/24/0780. The Weizmann Archives in Israel contains no record of her relationship to Prüfer and holds little material on her life; Nehama Chalom (curator) to the author, 17 Mar. 1983. Reinharz also has no knowledge of the connection.

19. According to her sister, Haya Weizmann-Lichtenstein, *Be-tsel Koratenu [In the Shadow of Our Roof]* (Tel-Aviv, 1948), 135, the younger sisters in the large Weizmann family tended to disagree with Chaim. He quoted with much pleasure and humor Minna's slogan to advance her assimilationist views against Zionism: "Let's not rely on history to tell us how to live our lives in the present." Note, moreover, Chaim Weizmann (in Geneva) to Catherine Dorfman, 4 May 1903, in Weizmann, *Letters,* A, II:298–99, which discusses his bitter opposition to the Bund and notes: "Everything is fine at home [in Russia]. My vagabonds are fine boys, studying hard and rendering their due to the cause. Only one sister is a Bundist (true, she is only 15) but the old folk take it hard." Minna Weizmann was born in Motele, White Russia, in 1888 or 1890; Reinharz to the author, 4 Mar. 1983. She is not mentioned in Chaim Weizmann's memoirs, *Trial and Error: The Autobiography of Chaim Weizmann* (London: Hamish Hamilton, 1950).

20. The first wave had begun with the pogroms in the 1880s; Levin, x–xii; and Laqueur, 124–25.

21. Her treatment, for example, provided an interesting contrast to that accorded Edith Cavell, a British nurse in Belgium executed (along with several Belgian colleagues) in October 1915 by the Germans for assisting Anglo-French soldiers in crossing the Dutch border; see Helen Judson, *Edith Cavell* (New York: Macmillan, 1941), 261, 281–83. Minna Weizmann, while on her way to Russia, gave the following explanation for her fate to the Turkish attaché in Bucharest, Nouri Zia Bey: "But she was so popular and respected in Cairo and Alexandria that one believed her steadfast denials [that she spied for the Germans]—the Russian consul vouched for her and ordered her returned to Russia." She repeatedly asked the attaché to instruct the German embassy in Constantinople about her fate, "and especially to advise Herr Prüfer of it." See Steinbach-Schuh to Dr. Ziemke, 2 Aug. 1915, GFMA-UM/24/0780. Whether Minna Weizmann escaped imprisonment on Malta because of her charming and forceful personality, as she suggested, is uncertain. I have found no evidence in the British or German archives that she was an Entente agent or that her brother intervened from London on her behalf. What is known is that Russian officials in Egypt were under considerable pressure from the British government to help pay for the several thousand destitute Russian Jews in Alexandria, expelled from Palestine by Djemal Pasha; see George Buchanan (British ambassador to Russia) to FO, 7 Feb. 1915, and FO (Eyre Crowe) to the British treasury, 13 Aug. 1915, FO 371/2355/14581, 110272.

22. Wangenheim to Bethmann, 2 Mar. 1915, GFMA-UM/23/0862; Wangenheim to AA, 4 Apr. 1915; Rudolf Nadolny (a reserve general staff officer), memo, 13 Apr. 1915; and AA, memo, n.d., GFMA-UM/24/0144, 0199, 0396. Regarding the Bulgarian spies, note FO to the British commissioner in Cairo, Henry McMahon, 26 Aug. 1915, FO 371/2356/118739.

23. See pp. 32–33 herein.

24. Note, for instance, the AA memo, "Aufgaben der Mission des Kaiserlichen Ministerresidenten Freiherrn von Oppenheim," 12 Mar. 1915, GFMA-UM/24/0027-28. Oppenheim, in requesting that Prüfer be assigned to him during his visit, wrote on 23 Mar. 1915, frame 0082: "I know him [Prüfer] from many years in Cairo, and he has also now proven again that he is excellently suited for carrying out our difficult work because of his precise knowledge of Arabic-Islamic relations as well as his conciliatory and well-considered nature."

25. See p. 32 herein; Kedourie, 48–52; Antonius, 126–34; Friedman, 65; and Zeine, 105–09.

26. The German negotiations with the Arabs have not been examined by historians. The most thorough account of Faisal's trip to Constantinople is still Antonius, 152–57, who nevertheless fails to mention Oppenheim. Kedourie, 57–58, incorrectly places Oppenheim in Turkey before the latter's attack on the canal in Feb. 1915. Oppenheim's "negotiations with Hussein" (through Faisal) are mentioned in Edouard Bremond, *Le Hedjaz dans la guerre mondiale* (Paris: Payot, 1931), 103.

27. Wangenheim to Bethmann, 22 May 1915, GFMA-UM/24/0516-17.

28. Wangenheim to AA, 6 June 1915, GFMA-UM/138/0064; Oppenheim to Jagow, 23 Feb. 1915, GFMA-UM/23/0782-83; Oppenheim to Bethmann, 4 June 1915, ibid., frames 0578-80; and Wangenheim to AA, 12 Feb. 1915, GFMA-UM/136/0594. Reports about Berlin paying the ex-Khedive include Fischer, *Germany's Aims,* 128, who claims Abbas Hilmi received four million gold francs; and a British intelligence file, "The Ex-Khedive and Bolo Pasha," 24 Apr. 1917, which speaks of four million marks, FO 371/2931/89236. Regarding Bolo Pasha's later trial in France for allegedly aiding the ex-Khedive in bribing the French press, note Herzfeld, 251.

29. AA to the embassy, 11 May 1915; and Wangenheim to AA, 5 May 1915, GFMA-UM/24/0400, 0378.

30. Antonius, 157–69; and Kedourie, 62.

31. See, for instance, his memo for Bethmann, 21 Nov. 1916, microfilm, "German Foreign Ministry Archives, 1867–1920," University of California (hereafter GFMA-UC), reel 476/frame 0359. According to the British, who kept Oppenheim's activities under close surveillance, he was "well supplied with cash." Note Rennell Rodd (British ambassador in Rome) to FO, 29 May 1915, FO 371/2489/68849.

32. Wratislaw (Salonica) to FO, 1 July 1915, quoting a WO intelligence report; and H. Bax-Ironside (British minister in Sofia) to FO, 8 June 1915, FO 371/2489/87754, 74465.

33. Neurath, memo, 23 Oct. 1915, GFMA-UM/25/0040.

34. AA, memo, 18 June, GFMA-UM/24/0618–19. On the trip into the Sinai, note Wangenheim to Bethmann, 17 Oct. 1915, GFMA-UM/25/0038.

35. Oppenheim to Bethmann, 10 Nov. 1915, GFMA-UM/25/0073–74.

36. Kedourie, 63–64; Antonius, 186–87; and Zeine, 113 n. 35. For Djemal's later defense of the Arabs, see his memoirs, 153.

37. Prüfer to Paul Count von Wolff-Metternich (the new German ambassador in Turkey following Wangenheim's death in the fall of 1915), 10 Dec. 1915, GFMA-UM/25/0153, containing his report to Djemal Pasha, written in French; and Friedman, 70–71. Other German officials in the provinces, such as Loytved Hardegg, also underestimated the prospect for an Arab revolt.

38. Prüfer to Metternich, 10 Dec. 1915, GFMA-UM/25/0152–53. On the mule corps, see Vladimir Jabotinsky, *The Story of the Jewish Legion* (New York: Bernard Ackerman, 1945), chaps. 1–2; and Friedman, 43–44. To what extent, if any, his views towards the Zionists resulted from his connection to Minna Weizmann (see pp. 42–43 herein), is unknown.

39. Zechlin, *Deutsche Politik und die Juden,* 347.

40. "Abschrift: Telegram des Militärattaches Pera Nr. 2333 vom 11.3 [1916]"; and Loytved Hardegg to Metternich, 26 Feb. 1916, GFMA-UM/25/0277, 0303–05.

41. Kress, 126–40; and Mühlmann, 92–93.

42. See p. 14 herein. The extensive literature on the subject, especially German economic interest in Central Africa during the war, includes Herzfeld, 169–70, 287; Fischer, *Germany's Aims,* 104–5, 109, 317–18, 586–89; and Jarausch, *Enigmatic Chancellor,* 190, 192, 196, 200, 205–6, 218, 259, 312.

43. Prüfer, "Vertraulich," 6 Aug. 1915, GFMA-UM/24/0791–97. On the German construction between 1915 and 1917 of a railroad into the Sinai, which Djemal urged against the conservative wishes of Kress, see Pinhas Walter Pick, "German Railway Constructions in the Middle East," in Wallach, ed., *Germany and the Middle East,* 79–83.

44. Prüfer, "Krieg," entry for 5 May 1916, OPC/KO; and Metternich to AA, 2 May 1916, GFMA-UM/25/0384.

45. Prüfer, "Krieg," entry for 28 May 1916, OPC/KO. I found no reference to this in the PRO's WO or FO files. Note p. 31 herein. This may have been an interesting psychological strategy of the British for dealing with German officials such as Prüfer. The report could likely have been false since the people he knew who had fallen into British hands as spies (e.g., Mors and Minna Weizmann)—although not officers—had not been executed.

46. Prüfer, "Krieg," entries for 6, 10, 22, 23, 28 May; 9, 20–21 June; and 8, 22 July 1916, OPC/KO; and Kress, 178–79. Many of the officers Prüfer befriended are mentioned by Kress and in "2. Bericht, Expedition nach Türkei," 1 Mar. 1915, GFMA-UM/24/0130–131.

47. Prüfer, "Krieg," entries for 5 Aug. and 27 July 1916, OPC/KO. Standard accounts of the battle are Macmunn and Falls, I:184–98; Mühlmann, 99–102; and Kress, chap. 12.

48. A. Prüfer, "Curt Prüfer," 23 Mar. 1959; and "Krieg," entries for 14 Aug.–23 Sept. 1916; regarding the cases of cholera, which numbered over two hundred, note Kress, 170.

49. Important sources include those in n. 42 above. The standard work is still Fischer, *Germany's Aims*, esp. 102–5, 109–10, and 586–91.

50. Oppenheim to Bethmann, 31 Dec. 1916; and his appended note, "Nachtrag zu meinem Bericht vom 31 Dezember 1916" ("betreffend: Die deutsche wirtschaftliche Propaganda in den Balkanländern und der Türkei und die Umwandlung der türkischen Nachrichtensaal-Organisation."), GFMA-UC/Reel 476/Frames 0347–52, 0353–54.

51. Max Freiherr von Oppenheim, "Die Nachrichtenstelle der Kaiserlich Deutschen Botschaft in Konstantinopel und die deutsche wirtschaftliche Propaganda in der Türkei" (Berlin: Reichsdruckerei, 1916), especially 7–11.

52. Kühlmann to AA, 8 Jan. 1917, requesting Prüfer's appointment at the embassy; Kühlmann to Bethmann, 19 Jan. 1917; Wesendonk to the embassy, 14 Mar. 1917; Prüfer to Rötger, 16 Feb. 1917; Prüfer to Wesendonk, 16 Feb. 1917; and Kühlmann to Bethmann, 1 May 1917, in GFMA-UC/476/0355, 0384–88, 0425, 0398, 0399–400, 0435, respectively.

53. See p. 46 herein.

54. Prüfer, "Vertraulich," 12 Apr. 1917, NARA/Microcopy T-149 (American Committee for the Study of War Documents, German Foreign Ministry Archives, Post-1914), roll 365/frames 0400–01.

55. Ibid., frame 0399, Eugen Mittwoch, memo (for Wesendonk), 26 Apr. 1917; and Rheinhaben, "Besprechungen in Konstantinopel vom 21. bis 23. April 1917.," GFMA-UC/476/0430–31.

56. Prüfer, "Krieg," entries for 26 May–11 July 1917, OPC/KO; and Trumpener, *Germany and the Ottoman Empire*, 156–65.

57. Prüfer, "Krieg," entries for 26, 30 June and 10 July 1917, OPC/KO. The nature of his intelligence activities for Djemal Pasha is unclear from his diary.

58. Waldburg (at the embassy in Constantinople) to AA, 21 Aug. 1917, GFMA-UM/137/0357.

59. German embassy Constantinople to Reich chancellor, Georg Count von Hertling, 11 Nov. 1917, GFMA-UM/138/0245.

60. Note p. 44 herein; AA to Romberg, 8 Dec. 1915; and Romberg to Bethmann, 15 Mar. 1916 ("Geheim!"), GFMA-UM/137/0098. On the date of Prüfer's assignment to the Khedive, note A. Prüfer, "Curt Prüfer," 23 Mar. 1959, OPC/KO.

61. See the FO memo, n.d.; A. Hirtzel (Switzerland) to Clerk, 26 Oct. 1915; and FO to McMahon, 29 Oct. 1915, FO 371/2357/162102, 159028. On the German rumors, note Romberg to AA, 14 Oct. 1915, GFMA-UM/24/0878; and Romberg to Bethmann, 13 Dec. 1915, GFMA-UM/137/0023.

62. Regarding Abd al Moneim, note FO to A. R. Green (the prince's tutor in Geneva), 2 May 1916, FO 371/2666/80303; Duff to FO, 17 Dec. 1915, noting that he found Abbas Hilmi "rather unusually shifty and vague"; FO to Duff, 3 Jan. 1916; and FO to McMahon, 3 Jan. 1916, FO 371/2357/196626. See, moreover, Sir Horace Rumbold to FO, 16 Dec. 1916; F. Villiers (British minister to Belgium) to Arthur Nicolson, 14 Apr. 1916; and McMahon to FO, 20 May 1916, FO 371/2672/254982, 73216, 96750.

63. Zimmermann to German embassy Constantinople, 23 July 1916; AA to embassy, 26 July 1916; Erzberger, memo, 10 Nov. 1916; and Romberg to AA, 16 Nov. 1916, GFMA-UM/137/0162–63, 0166, 0254, 0262, respectively. Apparently during the arrest in Switzerland of one of the ex-Khedive's advisers, police discovered documents implicating Erzberger in funneling money to Abbas Hilmi. The Germans feared the information would be used by the Entente to undermine the Center party leader's creditability as a negotiator "independent" of the Reich government. His questionable role in this capacity during the first years of the war is discussed in Klaus Epstein, *Matthias Erzberger and the Dilemma of German Democracy* (Princeton: Princeton University Press, 1959), 118–40.

64. The British, however, cared nothing for the nineteen-year-old prince, despite the German concern; see p. 55 herein. Moreover, note Romberg to Reich chancellor, 8 Aug. 1917; German embassy Constantinople to Hertling, 11 Dec. 1917, claiming that the Porte had lured the ex-Khedive to Constantinople to keep him under surveillance and undermine his influence; and Wedel (German embassy Vienna) to Bethmann, 24 Apr. 1917, GFMA-UM/138/0155, 0254, 0113. On the unrest in Egypt, a good summary is John Darwin, *Britain, Egypt and the Middle East: Imperial Policy in the Aftermath of War, 1918-1922* (New York: St. Martin's, 1981), 67.

65. For instance, German legation Bern to Reich chancellor, 22 Feb. 1918, GFMA-UM/138/0278; and Prüfer, "Krieg," especially entries for 20-21, 24, 30 June, 25-26 July, and 20 Aug. 1918, OPC/KO.

66. Prüfer, "Krieg," entry for 30 June 1918; and the copy of his article, "Ägypten," in *Süddeutsche Monatshefte* (July 1918), 269-72, OPC/KO.

67. Regarding the tie of the army to such civilian elements and the latters' massive membership figures, see Wehler, 213-16; Fischer, *Germany's Aims*, 431-34; and Hillgruber, *Germany and the Two World Wars*, 44. Pan-German membership rose to an all-time high in 1918; the Fatherland party counted 1.25 million members in July 1918, which surpassed the previous largest party, the SPD, in membership and even potential voting strength.

68. Prüfer, "Krieg," entry for 31 July 1918, OPC/KO; and Prüfer to AA, 1 Aug. 1918, GFMA-UM/138/0307.

69. Prüfer, "Krieg," entries for 16-17 Aug. 1918, OPC/KO; and the Imperial Prussian legation in Munich to Hertling, 17 Aug. 1918, GFMA-UM/138/0315.

70. Prüfer, "Krieg," entry for 21-30 Aug. 1918.

71. Throughout most of 1918, in fact, Britain had begun procedures to liquidate the ex-Khedive's property in Egypt and officially remove him and his son from the succession. Note Reginald Wingate (British commissioner in Cairo) to FO, 9 Feb., 7 July, 21 Oct., and 13 Nov. 1918, FO 371/3200/36431, 133692, 176350, 188576, respectively. See, too, Prüfer, "Krieg," entry for 1 Aug. 1918, OPC/KO.

72. Romberg to AA, 2 Oct. 1918, GFMA-UM/138/0339; and Prüfer, memo, 3 Sept. 1918, PA/*Nachlass* Prüfer/*Politische Aufsätze*. Prüfer remained "skeptical" of the venture from the beginning, although he never voiced his feelings to his superiors; Prüfer, "Krieg," entry for 17 Aug. 1918, OPC/KO.

73. For example, AA (Wesendonk) to the reserve general staff, 19 Oct. 1918, identifying a potential British spy; and Prüfer, memo, 23 Nov. 1918, GFMA-UM/25/0563, 0574.

Chapter Five

1. See his untitled loose-leaf diary notes for the spring of 1920 (hereafter "Prüfer diaries"), entry for 15 Mar., OPC/KO; Francis L. Carsten, *Revolution in Central Europe, 1918-1919* (Berkeley: University of California Press, 1972); and A. J. Ryder, *The German Revolution of 1918: A Study of German Socialism in War and Revolt* (London: Cambridge University Press, 1967).

2. Compare, for instance, the memoirs of the German diplomats, Ernst von Weizsäcker, *Memoirs of Ernst von Weizsäcker*, trans. John Andrews (Chicago: Henry Regnery, 1951), 40-45; Herbert von Dirksen, *Moscow, Tokyo, London: Twenty Years of German Foreign Policy* (Norman: University of Oklahoma Press, 1952), 11; and Ericht Kordt, *Nicht aus den Akten . . . Die Wilhelmstrasse in Frieden und Krieg. Erlebnisse, Begegnungen und Eindrücke 1928-1945* (Stuttgart: Deutsche Verlagsanstalt, 1950), 20-32, with the studies by Wolfgang Elben, *Das Problem der Kontinuität in der deutschen Revolution 1918/19. Die Politik der Staatssekretäre und der militärischen Führung vom November*

1918 bis Februar 1919 (Düsseldorf: Droste, 1965); and Eberhard Pikar, "Berufsbeamten-tum und Parteinenstaat: Eine Fallstudie," *Zeitschrift für Politik,* 7 (1960): 225–40.

3. Kurt Doss, *Das deutsche Auswärtige Amt im Übergang vom Kaiserreich zur Weimarer Republik. Die Schülersche Reform* (Düsseldorf: Droste, 1977), chaps. 1–2; Peter Krüger, *Die Aussenpolitik der Republik von Weimar* (Darmstadt: Wissenschaftliche Buch-gesellschaft, 1985), 23–27; Elben, 174–75; and Cecil, 324–25.

4. Doss, 215–86; Krüger, 27–29; Paul Gordon Lauren, *Diplomats and Bureaucrats: The First Institutional Responses to Twentieth-Century Diplomacy in France and Germany* (Stanford: Hoover Institution Press, 1976), 122–209; Hajo Holborn, "Diplomats and Di-plomacy in the Early Weimar Republic," in his *Germany and Europe* (Garden City, N.Y.: Doubleday, 1971), 184–93; and Gaines Post, Jr., *The Civil-Military Fabric of Weimar Foreign Policy* (Princeton: Princeton University Press, 1973), 18–21.

5. For example, Fischer, *Bündnis der Eliten,* 75–77; and Jarausch, "From Second Reich to Third Reich," 72–73.

6. The last memo I found written by Prüfer before his leave from the AA was dated 5 Dec. 1918, GFMA-UM/25/0583. See also, "Dr. phil. Curt Prüfer," in Dr. Klaus Weinandy (former director of the PA) to the author, 29 Jan. 1982; Doss, 188–200; Fischer, *Bündnis der Eliten,* 63; Holborn, 192; and Ludwig Zimmermann, *Deutsche Aussenpolitik in der Ära der Weimarer Republik* (Göttingen: Musterschmidt, 1958), p. 36, n.3. On the Nachrichtenstelle, see p. 26 herein.

7. Note, for instance, "Prüfer diaries," entry for 4 June 1920: "Fr[ances] moved and lives with me at present. Provided that I walk the straight and narrow." Also, see his lengthy letter to her, which he may not have sent (and which he did not publish), "Wie ich den Krieg sah: Offener Brief eines Deutschen an seine amerikanische Frau," February 1919, OPC/KO.

8. Mittwoch, memo, 8 Dec. 1919, GFMA-UM/25/0639; and mention of Prüfer's ac-tivities in FO to Ronald Graham (British ambassador to Rome), 22 Mar. 1922, FO 371/7743/E3129. He was also apparently in touch with Djemal and Enver Pasha, who fled to Germany immediately after the war; see his mention of them in "Prüfer diaries," entries for 24 Mar. and 20 May 1920, and note about Kress on 17 Mar., OPC/KO. On the escape of the Turkish leaders to Germany in November 1918 (especially with the aid of General Hans von Seeckt, the chief of the German high command from 1920–26), Enver's trips from there to Russia in 1919 and 1920, and Djemal's similar curious contact with Moscow until he was assassinated by Armenians in Tiflis in July 1922, see Trumpener, *Germany and the Ottoman Empire,* 362–64. Regarding Seeckt's wartime service in Turkey, see Trumpener, 69, 101–3, 359. Mention of Prüfer's arrest is in A. Prüfer, "Curt Prüfer," 23 Mar. 1959, OPC/KO; on Kress, see Heinrich Hillmayr, *Roter und Weisser Terror in Bayern nach 1918. Ursachen, Erscheinungsformen und Folgen der Gewalttätigkeiten im Verlauf revolutionären Ereignisse nach dem Ende des Ersten Weltkrieges* (Munich: Nusser Verlag, 1974), 161. Seeckt later appointed Kress Reichswehr commander in Bavaria; F. L. Car-sten, *The Reichswehr and Politics, 1918 to 1933* (Oxford: Clarendon, 1966), 185.

9. On Prüfer's relationship to the Sobernheims, O. Prufer interview, 27 June 1982. The attitudes of nineteenth-century German anti-Semites are analyzed in Uriel Tal, *Christians and Jews in Germany: Religion, Politics, and Ideology in the Second Reich, 1870–1914,* trans. Noah Jonathan Jacobs (Ithaca: Cornell University Press, 1975); George L. Mosse, *Germans and Jews: The Right, The Left, and the Search for a "Third Force" in Pre-Nazi Germany* (New York: Howard Fertig, 1970), 19, 39–42, 70–74, 108–13; Dennis Prager and Joseph Telushkin, *Why the Jews? The Reason for Antisemitism* (New York: Simon and Schuster, 1983), 152–53; Pulzer, 76–86; on the view towards Jews of the German intellec-tual, Paul de Lagarde, see Stern, 91–93; Glaser, 220–24, identifies this phenomenon as

part of a German "cultural schizophrenia"; and Gordon A. Craig, *Germany, 1866–1945* (New York: Oxford University Press, 1978), 154.

10. "Prüfer diaries," entry for 15 Mar. 1920, OPC/KO; and O. Prüfer interview, 27 June 1982. For a statement on the war's impact on the anti-Semitic attitudes of Germans, note Zechlin, *Deutsche Politik und die Juden,* 561. An analysis of the role of Jews in the German revolution is in Werner T. Angress, "Juden im politischen Leben der Revolutionszeit," in Werner E. Mosse and Arnold Paucker, eds., *Deutsches Judentum in Krieg und Revolution 1916–1923. Ein Sammelband* (Tübingen: Mohr, 1971), 137–316.

11. "Prüfer diaries," entry for 19 Mar. 1920, OPC/KO; Hentig, 215; and Holborn, 192. Turkey was officially placed under the jurisdiction of Abt. III (*Grossbritannien und Amerika, Orient, Koloniale Angelegenheiten*) on 7 Nov. 1921; Lauren, 243; and Doss, 223 n. 284. For Prüfer's promotion and pay increase to 1750 marks per year, note AA to Prüfer, 24 Sept. 1920, OPC/KO; and "Dr. phil. Curt Prüfer," in Weinandy to author, 29 Jan. 1982.

12. "Prüfer diaries," entry for 15 Mar. 1920, OPC/KO. For studies of the Kapp putsch and Communist uprising, note Johannes Erger, *Der Kapp-Lüttwitz Putsch. Ein Beitrag zur deutschen Innenpolitik 1919–20* (Düsseldorf: Droste, 1967); and George Eliasberg, *Der Ruhrkrieg von 1920* (Bad Godesberg: Verlag Neue Gesellschaft, 1974), especially 35–163.

13. "Prüfer diaries," entry for 20 Mar. 1920, OPC/KO.

14. Ibid., entry for 21 Mar. 1920. Details on the role of Schiffer and Hirsch during the putsch are in Angress, 207. A brief, but informative, selection of documents from the uprising is in Wolfgang Michalka and Gottfried Niedhart, eds., *Die ungeliebte Republik. Dokumentation zur Innen- und Aussenpolitik Weimars 1918–1933,* 2d ed. (Munich: Deutscher Taschenbuch Verlag, 1981), 76–82 (doc. nos. 41–46).

15. "Prüfer diaries," entry for 19 June 1920, OPC/KO; and Helmut Heiber, *Die Republik von Weimar,* 15th ed. (Munich: Deutscher Taschenbuch Verlag, 1982), chap. 3. For the negative impact of the Kapp putsch on German negotiations with the western powers regarding the Reich's disarmament and payment of reparations, the most important issues in foreign policy in 1920, note Krüger, 101.

16. Prüfer, "Wie ich den Krieg sah. . . ," February 1919, OPC/KO. His bitter defense of Germany resembled that presented by the German foreign minister, Ulrich von Brockdorff-Rantzau, prior to the German delegation's receiving the treaty from the Allies in Paris on 7 May 1919; see Erich J. C. Hahn, "The German Foreign Ministry and the Question of War Guilt in 1918–1919," in Carole Fink, Isabel V. Hull, and MacGregor Knox, eds., *German Nationalism and the European Response, 1890–1945* (Norman: University of Oklahoma Press, 1985), 59. Krüger, 45–76, provides a survey of the period between the armistice ending the war and the peace settlement and emphasizes the problem of German nationalism.

17. Regarding the "stab-in-the-back" myth and its origins, see Theodore Johnstone, "Dolchstoss: The Making of a Legend, 1890–1919," unpublished Ph.D. dissertation, University of Kansas (1974).

18. Imanuel Geiss, *Das Deutsche Reich,* 204–5; Hahn, 67–70; and Holborn, 163–72.

19. Prüfer, "Wie ich den Krieg sah. . . ," February 1919, OPC/KO.

20. Note his denunciation of the treaty and reparations in his autobiography, written in 1945 and 1946, pp. 7, 22, 24; the manuscript is in OPC/KO. On the inaccuracy of such claims, see Sally Marks, "The Myths of Reparations," *Central European History,* 11 (1978): 231–56, which notes that Article 231 "in fact makes no mention of war guilt"; and Gerhard L. Weinberg's important essay, "The Defeat of Germany in 1918 and the European Balance of Power," *Central European History,* 2 (1969): 248–60, which concludes that unlike Austria, certain factors in Germany's defeat in the war worked to consolidate

and even strengthen its position as a great power in Europe. Note, moreover, Hahn, 61; and Fritz Dickmann, "Die Kriegsschuldfrage auf der Friedenskonferenz von Paris 1919," *Historische Zeitschrift,* 197 (1963): 8–17.

21. Note U.S. Government, *The Treaty of Versailles and After: Annotations of the Text of the Treaty* (Washington, D.C.: U.S. Government Printing Office, 1947); on Prüfer's views, see pp. 70–77 herein.

22. To my knowledge, the only study that focuses on German policy in the Orient during the Weimar years is Glen Sharfman, "Next Year in Jerusalem? The Question of Assimilation and Palestine for German Jews in the Weimar Republic," unpublished M.A. thesis, University of North Carolina (1984). Krüger, for example, barely mentions the Middle East. The principal published sources are Lukasz Hirszowicz, "The Course of German Foreign Policy in the Middle East Between the World Wars," in Wallach, ed., *Germany and the Middle East, 1835–1939,* 175–89; and Bernd Philipp Schröder, *Deutschland und der Mittlere Osten im Zweiten Weltkrieg* (Göttingen: Musterschmidt, 1975), 17–28. The main objectives of German foreign policy after 1919 are in Werner Weidenfeld, *Die Englandpolitik Gustav Stresemanns. Theoretische und praktische Aspekte der Aussenpolitik* (Mainz: v. Hase & Koehler Verlag, 1972), 36–61.

23. "Prüfer diaries," entry for 15 Mar. 1920, OPC/KO; and Prüfer's affidavit, 16 Apr. 1946, Doc. Neurath-4, *IMG,* XL:454.

24. "Prüfer diaries," 19 June 1920, OPC/KO.

25. Examples, especially from Syria against French rule, are in Francis Nicosia, "Arab Nationalism and National Socialist Germany, 1933–1939: Ideological and Strategic Incompatibility," *International Journal of Middle East Studies,* 12 (1980): 351–52.

26. Prüfer, "Aufzeichnung," 28 Apr. 1920, PA/Abt. III/*Politische Beziehungen Indiens zu Deutschland.* The Oriental Institute was apparently subsidized by the AA, thereby helping the latter disguise its relationship to the refugees.

27. Ludwig W. Adamec, *Afghanistan's Foreign Affairs to the Mid-Twentieth Century: Relations with the USSR, Germany, and Britain* (Tucson: University of Arizona Press, 1974), 42–62. Regarding Schubert's pro-British and Western orientation, note Weidenfeld, 146–48; and Theodor Schieder, *Die Probleme des Rapallo-Vertrags. Eine Studie über die deutsch-russischen Beziehungen 1922–1926* (Cologne: Westdeutscher Verlag, 1956), 54–55.

28. AA to the embassy ("Geheim!"), 2 May 1921; Prüfer to Grobba, 29 Mar. 1921; and Prüfer to Hentig, Sebastian Beck, Max Krause, and v. Bassewitz, 7 Apr. 1921, PA/Abt. III/Serial L81 (*Politische Beziehungen Afghanistans zu Deutschland*); and Adamec, 62–64.

29. Adamec, 72–75, 98–106; Johannes Glasneck and Inge Kircheisen, *Türkei und Afghanistan—Brennpunkte der Orientpolitik im Zweiten Weltkrieg* ([East] Berlin: VEB Deutscher Verlag der Wissenschaften, 1968), 180–81; and on Siddiq, "Aufzeichnung über die Mitglieder der afghanischen Mission," n.d., PA/Abt. III/L81.

30. Despite the efforts of the Persians, who were financially dependent on Britain (and to a far lesser extent on Russia) and sought other sources of money, to establish close relations with a "third power," namely Germany; see Yair P. Hirschfeld, "German-Iranian Relations, 1921–1941," unpublished Ph.D. dissertation, Tel-Aviv University (1976), 13–20.

31. Note, for instance, AA, memo, 20 Dec. 1920; Sobernheim, memo, 19 Feb. 1921; German embassy London to AA, 11 and 12 July 1922; and Ulrich Schmid (Rome), "Vatikan und Zionismus," 4 July 1922, PA/Abt. III/Serial L1291 (*Politische Beziehungen zwischen England und Palästina*). See, moreover, J. C. Hurewitz, *The Struggle for Palestine* (New York: Greenwood Press, 1968; first pub. in 1950), 55–58; and Elizabeth Monroe,

Britain's Moment in the Middle East, 1914-1971 (Baltimore: Johns Hopkins University Press, 1981), chap. 2.

32. Nothing appears in the files of the AA, which is confirmed in the account of the meeting in David Yisraeli, "Germany and Zionism," 152-53. Weizmann's memoirs, 358-59, discuss only his meeting with Rathenau.

33. The Germans argued that reparations were contributing to their acute inflation by 1922, while Anglo-French officials agreed that Germany was deliberately ruining the mark, partly to avoid budgetary and currency reform, and especially to escape paying reparations. According to Marks, 238-39: "In this, the Entente experts were correct." See, furthermore, Charles S. Maier, *Recasting Bourgeois Europe: Stabilization in France, Germany, and Italy in the Decade after World War I* (Princeton: Princeton University Press, 1975), 249-304; Stephen A. Schuker, *The End of French Predominance in Europe* (Chapel Hill: University of North Carolina Press, 1976), 14-22; and Fritz K. Ringer, ed., *The German Inflation of 1923* (New York: Oxford University Press, 1969), 90-96. The well-known objective of each Weimar government and an overwhelming majority of the German people to recover German territories in Poland is discussed by Post, 14. On the Upper Silesian issue, see F. Gregory Campbell, "The Struggle for Upper Silesia, 1919-1922," *Journal of Modern History*, 42 (1970): 361-85.

34. Basic sources include Gerald Freund, *Unholy Alliance: Russian-German Relations from the Treaty of Brest-Litovsk to the Treaty of Berlin* (London: Chatto and Windus, 1957), 90-105; and Theodor Schieder, "Die Entstehungsgeschichte des Rapallo-Vertrages," *Historische Zeitschrift*, 204 (1967): 545-65.

35. Trade with Iran steadily increased, for example; Hirszowicz, "Course of German Foreign Policy," 175-76; Hirschfeld, "German-Iranian Relations," 25-29; and the general discussion of German-Arab ties in Schröder, 19-21. Regarding the Soviet-inspired attempt at a Communist revolution in Germany in October 1923, see Ruth Fischer, *Stalin and German Communism: A Study in the Origins of the State Party* (Cambridge, Mass.: Harvard University Press), 291-383.

36. The factors contributing to the recovery of German-Turkish relations, including the dissension among the Western powers regarding Turkey, are in Lothar Krecker, *Deutschland und die Türkei im zweiten Weltkrieg* (Frankfurt/Main: Klostermann, 1964), 11-12; and Heinz Gläsner, "Das Dritte Reich und der Mittlere Osten. Politische und Wirtschaftliche Beziehungen Deutschlands zur Türkei 1933-1939, zu Iran 1933-1941 und zu Afghanistan 1933-1941," unpublished Ph.D. dissertation, University of Würzburg (1976), 14-16.

37. Prüfer, "Aufzeichnung," 27 July 1923; German diplomatic representative for Transcaucasia to AA, 18 Oct. 1922, PA/Abt. III/Serial L101 (*Politische Beziehungen der Türkei zu Deutschland*); and Gläsner, 7-8.

38. Prüfer, "Aufzeichnung," 27 July 1923, PA/Abt. III/L101.

39. Ibid.

40. Prüfer to Ihsan Bey, 17 Nov. 1923; Prüfer, memo, 5 Nov. 1923, PA/Abt. III/Serial L106 (*Staatsmänner in der Türkei*); and Gläsner, 9.

41. Prüfer, memo, 4 Dec. 1923; and AA to Editora Internacional (Berlin), 3 Apr. 1924, PA/Abt. III/L101. A German edition of the book appeared the next year; see Rafael de Nogales y Mendez, *Vier Jahre unter dem Halbmond: Errinerungen aus dem Weltkrieg* (Berlin: R. Hobbing, 1925).

42. Gläsner, 15-24; Krecker, 11; Hirszowicz, "Course of German Foreign Policy," 175-76; and on the role of Prüfer and Oppenheim, AA, memo, n.d., *Akten zur deutschen auswärtige Politik 1918-1945*, Series B, 15 vols. (hereafter *ADAP*; Göttingen: Vandenhoeck und Ruprecht, 1966-81), III, document no. 14. Regarding Oppenheim's post-

war career, see Melka, 81–82. Note further, Freytag to AA, 12 and 23 Feb. 1924, PA/Abt. III/L101.

43. Note pp. 44, 52–55. On the reestablishment of the professional diplomats in the AA by 1924, see Post, 19; and Gordon A. Craig, *From Bismarck to Adenauer: Aspects of German Statecraft* (Baltimore: Johns Hopkins University Press, 1958), 108–9.

44. Darwin, 80–125; and Kramer, 73–75.

45. Prüfer, "Über Aegypten," n.d., PA/*Nachlass* Prüfer/*Politische Aufsätze*; and regarding the AA's propaganda campaign against the Allies before the signing of the Versailles treaty, see pp. 62, 63 herein.

46. Prüfer, "Aufzeichnung," 1 and 16 Sept. 1920; and German consulate general Zurich to AA, 18 Oct. 1920, PA/Abt. III/L1045 (*Politische Beziehungen zwischen England und Ägypten*).

47. In denying the funds for the paper, he informed the German embassy in Rome, 23 Dec. 1920, that "German policy obviously must refrain from any intervention in the internal affairs of Egypt." In addition, see Prüfer, "Aufzeichnung," 14 Dec. 1921, PA/Abt. III/L1045.

48. Defense security intelligence report, Cairo, 16 Nov. 1920 ("Notes on the opinion of Egyptians of the ex-Khedive."); Lord Curzon (British foreign secretary) to Lord Allenby (British high commissioner in Egypt), 14 Apr. 1920; and Allenby to Curzon, 15 Mar. 1920, FO 371/4982/E15729, E3095, E2368. Note, moreover, Schubert, "Aufzeichnung," 20 July 1922, T-120/4871/L309258, on the ex-Khedive's movements during the previous year.

49. Allenby to Curzon, 30 Nov. 1920, FO 371/4995/E15793.

50. He apparently owed the Germans 27,423 marks; Prüfer, memo, 16 Nov. 1920; Prussian army office for closed accounts to AA, 17 Mar. 1921; Prüfer, "Aufzeichnung," 13 Dec. 1921; and Prüfer to police presidium, 16 Dec. 1921, T-120/4871/L309244, L309252, L309253, L309254, respectively. Also on the smuggling of weapons, note Lord Granville (British minister in Athens) to FO, 27 May 1921; and FO, "Minute," 30 May 1921, FO 371/6283/E6114.

51. Darwin, 123–31. According to M. Woollcombe (SIS [Secret Intelligence Service] section Ia) to J. R. Murray (FO), 10 Feb. 1922: "The Ex-Khedive seems to be taking a strong interest in the latest turn of events in Egypt." See also, Scott (Cairo) to FO, 14 Feb. 1922; and Graham (Rome) to FO, 24 Feb. and 14 Mar. 1922, FO 371/7743/E1595, E1703, E2181, and E2852, respectively.

52. On Mertens's involvement, see Adamec, 74–75; and Kramer, 183–84.

53. See Dr. Conrad Marms, "Gutachtliche Äusserung über die gegenwärtige Rechtsstellung Ägyptens," 6 Apr. 1922; and Prüfer, "Aufzeichnung," 18 Mar. 1922, PA/Abt. III/1045.

54. D'Abernon to Eyre Crowe, 17 Mar. 1922, FO 371/7743/E3129. During his trips to Rome at the beginning of the 1920s—sometimes to visit his parents, who lived there and his sister, Helene, who worked at the German embassy—Prüfer became well-acquainted with the ambassador and later foreign minister under Hitler, Neurath; Prüfer affidavit, 16 Apr. 1946, Doc. Neurath-4, *IMG*, XL:454.

55. On the interest of the AA and the ex-Khedive in Syria, see Schubert, "Aufzeichnung," 20 July 1922; Abbas Hilmi to Prüfer, 18 July 1922; and German legation Bern (Adolf Müller) to AA, 19 June 1922, T-120/4871/L309258, L309257, L309255. Note, moreover, the denial by the foreign minister of France, Raymond Poincare, that Paris sought the ex-Khedive for the Syrian throne; Lord Hardinge (British ambassador to France) to FO, 24 Aug. 1922, FO 371/7852/E8457.

56. According to an FO official, "Minute," 18 Sept. 1922, FO 371/7745/E9282: "Everything seems to point to the organization of the attempts on the lives of British subjects

and officials in Egypt being initiated in Italy. But so far there is no documentary evidence."

57. To my knowledge, no detailed history of Egyptian politics exists for this period; summaries include Peter Mansfield, *The British in Egypt* (London: Weidenfeld and Nicolson, 1971), 245–52; J. C. B. Richmond, *Egypt 1798–1952: Her Advance Towards a Modern Identity* (New York: Columbia University Press, 1977), 192–94; and Kramer, 76–78.

58. By 1925, the British possessed far more evidence than previously (see above, n.50), including testimony of Hanafi Bey's son, in Allenby to Austen Chamberlain (British foreign minister), 11 Apr. 1925, and the accompanying FO "Minute," 5 May 1925, which observed that "Hag Ahmed had been arrested and a revolver found in his back yard which has been identified as having been used in some of the crimes." See FO 371/10904/J1135. On the Society of Vengeance, note the memoirs of Allenby's successor as British high commissioner in Egypt after 1925, Lord Lloyd, *Egypt Since Cromer,* 2 vols. (New York: AMS Press, 1970; first pub. 1934), II:38, 69.

59. The details are in the lengthy report, "Summary of Information Received up to 6th December 1923 Regarding the Activities of the Ex-Khedive," enclosed in British SIS to FO, 13 Dec. 1923, FO 371/8970/E12242.

60. Ibid. Note, furthermore, German legation Cairo (Mertens) to AA, 27 June 1923 ("Inhalt: Pläne des Ex-Khediven.") and 15 Nov. 1923, T-120/4871/L309303–305, L309317.

61. The ministry is not mentioned in SIS to FO, 13 Dec. 1923, FO 371/8970/E12242.

62. AA to Prussian ministry of interior, 7 Aug. 1923; Prüfer, memo, 25 June 1923; and a mysterious memo by Prüfer, 5 Feb. 1923, discussing the ex-Khedive's sending of "clothing" through Germany to Italy and Switzerland, which may have been a cover for the arms smuggling; T-120/4871/L309309–310, L309302, L309295. Also, note SIS to FO, 13 Dec. 1923, FO 371/8970/E12242; and the further British intelligence report in Allenby to Chamberlain, 11 Apr. 1925, FO 371/10904/J1135.

63. Allenby to Chamberlain, 11 Apr. 1925, FO 371/10904/J1135. According to British SIS to FO, 13 Dec. 1923, FO 371/8970/E12242, the ex-Khedive also attempted to purchase a couple of submarines from the Soviet government in August 1923.

64. Prüfer, memo, 19 Jan. 1924; Prüfer, "Aufzeichnung," 17 Dec. 1923; and German legation Athens to AA, 2 Jan. and 8 Feb. 1924, T-120/4871/L309330, L309320, L309321–323, L309331 respectively. Although there is no such evidence in the German or British diplomatic files, the AA may have sent Prüfer to the Mediterranean in January 1924 to mediate between the ex-Khedive and the German crew, possibly to keep the plot alive and/or limit the publicity surrounding the incident. According to A. Prüfer, "Curt Prüfer," 23 Mar. 1959, OPC/KO, he went to the Mediterranean that month for "recuperation" from his tuberculosis.

65. Legation de Suede (Constantinople) to AA, 10 May 1924; German legation Athens to AA, 8 Feb. 1924, T-120/4871/L309345, L309331; "Ein lästiger Ausländer," *Kieler Nachrichten,* 22 Aug. 1924; and Allenby to Chamberlain, 11 Apr. 1925, FO 371/10904/J1135.

66. Mansfield, 249–50; Richmond, 193; and Kramer, 77. Regarding Prüfer's appointment to Davos from the summer of 1924 to the end of 1925, note his affidavit, 16 Apr. 1946, Doc. Neurath-4, *IMG,* XL:454. According to A. Prüfer, "Curt Prüfer," 23 Mar. 1959, OPC/KO, the reason for his assignment was recuperation from tuberculosis. On the activity of Richthofen's father in prewar Egypt and his acquaintance with the ex-Khedive, see p. 21 herein; and Abbas Hilmi to Richthofen, 4 Sept. 1917, GFMA-UM/138/0205.

67. Yousri's request is in Kramer, 184. The others are in German embassy London to AA, 2 Sept. 1924; "Auszug aus einem Privatbrief des Botschaftsrat v. Prittwitz aus Rom vom 3. September d.J. an Staatssekretär von Maltzan"; and German embassy Paris to AA,

26 Sept. 1924, PA/Abt. III/Serial L1043 (*Politische Beziehungen Ägyptens zu Deutschland*).

68. Richthofen to German embassy Paris, 1 Oct. 1924; to German embassy Rome, 4 Oct. 1924; and to German legation Cairo, 1 Dec. 1924, PA/Abt. III/L1043. Further, note Richthofen to German embassy Rome, 19 Oct. 1924, T-120/4871/L309358.

69. Willy Hahn (Berlin lawyer) to Prüfer (Davos), 6 Nov. 1925; German legation Constantinople-Angora to AA, 10 Dec. 1924, emphasizing the view of the German minister, Hans Adolf von Moltke, and Wilhelm Padel, the consul general and acquaintance of the ex-Khedive, that Abbas Hilmi's trial should be quashed to preserve his allegedly good position with Turkey; Prüfer (Davos) to Richthofen, 23 Jan. 1925, calling the trial "abominable"; and de Haas to Prüfer (Davos), 26 Jan. 1925, T-120/4871/L309392-393, L309361, L309376-77, L309374, respectively. On the publicity that in fact surrounded the trial, note "Das verhängnisvolle Hoch," *Berliner Tageblatt*, 23 Feb. 1926; and "Ein feiner Khedive," *Deutsche Tageblatt*, 18 July 1926.

70. For example, in response to a report that Germany was intriguing to place the ex-Khedive in power in Turkey as Sultan, an FO official, D. A. Osborne, replied in a "Minute," 22 Aug. 1924: "I don't believe for an instant that the Germans would do anything of the sort. It is in any case too intractable a scheme for them to take up." Another exclaimed in a "Minute," 23 Aug. 1924: "Rubbish." See FO 371/10037/E7205. On the yacht's whereabouts and the evidence of German complicity, note FO to consul general Marseilles, 29 Jan. 1925; J. W. Keogh (consul general Nice) to FO, 28 May 1925; Eric Phipps (ambassador in Paris) to FO, 19 Feb. 1925; Nevile Henderson (Alexandria) to Herbert, 26 Sept. 1925; and Allenby to Chamberlain, 11 Apr. 1925, FO 371/10904/J292, J1547, J556/G, J2937, J1135, respectively. On the treaty and German trade with Egypt, note Kramer, 184; and Hirszowicz, "Course of German Foreign Policy," 176-77.

71. Lord Lloyd (Cairo) to FO, 15 June 1926, FO 371/11579/J1756.

72. Richthofen to German embassy Angora, 13 Dec. 1927; Padel to AA, 14 Dec. 1927; AA to the lawyers, Kröger and Riis, 13 Feb. 1928; and the lawyers to AA, 7 Feb. 1928, T-120/4871/L309477, L309449, L309453, L309452, respectively. According to Post, 19, the AA had already reasserted much of its autonomy against control by the republican institutions. See, furthermore, Hirszowicz, "Course of German Foreign Policy," 175-77.

Chapter Six

1. Most recent among the publications since the 1950s demolishing the myths surrounding Stresemann are Fischer, *Bündnis der Eliten*, 76; Krüger, 207-11, particularly noting the minister's reliance on careerists as leaders in the AA; Dirk Stegmann, " 'Mitteleuropa' 1925 bis 1934: Zum Problem der Kontinuität deutscher Aussenhandelspolitik von Stresemann bis Hitler," in Dirk Stegmann, Bernd-Jürgen Wendt, Peter-Christian Witt, eds., *Industrielle Gesellschaft und politisches System. Beiträge zur politischen Sozialgeschichte. Festschrift für Fritz Fischer zum 70. Geburtstag* (Bonn: Verlag Neue Gesellschaft, 1978), 203-11; and Post, 79-81.

2. See p. 68 herein; Krüger, 151-82, 266-69; Schieder, *Die Probleme des Rapallo-Vertrags*, 39-55; the heavily Marxist Alfred Anderle, *Die Deutsche Rapallo-Politik. Deutsch-Sowjetische Beziehungen 1922-1929* ([East] Berlin: Rütten & Loening, 1962), 53-199; Freund; and Kurt Rosenbaum, *Community of Fate: German-Soviet Diplomatic Relations, 1922-1928* (Syracuse: Syracuse University Press, 1965), 49-187.

3. In April 1925, amid massive press attention, the Germans convicted sixteen Communists of treason, declaring that they had cooperated in October 1923 in plotting the

overthrow of the Weimar Republic. The Russians retaliated a few months later by sentencing two German students, Karl Kindermann and Theodor Wolscht, arrested in Moscow for espionage, to death, and accusing a diplomat at the German embassy, Gustav Hilger, of complicity in the affair. See Rosenbaum, chap. 5; Freund, 150–234; Martin Walsdorff, *Westorientierung und Ostpolitik. Stresemanns Russlandpolitik in der Locarno Ära* (Bremen: Schuenemann Universitätsverlag, 1971), 78–155; Krüger, 282–84; Gustav Hilger and Alfred G. Meyer, *The Incompatible Allies: A Memoir-History of German-Soviet Relations, 1918–1941* (New York: Macmillan, 1953), 40–47; and Edward H. Carr, *German-Soviet Relations Between the Two World Wars, 1919–1939* (Baltimore: Johns Hopkins University Press, 1951), chap. 6.

4. Walsdorff, 121–30; Rosenbaum, 166–69; and Krüger, 322.

5. The details are in "Aufzeichnung des Reichsminister des Auswärtigen Stresemann," 22 Dec. 1925; and "Aufzeichnung des Staatssekretärs des Auswärtigen Amts von Schubert," 28 Jan. 1926, *ADAP*, B, II (pt. 1), nos. 15 and 51. Also, note Walsdorff, 129–30, 162, 309 n.29; Rosenbaum, 200–201; and Hilger and Meyer, 148–49. On the Wahlkonsuln, see Lauren, 173. For Prüfer's appointment to the consulate general in Tiflis, note AA to Prüfer, 31 Oct. 1925, OPC/KO.

6. "Aufzeichnung des Staatssekretärs des Auswärtigen Amts von Schubert," 30 Dec. 1925, *ADAP*, B, II (pt. 1), no. 22; Walsdorff, 309 n.29; and Rosenbaum, 201.

7. Brockdorff to AA, 14 Mar. 1926, PA/Abt. IV (*Russland*)/Serial L667 (*Deutsche diplomatische und konsularische Vertretung*); and Walsdorff, 169–77.

8. For example, Brockdorff to AA, 23 Mar. 1926, and other documents in PA/Abt. IV/ L667; and the AA correspondence from June–December 1926 in *ADAP*, B, II (pt. 2), nos. 5, 31, 34, 35, 48, 57, 64, 83, 99.

9. Fritz Grobba, *Männer und Mächte im Orient. 25 Jahre diplomatischer Tätigkeit im Orient* (Göttingen: Musterschmidt, 1967), 36; and on his relations with the Communist party leader and president of the Soviet Union, M. I. Kalinin, interview, O. Prüfer, 27 June 1982. Kalinin visited Tiflis in June 1927; note David M. Lang, *A Modern History of Soviet Georgia* (Westport, Conn.: Greenwood, 1975; first pub. 1962), 245–46.

10. Brockdorff to AA, 28 July 1926; and Prüfer's report quoted in Brockdorff to AA, 10 Apr. 1926, PA/Abt. IV/L667.

11. Brockdorff to AA, 10 Apr. 1926, PA/Abt. IV/L667.

12. The paper, the *Türkische Post,* borrowing an article from the Berlin *Deutsche Allgemeine Zeitung,* accused the Soviet secret police (Cheka) of having shot Djemal Pasha in Tiflis in 1922; German consulate general Tiflis to German embassy Moscow, 25 Sept. 1926. See, in addition, German embassy Moscow to AA, 20 Jan. 1926; and German consulate general Tiflis to embassy, 30 July 1926, 13 Nov. 1926, and 31 Jan. 1927, PA/ Abt. IVa/L658 (*Politische Beziehungen zwischen Russland und der Türkei*). On the Russo-Turkish treaty of 1925, note Rosenbaum, 203.

13. Relations between the two countries, however, gradually cooled after 1926. Note Post, 47–52; and Harvey L. Dyck, *Weimar Germany and Soviet Russia, 1926–1933: A Study in Diplomatic Instability* (New York: Columbia University Press, 1966), 13–19. Copies of the treaty of Berlin and Stresemann's press conference regarding it are in Michalka and Niedhart, 192–94 (numbers 100–101); Krüger, 315–19, provides a survey of the background to and consequences of the treaty.

14. About the marriage, note A. Prüfer, "Curt Prüfer," 23 Mar. 1959; and on the divorce from Francis Pinkham, see the court decision, "Im Namen des Volkes," 28 Sept. 1927, OPC/KO. Details of Anneliese Fehrmann's background are from interview, O. Prüfer, 27 June 1982. Inasmuch as Prüfer appeared to have no specific mission in Ethiopia,

one suspects as did Sidney Barton, the British minister in Addis Ababa, that he was sent there for reasons of health; Barton to A. Henderson, 11 June 1930, enclosing "Report on Heads of Foreign Missions at Addis Ababa," FO 371/14595/J1868.

15. Interviews, O. Prufer, 5 Apr. and 8 May 1986. The elder Prüfer always owned dogs; he also transported a baby hyena from French Somaliland to Berlin in 1930, where it lived in his apartment until its size forced him to place the animal in a zoo. In his "Notizen," I, 16 May 1943, OPC/KO, Prüfer mentioned seeing the hyena at the zoo. Also, while ambassador to Brazil during World War II (see chap. 10), he ordered the construction of a giant wire mesh birdhouse that began at the ground and stretched around several large trees, in which he could walk and keep numerous exotic birds.

16. When questioned on the subject, Olaf Prufer declared, "I have no recollection of their bedroom." Interview, O. Prufer, 5 Apr. 1986.

17. Most significant, he negotiated the dissolution of the inter-Allied military control commission, which had attempted to supervise the disarmament clauses of the peace, and through the Dawes and Young plans (1924, 1929) he smoothed the way for a reparations agreement advantageous to Germany. Finally, the foreign minister succeeded in obtaining the withdrawal of Allied troops from the west bank of the Rhine in 1930, five years before the date originally set.

18. According to his affidavit, 16 Apr. 1946, Doc. Neurath-4, IMG, XL:454.

19. George W. Baer, The Coming of the Italian-Ethiopian War (Cambridge, Mass.: Harvard University Press, 1967), 2–18; Robert L. Hess, Ethiopia: The Modernization of Autocracy (Ithaca: Cornell University Press, 1970), 57–58, 64–65; Angelo Del Boca, The Ethiopian War, 1935–1941, trans. P. D. Cummins (Chicago: University of Chicago Press, 1969), 12–13; and Esmonde M. Robertson, Mussolini as Empire-Builder: Europe and Africa, 1932–36 (London: Macmillan, 1977), 7–8.

20. Prüfer to AA, 8 Feb., 19 May, and 25 Aug. 1928, PA/Abt. III/Serial L78 (Politische Beziehungen zwischen fremden Staaten-Äthiopien).

21. Prüfer to AA, 31 July 1928, PA/Abt. III/Serial L78. As a condition for entry into the League, Ethiopia promised to work to abolish slavery, which was widespread in the country; Baer, 8–9.

22. Prüfer to AA, 23 Oct. 1928, PA/Abt. III/Serial L78; Baer, 20–21; Robertson, Mussolini, 8; and Hess, 66.

23. Note German legation Addis Ababa to AA, 2 May 1929; and the telegram of apology in English from Ras Guksa Wolie, 1 June 1929, PA/Abt. III/Serial 102 (Deutsche diplomatische und konsularische Vertretung in Äthiopien). The details of the expedition are in Prüfer, "Reise durch Nordabessinien und Eritrea," n.d., PA/Nachlass Prüfer/Politische Aufsätze.

24. Prüfer, "Reise durch Nordabessinien. . . ," n.d., PA/Nachlass Prüfer/Politische Aufsätze. Also on the payment of the chieftains by Britain and Italy, note Prüfer to AA, 15 Feb. 1930, PA/Abt. III/L78.

25. Prüfer to AA, 6 Apr. 1929, ADAP, B, XI, no. 159. Even as late as World War II, Germans had not forgotten Italy's breach of its alliance with Germany in 1915; Marlis G. Steinert, Hitler's War and the Germans: Public Mood and Attitude during the Second World War, ed. and trans. Thomas E. J. DeWitt (Athens: Ohio University Press, 1977), 68, 88. For mention of David Hall and German concern about the bankruptcy of his firm, see Grobba, memo, 22 Nov. 1929, PA/Abt. III/Serial M259 (Äthiopien: Militär-Angelegenheiten).

26. Prüfer to AA, 10 Dec. 1929 and 25 Feb. 1930, PA/Abt. III/L78.

27. Prüfer to AA, 14 Mar. 1928 and 6 June 1929, PA/Abt. III/L78. Details on Steffen's background are in Robertson, Mussolini, 111.

28. Barton to Henderson, 11 June 1930, enclosing "Report on Heads of Foreign Missions. . . ," FO 371/14595/J1868. Barton added about Prüfer: "His taste for secret service work has led him to make a study of the Russian agents who operate in this country, and, as a result, he has himself been described as a Bolshevik agent." Apparently, in Ethiopia Prüfer knew the former Russian policeman, Captain Paul Bolygin, head of the security force of the dowager Tsarina, Marie; Bolygin claimed in a book published in 1935 that his investigation of the deaths of the Tsar and Tsarina, Nicholas II and Alexandra, showed that they had escaped from the Communists in 1918. See Guy Richards, *The Hunt for the Czar* (Garden City, N.Y.: Doubleday, 1970), 193, 195–97; and interview, O. Prufer, 27 June 1982.

29. Which was done, Barton to Henderson, 15 Sept. 1930; and on the incident with the Aden police and the British apology, Barton to Wilhelm Melchers, 30 October 1930, FO 371/14481/E5388, E5988. Other information is in Prüfer's memo, 11 Sept. 1930, discussing the trip, *ADAP*, B, XV, no. 213; and Prüfer's diaries written during the journey, 18 June-15 Aug. 1930, OPC/KO. While in Aden, Prüfer took an interest in the wife of an English captain. He observed in his diary entry for 22 June: "I ate lunch at Medicis [the Italian consul] with a couple of Italians and an English captain and his wife, whose female half is undoubtedly Medici's sweetheart. That did not prevent her at all, however, from showing affection for other men, e.g. she gave me a loving glance." That evening, the English couple, Medici, and Prüfer rode in an auto to the nearby seashore, about which the German minister remarked: "The discussion was gloomy and slow. I had the feeling that at least two men too many were there, certainly the brave captain."

30. For instance, Gerhard Köpke headed Abt. II (Western and Southeastern Europe); Hans Heinrich Dieckhoff Abt. III; Oskar Trautmann Abt. IV (Eastern Europe, Scandanavia, and Russia); Friedrich Gaus Abt. V (legal division); and Hans Freytag Abt. VI (cultural division). See Post, 19–20; Krüger, 518–19; and Craig, *From Bismarck to Adenauer*, 107–10. According to Seabury, 16, the careerists had dominated the divisions anew by 1922; the chiefs of all eight divisions were from the prewar era, having entered the ministry between 1896 and 1906.

31. Sander A. Diamond, *The Nazi Movement in the United States, 1924–1941* (Ithaca: Cornell University Press, 1974), 284–85; Warren F. Kimball, "Dieckhoff and America: A German's View of German-American Relations," *The Historian*, 27 (1965): 219, 242; Manfred Jonas, "Prophet without Honor: Hans Heinrich Dieckhoff's Reports from Washington," *Mid-America*, 47 (1965): 232; and Dirksen, 33. According to Heinemann, 144, Dieckhoff "was a good man who lacked energy." A more cautious view towards the ambassador is in Gerhard L. Weinberg, *The Foreign Policy of Hitler's Germany*, vol. 2, *Starting World War II, 1937–1939* (Chicago: University of Chicago Press, 1980), 11, 252 n. 11. For the importance after 1930 in the AA of "discipline" and efficiency in carrying out assigned functions at the expense of "independence and originality," note Krüger, 519.

32. Brief, but key and revealing, excerpts of documents are in Michalka and Niedhart, 290–92, 307–8, 323–25, 364–70 (especially numbers 157, 168, 176, 208–18). There is also an extensive secondary literature on this subject. Especially useful are Krüger, 507–50; Reinhard Frommelt, *Paneuropa oder Mitteleuropa. Einigungsbestrebungen im Kalkül deutscher Wirtschaft und Politik 1925–1933* (Stuttgart: Deutsche Verlags-Anstalt, 1977), 73–97; Fischer, *Bündnis der Eliten*, 75–80; Stegmann, 208–20; Post, 265–90; and Hillgruber, *Germany and the Two World Wars*, 53–55, 76. For further details, see the standard works by Edward W. Bennett, *German Rearmament and the West, 1932–1933* (Princeton: Princeton University Press, 1979), chaps. 1–6; and *Germany and the Diplomacy of the Financial Crisis* (Cambridge, Mass.: Harvard University Press, 1962).

33. As examples, Prüfer, memo, 3 and 6 Oct. 1931; and AA, "Program-Entwurf für

den Besuch Ihrer Exzellenzen des Kgl. Britischen Ministerpräsidenten und des Kgl. Britischen Ministers des Auswärtigen," n.d., PA/*Büro Reichsminister*/Serials 1460, 2368 (*England*).

34. Including a refusal to invite the leading Indian nationalist, Mohandas Gandhi, to Germany in the fall of 1931; see Grobba, memo, 21 Oct. 1930 and 30 Oct. 1931; and AA to German consulate general Calcutta, 7 Oct. 1931; PA/Abt. III/*Politische Beziehungen Indiens zu Deutschland*. A survey of German-Indian relations before 1933 is Milan Hauner, *India in Axis Strategy: Germany, Japan, and Indian Nationalists in the Second World War* (Stuttgart: Klett-Cotta, 1981), 56–89.

35. Information on the arms convention is in AA, "Kontrolle des Waffenhandels in und von Abessinien," 21 Aug. 1930, PA/Abt. III/L78; and AA to Reich ministries, 6 Apr. 1932, PA/Abt. III/Serials 8025, M219 (*Militärangelegenheiten Äthiopien*). Allegations concerning Steffen's activity are in German legation Addis Ababa to AA, 9 Feb. 1931; and Steffen to Prüfer, 13 Feb. 1931, PA/Abt. III/Serials 8014, L77 (*Politische Beziehungen Äthiopien zu Deutschland*). For more on the arms issue, note Baer, 11; and Hess, 66.

36. See pp. 70–77 herein; and Prüfer, memo, 7 Oct. 1930, PA/Abt. III/M259.

37. Kramer, 72, 79–82; and Prüfer to Grobba, 2 May 1931, T-120/4871/L309484–485. Details on the Syrian rumors are in Percy Loraine (British commissioner in Cairo) to FO, 29 Nov. 1931, FO 371/15364/E6079.

38. Loraine to FO, 21 Dec. 1931, FO 371/15364/E6413; Prüfer, memo ("Hiermit über Herrn Min. Dir. Dieckhoff dem Herrn Staatssekretär erg. vorgelegt."), 29 Apr. 1932; and Prüfer to Prussian ministry of interior, 31 May and 24 Nov. 1932, T-120/4871/L309539–540, L309549–551.

39. Ahmad Mahrad, "Die deutsch-persischen Beziehungen, 1918–1933," unpublished Ph.D. dissertation, Freie Universität Berlin (1973), 74–187, 246–54; and Yair Hirschfeld, "German Policy Towards Iran: Continuity and Change from Weimar to Hitler, 1919–1939," in Wallach, ed., *Germany and the Middle East, 1835–1939*, 117–23.

40. "Die Vorgeschichte des deutsch-persischen Konflikts," 27 Oct. 1931, PA/Abt. III/Serial L88 (*Politische Beziehungen Persiens zu Deutschland*).

41. Ibid. The literature on this episode is inconsistent and contradictory. Hirschfeld, "German Policy Toward Iran," 124, mentions nothing about the efforts of the German government to suppress the Persian students. Two dissertations, however, note the AA's concern over the students: Mahrad, 331–83; and Gläsner, 188–89.

42. On Prüfer's views in this connection, note pp. 59–61 herein. Regarding Dieckhoff's attitude, see his memo, 6 Aug. 1931 ("Betrifft: Kommunistische Propaganda des persischen Studenten Alavi, Angriff gegen den Schah."), PA/Abt. III/L88.

43. Prüfer, memo, 21 Oct. 1931; Köpke to Diplogerma Tehran, 23 Oct. 1931; and "Die Vorgeschichte. . . . ," 27 Oct. 1931, PA/Abt. III/L88.

44. Prüfer to Dieckhoff, 23 Oct. 1931; and Diplogerma Tehran to AA, 25 Oct. 1931, PA/Abt. III/L88.

45. Prüfer, memo, 26 Oct. 1931, PA/Abt. III/L88. Press articles included "Ein deutsch-persischer Zwischenfall," *Frankfurter Zeitung*, 24 Oct. 1931; and "Ein deutsch-persischer Streitfall," *Kölnische Zeitung*, 24 Oct. 1931.

46. Grobba, memo, 5 Mar. 1932, for Dieckhoff and Prüfer, PA/Abt. III/L88.

47. Dieckhoff to Berlin police president, 8 Mar. 1932; Dieckhoff to Prussian ministry of interior, 8 Mar. 1932; Prüfer to Diplogerma Tehran, 8 Mar. 1932; German legation Tehran to AA ("Inhalt: Persische Kommunisten in Berlin."), 28 May 1932, ibid.; and "Die verbotene persische Emigrantenzeitung," *Berliner Börsen-Zeitung*, 9 Apr. 1932. Erich Rinka, the editor, was suspected by the AA of being a part of Willi Münzenberg's Communist propaganda concern; regarding Münzenberg, see Helmut Gruber, "Willi Münzen-

berg's German Communist Propaganda Empire, 1921–1933," *Journal of Modern History*, 38 (1966): 278–99.

48. Kalisch, "Aufzeichnung," 19 June 1932; and German legation Tehran to AA, 9 June 1932, PA/Abt. III/L88.

49. AA to Prussian ministry of interior, 16 June 1932, PA/Abt. III/L88.

50. Prüfer, memo, 6 July 1932; Dieckhoff to Diplogerma Tehran, 16 June 1932; and Prussian ministry of interior to AA, 15 June 1932, PA/Abt. III/L88.

51. German legation Tehran to AA, 25 June 1933, PA/Abt. III/L88.

52. For criticism in the press, see "Der Hauptzeuge—ausgewiesen," *Berliner Tageblatt*, 30 June 1932.

53. "Jüdische Hetze stört deutsche Auslandsbeziehungen," *Der Angriff*, 4 July 1932.

54. Note the letters, seen by Dieckhoff and Prüfer, Pillai to Hitler, 10 Dec. 1931; and Hitler (signed "Private Secretary," but unidentified) to Pillai, 24 Dec. 1931, PA/Abt. III/ *Politische Beziehungen Indiens zu Deutschland.*

55. See document no. 51 in Arnold Paucker, *Der jüdische Abwehrkampf gegen Antisemitismus und Nationalsozialismus in den letzten Jahren der Weimarer Republik* (Hamburg: Leibniz-Verlag, 1968), 221.

56. Ibid.

57. Louis Rittenberg to Paul Schwarz (German consul general New York), 14 July 1932; German consulate general Antwerp to AA, 20 July 1932; German embassy Paris to AA, 4 Aug. 1932; German legation Cairo to AA, 14 July 1932; and German consulate general Jerusalem to AA, 25 June 1932, PA/Abt. III/Serial L1279 (*Jüdische-politische Angelegenheiten-Allgemeines*). For examples of Nazi attacks in the fall of 1932 against Jews, note Richard Bessel, *Political Violence and the Rise of Nazism: The Storm Troopers in Eastern Germany, 1925–1934* (New Haven: Yale University Press, 1984), 89; Martin Gilbert, *The Holocaust: A History of the Jews of Europe during the Second World War* (New York: Holt, Rinehart and Winston, 1985), 30–31; and on Nazi violence in general, Volker Hentschel, *Weimars letzte Monate. Hitler und der Untergang der Republik* (Düsseldorf: Droste, 1978), passim.

58. Reich ministry of interior to AA, 15 Sept. 1932, PA/Abt. III/L1279.

59. Sobernheim to Prüfer, 2 Aug. 1932; and Prüfer, memo, 4 Aug. 1932, PA/Abt. III/ L1279.

60. This incident is not mentioned in Herbert S. Levine, "A Jewish Collaborator in Nazi Germany: The Strange Career of Georg Kareski, 1933–37," *Central European History,* 8 (1975): 256–57, 265, n.36. See, moreover, Prüfer to Sobernheim, 9 Aug. 1932, PA/Abt. III/Serial L1287 (*Prof. Sobernheim: Verschiedenes, 1929–1932*).

61. Sobernheim, "Bericht über die jüdische Weltkonferenz vom 14.–16. August 1932 in Genf.," n.d., PA/Abt. III/L1279.

62. The consulate to AA, 22 Aug. 1932, PA/Abt. III/L1279. The press reports appeared to bear out the consulate's assessment; note "Say Palestine Jews have Best Conditions," *The New York Times,* 16 Aug. 1932; and "The Jewish Conference," *The Times* (London), 18 Aug. 1932, which noted only that the conference "strongly protests against the anti-Jewish measures some states are still practising, and against attacks on Jews in some countries."

63. Such behavior was apparently typical of Kareski's style as "a wheeler and dealer" in both business and politics and which contributed to his collaboration with the Nazis during the Third Reich; Levine, 264–81. Note, further, Prüfer to German consulate general Antwerp, 23 Sept. 1932, PA/Abt. III/L1279.

64. Prüfer entered the party in 1937; see p. 135 herein. Deickhoff joined in 1941; see Jacobsen, 632. Regarding Neurath's appointment in May 1932, note Heinemann, 43–45.

65. The most significant examples were the growing power of the government bureaucracy during the last years of the republic; Brüning's continuous use of the authoritarian article 48 of the Weimar constitution to govern without the Reichstag; and Papen's coup on 20 July 1932, in which he seized as chancellor control over the state government in Prussia from the SPD leadership. The best discussion remains Karl Dietrich Bracher, *Die Auflösung der Weimarer Republik. Eine Studie zum Problem des Machtverfalls in der Demokratie,* 4th ed. (Villingen/Schwarzwald: Ring Verlag, 1964), 179-98, 331-600.

Chapter Seven

1. From his affidavit to the Nuremberg tribunal in defense of Hitler's first foreign minister, Neurath, 16 Apr. 1946, Doc. Neurath-4, *IMG,* XL:457. Also, see his much more fervent support of the Germans and himself in his autobiography, especially 24-33, 54-76, 149-76, written in 1945 and 1946, manuscript in OPC/KO. For the series of wars that Hitler planned to wage, first discussed by him in the 1920s in his memoir, *Mein Kampf,* and elsewhere publicly, note Weinberg, *Foreign Policy,* I:7-8, 14-21; Günter Wollstein, *Vom Weimarer Revisionismus zu Hitler. Das Deutsche Reich und die Grossmächte in der Anfangsphase der nationalsozialistischen Herrschaft in Deutschland* (Bonn: Voggenreiter, 1973), 12-13; and Hillgruber, *Germany and the Two World Wars,* 50-51.
2. For examples of other diplomats who disclaimed their service to Hitler note Weizsäcker, 50; Dirksen, 49; Zechlin, *Pressechef,* 57; and Kordt, 32-50.
3. See Neurath's report, based on a memo of Bülow's, to the conference of ministers that met with Hitler on 7 Apr. 1933, *Documents on German Foreign Policy, 1918-1945,* Series C, 6 vols. (hereafter *DGFP;* Washington, D.C.: U.S. Government Printing Office, 1957–), I, doc. no. 142. This discourse, together with Hitler's announcement to his military leaders on 3 Feb. 1933 of his intention to conquer "living space" (*Lebensraum*) in the East (see an excerpt of General Liebmann's memo on the meeting in Michalka and Niedhart, 372-73 [no. 219]), formed the guiding principles of the new regime. Note further, Wollstein, 14-17, 18, 27-30; Weinberg, *Foreign Policy,* I:9-11; Jacobsen, 28-34, 466; and Hillgruber, *Germany and the Two World Wars,* 76-77.
4. Prüfer's claims in this regard are in his "Schweizer Tagebuch," entry for 18 Apr. 1945, OPC/KO. See, moreover, Kordt, 50-51; Weizsäcker, 85-87; Hentig, 289-92; and Dirksen, 107-8. An excellent rebuttal to the view that the conservatives would moderate or oust Hitler is in Weinberg, *Foreign Policy,* I:28, n. 14. According to the figures of the AA itself, only sixty-four of the roughly 2,500 employees of the ministry and its foreign missions were Nazi members before 1933; AA, "Parteimitglieder, Stand 30.6.1937," T-120/78/60148. Note, moreover, Jacobsen, 137; Seabury, 28-33; Donald M. McKale, *The Swastika Outside Germany* (Kent, Ohio: Kent State University Press, 1977), 40-41; and Kordt, 44-45. Hitler's view of the diplomats is in Andreas Hillgruber, ed., *Henry Picker. Hitlers Tischgespräche im Führerhauptquartier 1941-1942* (Munich: Deutscher Taschenbuch Verlag, 1968), 180 (entry for 7 June 1942), 224 (entry for 6 July 1942).
5. This is a theme in his autobiography, especially 24-25, OPC/KO.
6. Peter Krüger and Eric J. C. Hahn, "Der Loyalitätskonflikt des Staatssekretärs Bernhard Wilhelm von Bülow im Frühjahr 1933," *Vierteljahrshefte für Zeitgeschichte,* 20 (1972): 376-410; and Wollstein, 29. See, moreover, Weizsäcker, 87, 89, 270-71; Dirksen, 110-11; and Hentig, 274. Only the reminiscences written by diplomats during the Third Reich revealed the anti-Semitism among them; an example is Kurt Ziemke, *Als deutscher Gesandter in Afghanistan* (Stuttgart, Berlin: Deutsche Verlagsanstalt, 1939), 111.
7. Regarding the attitude in 1933 of Neurath, Bülow, the latter's cousin Vico von Bülow-Schwante, and some of the AA division chiefs, note Christopher R. Browning, *The*

Final Solution and the German Foreign Office: A Study of Referat D III of Abteilung Deutschland, 1940–1943 (New York: Holmes and Meier, 1978), 11–14. Compare his conclusions with the far more favorable assessments of Bülow by Weizsäcker, 106; Craig, *From Bismarck to Adenauer,* 110–11; and Jacobsen, 32–33. Dirksen, 169, for example, noted that the "thinly veiled anti-Nazi sentiments" of Bülow and Neurath "were common knowledge."

8. An element that Weinberg, *Foreign Policy,* I:23–24, observed about many Germans in 1933.

9. Note, for example, his bitterness at Germany's loss of territory to Poland after World War II and the Allied refusal in 1919 to approve the Anschluss, in his autobiography, pp. 70–76; and his letter, "Wie ich den Krieg sah. . . ," February 1919, OPC/KO. See, moreover, Prüfer to the legation in Rio, 1 Feb. 1933, PA/Abt. III/Serial 8709 (*Politische Beziehungen Brasiliens zu Deutschland*).

10. The message to Arslan was in Prüfer to German consulate Geneva, 26 Oct. 1933, PA/Abt. III/L1279.

11. See Kress, "Bestätigung," 24 May 1933; and Heemskerck, "Bescheinigung," 27 May 1933, OPC/KO. Regarding the law, note Hans Mommsen, *Beamtentum im Dritten Reich. Mit ausgewählten Quellen zur nationalsozialistischen Beamtenpolitik* (Stuttgart: Deutsche Verlags-Anstalt, 1966), 39–62, and especially 56 for figures on those purged; Schleunes, 92–110; Schoenbaum, 195–96; Hofer, 176; and Lucy S. Dawidowicz, *The War Against the Jews, 1933–1945* (New York: Holt, Rinehart and Winston, 1975), 55–61. Uwe Dietrich Adam, *Judenpolitik im Dritten Reich* (Königstein/Ts./Düsseldorf: Athenäum/ Droste Taschenbücher, 1979), 63 n. 196 and 89 n. 118, provides little evidence for the claim that it was Neurath and Papen who intervened with Hindenburg to persuade the latter to oppose the law. The best account of the Nazi takeover remains Karl Dietrich Bracher, Wolfgang Sauer, and Gerhard Schulz, *Die nationalsozialistische Machtergreifung. Studien zur Errichtung des totalitären Herrschaftssystems in Deutschland 1933/34,* 2d ed. (Cologne: Westdeutscher Verlag, 1962).

12. On proving Aryan descent, a good summary is Raul Hilberg, *The Destruction of the European Jews* (Chicago: Quadrangle, 1967), 45, 49.

13. Prüfer's son, Olaf Prufer, explained in several interviews that he received this information after 1959, subsequent to Curt Prüfer's death, from his mother. "My mother had discovered these details when Hitler required them in various degrees," he recalled. "In revealing such matters, she was not quite certain where in the genealogical tree the 'Jewishness' lay. She had grown up in an intensely Jewish environment in Berlin; morcover, her father, Friedrich Fehrmann, was closely associated with local Jews (including Leo Blech, the composer) and Jewish businessmen." Anneliese Prüfer's sisters confirmed this to O. Prufer while visiting him in 1982; interviews, O. Prufer, 27, 29 June 1982 and 5 Apr. 1986. Furthermore, during her childhood years, Anneliese Prüfer (née Fehrmann) had numerous schoolmates in Berlin who were Jews; note her small album, "Poesie," 24 Oct. 1912 to 2 Oct. 1923, OPC/KO, which contains the names of her friends and effusions from them. Later, during World War II and after, O. Prufer knew several of these persons.

14. See "Ahnenpass" for O. Prufer, OPC/KO, showing Hirschfeld's death in 1830; interview, O. Prufer, 27 June 1982. Also according to O. Prufer, his father contributed along with the prestigious German Oriental Society (*Deutsche Morgenländische Gesellschaft,* or DMG) to helping safeguard Prüfer's prewar mentor, Baron von Oppenheim, from the regime. Prüfer was chairman of the DMG from January 1934 to August 1939; see Kahle, 2–3. According to Melka, 82: "The advent of the Nazi regime in 1933 might have spelled ruin for von Oppenheim, whose Jewish ancestry was well known. Whether or not, as a frequently encountered story had it, the Nazi leadership considered him an 'honorary

Aryan' by reason of his loyal services to Germany, it is a fact that he was not troubled because of his 'racial' origins, but rather continued his scholarly and . . . political activities, unhindered by and indeed with the active support of the Nazi government."

15. Heinemann, 135–36; Jacobsen, 25–26, 467–68; and Seabury, 28–30. Diplomats who joined the party in 1933 and 1934 are noted in Jacobsen, 627–32. The few diplomats removed for "political" reasons (such as the Jew, Paul Schwarz, consul general in New York) or who resigned in protest against the Nazi regime (for example, Prittwitz-Gaffron, ambassador to the United States) are in Seabury and Jacobsen.

16. Details on the nature of Prüfer's relationship with Bohle are in interview, O. Prufer, 29 June 1982. An example of Prüfer's latent disrespect for Bohle, despite their apparent friendship, is in his "Notizen," I, entry for 19 Nov. 1942, OPC/KO, which notes that Rudolf Hess's flight in May 1941 to England "almost ended his [Bohle's] career—which might have been good." On Bohle and the AO, note Jacobsen; and McKale, *Swastika Outside Germany.*

17. Emil Ehrich (Bohle's adjutant) to Prüfer, 5 July 1938, PA/*Chef* AO/Folder 42 (*Beamte des AA*); and "N.S.-Ortsgruppenleiter aus dem Auslande beim Führer," *Völkischer Beobachter* (hereafter *VB*), 6 July 1933.

18. Bohle to Hess, 26 Feb. 1934 ("Betr.: Personal-Abteilung des Auswärtigen Amts."), *Bundesarchiv* Koblenz (hereafter BA)/Zsg. (*Zeitgeschichtliche*) 133 (*Sammlung Jacobsen*)/ no. 5 (*Personalpolitik 1933–34*); Jacobsen, 469; and Heinemann, 136.

19. I have been unable to locate much on this in the German records; it is noted in A. Prüfer, "Curt Prüfer," 23 Mar. 1959. Dieckhoff mentions Prüfer's absence from the office in a letter to the German legation in Vienna, 28 May 1935, PA/Abt. III/*Politische Beziehungen Indiens zu Deutschland.*

20. Rumbold to Sir John Simon, 3 Mar. 1933, *Documents on British Foreign Policy, 1919–1939,* 2d series, (London: HMSO, 1947–), vol. IV, doc. no. 254; and also on Neurath's role in defending the regime's anti-Semitism, Wollstein, 57. See, further, Adam, 46–48; and for SA attacks against Jews in Eastern Germany, note Bessel, 105–9. The outcry abroad is detailed in Weinberg, *Foreign Policy,* I:38–40.

21. Eliahu Ben-Elissar, *La Diplomatie du IIIe Reich et les Juifs (1933–1939)* (Paris: Julliard, 1969), 26.

22. Browning, *Final Solution,* 11–13.

23. Dieckhoff to Hoesch, 27 Mar. 1933; and Hoesch's protests against the German behavior mentioned in German embassy London to AA, 21, 22, 25, 29, 31 Mar. 1933, PA/ Abt. III/Serial 5740 (*Politische Beziehungen zwischen England und Deutschland*). Bülow-Schwante's distribution of the propaganda to the AA is in Browning, *Final Solution,* 227 n.5. See, too, Wollstein, 57, 80–81; Eugene R. McCane, "Anglo-German Diplomatic Relations, January 1933–March 1936," unpublished Ph.D. dissertation, University of Kentucky (1982), 55–60; and Barbara Benge Kehoe, "The British Press and Nazi Germany," unpublished Ph.D. dissertation, University of Illinois (Chicago Circle) (1980), 75–82, for the details on the British opposition to the persecution of the Jews.

24. In light of the Holocaust, which the Nazis eventually perpetrated against the Jews and other peoples, a further statement in the letter was tragic in the most extreme sense: "We have come across certain reports giving details about women being assaulted, even little children being burnt. These reports are absolutely untrue and may, if reprinted, do very much harm to our cause." Note Ludwig Tietz and R. Lichtheim to board of deputies of British Jews and Anglo-Jewish association (London), 2 Apr. 1933; and German embassy London to AA, 3 Apr. 1933 ("Inhalt: Jüdische Delegation in London."), PA/Abt. III/ 5740. Regarding those present to discuss the protests in the United States, see "Besprechung im Auswärtigen Amt am 30. März 1933," PA/Abt. III/Serial 5747 (*Politische*

Beziehungen der Vereinigten Staaten von Amerika zu Deutschland). On the alleged complaint by Hindenburg and "non-Nazis in the Cabinet" about the boycott, see Adam, 62–63; and Dawidowicz, 54.

25. For more details in this regard, see chap. 8 herein.

26. Dieckhoff, memo, 25 May 1934, mentioning Prüfer's agreement; and Prüfer, memo, 22 Sept. 1933, on Moore's visit with Hitler, PA/Abt. III/5740. Regarding the visit of Moore and the array of other influential British officials with Hitler and the significance for German policy, note Josef Henke, *England in Hitlers politischem Kalkül 1935–1939* (Boppard/Rhein: Boldt Verlag, 1973), 32–33.

27. Gestapo to AA, 19 Sept. 1934 ("Geheim! Betrifft: Bericht über die III. Jüdische Weltkonferenz in Genf von 20. bis 23. August 1934."); and many more examples in PA/Abt. III/L1279. Other sources have noted the division's anti-Jewish views, including Gläsner, 190; and Heinz Tillmann, *Deutschlands Araberpolitik im Zweiten Weltkrieg* ([East] Berlin: VEB Deutscher Verlag der Wissenschaften, 1965), 68 n.264. On the habituation of the AA to the premise that the world's Jews were Germany's enemies, note Ben-Elissar, 135–41.

28. Diewerge to Prüfer, 29 Sept. 1933; Prüfer, memo, 15 June 1933; German legation Cairo (Stohrer) to AA, 31 Mar. and 3, 12, 19, 21 Apr. 1933, PA/Abt. III/L1043.

29. "Übersetzung. Eine Rundfunkrede des Ägyptischen Gesandten in Berlin in arabischen Sprache.," 29 Jan. 1934; Prüfer to Nachat Pasha, 20 Jan. 1934; German legation Cairo (Stohrer) to AA, 4 Dec. 1933; Prüfer, memo, 6 Nov. 1933; and AA (Prüfer) to German legation Cairo, 10 Nov. 1933, PA/Abt. III/L1043.

30. For instance, note his work in renaming a street in Berlin for Simon Bolivar, to honor Venezuela, Prüfer, memo, 9 May 1935, PA/Abt. III/Serial 8706 (*Politische Beziehungen Venezuelas zu Deutschland*); his handling of the problems surrounding the beating in Colombia of the German minister there, Werner Otto von Hentig, Prüfer, "Aufzeichnung," 18 July 1935, PA/Abt. III/*Politische Beziehungen Columbiens zu Deutschland;* and his involvement in the *Bremen* affair, in which an anti-German crowd in New York tore an emblem from a German passenger liner, Prüfer to German embassy Washington, 29 July 1935, PA/Abt. III/5747.

31. "Rabbi Isserman Reports Mumbling in Ranks of Nazis," St. Louis *Globe-Democrat*, 26 Sept. 1935; and Prüfer to German missions in Europe, 13 Aug. 1935, PA/Abt. III/5747.

32. Prüfer to German consulate Geneva, 26 Oct. 1933; and the anti-Zionist stance in his lecture to German war veterans in Berlin, "Die politische Entwicklung der arabischen Nachfolgestaaten der osmanischen Türkei in der Nachkriegzeit," 28 Nov. 1933, PA/Abt. III/Serials 8621, M214 (*Politische Beziehungen der Türkei zu fremden Staaten*). Later, he apparently believed that the Jews should be shipped to Kenya, near former German East Africa; interview, O. Prufer, 27 June 1982. Details on the Haavara agreement are in Werner Feilchenfeld, Dolf Michaelis, and Ludwig Pinner, *Haavara Transfer nach Palästina und Einwanderung deutscher Juden 1933–1939* (Tübingen: Mohr, 1972); David Yisraeli, "The Third Reich and Palestine," *Middle Eastern Studies*, 7 (1971): 343–55; and Francis R. Nicosia, *The Third Reich and the Palestine Question* (Austin: University of Texas Press, 1985), especially chap. 3. Regarding the divisions and lack of coordination in Nazi Jewish policy from the April boycott of 1933 till the end of 1938, see Schleunes, 92–213; Dawidowicz, 61–69, 82–87; Hofer, 178–80; Yehuda Bauer, *A History of the Holocaust* (New York: Franklin Watts, 1982), 101–6; and Adam, especially 204–12.

33. Prüfer, memo, 18 Apr. 1935, at the end of which Bülow scrawled, "Danke nein. B."; and Prüfer, "zu III.0.1788," 24 Apr. 1935, PA/Abt. III/L1279. For background material on the Hilfsverein, note Dawidowicz, 189–90, 193. Bauer, 122, and Max M.

Warburg, *Aus meinem Aufzeichnungen* (New York: Eric M. Warburg, 1952), 151–55, discuss Warburg's prominent role by 1935 in encouraging Jewish emigration.

34. Prüfer, "Die politische Entwicklung der arabische Nachfolgestaaten . . . ," 28 Nov. 1933, PA/Abt. III/8621, M214; Schleunes, 57–58, on the "type of armchair anti-Semitism which resisted self-inspired action, but failed to resist the action of others"; and Glaser, 223, on the "fashionable anti-Semites" who went along with the Nazis and shared significant responsibility for what happened.

35. Wollstein, 57; Adam, 46–47, 89–90; and Browning, *Final Solution,* 11–13.

Chapter Eight

1. An example of the older view that has now been superseded is Axel Kuhn, *Hitlers aussenpolitisches Programm. Entstehung und Entwicklung 1919–1939* (Stuttgart: Klett Verlag, 1970), chaps. 7–12.

2. Gerhard L. Weinberg, "Hitler and England, 1933–1945: Pretense and Reality," *German Studies Review,* 8 (1985): 299–300; Wolfgang Michalka, *Ribbentrop und die Deutsche Weltpolitik 1933–1940. Aussenpolitische Konzeptionen und Entscheidungsprozesse im Dritten Reich* (Munich: Wilhelm Fink, 1980), especially 191–92; and Henke, 30, 40–68.

3. As, for instance, Neurath's report to the conference of ministers and Hitler on 7 Apr. 1933, *DGFP,* C, I, no. 142; and Wollstein, 27–30.

4. Hans v. Kotze, memo, 27 Oct. 1933; Himmler to Reich chancellery, AA, and other government offices, 26 Oct. 1933 ("Betrifft: Spionageverdacht gegen Ackermann, Josef und Panter, Noel Douglas."), PA/Abt. III/Serials 5745, 7287, 7720 (*England: Fall Noel Panter*); and "20,000 Men 'Goose-Step' Before Hitler," *Daily Telegraph,* 23 Oct. 1933. Apparently the *Telegraph* had traditionally been the most critical among Britain's conservative papers towards the Nazi regime; see Rolf Kieser, *Englands Appeasementpolitik und der Aufstieg des Dritten Reiches im Spiegel der britischen Presse (1933–1939). Ein Beitrag zur Vorgeschichte des Zweiten Weltkrieges* (Winterthur: Verlag P. G. Keller, 1964), 23, 26; and McCane, 52. Curiously, neither mentions the Panter incident, which received widespread coverage in the British press and even received Hitler's attention. On the role of the SA in German rearmament plans in 1933, note Bennett, *German Rearmament,* 346–54; and regarding French concern about the arming of the SA as auxiliary police and its potential for expanding the Reichswehr, see Wollstein, 49–50, 77.

5. Prüfer, "Aufzeichnung," 3 Nov. 1933 (sent to Bülow and Neurath); German embassy London to AA, 27 Oct. and 3, 4 Nov. 1933; Prüfer, memos, 31 Oct. and 1 Nov. 1933; Neurath to Reich governor of Bavaria, 1 Nov. 1933; and Phipps to Neurath, 30 Oct. 1933, PA/Abt. III/5745, 7287, 7720. See, moreover, "An Unwarranted Expulsion," *The Times* (London), 3 Nov. 1933.

6. Michalka, 75–79; and Wollstein, 50–56, 229–38.

7. Prüfer, memo, 15 May 1935; Reich war ministry to Prüfer, 13 June 1935; and Prüfer, "Über den Herrn Staatssekretär dem Herrn Reichsminister gehorsamst vorgelegt," 14 June 1935; German embassy London to AA, 18 July 1935 ("Inhalt: Besuch englischer Frontkämpfer in Deutschland."), PA/Abt. III/5740; "British Legion and Stahlhelm," *News Chronicle* (London); and "Ex-Service Men and Germany," *The Times* (London), 20 June 1935. Such visits were begun in 1933 and 1934 with French war veterans and were especially pushed in a speech by Rudolf Hess in July 1934 in regard to England; note Weinberg, *Foreign Policy,* I:170, 173–74, 199–200; Michalka, 69; and Henke, 30.

8. Weinberg, "Hitler and England," 299–301.

9. Prüfer, "Hiermit über Herrn Ministerialdirektor Dieckhoff dem Herrn Staatssekretär gehorsamst vorgelegt," 13 Aug. 1935; Prüfer, memo, 21 Jan. 1936, PA/Abt. III/5740; and Henke, 43.

10. Prüfer, "Die politische Entwicklung der arabischen Nachfolgestaaten . . . ," 28 Nov. 1933, PA/Abt. III/8621, M214; Nicosia, "Arab Nationalism," 351–53; and Hirszowicz, "Course of German Foreign Policy," 179–80.

11. Except for the anti-British view, the major themes are addressed in "Die politische Entwicklung der arabischen Nachfolgestaaten . . . ," 28 Nov. 1933, PA/Abt. III/8621, M214. Useful for tracing his thinking regarding Arab unity and bitterness towards Anglo-French control in North Africa and the Middle East is his memo, "Über Aegypten," n.d. (but is clearly 1919), PA/*Nachlass* Prüfer/*Politische Aufsätze*.

12. Haim Shamir, "The Middle East in the Nazi Conception," in Wallach, ed., *Germany and the Middle East, 1835–1939*, 172–73. When political circumstances demanded it by the end of the 1930s and beginning of World War II, the Nazis set out to rehabilitate the "racial" image of the Arabs.

13. German consulate Beirut to AA, 27 Apr. 1935 ("Inhalt: Besuch des Nationalisten Hozek."); Dieckhoff to German consulate Beirut, 24 Aug. 1933; Walther to Ziemke, 15 Aug. 1933, PA/Abt. III/L1246 (*Politische Beziehungen Syriens zu Deutschland*); and Nicosia, "Arab Nationalism," 353–54, 368 n.21. For the views of Arslan and his reduction by the French to a generally impotent exile by the beginning of the 1930s, note Philip S. Khoury, "Factionalism among Syrian Nationalists during the French Mandate," *International Journal of Middle East Studies*, 13 (1981): 444–49, 463.

14. Dieckhoff to Diplogerma Baghdad, 12 Feb. 1935; German legation Baghdad to Prüfer, 2 Feb. 1935; Prüfer to Edgar Pröbster, 30 Apr. 1935; Pröbster to Prüfer, 5 May 1935, PA/Abt. III/L1294 (*Zwischenstaatliche aussenpolitische Probleme: Panarabische Bund*); and Nicosia, "Arab Nationalism," 355.

15. Prüfer, memo, 10 Oct. 1933, PA/Abt. III/L87 (*Irak: Politsche Beziehungen zwischen fremden Staaten*); and on the demands regarding the German minorities in Upper Silesia, Polish corridor, and Memelland, note Christoph M. Kimmich, *Germany and the League of Nations* (Chicago: University of Chicago Press, 1976), chap. 7; and Carole Fink, "Defender of Minorities: Germany in the League of Nations, 1926–1933," *Central European History*, 5 (1972): 352–56. The latter emphasizes that Germany could hardly continue to pose as the champion of minorities following the Nazi government's anti-Jewish legislation in 1933.

16. See p. 94 herein; and Hauner, *India in Axis Strategy*, 56–58.

17. Prüfer, memo, 25 July 1933 ("Hiermit Herrn Ministerialdirektor Dieckhoff erg. vorgelegt."); Dieckhoff, memo, 26 July 1933; Prüfer to Prussian ministry of interior, 25 Nov. 1933; Prüfer to Berlin police president, 31 July 1933; Rumbold (British ambassador in Berlin) to Neurath, 28 Mar. 1933; Neurath to Goering, 11 Mar. 1933; German consulate general Calcutta to AA, 24 July and 9 Nov. 1933, PA/Abt. III/*Politische Beziehungen Indiens zu Deutschland;* and Johannes H. Voigt, *Indien im Zweiten Weltkrieg* (Stuttgart: Deutsche Verlags-Anstalt, 1978), 34.

18. Prüfer to Franz Theirfelder (head of the German academy in Munich), 13 Mar. 1936; Dieckhoff, memo, 14 Jan. 1936; and Bose to Prüfer, 2 Feb. and 7 May 1935, PA/Abt. III/*Politische Beziehungen Indiens zu Deutschland*. Note, further, Voigt, 34; Hauner, *India in Axis Strategy*, 58–64; and "Rasse und wissenschaftlicher Genius," *VB*, 15 Mar. 1935.

19. Bose to Thierfelder, 25 May 1936, PA/Abt. III/*Politische Beziehungen Indiens zu Deutschland*.

20. For his attempts to negotiate with Britain a return to Egypt, see, for instance, FO to Miles Lampson (Cairo), 15 July 1936, FO 371/20151/J5738. Details of Prüfer's help with the ex-Khedive's new yacht are in Prüfer to Reich economics ministry, 12 Aug. 1933; and Prüfer to Reich finance ministry, 22 May 1934, T-120/4871/L309595–96, L309622. The broad outlines of the Egyptian crisis are in Kramer, 82–84. Regarding Prüfer's ties to the ex-Khedive during the Weimar republic, note pp. 70–77, 90–91 herein.

21. See chaps. 5–6 herein.

22. The details are in a vast literature that includes Gläsner, 55–59; Glasneck and Kircheisen, 25–26; Zehra Oendra, *Die türkische Aussenpolitik im Zweiten Weltkrieg* (Munich: R. Oldenbourg, 1977), 14–16; Krecker, 23–24; and Tillmann, 22. According to these sources, German trade with Turkey increased dramatically beginning in 1935.

On Prüfer's involvement, note his telegram to Diplogerma Ankara, 10 May 1935, PA/ Abt. III/Serial 9842 (*Militärangelegenheiten in der Türkei*). Records of his participation in negotiating for the Turkish export of hides and other agrarian products to Germany are Reich minister for food and agriculture to AA, 28 Feb. 1934 ("Betrifft: Wirtschaftsverhandlungen mit der Türkei."); and Turkish chamber of commerce for Germany to Prüfer, 27 June 1934, PA/*Sonderreferat W[irtschaft]*./Serial 8622 (*Das Handelsvertragsverhältnis der Türkei zu Deutschland*). Regarding his presence in the delegation to Ankara, see AA to Zoelch (counselor of legation in Teheran), 3 Mar. 1934, PA/Abt. III/ *Handelsbeziehungen Persiens zu Deutschland;* and Hans Kroll, *Lebenserinnerungen eines Botschafters* (Cologne: Kiepenheuer und Witsch, 1968), 87. For his dislike of the Turkish foreign minister, Tewfik Rüshdi Bey, and Turkish policy, note German embassy Therapia to AA, 7 Aug. 1933, PA/Abt. III/L101, which he dispatched as an "information telegram" to German missions abroad.

23. Shamir, 171.

24. Dieckhoff, memo, 10 July 1933; Prüfer, "Hiermit Herrn Ministerialdirektor Dieckhoff erg. vorgelegt.," 13 July 1933; the lack of success with the interview in German embassy Therapia to AA, 25 July 1933, PA/Abt. III/L101; and Gläsner, 25, 28–33.

25. Bormann to AA, 20 Aug. 1934; and Prüfer to German embassy Therapia, 23 Aug. 1934, PA/Abt. III/L1279.

26. Gläsner, 190–93; and Hirschfeld, "German Policy Towards Iran," 125–26.

27. Prüfer to the NSDAP liaison staff (*Verbindungsstab*), 23 Dec. 1933; Prüfer to propaganda ministry, 31 Jan. 1934, PA/Abt. III/L88, L1145; and Hirschfeld, "German Policy Towards Iran," 125–26.

28. Prüfer, memo, 27 July 1934, PA/Abt. III/*Deutscher Orient Verein*.

29. Gläsner, 219–31; Tillmann, 18–19; Hirszowicz, "Course of German Foreign Policy," 175–76; Wipert von Blücher, *Zeitwende in Iran. Erlebnisse und Beobachtungen* (Biberach/Riss: Köhler & Voigtländer, 1949), 320–32; Prüfer, memos, 15 May 1934 ("Hiermit Herrn Ministerialdirektor Dieckhoff erg. vorgelegt.") and 26 Oct. 1934 ("Hiermit über Herrn Ministerialdirektor Dieckhoff dem Herrn Staatssekretär gehorsamst vorgelegt."); and Prüfer to Iranian legation, 25 May 1934, PA/Abt. III/L1145.

30. For a discussion of economic ties with Afghanistan, see Hauner, *India in Axis Strategy,* 73.

31. Dieckhoff, "Aufzeichnung," 6 Nov. 1934 ("Hiermit über Herrn Staatssekretär dem Herrn Reichsminister vorzulegen."), PA/Abt. III/*Politische Beziehungen Afghanistans zu Deutschland;* Adamec, 196–97; Glasneck and Kircheisen, 182–83; and Gläsner, 441–46.

32. Prüfer, memo, 13 Nov. 1934 ("Hiermit dem Herrn Staatssekretär gehorsamst vorgelegt."); and German legation Kabul to AA, 19 Sept. 1933 and 30 Oct. 1934, PA/Abt. III/ *Politische Beziehungen Afghanistans zu Deutschland*.

33. Gläsner, 453, 462–96; Glasneck and Kircheisen, 183–95; Alfred Rosenberg, *Das politische Tagebuch Alfred Rosenbergs aus den Jahren 1934/35 und 1939/40,* ed. Hans-

Günther Seraphim (Göttingen: Musterschmidt, 1956), 235; and Dieckhoff to Gestapo, 30 Sept. 1935, PA/Abt. III/*Politische Beziehungen Afghanistans zu Deutschland.*

34. Note pp. 84–86 herein.

35. Prüfer to Diplogerma Addis Ababa, 31 Oct. 1934; Schoen to AA, 28 Oct. 1934, T-120/3299/E577711, E577712; Robertson, *Mussolini,* 97–103; and Baer, chap. 2.

36. Compare Neurath's memo, 31 Oct. 1934 ("Der Herr Reichskanzler hat Kenntnis."), T-120/3299/E577872-875, with Prüfer's, 31 Oct. 1934 (sent to Dieckhoff, Bülow, and Neurath), PA/Abt. III/Serial 8015 (*Politische Beziehungen zwischen Äthiopien und Italien*). Further, see Jens Petersen, *Hitler-Mussolini. Die Entstehung der Achse Berlin-Rom 1933–1936* (Tübingen: Max Niemeyer Verlag, 1973), 388.

37. Prüfer, memo, 13 Dec. 1934, PA/Abt. III/8015. Lengthy accounts of the Wal Wal incident are in Robertson, *Mussolini,* 105–10; and Baer, chap. 3.

38. Prüfer, memo, 10 Jan. 1935, PA/Abt. III/8015; Petersen, 389; Unverfehrt to AA, 26 Dec. 1934; *DGFP,* C, III, no. 402; and Robertson, *Mussolini,* 110–11.

39. As examples, Prüfer to German legation Ethiopia, 13 Feb. 1935; PA/Abt. III/8015; Bülow to Diplogerma Washington, 26 Mar. 1935; Prüfer to German embassy Paris, 26 Apr. 1935; Prüfer, memo, 13 May, 15 July 1935; Prüfer to Diplogerma Washington, 13 July 1935, PA/Abt. III/8025, M219; Dieckhoff to Diplogerma Addis Ababa, 22 Mar. 1935; and Bülow to Diplogerma Rome, 26 Mar. 1935, T-120/3299/E577714, E577718-719. According to Petersen, 391, the Germans refused to allow a Bavarian major, Eugen Frauenholz, to act as a military adviser in Ethiopia, and rejected a proposal by Haile Selassie to settle German youth in Ethiopia for political and military purposes. On how the Italians discovered Steffen's activities, see Manfred Funke, *Sanktionen und Kanonen. Hitler, Mussolini und der internationale Abessinienkonflikt 1934–36* (Düsseldorf: Droste Verlag, 1970), 37–38.

40. KPA (Dr. K. Jung) to Fritz Wiedemann (Hitler's adjutant), 5 Oct. 1935, in Klaus Hildebrand, *Vom Reich zum Weltreich. Hitler, NSDAP und koloniale Frage 1919–1945* (Munich: Wilhelm Fink, 1969), 891; Prüfer, memo, 30 Apr. 1935, PA/Abt. III/8015.

41. German legation Addis Ababa to AA, 10 July 1935, NA/T-120/3299/E577747; Funke, 39–43; and Robertson, *Mussolini,* 142–43.

42. Bülow to Neurath, 18 July 1935, *DGFP,* C, IV, no. 212.

43. According to Prüfer, Hitler personally approved the loan, the payments occurred in Prüfer's office, and apparently for the sake of secrecy, Neurath directed him to keep the copy of the receipts in his personal file; Prüfer, "Schweizer und Indisches Tagebuch," entry for 2 Sept. 1946, OPC/KO. See, furthermore, the receipts for three payments of one million reichsmarks each, AA, "Copie.," 23 Aug., 4 and 23 Sept. 1935, OPC/KO; Funke, 43–44; and Robertson, *Mussolini,* 151–52.

44. Funke, 68–69; and Robertson, *Mussolini,* 152–53. Note, too, Kirchholtes to Prüfer, 12 Aug. 1935, referring to the agreement as "Gracord Menelik"; and Prüfer, "Schweizer und Indisches Tagebuch," entry for 2 Sept. 1946, both in OPC/KO.

45. He chaired the DMG from 1934 to 1939. Note, on the spy affair, German embassy Rome to AA, 27 Sept. 1935 ("Inhalt: Italienische Agenten in Abessinien."), PA/Abt. III/8025; Prüfer, memos, 19 Dec. 1935 ("Hiermit dem Herrn Staatssekretär gehorsamst vorgelegt.") and 24 Jan. 1936; German legation Addis Ababa to AA, 30 Jan. 1936; and Prüfer to Diplogerma Budapest, 24 Dec. 1935, PA/Abt. III/M259. Regarding the changes in Hitler's policy towards Italy between 1934 and 1936, particularly his favoring of Mussolini after Sept. 1935, note Esmonde Robertson, "Hitler and Sanctions: Mussolini and the Rhineland," *European Studies Review,* 7 (1977): 409–35.

46. Prüfer, memo, 4 Dec. 1935, PA/Abt. III/8015; and for the angry remarks against the Italians, mainly by Dieckhoff, note R. Ambasciata d'Italia, Berlino, "Aufziechnung," 28 and 30 Aug. 1935, T-120/3299/E577752, E577753. On one of the Italian memoran-

dums, Dieckhoff scrawled: "What is this? We don't need to discuss anything with the Italians. What right do they have to such presumptuous queries?"

47. See Henke, 95–99; and the survey in Weinberg, *Foreign Policy,* I:218–38.

48. Stressed by Henke, 41–44.

Chapter Nine

1. See his "Notizen," I, entry for 19 July 1943, OPC/KO, praising Hitler's accomplishments from 1933 to 1941. This is also the view in his autobiography, OPC/KO. Regarding the problems of the German civil service in general under the Nazis while maintaining its strong support, (including support of the regime's Jewish policy) before World War II, see Kershaw, *Popular Opinion,* 140–43. According to Kater, 106, higher civil servants joined the NSDAP in large numbers in 1933; they lost interest in 1935, showed a renewed concern for entering the party in 1937, and again stayed away from it in 1938.

2. On the party's temporary membership ban of 1 May 1933, see NSDAP, Reich treasurer, *Verordnungsblatt der Reichsleitung der Nationalsozialistischen Deutschen Arbeiterpartei,* Nr. 45/46, 30 Apr. 1933; "Verfügung," *VB,* 8 July and 9 Sept. 1933; and McKale, *Swastika Outside Germany,* 61. For a list of the new mission leaders who joined the NSDAP in 1933 and 1934, which included Edmund Freiherr von Thermann (Argentina), Ulrich von Hassell (Italy), Viktor Prinz zu Wied (Sweden), and Emil Wiehl (Southwest Africa), note Jacobsen, 627–32.

3. Heinemann, 137; and Seabury, 32–35. Most of the AA's personnel records were destroyed during an Allied air raid on Berlin on 23 Nov. 1943, when the Wilhelmstrasse quarters were severely bombed; Frank, 192–93. The bulk of such records that survived World War II remain closed in the PA to scholars.

4. AA (Grünau) to legations and consulates, 15 July 1935; and Grünau, memo, 19 Mar. 1935 ("Hiermit über den Herrn Staatssekretär dem Herrn Reichsminister vorgelegt."), BA/Zsg. 133/no. 6 (*Personalpolitik 1935–38*).

5. Ribbentrop, "Geplante Reorganisation der Auswärtigen Amtes," 1936–37, in Jacobsen, 315. For a brief summary of the reorganization of the AA announced by Neurath on 30 Apr. 1936, note Frank, 105–6.

6. See pp. 104–9 herein. Moreover, note Heinemann, 139–40; Adam, 125–31; and Hofer, 178–79.

7. Bohle, "Einladungen zum Reichsparteitag," 1935, BA/Zsg. 133/6; and the information on Meyer and Köpke in Heinemann, 139, who also notes that Hitler accused Köpke of having expressed strong reservations about Nazi policy and of uttering "disparaging remarks concerning his [Hitler's] special commissioner and ambassador, Joachim von Ribbentrop."

8. Jacobsen, 122–27; and Bohle's proposal for Hitler and Hess regarding combining the party and diplomatic offices, "Vorschlag für die Schaffung der Einheit von Partei und Staat in der Bearbeitung des Auslandsdeutschtums," 26 Feb. 1936, T-120/1624/E000057-065.

9. Heinemann, 140–45; Jacobsen, 33–34; Michalka, 156–59, 210–19; Weinberg, "Hitler and England," 301–3; and Henke, 47–48, 31, 53, which claims with little justification that Hitler sent Ribbentrop to London "to make the final attempt to arrive at an alliance and partnership with the island kingdom."

10. Prüfer to A. Prüfer, 10 Sept. 1936, OPC/KO; and Hess to Neurath, 8 Apr. 1936 ("Betrifft: Beamtenernennungen."), BA/Zsg. 133/6. On Hitler's speeches at the party rally, note Norman H. Baynes, ed., *The Speeches of Adolf Hitler, April 1922–August 1939,* 2 vols. (New York: Howard Fertig, 1969; first pub. in 1942), I:692, II:1357–59.

11. Jacobsen, 627–32; and Bohle, "Aufzeichnung," 24 Nov. 1937 ("Betr. Legationsrat Schröder."), BA/Zsg. 133/6. Pressure by the party on bureaucrats and government agencies was hardly uncommon; see Mommsen, 39–126.

12. McKale, *Swastika Outside Germany,* 108–9; and Jacobsen, 132–33.

13. The AO's activities were investigated by the Nuremberg tribunals; Neurath, "Affidavit," 19 Sept. 1946, Nuremberg Document 163–NG, NARA/Case No. 11 (*United States v. Ernst von Weizsäcker et al.*)/RG (Record Group) 238 (Collection of World War II War Crimes Records [Nuremberg]); and Frank, 175. On Spain, see Manfred Merkes, *Die deutsche Politik gegenüber dem spanischen Bürgerkrieg 1936–1939* (Bonn: Rohrscheid, 1961), passim, which is often inadequate; and Weinberg, *Foreign Policy,* I:288–89. Regarding the AO in Austria and the other countries, note Daniel Bourgeois, *Le Troisième Reich et la Suisse 1933–1941* (Neuchâtel [Switzerland]: Editions de la Baconnière, 1974), 53–57; Günter Lachmann, "Der Nationalsozialismus in der Schweiz 1931–1945. Ein Beitrag zur Geschichte der Auslandsorganisation der NSDAP," unpublished Ph.D. dissertation, Freie Universität Berlin (1962), passim; Horst Kühne, "Die Fünfte Kolonne des faschistischen deutschen Imperialismus in Südwestafrika (1933–1939)," *Zeitschrift für Geschichtswissenschaft,* 8 (1960): 765–90; McKale, *Swastika Outside Germany,* 105–8; and Diamond, passim.

14. For details on his meeting with Hitler and Hess on the AO in Austria, note Bohle to Reich chancellery, 9 Feb. 1937, Nuremberg Document 2794–NG, NARA/Case 11/RG 238.

15. Mommsen, 91–126; and Frank, 158–60.

16. The procedure is outlined in Andor Hencke, "Einfluss der Parteikanzlei auf Beamtenernennenungen und auf aussenpolitische Fragen," n.d., NARA/Microcopy M–679 (Records of the Department of State Special Interrogation Mission to Germany, 1945–46), roll 2/frame 0484.

17. Bohle to Prüfer, 13 May and 28 Oct. 1937, PA/*Chef* AO/42; Bohle, "Besprechung mit Herrn Min. Dir. Dr. Prüfer im Auswärtigen Amt am 8. Dez. 1937.," PA/*Chef* AO/Folder 96 (*Min.-Dir. Dr. Prüfer*); Bohle, "Aufzeichnung für Herrn Ministerialdirektor Dr. Prüfer," 8 Oct. 1937; and Bohle to Prüfer, 13 Oct. 1937, BA/Zsg. 133/6.

18. See *Mitteilungsblatt der Leitung der Auslands-Organisation der Nationalsozialistischen Deutschen Arbeiterpartei,* 45 (Jan. 1937): 3; 46 (Feb. 1937): 3; 48 (Apr. 1937): 3; 49 (May 1937): 2; 51 (Aug./Sept. 1937): 1; 53 (Nov. 1937): 1; 54 (Dec. 1937), 1. Further, note Bohle to AO, 17 Aug. 1937, T–120/1382/D535587; and Jacobsen, 474–76.

19. "Aufzeichnung für Herrn Ministerialdirektor Dr. Prüfer," 8 Oct. 1937; and German consulate St. Gallen to AA, 12 July 1937, BA/Zsg. 133/6.

20. Georg Vogel, *Diplomat unter Hitler und Adenauer* (Düsseldorf: Econ, 1969), 45–47, 50–51; Bernhard Ruberg (AO official) to Nazi local group Dublin, 6 July 1937, T–120/2956/E471481–482; Jacobsen, 471; and Bohle to AO, 17 Aug. 1937, T–120/1382/D535587.

21. Hentig, 316–17.

22. Prüfer to all officials of the AA, 31 Oct. 1937, PA/*Chef* AO/Folder 41 (*Beamte: Allgemeines*); Haas, "Affidavit," 2 Mar. 1948, Nuremberg Document 13 (Defense Exhibit Bohle), NARA/Case 11/RG 238; Ehrich, "Bericht," 27 Feb. 1937, T–120/368/281487–488; and Hentig, 317.

23. Prüfer to Bohle, 9 June 1937, PA/*Nachlass* Prüfer/*Politische Aufsätze;* and on his attitude toward Haavara, note pp. 107–8 herein. Details on the Pro-Palestine Committee and its origins are in Eva G. Reichmann, "Der Bewusstseinswandel der deutschen Juden," in Werner E. Mosse and Arnold Paucker, eds., *Deutsches Judentum in Krieg und Revolution 1916–1923* (Tübingen: Mohr, 1971), 546–48; and Yisraeli, "Germany and Zionism," 151–52.

24. Of the 330 "personal questionnaires" completed by diplomats surveyed by the Reich government in the summer and fall of 1944, apparently for the purpose of purging the AA following the attempt on Hitler's life, only forty-one had joined the ministry between 1936 and 1938; of those, thirty-three had already belonged to the NSDAP and only twelve held university degrees; see the "Personalbogen," listed alphabetically, in T-120/rolls 2537–2540. Note further, regarding the conflict over the examinations, Fritz Gebhardt von Hahn, "Bericht zur Frage der Benennung eines Mitarbeiters aus dem Stabe des Stellvertreters des Führers als Mitglied der Prüfungskommission für die Sprachen-Vorprüfung des Auswärtigen Amtes," 11 Feb. 1937 ("Streng Vertraulich! Nicht zur Kenntnisnahme des Auswärtigen Amtes."), PA/*Chef* AO/41; and Frank, 166.

25. Of the ninety-two higher officials in Berlin, seven were Nazi members before 1933, twenty-six more joined by 1937, and no records exist regarding the party membership of twenty-one; Jacobsen, 28. By the summer of 1937, 881 of the AA's 2,665 employees had entered the NSDAP or applied for membership; AO, "Parteimitglieder. Stand 30.6.1937," T-120/78/60148.

26. See the "Personalbogen," T-120/rolls 2537–2540; AO to *Chef* AO, 12 May and 29 June 1937, PA/*Chef* AO/42; and Prüfer's party membership card, Berlin Document Center (hereafter BDC)/Master File/*Curt Prüfer*.

27. Prüfer to all leaders of work units in the AA office, 27 Jan. 1938, PA/*Chef* AO/41; and AA memo to officials, employees, and workers in the Berlin office, 30 Apr. 1937, T-120/3968/E044100.

28. Bohle to Prüfer, 21 Dec. 1937, PA/*Chef* AO/42.

29. One can hardly begin to appreciate the immensity of Prüfer's hatred for Ribbentrop in the former's affidavit, 16 Apr. 1946, Doc. Neurath-4, *IMG,* XL:458–59. Much more revealing is his tirade against the minister in his autobiography, especially 33–53, OPC/KO. For the general view of the diplomats towards Ribbentrop, note Seabury, 51.

30. Jacobsen, 627–32; and McKale, *Swastika Outside Germany,* 117.

31. "Strengst vertraulich. Nur zur persönlichen Verfügung des Reichsministers," 2 Mar. 1938, BA/Zsg. 133/6. I have been unable to identify the author of this document.

32. Which infuriated Hess; see Hess's letter to Ribbentrop, 23 May 1938 ("Betrifft: Neuorganisation der Parteigenossen im Auswärtigen Amt."), BA/Zsg. 133/6; and Hitler, "Anordnung Nr. 62/38," 23 May 1938, BDC/*Sammlung Schumacher/Ordner* 378 (*Partei-Mitgliedswesen: Sonderfälle*).

33. The incident is recounted in Kroll, 134–35. Papen was sent in April 1939 as ambassador to Turkey.

34. Browning, 25; Seabury, 74; Bormann to OPG, 23 Aug. 1938; and NSDAP to OPG, 4 Oct. 1938; BDC/OPG/*Martin Luther.* Bormann's marriage to Gerda Buch is in Donald M. McKale, *The Nazi Party Courts: Hitler's Management of Conflict in His Movement, 1921–1945* (Lawrence: The University Press of Kansas, 1974), 61.

35. Prüfer to all missions and honorary consulates, 1 July 1938, PA/*Chef* AO/41; Prüfer to all AA officials, 14 Nov. 1938, PA/*Chef* AO/Folder 100 (*Verschiedenes 1937–39*); and Prüfer to all AA officials, employees, and workers, 30 Sept. 1938, BA/Zsg. 133/6. On the continued dealings between Prüfer and Bohle about lower echelon appointments, note Bohle to Prüfer, 2 Mar. 1938, PA/*Chef* AO/42.

36. Interview, O. Prufer, 29 June 1982.

37. Seabury, 70–71; Jacobsen, 27: Frank, 177, 195–201; and Prüfer's testimony regarding the official date of his removal, "Eidesstaatliche Versicherung," 7 June 1948, Nuremberg Document No. 58 (Defense Exhibit Bohle), NARA/Case 11/RG 238.

38. British power and influence were not as strong in Iran, Afghanistan, and Turkey as in the Arab lands; through such trade, the Nazis sought to acquire fuels, minerals and, in

the case of Egypt, cotton. See Nicosia, "Arab Nationalism," 362–63; and Tillmann, 17–27. What made Berlin more cautious towards and less dependent on the Middle East, however, was the development of its synthetic oil and fiber industries and its increasing reliance on Rumanian oil supplies; Weinberg, *Foreign Policy,* II:242–43. Prüfer's poor health is discussed in his autobiography, 76, OPC/KO; and for his vacation leave that apparently occurred in July 1938, note Ehrich to Prüfer, 5 July 1938, PA/*Chef* AO/42.

39. Weinberg, *Foreign Policy,* II:243–44; Tillmann, 28–31; Hentig, memo, 27 Aug. 1938, *Documents on German Foreign Policy, 1918–1945,* Series D, 13 vols. (hereafter *DGFP;* Washington, D.C.: U.S. Government Printing Office, 1949–), D, V, doc. no. 582; Lukasz Hirszowicz, "Course of German Foreign Policy," 183–86; and Nicosia, "Arab Nationalism," 363–64. According to Hentig, 319, Prüfer sought to encourage the arms business in the Middle East.

40. British embassy Berlin to FO, 30 July 1938, FO 371/22257/N3817.

41. Prüfer to Diplogerma Warsaw, 19 Oct. 1938, T-120/1004/391081; and the background in Weinberg, *Foreign Policy,* II:479.

42. A. Prüfer, "Curt Prüfer," 23 Mar. 1959, OPC/KO.

43. The standard accounts include Stanley E. Hilton, *Brazil and the Great Powers, 1930–1939: The Politics of Trade Rivalry* (Austin: University of Texas Press, 1975), 41–43, 63, 84–85, 141–46; Käte Harms-Baltzer, *Die Nationalisierung der deutschen Einwanderer und ihrer Nachkommen in Brasilien als Problem der deutsch-brasilianischen Beziehungen 1930–1938* (Berlin: Colloquium Verlag, 1970), 8–14, 21–30; Heinz Sanke, ed., *Der deutsche Faschismus in Lateinamerika 1933–1943* ([East] Berlin: Humboldt-Universität, 1966), 9–22, 25, 114; Weinberg, *Foreign Policy,* II:255–59; and especially on the growing concern of the United States for the German penetration of Latin America, Hans-Jürgen Schröder, *Deutschland und die Vereinigten Staaten 1933–1939. Wirtschaft und Politik in der Entwicklung des Deutsch-Amerikanischen Gegensatzes* (Wiesbaden: F. Steiner, 1970), 221–35, 238–39. Regarding events in Argentina, note Arnold Ebel, *Das Dritte Reich und Argentinien. Die diplomatischen Beziehungen unter besonderer Berücksichtigung der Handelspolitik (1933–1939)* (Cologne: Boehlau Verlag, 1971), 401–10.

44. Hilton, *Brazil and the Great Powers,* 65–66, 110–31; and Frank D. McCann, Jr., *The Brazilian-American Alliance, 1937–1945* (Princeton: Princeton University Press, 1973), 54–55.

45. The quotations from the Brazilians are in McCann, 177–78. Alton Frye, *Nazi Germany and the American Hemisphere, 1933–1941* (New Haven: Yale University Press, 1967), 113, called Prüfer a "loyal Nazi." On Prüfer's date of appointment, note "Dr. phil. Curt Prüfer," in Weinandy to author, 29 Jan. 1982.

46. Prüfer autobiography, 78, OPC/KO. On Prüfer's attendance at the meeting, see "Niederschrift über die erste Sitzung der Lateinamerika-Konferenz am 12. Juni 1939 im Auswärtigen Amt (Bundesratssaal).," T-120/64/51571–584. A comprehensive discussion of the conference is in Ebel, 418–23.

Chapter Ten

1. Reiner Pommerin, *Das Dritte Reich und Lateinamerika. Die deutsche Politik gegenüber Süd- und Mittelamerika 1939–1942* (Düsseldorf: Droste, 1977), 82–85; Hans Wilhelm Freytag, memo, 17 Sept. 1939, *DGFP,* D, VIII, no. 86; and Prüfer autobiography, 78, OPC/KO.

2. The idea of defeating the United States and ruling the world had been present in Hitler's thinking since the 1920s. Note Hillgruber, *Germany and the Two World Wars,* 51, 88–89; Weinberg, *Foreign Policy,* I:21–22; and Milan Hauner, "Did Hitler Want a World

Dominion?" *Journal of Contemporary History,* 13 (1978): 15–18. Kuhn, 131–35, omits important sources and mentions nothing of Hitler's ultimate aim towards America.

3. Knox to FO, 29 Aug. 1940, FO 371/24174/A4259.

4. A. Prüfer (Rio) to her family ("Alle meine Lieben") in Berlin, 24 Aug. 1941, and a similar letter from 22 May 1941, noting such punishment, in OPC/KO; and interviews, O. Prüfer, 5 and 11 Apr. 1986.

5. The trip took place from 19–23 Jan. 1940; see the book of newspaper clippings on the visit, compiled by O. Prufer for his father in 1957, in OPC/KO. Note, furthermore, McCann, 178; and Prüfer to AA, 1, 22, 23 Apr. and 27 June 1940, T-120/225/171151, 171162, 171163, 171182, respectively.

6. Pommerin, 87–90; John L. Snell, *Illusion and Necessity: The Diplomacy of Global War, 1939–1945* (Boston: Houghton Mifflin, 1963), 103–4; and Knox to FO, 29 Aug. 1940, FO 371/24174/A4259.

7. Prüfer to AA, 3 Oct. 1939 and 8 Mar. 1940, T-120/223/157078, 157106.

8. Prüfer to AA, 26 Mar. and 21 Aug. 1940, T-120/223/157109, 157154; and Pommerin, 100–105.

9. McCann, 178, 182–84, 190; and Prüfer to AA, 22 Dec. 1939, T-120/223/157088.

10. Woermann to embassy, 18 May 1940, T-120/223/157118; Pommerin, 129–45; and McKale, *Swastika Outside Germany,* 165–66.

11. Prüfer to AA, 8 June 1940, T-120/223/157128; McCann, 181–82, 185–87, 201–6; and Stetson Conn and Byron Fairchild, *The Framework of Hemisphere Defense* (Washington, D.C.: United States Government Printing Office, 1960), 269–71. Woermann had been alerted much earlier by the Brazilian ambassador in Berlin, Cyro Freitas-Valle, to the likelihood of Rio's purchasing more of its weapons elsewhere if the German deliveries were not forthcoming; Pommerin, 98, 104.

12. Prüfer to AA, 18, 21 June 1940; and AA to embassy, 19 June 1940, *DGFP,* D, IX, nos. 470, 518, 498, respectively. This meeting and the subsequent feverish German efforts to conclude an accord with Rio are discussed in McCann, 190–98; and Frye, 127–29.

13. Prüfer to AA, 13 July 1940, T-120/223/157136–137, noting "the plutocratic-oriented and Americanophile foreign minister." On the Havana meeting, which provided for the protection of European colonies in Latin America from the Axis, for inter-American cooperation in suppressing subversive activity in the Americas, and for the collective rather than unilateral enforcement of the Monroe doctrine, note Snell, 104.

14. Prüfer to AA, 3 Sept. 1940, T-120/223/157157; the correspondence in *DGFP,* D, X, nos. 41, 89, 90, 92 (Ribbentrop's circular to all Latin American mission leaders urging them to use trade as a weapon against Anglo-American influence), 118, 299; and the accounts in McCann and Frye. Regarding Olavo Aranha, note Prüfer to AA, 14, Aug. and 5 Oct. 1940, T-120/181/137645–48, 137706.

15. Prüfer to AA, 19 Oct. 1940, T-120/181/137730; and Prüfer to AA, 17 Oct. 1940, *DGFP,* D, XI, no. 182.

16. Prüfer to AA, 25 Oct. 1940, T-120/181/137738; and Conn and Fairchild, 274–78. On Aranha's assurances, Prüfer to AA, 20 Nov. 1940, *DGFP,* D, XI, no. 361; and Prüfer to AA, 29 Nov. 1940, T-120/223/157167.

17. Stanley E. Hilton, *Hitler's Secret War in South America, 1939–1945: German Military Espionage and Allied Counterespionage in Brazil* (Baton Rouge: Louisiana State University Press, 1981), chap. 2.

18. Prüfer to AA, 7 Dec. 1940, T-120/223/157171; McCann, 209–10, 212; and Conn and Fairchild, 277–78.

19. Pommerin, 216–22.

20. Prüfer to AA, 12 Dec. 1940, T-120/181/137843; and on Hitler's speech, Max Domarus, *Hitler. Reden und Proklamationen 1932–1945. Kommentiert von einem deutschen*

Zeitgenossen, 2 vols. (Neustadt/Aisch: Verlagsdruckerei Schmidt, 1963), II:1629.

21. Prüfer to AA, 17 Jan. 1941, T-120/223/157178; and the account of the feud in McCann, 225–26, 240–41.

22. McCann, 246–50. On the raw materials agreement, see Jefferson Caffery (U.S. ambassador in Brazil) to secretary of state, 14 and 15 May 1941, *Foreign Relations of the United States,* 1941, 7 vols. (hereafter *FRUS,* 1941; Washington, D.C.: United States Government Printing Office, 1963), VI:541; and Prüfer to AA, 8 Feb. 1941, T-120/181/137923.

23. Prüfer to AA, 7 Feb. 1941, T-120/223/157182. Regarding his talks with Aranha and Ishii, see the typewritten diaries, which should be used with caution because of the possibility that Prüfer edited them after the war, the entries for 27 Jan. and 6 Feb. 1941, "Tagebücher Band I: 1. Jan. 1941–31. Dez. 1941" (hereafter "Tagebücher Band I"), PA/*Nachlass* Prüfer. About Aranha's remark, Prüfer noted: "Today Oswald was very pessimistic with me for the first time regarding America's entry into the war."

24. Prüfer, "Tagebücher Band I," entries for 4, 12, 30 Jan. 1941, PA/*Nachlass* Prüfer.

25. Regarding Engling, see AA to Diplogerma Rio, 18 Apr. 1941; and Prüfer (and Engling) to AA, 27 Sept. 1941, T-120/181/138094, 138432–433. Note, moreover, "Tagebücher Band I," entry for 30 Jan. 1941, PA/*Nachlass* Prüfer.

26. Twice during the first half of 1941, as Hitler was preparing for the invasion of Russia, he stated publicly that he was unconcerned about Latin America. See his speech on 30 Jan. 1941 in the Berlin Sportpalast, in Domarus, II:1661; and his interview on 23 May 1941 with the diplomat, John Cudahy, in Andreas Hillgruber, ed., *Staatsmänner und Diplomaten bei Hitler: Vertrauliche Aufzeichnungen über Unterredungen mit Vertretern des Auslandes,* 2 vols. (Frankfurt/Main: Bernard & Graefe, 1967), II:551–53.

27. Prüfer to AA, 20 Apr. and 31 Jan. 1941, T-120/223/157198, 157180; Prüfer to AA, 21 Jan. 1941, T-120/181/137887; Pommerin, 235–41; and McCann, 217–18.

28. Prüfer, entry for 28 June 1941, "Tagebücher Band I," PA/*Nachlass* Prüfer; Prüfer, "Notizen," III, entry for 22 Sept. 1944, OPC/KO; Hilton, *Hitler's Secret War,* 208; and McCann, 53. For examples of Caffery's relationship to Aranha, see *FRUS,* 1941, VI:494, 502, 510, 511. Prüfer called many persons he disliked, including his own embassy officials, "homosexuals"; note, for example, references to their alleged behavior in entries for 28 May, 10 June, and 13 Oct. 1941, Prüfer, "Tagebücher Band I." See, too, in this regard, p. 3 herein. On the significance of the Lend-Lease program for American policy, note William L. Langer and S. Everett Gleason, *The Undeclared War, 1940–1941* (New York: Harper, 1953), 252–90; and David Reynolds, *The Creation of the Anglo-American Alliance, 1937–41: A Study in Competitive Co-operation* (Chapel Hill: University of North Carolina Press, 1982), 145–68, 195–221, which refers to Roosevelt's "war in masquerade."

29. The weapons that were eventually bought were not delivered until a year later, however; Conn and Fairchild, 280. Prüfer mentioned nothing of such arms agreements, either in his dispatches to the AA or in his diaries, till 3 July 1941; see his telegram to the AA of that date, T-120/181/138265.

30. Prüfer to AA, 18 June 1941, T-120/223/157218–219; Conn and Fairchild, 296–97; and McCann, 221–31, 234–35. Regarding Alvarenga, see Hilton, *Hitler's Secret War,* 287.

31. Pommerin, 250–64. On the negative effect which such ideas had on German-Latin American relations, see pp. 146–49 herein.

32. Prüfer, "Tagebücher Band I," entry for 1 July 1941, PA/*Nachlass* Prüfer; and Hilton, *Hitler's Secret War,* 39–40.

33. Prüfer to AA, 3 July 1941, T-120/181/138265; and Prüfer, "Tagebücher Band I," entries for 29 June and 2, 4, July 1941, PA/*Nachlass* Prüfer.

34. Prüfer, "Tagebücher Band I," entry for 2 July 1941, PA/*Nachlass* Prüfer.

35. Prüfer to AA, 11 July 1941, T-120/181/138317.

36. Prüfer, "Tagebücher Band I," entries for 19, 22 June, 11 July, and 28 Aug. 1941, PA/*Nachlass* Prüfer.

37. The quotes are from "Tagebücher Band I," entries for 13 Jan. and 31 Mar. 1941, PA/*Nachlass* Prüfer. For his meetings with Aranha, see the entries for 7 Feb., 9, 13 Mar. 1941; and Prüfer to AA, 9 May 1941, T-120/223/157202-203.

38. Such as Colonel Gustavo Cordeiro de Farias, head of the Brazilian arms-purchasing commission in Essen, who returned to Brazil in the spring of 1941; McCann, 241. In addition to McCann's mention of Góes Monteiro's change, note the role of the chief of staff in the negotiations with the United States, *FRUS,* 1941, VI:490, 497. The embassy's few contacts with him were through Niedenführ; see Prüfer to AA, 23 Apr. 1941, T-120/181/138104-105; and Prüfer to AA, 26 Aug. 1941, T-120/223/157273-274. Prüfer met the staff chief on 6 Jan., 28 May, and 7 June 1941, "Tagebücher Band I," PA/*Nachlass* Prüfer.

39. This is the view in McCann, 227; Hilton, *Hitler's Secret War,* 22-24; and Frye, 127-29.

40. Caffery to secretary of state, 27 June 1941, *FRUS,* 1941, VI:502.

41. For example, Prüfer, "Tagebücher Band I," entry for 12 Feb. 1941, PA/*Nachlass* Prüfer; and Hilton, *Hitler's Secret War,* 287. On Vergara, Prüfer informed the AA on 24 Mar. 1941, T-120/223/157191: "V. is friendly to Germany and has connections to the embassy."

42. Prüfer, "Tagebücher Band I," entry for 21 June 1941, PA/*Nachlass* Prüfer. This was the first of several references to race that Prüfer made in his diaries; for its possible significance in his political attitudes, see pp. 158, 180, 185 herein.

43. Prüfer to AA, 7, 18 June 1941; and Ribbentrop to embassy, 11 June 1941, *DGFP,* D, XII, nos. 601, 642, 613, respectively. On Vargas's sincerity, Prüfer to AA, 18 June 1941, *DGFP,* D, XII, no. 642: "I had the impression that the President is also very much concerned about the situation here."

44. Wiehl, memo, 10 June 1941, *DGFP,* D, XII, no. 612. On Ribbentrop's disagreement with Hitler, note Seabury, 115-18; Robert Cecil, *Hitler's Decision to Invade Russia 1941* (London: Davis-Poynter, 1975), 105; and Barton Whaley, *Codeword Barbarossa* (Cambridge: MIT Press, 1973), 17.

45. Pommerin, 118-19, 293-94; AA to Diplogerma Rio, 23 June 1941; and Prüfer to AA, 22 June 1941, T-120/181/138275, 138272. On the *Windhuk,* see Prüfer to AA, 25 Oct. 1941, T-120/223/157284-285; and Pommerin, 294.

46. This particularly emerged in September 1941. Note Conn and Fairchild, 133-35; Michael Salewski, *Die deutsche Seekriegsleitung 1935-1945,* 3 vols. (Frankfurt/Main: Bernard & Graefe, 1970), I:503-5; Reynolds, 216-21; and Langer and Gleason, 677-92, 742-60.

47. See McCann, 232, 242-46; Conn and Fairchild, 290-301; and "Lend-Lease Agreement Between the United States and Brazil, Signed at Washington, October 1, 1941," *FRUS,* 1941, VI:534-36.

48. For Dutra's complaint see Prüfer to AA, 9, 10 Nov. 1941, T-120/223/157296-297, 157301-303; and Prüfer to AA, 6 Nov. 1941, *DGFP,* D, XIII, no. 450. For mention of the problems by the Americans, note Caffery to secretary of state, 3 Nov. 1941, *FRUS,* 1941, VI:538. It is uncertain whether Dutra threatened to resign; McCann, 255, mentions nothing of this episode, but says that the war minister considered leaving the government during the Rio conference of American foreign ministers in January 1942.

49. Prüfer to AA, 11 Nov. 1941, T-120/223/157307-308; and McCann, 250.

50. Prüfer to AA, 29 Nov. 1941, *DGFP,* D, XIII, no. 520; and Prüfer to AA, 13, 16, 22 Nov. 1941, T-120/223/157309-310, 157313, 157321.

51. The best studies on Hitler's motives are Gerhard L. Weinberg, *World in the Balance: Behind the Scenes of World War II* (Hanover, N.H. and London: University Press of New England, 1981), 75–95; Hauner, "Did Hitler Want a World Dominion?" 15–32; Holger H. Herwig, "Prelude to *Weltblitzkrieg:* Germany's Naval Policy Towards the United States, 1939–41," *Journal of Modern History,* 43 (1971): 667–68; and Hillgruber, *Germany and the Two World Wars,* 94–95, which emphasizes the strategic nature of the dictator's decision.

52. Caffery to secretary of state, 8 Dec. 1941, *FRUS,* 1941, VI:73–74; McCann, 250; and Snell, 105.

53. Prüfer to AA, 9, 10, 11, 15, 20 Dec. 1941, T-120/223/157336, 157338–340, 157342, 157346–349, 157354, respectively. On the suspension of the Lati flights, note Caffery to secretary of state, 23 Dec. 1941, *FRUS,* 1941, VI:528; Conn and Fairchild, 248; and Pommerin, 245. For the British judgment of Nobre de Mello, see Knox to FO, 29 Aug. 1940, FO 371/24174/A4259; and Sir N. Charles (Rio de Janeiro) to FO, 29 Mar. 1943, FO 371/33651/A3706.

54. Prüfer to AA, 21 Dec. 1941, T-120/223/157357; Hilton, *Hitler's Secret War,* 156–57, 221–22, 242; and Prüfer, "Tagebücher Band I," entries for 16, 17, 24, 31 Dec. 1941, PA/*Nachlass* Prüfer.

55. Pommerin, 295; and Prüfer to AA, 12 Dec. 1941, T-120/223/157343.

56. Prüfer to AA, 9 Dec. 1941, T-120/223/157334, 157337. Details on the use of bribery by some German diplomats and on Ribbentrop's propaganda offensive for the Rio conference are in Pommerin, 311, 318–20. A discussion of the German efforts to employ Spain and Portugal to influence matters is in Klaus-Jörg Ruhl, *Spanien im Zweiten Weltkrieg. Franco, die Falange und das 'Dritte Reich'* (Hamburg: Hofmann und Campe Verlag, 1975), 78–79.

57. Prüfer, "Tagebücher Band I," entry for 12 Dec. 1941, PA/*Nachlass* Prüfer.

58. Ibid., entry for 20 Dec. 1941.

59. Prüfer, "Tagebücher Band II: 2. Januar 1942–16.8.1942" (hereafter "Tagebücher Band II"), entry for 2 Jan. 1942, PA/*Nachlass* Prüfer; and McCann, 252.

60. Prüfer to AA, 16, 17 Jan. 1942, T-120/223/157391, 157395.

61. Prüfer to AA, 17 Jan. 1942, T-120/223/157392.

62. McCann, 254; Prüfer and Bohny to AA, 17 Jan. 1942, T-120/223/157393.

63. Prüfer, "Tagebücher Band II," entry for 21 Jan. 1942, PA/*Nachlass* Prüfer; Prüfer to AA, 20, 21 Jan. 1942, T-120/223/157396, 157398; and Woermann, memo, 22 Jan. 1942, T-120/223/157401.

64. Prüfer to AA, 27 Jan. 1942, T-120/223/157412; and McCann, 254–56.

65. McCann, 255–56; Pommerin, 324–33; Snell, 105; and Thomas A. Bailey, *A Diplomatic History of the American People* (New York: Appleton-Century-Crofts, 1955), 830.

66. Prüfer, "Tagebücher Band II," entry for 11 Feb. 1942, PA/*Nachlass* Prüfer; Hilton, *Hitler's Secret War,* 181; and mention of Aranha's assurances through Nabuco of fair treatment in Prüfer to AA, 28 Jan. 1942, T-120/223/157415.

67. On the confinement to the embassy, see German embassy Madrid to AA, 26 Feb. 1942; Woermann, memo, 14, 27 Feb. 1942, T-120/223/157444, 157437–438, 157448; and McCann, 275–76.

68. Hilton, *Hitler's Secret War,* chap. 9.

69. Prüfer, "Tagebücher Band II," entry for 12 Mar. 1942, PA/*Nachlass* Prüfer; and Hilton, 236.

70. Hilton, 237–39, 242, 250–51; and Caffery to secretary of state, 27 Mar. 1942, *Frus,* 1942, V:191.

71. Hilton, pp. 262–74.

72. "Brasilien und die Achsenmächte," *Neue Zürcher Zeitung,* 8 May 1942; and Prüfer, "Tagebücher Band II," entries for 10, 16, 19, 23, 24 Apr. and 2 May 1942, PA/*Nachlass* Prüfer.

73. Prüfer, "Tagebücher Band II," entry for 2 June 1942, PA/*Nachlass* Prüfer.

74. Ibid., entry for 11 May 1942.

75. "Perhaps the fall of Tobruk will ease the fate of the prisoners," he wrote in his diary. See ibid., entries for 10, 16, 18, 22 June 1942; and Hilton, *Hitler's Secret War,* 255–57.

76. Louis P. Lochner, ed., *The Goebbels Diaries* (New York: Doubleday, 1948), 145 (entry for 26 Mar. 1942); and Hilton, *Hitler's Secret War,* 257–58.

77. Regarding Prüfer's criticism of the German radio's attack on Aranha, see his "Tagebücher Band II," entry for 7 June 1942, PA/*Nachlass* Prüfer; and on his differences with Niedenführ, entry for 17 Apr. 1942.

78. Ibid., entry for 4 Aug. 1942.

79. For Prüfer's claim that he sent the telegram, see the version of his diaries that he "revised" after the war and for a brief time intended to publish, entry for 18 Oct. 1942, OPC/KO. He made no mention of contacting Berlin in his Brazil diaries, "Tagebücher Band II," entries for 4–16 Aug. 1942, PA/*Nachlass* Prüfer.

80. He wrote on 11 Aug. 1942: "The collapse of the Russians in the Caucasus, the Japanese sea victory near the Solomon islands, and the Indian revolution begin to make themselves powerfully felt in the local press. The all too wild attacks on Germany have abated. . . ." See "Tagebücher Band II," entries for 10, 11, 13 Aug. 1942. Nascimento was arrested and his spy ring destroyed in Sept.; Hilton, *Hitler's Secret War,* 261, 275–76.

Chapter Eleven

1. "Die Heimkehrer aus Brasilien," *Frankfurter Zeitung,* 18 Oct. 1942; and "Empfang der deutschen Heimkehrer aus Brasilien," *Deutsche Allgemeine Zeitung,* 16 Oct. 1942.

2. According to Prüfer's account, which is not verified in the AA records, the telegram was later found buried and unnoticed in a file of a member of Ribbentrop's personal staff, Gustav Adolf Steengracht von Moyland. Note Prüfer's "revised" diaries, entries for 18, 22, 23, 25 Oct. 1942, OPC/KO; and p. 163 herein.

3. See, for example, the secret public opinion report of the SS security service (*Sicherheitsdienst,* or SD), Nr. 314, 3 Sept. 1942, Heinz Boberach, ed., *Meldungen aus dem Reich: Die geheimen Lageberichte des Sicherheitsdienstes der SS 1938–1945,* 17 vols. (Herrsching: Pawlak Verlag, 1984), XI:4164–65. The standard works on German public opinion during this part of the war are Steinert, 166–68; and Kershaw, *Popular Opinion,* chaps. 7–9. Also see Earl R. Beck, *Under the Bombs: The German Home Front, 1942–1945* (Lexington: University of Kentucky Press, 1986). Regarding Prüfer's lifestyle in Germany from November 1942 to September 1943, see his "Notizen," I, passim, OPC/KO.

4. Prüfer, "Notizen," I, entry for 11 Nov. 1942, OPC/KO.

5. Seabury, chaps. 4–6; and Frank, 124–30, 135–36. The figures for the expansion of the ministry under Ribbentrop are from Jacobsen, 24.

6. Prüfer, "Notizen," I, entries for 13, 17, 24 Nov. 1942, OPC/KO. On the dispute, see pp. 169–73 herein.

7. Browning, *Final Solution;* Schröder, 215–18; and George H. Stein, *The Waffen SS: Hitler's Elite Guard at War, 1939–1945* (Ithaca: Cornell University Press, 1966), 179–90.

8. Prüfer, "Notizen," I, entries for 8, 16, Dec. 1942, OPC/KO.

9. The literature on this is vast and includes Tillmann, 227–423; Schröder, passim; Lukasz Hirszowicz, *The Third Reich and the Arab East* (London: Routledge & Kegan Paul, 1966), 74–268; Mohamed-Kamal Al-Dessouki, "Hitler und der Nahe Osten," unpublished Ph.D. dissertation, Freie Universität Berlin (1963), 33–136; Joseph Nevo, "Al-Hajj Amin and the British in World War II," *Middle Eastern Studies,* 20 (1984): 9–14; J. C. Hurewitz, *The Struggle for Palestine* (New York: Greenwood, 1968; first pub. 1950), 146–55; Anthony R. De Luca, " 'Der Grossmufti' in Berlin: The Politics of Collaboration," *International Journal of Middle East Studies,* 10 (1979): 127–33; and Nicholas Bethell, *The Palestine Triangle: The Struggle for the Holy Land, 1935–1948* (New York: G. P. Putnam's Sons, 1979), 105–9.

10. Tillmann, 426–27; De Luca, 133; Grobba, 281–89; and Hirszowicz, *Third Reich and the Arab East,* 259–68. See, too, Grobba, memo ("Inhalt: Stellungnahme zu der Niederschrift des Gesandter Ettel betreffend Anerkennung des Grossmufti als Leiter der Geheimorganisation 'Die Arabische Nation.' "), 19 Oct. 1942; and Ettel, "Übersetzung einer Denkschrift, die der Grossmufti Anfang Oktober 1942 dem Gesandten Ettel in Rom übergab," n.d., PA/*Handakten* Ettel/Serials 1473, 1642 (*Grossmufti, 1942*).

11. Prüfer, "Notizen," I, entry for 23 Nov. 1942, OPC/KO; Schröder, 220–28; Tillmann, 428, which discusses the meeting between the AA and OKW based on materials from the *Deutsches Zentralarchiv* in Potsdam; Husayni, "Denkschrift über die Verlegung des Lagers Sunion," 29 Aug. 1942; and Ettel, "Aufzeichnung," 20 Oct. 1942, PA/*Handakten* Ettel/1473, 1642.

12. His memo for Weizsäcker and Woermann of 3 Dec. 1942 is in Tillmann, 432–33. Regarding Rahn, see Hirszowicz, *Third Reich and the Arab East,* 271–87; and Rudolf Rahn, *Ruheloses Leben: Aufzeichnungen und Erinnerungen* (Düsseldorf: Diderichs Verlag, 1949), 198–215. A good summary of nationalism in the Maghreb and its relation to Germany in the war is George Kirk, *Survey of International Affairs, 1939–1946: The Middle East in the War* (London: Oxford University Press, 1953), 405–14.

13. Prüfer, "Notizen," I, entry for 9 Dec. 1942, OPC/KO; and Weizsäcker, memo, 10 Dec. 1942, PA/*Handakten* Ettel/Serials 1433, 1642 (*Tunis: Arab. Lehrabt. d. Grossmufti 1942–43*).

14. Tillmann, 437; and Hirszowicz, *Third Reich and Arab East,* 289–90.

15. Woermann, memo, 14 Dec. 1942 ("Hiermit Herrn Botschafter Prüfer mit der Bitte, einen Vorschlag für einen Ausweg zu machen."), PA/*Handakten* Ettel/Serial 930 (*Grossmufti: allgem. alphab. 1942–44*).

16. Grobba to Prüfer, 28, 29 Dec. 1942, T-120/4367/371699–700, 371701. Note further, Melchers, memo, 16 Dec. 1942; Ettel, memo, 16 Dec. 1942; Prüfer, memo ("Hiermit Herrn U.St.S.Pol."), 15 Dec. 1942, PA/*Handakten* Ettel/930 Prüfer, "Notizen," I, entry for 18 Dec. 1942, OPC/KO; and Schröder, 228.

17. Prüfer, "Notizen," I, entry for 14 Dec. 1942, OPC/KO; and Prüfer, "Eidesstaatliche Versicherung," 27 Apr. 1948, Steengracht defense document no. 6, NARA/Case 11/RG 238.

18. See the sources below in note 23.

19. Grobba, "Dienstliche Äusserung des Gesandten Grobba zu seiner an den Reichsführer gelangten Niederschrift vom 2. November 1942 über die arabische Frage," 5 Feb. 1943, T-120/4367/371629–632; Ettel, memo, 28 Jan. 1943 ("Hiermit Herrn Botschafter Prüfer vorgelegt."); and Ettel, "Notiz," n.d., PA/*Handakten* Ettel/1473, 1642.

20. Prüfer, memo, 25 Jan. 1943 ("Hiermit über Herrn Staatssekretär von Weizsäcker dem Herrn Reichsaussenminister vorgelegt."), PA/*Handakten* Ettel/1473, 1642.

21. Prüfer, "Über Herrn U.St.S. Woermann dem Herrn Staatssekretär von Weizsäcker," 3 Feb. 1943, enclosing Arslan's letter, 15 Jan. 1943, T-120/4367/371660–665;

Hirszowicz, *Third Reich and the Arab East*, 290–98; Schröder, 212; and Tillmann, 443.

22. Prüfer, "Eidesstaatliche Versicherung," 27 Apr. 1948, Steengracht defense doc. no. 6, NARA/Case 11/RG 238.

23. Ibid.; Christopher R. Browning, "Unterstaatssekretär Martin Luther and the Ribbentrop Foreign Office," *Journal of Contemporary History,* 12 (1977): 337–40, 343 n.50; Heinz Höhne, *The Order of the Death's Head: The Story of Hitler's S.S.,* trans. Richard Barry (London: Secker and Warburg, 1969), 521–22; and Seabury, 131–34.

24. Goebbels, 289 (entry for 9 Mar. 1943); and Prüfer, "Notizen," I, entry for 27 Jan. 1943, OPC/KO.

25. Discussed most recently by Jäckel, 90: "Perhaps nothing characterizes the relationship of the Germans to Hitler so aptly as a phrase that was making the rounds in those days and went like this: 'If only the führer knew about that!' Being applicable and indeed applied to the petty nuisances of daily life as well as to the great horrors of the regime, it absolved the führer (who after all could not concern himself with everything) of responsibility for specific events and also elevated him to the ranks of the unimpeachable."

26. Seabury, 109–10; and Prüfer, "Notizen," I, entries for 11, 21, 23 Jan. and 3 Feb. 1943, OPC/KO.

27. While she and Prüfer were in Switzerland in June 1943, for example, he noted in his diary that she "is very nervous; her mother's presence does not help." See Prüfer, "Notizen," I, entries for 16–17, 19 Jan.; 1, 3, 17 Feb.; 22 Mar.; 7–8 Apr.; and 11 June 1943, OPC/KO. Her father, Friedrich Fehrmann, died in 1941; interview, O. Prufer, 17 Oct. 1985. Information regarding Prüfer's infidelity, and particularly his affair with a secretary, Fraulein Rohde, is from interview, O. Prufer, 27 June 1982. Best was charged after the war with complicity in the murder of Jews and Poles in occupied Poland; after November 1942 he became Nazi Commissioner in Denmark.

28. According to Prüfer's son, Olaf, Anneliese Prüfer's deteriorating health may also have resulted from her concern for the fate of her former childhood friends in Berlin who were Jewish and who still lived in the capital. O. Prufer recalled knowing several of these persons (e.g. Tilla Münchhausen); interview, O. Prufer, 5 Apr. 1986; and p. 221 n.13 herein.

29. See the "revised" version of his diaries, written after the war, entry for 16 Oct. 1942, OPC/KO.

30. Prüfer, "Notizen," I, entry for 22 Nov. 1942, OPC/KO. A wide circle of AA officials knew about the extermination of the Jews; note Browning, *Final Solution,* 54–55, 72–75. On the general knowledge of the government bureaucracy, note Strauss, 229.

31. Interview, O. Prufer, 5 Apr. 1986; and p. 183 herein. The deportation of Jews from Baden to France and to extermination camps during the war and the state's seizure of their property is in Grill, 355. Regarding the extensive requests from the German civilian administration for goods "from the Jewish remnants" seized at the Lublin death camp, note Scheffler, 196.

32. His example raises questions about the studies of German public opinion in the Nazi era, and particularly the war, which suggest that large numbers of Germans were indifferent to what happened to the Jews. The implication is that such persons were not vigorous anti-Semites or supporters of the regime's anti-Jewish policies. Such accounts, which divide anti-Semites into categories and rate those who appeared apathetic the mildest, include Steinert, 132–47; Gordon, 186–97; Kershaw, *Popular Opinion,* 231–45, 362–68; William S. Allen, *The Nazi Seizure of Power: The Experience of a Single German Town, 1922–1945,* rev. ed. (New York: Franklin Watts, 1984), 291; and Lawrence D. Stokes, "The German People and the Destruction of the European Jews," *Central European History,* 6 (1973): 189–91.

33. This offers further support for those scholars who maintain that public ardor for anti-Semitism resulted in the passivity of many Germans towards what was occurring and that such enthusiasm remained throughout the regime (and, in Prüfer's case, it even survived the Nazi defeat; note in this connection chap. 12 herein). See Hofer, 172–76; Scheffler, 188–97; Strauss, 228–31; Kater, 28, 30, 56, 102, 107, 110–14; Grill, 355–56; Jäckel, 91; and Weinberg, *Diplomatic Revolution,* I:23–24.

34. Stein, 179–84; Schröder, 224; and on the mention of Prüfer and Melchers in connection with the Mufti's activities, Ettel, "Aufzeichnung," 16 Apr. 1943, PA/*Handakten* Ettel/Serials 1474, 1642 (*Geheim u. Geh. Reichssachen* 1943).

35. Andor Hencke (under-secretary of state in the AA), memo, 12 May 1943 (copy to Prüfer), *Institut für Zeitgeschichte,* Munich/*Eichmann Prozess*/No. 1308; Frederick B. Chary, *The Bulgarian Jews and the Final Solution, 1940–1944* (Pittsburgh: University of Pittsburgh Press, 1972), 137; Robert Kempner, *Eichmann und Komplizen* (Zurich: Europa Verlag, 1961), 395–401; Randolph L. Braham, *The Politics of Genocide: The Holocaust in Hungary,* 2 vols. (New York: Columbia University Press, 1981), II:945, 1081; and Gilbert, 578.

36. Prüfer, "Notizen," I, entry for 13 May 1943, OPC/KO.

37. Ibid., entries for 7 Apr.; 8, 17 May; and 18 June 1943. Details of the peace feelers in Stockholm are in Vojtech Mastny, "Stalin and the Prospects of a Separate Peace in World War II," *American Historical Review,* 77 (1972): 1365–88.

38. "Botschafter Dr. Prüfer, Nr. 14," 17 June 1943 ("Geheime Reichssache"), T-120/4367/371616–628; and Hirszowicz, *Third Reich and the Arab East,* 308. Regarding Abbas Hilmi's approach to the Germans in the spring of 1941 as Rommel had forced the British to withdraw from Libya into Egypt, note Schröder, 56–60; and Al-Dessouki, 89–91. Berlin rebuffed the ex-Khedive because it feared alienating the king of Egypt, Farouk, and Egyptian nationalists, with whom it was secretly negotiating for support against Britain.

39. Brenner, "Büro RAM über St.S. U.St.S. Pol. vorgelegt," 9 July 1943; and Prüfer, memo, 19 July 1943 ("Geheime Reichssache"), T-120/4367/371611–613. Although it cannot be substantiated in the AA records, it is worth noting that in an interview on 5 Apr. 1986, O. Prufer recalled that in 1943 (when he was thirteen) he had overheard his father mention that his trip to Switzerland also involved an "economic mission." The son remembered hearing the name of Brown-Bovery, which was a firm that made precision gun-sights, and he recalls that part of Curt Prüfer's task was to trade coal for such sophisticated instruments.

40. See, for instance, p. 174 herein.

41. Prüfer, "Notizen," I, entry for 19 July 1943, OPC/KO.

Chapter Twelve

1. Ian Kershaw, *Der Hitler-Mythos. Volksmeinung und Propaganda im Dritten Reich* (Stuttgart: Deutsche Verlags-Anstalt, 1980), 181; and Steinert, 226–39, 261, 292–93. Regarding Goebbels's speech and campaign for "total war," see Robert Edwin Herzstein, *The War That Hitler Won: The Most Infamous Propaganda Campaign in History* (New York: G. P. Putnam's, 1978), 83–111; and Jay W. Baird, *The Mythical World of Nazi War Propaganda, 1939–1945* (Minneapolis: University of Minnesota Press, 1974), 192–94.

2. On his retirement, note "Dr. phil. Curt Prüfer," in Weinandy to author, 29 Jan. 1982. His personal difficulties are discussed throughout his diaries from the end of 1943 till the close of the war, "Notizen," vols. I–III, OPC/KO. Köcher's suicide in an American prison camp at Ludwigsburg on 27 Dec. 1945 because of his distress over the accusations that he had stolen substantial amounts from the legation, is discussed in Jürg Fink, *Die*

Schweiz aus der Sicht des Dritten Reiches 1933-1945. Einschätzung und Beurteilung der Schweiz durch die oberste deutsche Führung seit der Machtergreifung Hitlers—Stellenwert des Kleinstaates Schweiz im Kalkül der nationalsozialistischen Exponenten in Staat, Diplomatie, Wehrmacht, SS, Nachrichtendiensten und Presse (Zurich: Schulthess Polygraphischer Verlag, 1985), 133 n. 76. Köcher's antagonism towards Prüfer may also have resulted from the minister's belief that Prüfer was mainly in Switzerland on a spy mission. By the summer of 1943, according to Fink, 156, Köcher sought to preserve Swiss economic collaboration with the Reich by halting German intelligence activities in the country. Shortly after the family moved from Davos to Geneva at the end of Feb. 1944, Anneliese Prüfer entered a hospital, where she remained for several months; see "Notizen," II, entry for 15 Mar. 1944. Despite his problems, Prüfer found time to continue his philandering; note, for example, the entry for 8 Feb. 1944.

3. "Would Franzchen be the man?" he asked in his "Notizen," I, entry for 14 Nov. 1943, OPC/KO. Compare his vague program to similar ones of conservative resistance leaders such as Ulrich von Hassell and Carl Goerdeler, in Peter Hoffmann, *The History of the German Resistance, 1933-1945,* trans. Richard Barry (Cambridge, Mass.: MIT Press, 1977), 178-79, 184-91.

4. Prüfer, "Notizen," I, entry for 4 Nov. 1943; and II, entries for 18 Feb. and 14 Aug. 1944, OPC/KO. The racial remarks in his World War II diaries do not indicate that his anti-Semitism had become racist in nature. For other examples, see pp. 158, 185 herein.

5. Prüfer, "Notizen," II, entry for 18 Feb. 1944, OPC/KO.

6. Prüfer, "Notizen," I, entries for 16 Dec. 1943 and 7 Jan. 1944, OPC/KO. Regarding the continuation of the German deportation of the Jews to Poland, particularly from Hungary in 1944, and the growing hesitancy of General Antonescu, the dictator of Rumania, one of the Reich's satellites in Southeastern Europe, to cooperate, fearing retribution, note Gilbert, 637, 662-731.

7. Prüfer, "Notizen," II, entry for 31 Aug. 1944, OPC/KO.

8. Prüfer, "Schweizer Tagebuch," entry for 4 Dec. 1944, OPC/KO.

9. Prüfer, "Notizen," III, entry for 23 Mar. 1945, OPC/KO.

10. Prüfer, "Notizen," I, entry for 26 Oct. 1943, OPC/KO.

11. Ibid., entry for 24 Nov. 1943. The negative effects of the overdose of Nazi war propaganda on German opinion, especially by 1943 and 1944, are in Ian Kershaw, "How Effective Was Nazi Propaganda?" in David Welch, ed., *Nazi Propaganda: The Power and the Limitations* (London: Croom Helm, 1983), 194-205; Herzstein, chap. 12; and Baird, chaps. 14-16.

12. Prüfer, "Notizen," I, entry for 24 Nov. 1943; and Prüfer, "Notizen," II, entry for 21 July 1944, OPC/KO. For German opinion regarding the person of Hitler and his image during the final phase of the war, see Kershaw, *Hitler-Mythos,* 176-94.

13. Prüfer, "Notizen," III, entries for 13, 20 Apr. 1945, OPC/KO.

14. Prüfer, "Notizen," IV, entry for 15 Oct. 1946, and other passages throughout the diaries, OPC/KO. Also in the same collection, note Prüfer to Cardinal Luigi Maglione, the Vatican secretary of state, 10 Oct. 1945.

15. On German disapproval of anti-Jewish acts, see the analysis of the studies conducted by the American government after the war, the so-called OMGUS (Office of Military Government for Germany, United States) surveys, in Gordon, 197-206. The studies are published in Anna J. and Richard L. Merritt, eds., *Public Opinion in Occupied Germany: The OMGUS Surveys, 1945-1949* (Urbana: University of Illinois Press, 1970). Another source on postwar German attitudes is Elisabeth Nölle and Erich Peter Neumann, eds., *The Germans: Public Opinion Polls, 1947-1966,* trans. Gerard Finan (Allensbach and Bonn: Verlag für Demoskopie, 1967), 186-87. On the continuation of stereotypes, accord-

ing to Klaus-Henning Rosen, "Vorurteile im Verborgenen: Zum Antisemitismus in der Bundesrepublik Deutschland," in Herbert A. Strauss and Norbert Kampe, eds., *Antisemitismus. Von der Judenfeindschaft zum Holocaust* (Frankfurt: Campus Verlag, 1985), 257: "Germany is a country without Jews—nevertheless, there is reason to speak of anti-Semitism." Prüfer's example lends credence to Gordon's conclusion, 199, regarding the *OMGUS* surveys: that anti-Semitism remained in Germany after 1945, but that the persons interviewed "may have been particularly reluctant to give 'unfavorable' answers to Americans."

16. Prüfer, "Schweizer und Indisches Tagebuch," entry for 7 June 1946, OPC/KO. For the falsehood of this statement, see p. 175 herein.

17. Prüfer, "Schweizer und Indisches Tagebuch," entry for 24 Dec. 1947, OPC/KO; Prüfer's affidavit, 16 Apr. 1946, Doc. Neurath-4, *IMG,* XL:450-60; and Prüfer, "Eidesstaatliche Versicherung," 7 June 1948, Nuremberg doc. no. 58 (Defense Exhibit Bohle), NARA/Case 11/RG 238.

18. According to interview, O. Prufer, 5 Apr. 1986, regarding this incident: "Endless negotiations; my father displayed public friendship for her, but privately he was anti-Semitic. I was a witness to this in Geneva. Outcome: the property went to Mrs. Kleinmann, although there was some kind of settlement." Moreover, see p. 175 herein; Lachmann, 85; Urs Schwarz, *The Eye of the Hurricane: Switzerland in World War Two* (Boulder, Colo.: Westview Press, 1980), 126; and Prüfer, "Schweizer und Indisches Tagebuch," entries for 7 June 1946 and 28 June 1947, OPC/KO.

19. Quoted from his "Notizen," III, entry for 17 Nov. 1945, OPC/KO.

20. See especially Prüfer, "Notizen," IV, entries for 1 May-4 Aug. 1946; and III, entry for 10 July 1945, OPC/KO. According to interview, O. Prufer, 5 Apr. 1986, Schwarz was the "Bubi" mentioned by Prüfer in the entry for 5 Dec. 1946 and elsewhere; the two apparently also collaborated on a book manuscript (different from the one Prüfer completed by himself in Switzerland) that was never published.

21. Prüfer, "Notizen," IV, entries for 1 July 1946; and 5, 12 June and 19 Dec. 1947, OPC/KO. Regarding the German loan to Haile Selassie in 1935, see pp. 125-26 herein.

22. See pp. 115-16 herein; and Prüfer, "Notizen," IV, entries for 13 Feb. and 14 Apr. 1948, OPC/KO.

23. Prüfer, "Notizen," IV, entry for 25 Oct. 1948, OPC/KO. Summaries of Bose's fate and that of his Indian National Army in Southeast Asia, which he intended to use to invade India and free it from British rule, are in Voigt, 210, 248-58, 293-94, 297-309; Hauner, *India in Axis Strategy,* 592-617; and Bernd Martin, *Deutschland und Japan im Zweiten Weltkrieg. Vom Angriff auf Pearl Harbor bis zur deutschen Kapitulationen* (Göttingen: Musterschmidt, 1969), 80-81, 200-202.

24. From there, O. Prufer went to the United States in the fall of 1954 and studied archaeology at Harvard University. See interviews, O. Prufer, 28 June 1982 and 5 Apr. 1986; O. Prufer to author, 18 Mar. 1983; Prüfer, "Tagebuch. Indien/Heimreise," entry for 27 Feb. 1951; Prüfer, "Notizen New Delhi," entries for 13 Apr. and 27 May 1949, OPC/KO; Voigt, 309; and William J. Barnds, *India, Pakistan, and the Great Powers* (New York: Praeger, 1972), 57-59.

25. Prüfer, "Tagebuch. Indien/Heimreise," entry for 27 May 1951, OPC/KO.

26. Prüfer, "Notizen New Delhi," entries for 29 Nov. and 3 Dec. 1950, OPC/KO. For his other racial comments, see pp. 155, 158, 180 herein.

27. Prüfer, "Notizen New Delhi," entries for 27 July 1951 and 19 Oct.-3 Nov. 1952, OPC/KO.

28. On the trial, note "Die Galal-Vorstellung," *Der Spiegel,* Nr. 17 (22 Apr. 1959), 19-20; and Prüfer, "Notizen New Delhi," entries for 4 Aug. 1951-20 Oct. 1954. A. Prüfer,

"Curt Prüfer," 23 Mar. 1959, OPC/KO, was later uncertain of the date of his meeting with Haile Selassie, but the emperor's visit to Europe lasted from October to December 1954. Regarding Germany's resistance to reform of its civil service after 1945, which coincided with the hiring of many former bureaucrats from the Nazi era, see Wolfgang Benz, "Versuche zur Reform des öffentlichen Dienstes in Deutschland 1945–1952: Deutsche Opposition gegen alliierte Initiativen," *Vierteljahrshefte für Zeitgeschichte,* 29 (1981): 216–45.

29. A. Prüfer, "Curt Prüfer," 23 Mar. 1959, OPC/KO.

30. See Christoph Dipper, "Deutsche Widerstand und die Juden," *Geschichte und Gesellschaft* 9 (1985): 349–80. Regarding the territories demanded for Germany by the conservative-nationalist resistance, see Hoffmann, 178–79, 184–91; and Lothar Gruchmann, *Der Zweite Weltkrieg. Kriegführung und Politik,* 6th ed. (Munich: Deutsche Taschenbuch Verlag, 1979), 332–34.

Bibliography

1. A Comment on Archival Sources

Much of this study is based on the diaries and other papers of Curt Max Prüfer, which are in the possession of Olaf H. Prufer in Kent, Ohio (abbreviated OPC/KO herein). Following the publication of the book, this collection will be placed for public use in the Hoover Institution on War, Revolution, and Peace at Stanford University. The collection contains diaries from World War I, the Kapp putsch and its aftermath in 1920, Prüfer's trip through eastern Africa in 1929, World War II (1941–45), and the postwar era. Also in the OPC/KO is an autobiography that includes a version of Prüfer's diaries from 1942–43, which he wrote after the war and changed from the original. More than any other group of records, these provide a source for examining how Prüfer's mind worked.

Crucial to this book, in addition, are the relevant portions of the German archives from 1920 to 1945, microfilmed after World War II, with the most extensive collection of films (nearly 30,000 rolls) located in the National Archives and Records Administration (NARA). Microfilms used in this study are cited according to their microcopy, roll, and frame numbers (e.g., T-120/2539/E309772). The microfilmed records originate primarily from the German foreign ministry (AA) and the offices of the Nazi party (NSDAP) inside and outside

Germany (including the *Auslands-Organisation*, AO). Records of the ministry before 1920, which include documents from World War I, were also microfilmed by the joint Anglo-American and French team in England as well as by the University of California, the University of Michigan, and other schools and institutions; the films from these collections are cited similarly (e.g., GFMA-UC/ 476/0359).

Most of the unfilmed documents dealing with Prüfer may be found in the *Politisches Archiv des Auswärtigen Amts* in Bonn (PA); of greatest value for this study were the collections titled *Aktengruppe Weltkrieg; Abteilung III* (*Grossbritannien und Amerika, Orient, Koloniale Angelegenheiten*); *Abteilung IV* (*Russland*); Chef AO; and *Büro Reichsminister.* Other unfilmed records include a few materials, such as Prüfer's typewritten Latin American diaries, provided to me by the PA from his *Nachlass*; the tiny remnant of the ministry's personnel files, most of which were destroyed during World War II, in the *Bundesarchiv* in Koblenz (originally collected by Hans-Adolf Jacobsen); a handful of documents from the Eichmann trial in the *Institut für Zeitgeschichte* in Munich; and Prüfer's party membership papers at the Berlin Document Center. The *Institut* possesses an outstanding group of German newspapers, memoirs, diaries, books, and pamphlets from the Nazi period. German documents captured by the Soviet Union that are stored in East Germany in the *Deutsches Zentralarchiv* in Potsdam are cited here only at second hand from East German publications.

Masses of German documents and postwar interrogations were also collected for the Nuremberg trials; these are available in the Captured Records Branch of the NARA. Of use for this project were the papers of the special State Department mission to Germany under DeWitt C. Poole (microcopy M-679) and the original records or reproductions of prosecution and defense documents (which include several interrogations of Prüfer), court transcripts, and court files of the "Ministries Case" at Nuremberg, the *United States of America v. Ernst von Weizsäcker, et al.* (Case 11/RG 238), which dealt with or involved many of the figures in this study. The main group of documents used in the case was the Nazi Government Ministries series (NG).

Especially valuable for examining Prüfer's career before and during World War I in Egypt, Palestine, and Syria is the collection of political papers of the British Foreign Office (FO 371), available at the Public Record Office in London. These documents also provided extensive information on the relationship of Prüfer and the German government to the ex-Khedive of Egypt in the 1920s. Of further use were the War Office files (WO 32 and WO 106).

2. Guides, Archives Inventories, Bibliographies, and Other Reference Works

American Historical Association, Committee for the Study of War Documents. *A Catalogue of Files and Microfilms of the German Foreign Ministry Archives, 1867–1920.* New York: Oxford University Press, 1959.

American Historical Association, Committee for the Study of War Documents, and National Archives and Records Administration. "Guides to German Documents Microfilmed at Alexandria, Va." Washington, D.C.: National Archives, 1958–.

Bracher, Karl Dietrich, Jacobsen, Hans-Adolf, and Tyrell, Albrecht, eds. *Bibliographie zur Politik in Theorie und Praxis*. Düsseldorf: Athenäum/Droste Taschenbücher Geschichte, 1982.

Facius, Fredrich, Booms, Hans, and Boberach, Heinz. *Das Bundesarchiv und seine Bestände*. 2d ed. Boppard/Rhine: Harold Boldt, 1968.

Heinz, Grete and Peterson, Agnes F. *NSDAP Hauptarchiv: Guide to the Hoover Institution Microfilm Collection*. Stanford, Calif.: Hoover Institution, 1964.

Kehr, Helen and Langmaid, Janet, eds. *The Nazi Era, 1919–1945: A Select Bibliography of Published Works from the Early Roots to 1980*. London: Mansell, 1982.

Kent, George O. *A Catalog of the Files and Microfilms of the German Foreign Ministry Archives, 1920–1945*. 4 vols. Stanford, Calif.: Hoover Institution, 1962–73.

3. Newspapers, Journals, and Other Serials

Ägyptische Nachrichten (Berlin)
Der Angriff (Berlin)
Beilage zur Vossische Zeitung (Berlin)
Berliner Börsen-Zeitung
Berliner Lokal-Anzeiger
Berliner Tageblatt
Daily Telegraph (London)
Deutsche Allgemeine Zeitung (Berlin)
Deutsche Tageblatt (Berlin)
Egyptian Daily Post (Cairo)
Frankfurter Zeitung
Globe-Democrat (St. Louis)
Hamburger Fremdenblatt
Kieler Nachrichten
Kölnische Zeitung
Mitteilungsblatt der Leitung der Auslands-Organisation der Nationalsozialistischen Deutschen Arbeiterpartei
The New York Times
News Chronicle (London)
Der Spiegel
Der Tag (Berlin)
The Times (London)
Verordnungsblatt der Reichsleitung der Nationalsozialistischen Deutschen Arbeiterpartei
Völkischer Beobachter (Berlin edition)

4. Memoirs, Diaries, Handbooks, and Pamphlets

Blücher, Wipert von. *Zeitwende in Iran. Erlebnisse und Beobachtungen*. Biberach/Riss: Köhler & Voigtländer, 1949.

Dirksen, Herbert von. *Moscow, Tokyo, London: Twenty Years of German Foreign Policy.* Norman: University of Oklahoma Press, 1952.

Djemal Pasha. *Memories of a Turkish Statesman, 1913–1919.* London: Hutchinson, n.d.

Goebbels, Joseph. *The Goebbels Diaries.* Ed. Louis P. Lochner. New York: Doubleday, 1948.

Grobba, Fritz. *Männer und Mächte im Orient. 25 Jahre diplomatischer Tätigkeit im Orient.* Göttingen: Musterschmidt, 1967.

Hentig, Werner Otto von. *Mein Leben—Eine Dienstreise.* 2d ed. Göttingen: Vandenhoeck und Ruprecht, 1963.

Hilger, Gustav and Meyer, Alfred G. *The Incompatible Allies: A Memoir-History of German-Soviet Relations, 1918–1941.* New York: Macmillan, 1953.

Kordt, Erich. *Nicht aus den Akten . . . Die Wilhelmstrasse in Frieden und Krieg. Erlebnisse, Begegnungen und Eindrücke 1928–1945.* Stuttgart: Deutsche Verlagsanstalt, 1950.

Kress von Kressenstein, Friedrich Freiherr. *Mit den Türken zum Suezkanal.* Berlin: Vorhut-Verlag, 1938.

Kroll, Hans. *Lebenserinnerungen eines Botschafters.* Cologne: Kiepenheuer und Witsch, 1968.

Lloyd, Lord. *Egypt Since Cromer.* 2 vols. New York: AMS Press, 1970; first pub. 1934.

Niedermayer, Oskar von. *In Weltkreig vor Indiens Tor. Der Wüstenzug der deutschen Expedition nach Persien und Afghanistan.* 2d ed. Hamburg: Hanseatische Verlagsanstalt, 1936.

Oppenheim, Max Freiherr von. "Die Nachrichtenstelle der Kaiserlich Deutschen Botschaft in Konstantinopel und die deutsche wirtschaftliche Propaganda in der Türkei." Berlin: Reichsdruckerei, 1916.

Prüfer, Curt. "Der arabische Dialekt von Ägypten," *Bädekers Ägypten.* Leipzig: Verlag von Karl Bädeker, 1913, xxviii–xlv.

Rahn, Rudolf. *Ruheloses Leben. Aufzeichnungen und Erinnerungen.* Düsseldorf: Diderichs Verlag, 1949.

Rosenberg, Alfred. *Das politische Tagebuch Alfred Rosenbergs aus den Jahren 1934/35 und 1939/40.* Ed. Hans-Günther Seraphim. Göttingen: Musterschmidt, 1956.

Storrs, Ronald. *Orientations.* London: Nicholson & Watson, 1943.

Vogel, Georg. *Diplomat unter Hitler und Adenauer.* Düsseldorf: Econ, 1969.

Warburg, Max M. *Aus meinem Aufzeichnungen.* New York: Eric M. Warburg, 1952.

Weizmann, Chaim. *Trial and Error: The Autobiography of Chaim Weizmann.* London: Hamish Hamilton, 1950.

Weizmann-Lichtenstein, Haya. *Be-tsel Koratenu [In the Shadow of Our Roof].* Tel-Aviv, 1948.

Weizsäcker, Ernst von. *Memoirs of Ernst von Weizsäcker.* Trans. John Andrews. Chicago: Henry Regnery, 1951.

Zechlin, Walter. *Pressechef bei Ebert, Hindenburg und Kopf. Erlebnisse eines*

Pressechefs und Diplomaten. Hannover: Schlütersche Verlagsanstalt und Buchdruckerei, 1956.

Ziemke, Kurt. *Als deutscher Gesandter in Afghanistan.* Stuttgart, Berlin: Deutsche Verlagsanstalt, 1939.

5. Document Collections

Akten zur deutschen auswärtigen Politik 1918-1945. Series B. 15 vols. Göttingen: Vandenhoeck und Ruprecht, 1966-81.

Baynes, Norman H., ed. *The Speeches of Adolf Hitler: April 1922-August 1939.* 2 vols. London: Oxford University Press, 1942.

Boberach, Heinz, ed. *Meldungen aus dem Reich. Die geheimen Lageberichte des Sicherheitsdienstes der SS 1938-1945.* 17 vols. Herrsching: Pawlak Verlag, 1984.

Documents on German Foreign Policy, 1918-1945. Series C. 6 vols. Washington, D.C.: U.S. Government Printing Office, 1957-. Series D. 13 vols. Washington, D.C.: U.S. Government Printing Office, 1949-.

Domarus, Max. *Hitler. Reden und Proklamationen 1932-1945. Kommentiert von einem deutschen Zeitgenossen.* 2 vols. Neustadt/Aisch: Verlagsdruckerei Schmidt, 1963.

Geiss, Imanuel, ed. *July 1914, The Outbreak of the First World War: Selected Documents.* New York: Charles Scribner's Sons, 1967.

Great Britain. *Documents on British Foreign Policy, 1919-1939.* 2d Series. 8 vols. London: His Majesty's Stationery Office, 1947-.

Great Britain. Foreign Office. *Correspondence Respecting Events Leading to the Rupture of Relations with Turkey, November 1914.* London: His Majesty's Stationery Office, 1914.

Die Grosse Politik der Europäischen Kabinette 1871-1914. Sammlung der Diplomatischen Akten des Auswärtigen Amtes. Ed. Johannes Lepsius, Albrecht Mendelssohn Bartholdy, and Friedrich Thimme. 40 vols. Berlin: Deutsche Verlagsgesellschaft für Politik und Geschichte, 1925-26.

Hill, Leonidas E., ed. *Die Weizsäcker Papiere 1933-1950.* Berlin: Propyläen Verlag, 1974.

Hillgruber, Andreas, ed. *Henry Picker. Hitlers Tischgespräche im Führerhauptquartier 1941-1942.* Munich: Deutscher Taschenbuch Verlag, 1968.

————. *Staatsmänner und Diplomaten bei Hitler. Vertrauliche Aufzeichnungen über Unterredungen mit Vertretern des Auslandes.* 2 vols. Frankfurt/Main: Bernard & Graefe, 1967.

Jäckel, Eberhard and Kuhn, Axel., eds. *Hitler. Sämtliche Aufzeichnungen 1905-1924.* Stuttgart: Deutsche Verlags-Anstalt, 1980.

Merritt, Anna J. and Richard L., eds. *Public Opinion in Occupied Germany: The OMGUS Surveys, 1945-1949.* Urbana: University of Illinois Press, 1970.

Michalka, Wolfgang and Niedhart, Gottfried, eds. *Die ungeliebte Republik. Dokumentation zur Innen- und Aussenpolitik Weimars 1918-1933.* 2d ed. Munich: Deutscher Taschenbuch Verlag, 1981.

Nölle, Elisabeth and Neumann, Erich Peter, eds. *The Germans: Public Opinion Polls, 1947–1966.* Trans. Gerard Finan. Allensbach and Bonn: Verlag für Demoskopie, 1967.

Der Prozess gegen die Hauptkriegsverbrecher vor dem Internationalen Militärgerichtshof Nürnberg 14. November 1945–1. Oktober 1946. 42 vols. Nuremberg, 1948.

Ringer, Fritz K., ed. *The German Inflation of 1923.* New York: Oxford University Press, 1969.

United States. Department of State. *The Treaty of Versailles and After: Annotations of the Text of the Treaty.* Washington, D.C.: U.S. Government Printing Office, 1947.

United States. *Foreign Relations of the United States,* 1941. 7 vols. Washington, D.C.: U.S. Government Printing Office, 1963.

United States. *Foreign Relations of the United States,* 1942. 6 vols. Washington, D.C.: U.S. Government Printing Office, 1962.

Weizmann, Chaim. *The Letters and Papers of Chaim Weizmann.* Ed. Meyer W. Weisgal, Gedalia Yogev, and Barnett Litvinov. Series A. 3 vols. London: Oxford University Press, 1971.

6. Secondary Sources

Adam, Uwe-Dietrich. *Judenpolitik im Dritten Reich.* Königstein/Ts./Düsseldorf: Athenäum/Droste Taschenbücher, 1979.

Adamec, Ludwig W. *Afghanistan's Foreign Affairs to the Mid-Twentieth Century: Relations with the USSR, Germany, and Britain.* Tucson: University of Arizona Press, 1974.

Albisetti, James C. *Secondary School Reform in Imperial Germany.* Princeton: Princeton University Press, 1983.

Al-Dessouki, Mohamed-Kamal. "Hitler und der Nahe Osten." Unpublished Ph.D. dissertation. Freie Universität, 1963.

Allen, William S. *The Nazi Seizure of Power: The Experience of a Single German Town, 1922–1945.* Rev. ed. New York: Franklin Watts, 1984.

Anderle, Alfred. *Die Deutsche Rapallo-Politik. Deutsch-Sowjetische Beziehungen 1922–1929.* [East] Berlin: Rütten & Leoning, 1962.

Anderson, M. S. *The Eastern Question, 1774–1923: A Study in International Relations.* New York: Macmillan, 1966.

Angress, Werner T. "Juden im politischen Leben der Revolutionszeit." In Werner E. Mosse and Arnold Paucker, eds., *Deutsches Judentum in Krieg und Revolution 1916–1923. Ein Sammelband.* Tübingen: Mohr, 1971, 137–316.

Antonius, George. *The Arab Awakening: The Story of the Arab National Movement.* Philadelphia: Lippincott, 1939.

Aycoberry, Pierre. *The Nazi Question: An Essay on the Interpretations of National Socialism (1922–1975).* Trans. Robert Hurley. New York: Pantheon, 1981.

Baer, George W. *The Coming of the Italian-Ethiopian War.* Cambridge, Mass.: Harvard University Press, 1967.

Bailey, Thomas A. *A Diplomatic History of the American People.* New York: Appleton-Century-Crofts, 1955.

Baird, Jay W. *The Mythical World of Nazi War Propaganda, 1939–1945.* Minneapolis: University of Minnesota Press, 1974.

Barnds, William J. *India, Pakistan, and the Great Powers.* New York: Praeger, 1972.

Bauer, Yehuda. *A History of the Holocaust.* New York: Franklin Watts, 1982.

Beck, Earl R. *Under the Bombs: The German Home Front, 1942–1945.* Lexington: University of Kentucky Press, 1986.

Ben-Elissar, Eliahu. *La Diplomatie du IIIe Reich et les Juifs (1933–1939).* Paris: Julliard, 1969.

Bennett, Edward W. *German Rearmament and the West, 1932–1933.* Princeton: Princeton University Press, 1979.

————. *Germany and the Diplomacy of the Financial Crisis.* Cambridge, Mass.: Harvard University Press, 1962.

Benz, Wolfgang. "Versuche zur Reform des öffentlichen Dienstes in Deutschland 1945–1952: Deutsche Opposition gegen alliierte Initiativen," *Vierteljahrshefte für Zeitgeschichte,* 29 (1981): 216–45.

Bessel, Richard. *Political Violence and the Rise of Nazism: The Storm Troopers in Eastern Germany, 1925–1934.* New Haven: Yale University Press, 1984.

Bethell, Nicholas. *The Palestine Triangle: The Struggle for the Holy Land, 1935–1948.* New York: G. P. Putnam's Sons, 1979.

Black, Edwin. *The Transfer Agreement: The Untold Story of the Secret Pact Between the Third Reich and Jewish Palestine.* New York: Macmillan, 1984.

Bourgeois, Daniel. *Le Troisième Reich et la Suisse 1933–1941.* Neuchâtel [Switzerland]: Editions de la Baconnière, 1974.

Bracher, Karl Dietrich. *Die Auflösung der Weimarer Republik. Eine Studie zum Problem des Machtverfalls in der Demokratie.* 4th ed. Villingen/Schwarzwald: Ring Verlag, 1964.

Bracher, Karl Dietrich; Sauer, Wolfgang; and Schulz, Gerhard. *Die nationalsozialistische Machtergreifung. Studien zur Errichtung des totalitären Herrschaftssystems in Deutschland 1933/34.* 2d ed. Cologne: Westdeutscher Verlag, 1962.

Braham, Randolph L. *The Politics of Genocide: The Holocaust in Hungary.* 2 vols. New York: Columbia University Press, 1981.

Bremond, Edouard. *Le Hedjaz dans la guerre mondiale.* Paris: Payot, 1931.

Browning, Christopher R. *The Final Solution and the German Foreign Office: A Study of Referat D III of Abteilung Deutschland, 1940–43.* New York: Holmes and Meier, 1978.

————. "Unterstaatssekretär Martin Luther and the Ribbentrop Foreign Office," *Journal of Contemporary History,* 12 (1977): 313–44.

Calleo, David. *The German Problem Reconsidered: Germany and the World Order, 1870 to the Present.* Cambridge and London: Cambridge University Press, 1978.

Campbell, F. Gregory. "The Struggle for Upper Silesia, 1919–1922," *Journal of Modern History,* 42 (1970): 361–85.

Carr, Edward H. *German-Soviet Relations Between the Two World Wars, 1919–1939*. Baltimore: Johns Hopkins University Press, 1951.

Carsten, Francis L. *The Reichswehr and Politics, 1918 to 1933*. Oxford: Clarendon, 1966.

———. *Revolution in Central Europe, 1918–1919*. Berkeley: University of California Press, 1972.

Cecil, Lamar. *The German Diplomatic Service, 1871–1914*. Princeton: Princeton University Press, 1976.

Cecil, Robert. *Hitler's Decision to Invade Russia 1941*. London: Davis-Poynter, 1975.

Chary, Frederick B. *The Bulgarian Jews and the Final Solution, 1940–1944*. Pittsburgh: University of Pittsburgh Press, 1972.

Chickering, Roger. *We Men Who Feel Most German: A Cultural Study of the Pan German League, 1886–1914*. Boston: Allen and Unwin, 1984.

Childers, Thomas. *The Nazi Voter: The Social Foundations of Fascism in Germany, 1919–1933*. Chapel Hill: University of North Carolina Press, 1983.

Cockfield, Jamie. "Germany and the Fashoda Crisis, 1898–99," *Central European History*, 16 (1983): 256–75.

Conn, Stetson and Fairchild, Byron. *The Framework of Hemisphere Defense*. Washington, D.C.: U.S. Government Printing Office, 1960.

Craig, Gordon A. *From Bismarck to Adenauer: Aspects of German Statecraft*. Baltimore: Johns Hopkins University Press, 1958.

———. *Germany, 1866–1945*. New York: Oxford University Press, 1978.

———. *Politics of the Prussian Army, 1640–1945*. New York: Oxford University Press, 1964.

Dann, Uriel. "Lawrence 'of Arabia'—One More Appraisal," *Middle Eastern Studies*, 15 (1979): 154–62.

Darwin, John. *Britain, Egypt and the Middle East: Imperial Policy in the Aftermath of the War, 1918–1922*. New York: St. Martin's, 1981.

Dawidowicz, Lucy S. *The War Against the Jews, 1933–1945*. New York: Holt, Rinehart and Winston, 1975.

Deak, Istvan. "How Guilty Were the Germans?" *The New York Times Review of Books*, 31 May 1984, 37–42.

De Luca, Anthony R. " 'Der Grossmufti' in Berlin: The Politics of Collaboration," *International Journal of Middle East Studies*, 10 (1979): 125–38.

Del Boca, Angelo. *The Ethiopian War, 1935–1941*. Trans. P. D. Cummins. Chicago: University of Chicago Press, 1969.

Diamond, Sander A. *The Nazi Movement in the United States, 1924–1941*. Ithaca: Cornell University Press, 1974.

Dickmann, Fritz. "Die Kriegsschuldfrage auf der Friedenskonferenz von Paris 1919," *Historische Zeitschrift*, 197 (1963): 1–101.

Dipper, Christoph. "Deutsche Widerstand und die Juden," *Geschichte und Gesellschaft* 9 (1983): 349–80.

Doss, Kurt. *Das deutsche Auswärtige Amt im Übergang vom Kaiserreich zur Weimarer Republik. Die Schülersche Reform*. Düsseldorf: Droste, 1977.

Dyck, Harvey L. *Weimar Germany and Soviet Russia, 1926–1933: A Study in Diplomatic Instability.* New York: Columbia University Press, 1966.

Ebel, Arnold. *Das Dritte Reich und Argentinien. Die diplomatischen Beziehungen unter besonderer Berücksichtigung der Handelspolitik (1933–1939).* Cologne: Boehlau Verlag, 1971.

Elben, Wolfgang. *Das Problem der Kontinuität in der deutschen Revolution 1918/ 19. Die Politik der Staatssekretäre und der militärischen Führung von November 1918 bis Februar 1919.* Düsseldorf: Droste, 1965.

Eley, Geoff. "The Wilhelmine Right: How it Changed." In Richard J. Evans, ed., *Society and Politics in Wilhelmine Germany.* London: Croom Helm, 1978, 112–35.

Eliasberg, George. *Der Ruhrkrieg von 1920.* Bad Godesberg: Verlag Neue Gesellschaft, 1974.

Erger, Johannes. *Der Kapp-Lüttwitz Putsch. Ein Beitrag zur deutschen Innenpolitik 1919–20.* Düsseldorf: Droste, 1967.

Feilchenfeld, Werner; Michaelis, Dolf; and Pinner, Ludwig. *Haavara Transfer nach Palästina und Einwanderung deutscher Juden 1933–1939.* Tübingen: Mohr, 1972.

Fink, Carole. "Defender of Minorities: Germany in the League of Nations, 1926–1933," *Central European History,* 5 (1972): 330–57.

Fink, Jürg. *Die Schweiz aus der Sicht des Dritten Reiches 1933–1945. Einschätzung und Beurteilung der Schweiz durch die oberste deutsche Führung seit der Machtergreifung Hitlers—Stellenwert des Kleinstaates Schweiz im Kalkül der nationalsozialistischen Exponenten in Staat, Diplomatie, Wehrmacht, SS, Nachrichtendiensten und Presse.* Zurich: Schulthess Polygraphischer Verlag, 1985.

Fischer, Fritz. *Bündnis der Eliten. Zur Kontinuität der Machtstrukturen in Deutschland 1871–1945.* Düsseldorf: Droste, 1979.

———. *Germany's Aims in the First World War.* New York: Norton, 1967.

Fischer, Ruth. *Stalin and German Communism: A Study in the Origins of the State Party.* Cambridge, Mass.: Harvard University Press, 1948.

Frank, Elke. "The Wilhelmstrasse During the Third Reich: Changes in Its Organizational Structure and Personnel Policies." Unpublished Ph.D. dissertation. Harvard University, 1963.

Freund, Gerald. *Unholy Alliance: Russian-German Relations from the Treaty of Brest-Litovsk to the Treaty of Berlin.* London: Chatto and Windus, 1957.

Friedman, Isaiah. *The Question of Palestine, 1914–1918: British-Jewish-Arab Relations.* New York: Shocken, 1973.

Frommelt, Reinhard. *Paneuropa oder Mitteleuropa. Einigungsbestrebungen im Kalkül deutscher Wirtschaft und Politik 1925–1933.* Stuttgart: Deutsche Verlags-Anstalt, 1977.

Frye, Alton. *Nazi Germany and the American Hemisphere, 1933–1941.* New Haven: Yale University Press, 1967.

Funke, Manfred. *Sanktionen und Kanonen. Hitler, Mussolini und der internationale Abessinienkonflikt 1934–36.* Düsseldorf: Droste Verlag, 1970.

Gehrke, Ulrich. "Germany and Persia up to 1919." In Jehuda L. Wallach, ed., *Germany and the Middle East, 1835–1939.* Tel-Aviv: Israel Press, 1975, 104–16.

Geiss, Imanuel. *Das Deutsche Reich und die Vorgeschichte des Ersten Weltkriegs.* Munich: Carl Hanser Verlag, 1978.

Gilbert, Martin. *The Holocaust: A History of the Jews of Europe During the Second World War.* New York: Holt, Rinehart and Winston, 1985.

Glaser, Hermann. *The Cultural Roots of National Socialism.* Trans. Ernest A. Menze. Austin: University of Texas Press, 1978.

Glasneck, Johannes and Kircheisen, Inge. *Türkei und Afghanistan—Brennpunkte der Orientpolitik im Zweiten Weltkrieg.* [East] Berlin: VEB Deutscher Verlag der Wissenschaften, 1968.

Gläsner, Heinz. "Das Dritte Reich und der Mittlere Osten. Politische und Wirtschaftliche Beziehungen Deutschlands zur Türkei 1933–1939, zu Iran 1933–1941 und zu Afghanistan 1933–1945." Unpublished Ph.D. dissertation, Universität Würzburg, 1976.

Gordon, Sarah. *Hitler, Germans and the "Jewish Question."* Princeton: Princeton University Press, 1984.

Gottlieb, W. W. *Studies in Secret Diplomacy.* London: Allen and Unwin, 1957.

Gruber, Helmut. "Willi Münzenberg's German Communist Propaganda Empire, 1921–1933," *Journal of Modern History,* 38 (1966): 278–99.

Gruchmann, Lothar. *Der Zweite Weltkrieg. Kriegführung und Politik.* 6th ed. Munich: Deutsche Taschenbuch Verlag, 1979.

Grunwald, Kurt. "Penetration Pacifique—The Financial Vehicles of Germany's 'Drang nach dem Osten.' " In Jehuda L. Wallach, ed., *Germany and the Middle East, 1835–1939.* Tel-Aviv: Israel Press, 1975, 85–101.

Guillen, Pierre. "The Entente of 1904 as a Colonial Settlement." In Prosser Gifford and William Roger Louis, eds., *France and Britain in Africa: Imperial Rivalry and Colonial Rule.* New Haven: Yale University Press, 1971, 333–68.

Hahn, Eric J. C. "The German Foreign Ministry and the Question of War Guilt in 1918–1919." In Carole Fink, Isabel V. Hull, and MacGregor Knox, eds., *German Nationalism and the European Response, 1890–1945.* Norman: University of Oklahoma Press, 1985.

Hamilton, Richard F. *Who Voted for Hitler?* Princeton: Princeton University Press, 1982.

Harms-Baltzer, Käte. *Die Nationalisierung der deutschen Einwanderer und ihrer Nachkommen in Brasilien als Problem der deutsch-brasilianischen Beziehungen 1930–1938.* Berlin: Colloquium Verlag, 1970.

Hauner, Milan. "Did Hitler Want a World Dominion?" *Journal of Contemporary History,* 13 (1978): 15–32.

———. *India in Axis Strategy: Germany, Japan, and Indian Nationalists in the Second World War.* Stuttgart: Klett-Cotta, 1981.

Heiber, Helmut. *Die Republik von Weimar.* 15th ed. Munich: Deutscher Taschenbuch Verlag, 1982.

Heinemann, John L. *Hitler's First Foreign Minister: Constantin von Neurath, Diplomat and Statesman.* Berkeley: University of California Press, 1979.

Henke, Josef. *England in Hitlers politischem Kalkül 1935–1939*. Boppard/Rhein: Boldt Verlag, 1973.

Hentschel, Volker. *Weimars letzte Monate. Hitler und der Untergang der Republik*. Düsseldorf: Droste, 1978.

Herwig, Holger. *Luxury Fleet: The Imperial German Navy, 1888–1918*. Winchester, Mass.: Allen & Unwin, 1980.

———. "Prelude to *Weltblitzkrieg*: Germany's Naval Policy Towards the United States, 1939–41," *Journal of Modern History*, 43 (1971): 649–69.

Herzfeld, Hans. *Der Erste Weltkrieg*. 6th ed. Munich: Deutsche Taschenbuch Verlag, 1982.

Herzstein, Robert Edwin. *The War That Hitler Won: The Most Infamous Propaganda Campaign in History*. New York: G. P. Putnam's, 1978.

Hess, Robert L. *Ethiopia: The Modernization of Autocracy*. Ithaca: Cornell University Press, 1970.

Hilberg, Raul. *The Destruction of the European Jews*. Chicago: Quadrangle, 1967.

Hildebrand, Klaus. *Vom Reich zum Weltreich. Hitler, NSDAP und koloniale Frage 1919–1945*. Munich: Wilhelm Fink, 1969.

Hillgruber, Andreas. *Germany and the Two World Wars*. Trans. William C. Kirby. Cambridge, Mass.: Harvard University Press, 1981.

Hillmayr, Heinrich. *Roter und Weisser Terror in Bayern nach 1918. Ursachen, Erscheinungsformen und Folgen der Gewalttätigkeiten im Verlauf revolutionären Ereignisse nach dem Ende des Ersten Weltkrieges*. Munich: Nusser Verlag, 1974.

Hilton, Stanley E. *Brazil and the Great Powers, 1930–1939: The Politics of Trade Rivalry*. Austin: University of Texas Press, 1975.

———. *Hitler's Secret War in South America, 1939–1945: German Military Espionage and Allied Counterespionage in Brazil*. Baton Rouge: Louisiana State University Press, 1981.

Hirschfeld, Yair P. "German-Iranian Relations, 1921–1941." Unpublished Ph.D. dissertation, Tel-Aviv University, 1976.

———. "German Policy Towards Iran: Continuity and Change from Weimar to Hitler, 1919–1939." In Jehuda L. Wallach, ed., *Germany and the Middle East, 1835–1939*. Tel-Aviv: Israel Press, 1975, 117–40.

Hirszowicz, Lukasz. "The Course of German Foreign Policy in the Middle East Between the World Wars." In Jehuda L. Wallach, ed., *Germany and the Middle East, 1835-1939*. Tel-Aviv: Israel Press, 1975, 175–89.

———. *The Third Reich and the Arab East*. London: Routledge & Kegan Paul, 1966.

Hofer, Walther. "Stufen der Judenverfolgung im Dritten Reich 1933–1939." In Herbert A. Strauss and Norbert Kampe, eds., *Antisemitismus. Von der Judenfeindschaft zum Holocaust*. Frankfurt: Campus Verlag, 1985, 172–85.

Hoffmann, Peter. *The History of the German Resistance, 1933–1945*. Trans. Richard Barry. Cambridge, Mass.: MIT Press, 1977.

Höhne, Heinz. *The Order of the Death's Head: The Story of Hitler's S.S.* Trans. Richard Barry. London: Secker and Warburg, 1969.

Holborn, Hajo. "Diplomats and Diplomacy in the Early Weimar Republic." In Hajo Holborn, *Germany and Europe*. Garden City, N.Y.: Doubleday, 1971, 155–212.

Hurewitz, J. C. *The Struggle for Palestine*. New York: Greenwood Press, 1968; first pub. in 1950.

Jabotinsky, Vladimir. *The Story of the Jewish Legion*. New York: Bernard Ackerman, 1945.

Jäckel, Eberhard. *Hitler in History*. Hanover, N.H.: University Press of New England, 1984.

Jacobsen, Hans-Adolf. *Nationalsozialistische Aussenpolitik 1933–1938*. Frankfurt/Main: Alfred Metzner Verlag, 1968.

Jarausch, Konrad H. *The Enigmatic Chancellor: Bethmann Hollweg and the Hubris of Imperial Germany*. New Haven: Yale University Press, 1973.

———. "From Second to Third Reich: The Problem of Continuity in German Foreign Policy," *Central European History*, 12 (1979): 68–82.

———. "Liberal Education as Illiberal Socialization: The Case of Students in Imperial Germany," *Journal of Modern History*, 50 (1978): 609–30.

———. *Students, Society and Politics in Imperial Germany: The Rise of Academic Illiberalism*. Princeton: Princeton University Press, 1982.

Johnstone, Theodore. "Dolchstoss: The Making of a Legend, 1890–1919." Unpublished Ph.D. dissertation. University of Kansas, 1974.

Jonas, Manfred. "Prophet without Honor: Hans Heinrich Dieckhoff's Reports from Washington," *Mid-America*, 47 (1965): 222–33.

Judson, Helen. *Edith Cavell*. New York: Macmillan, 1941.

Kaelble, Hartmut. "Social Mobility in Germany, 1900–1960," *Journal of Modern History*, 50 (1978): 439–61.

Kahle, Paul. "Curt Prüfer (26.7.1881–30.1.1959)," *Zeitschrift der Deutschen Morgenländischen Gesellschaft*, 111 (1961), 1–4.

Kater, Michael H. *The Nazi Party: A Social Profile of Members and Leaders, 1919–1945*. Cambridge, Mass.: Harvard University Press, 1983.

Kedourie, Elie. *England and the Middle East: The Destruction of the Ottoman Empire, 1914–1921*. London: Bowes and Bowes, 1956.

Kehoe, Barbara Benge. "The British Press and Nazi Germany." Unpublished Ph.D. dissertation. University of Illinois at Chicago Circle, 1980.

Kehr, Eckart. *Schlachtflottenbau und Parteipolitik 1894–1901*. Berlin, 1930.

Kempner, Robert. *Eichmann und Komplizen*. Zurich: Europa Verlag, 1961.

Kennedy, Paul M. *The Rise of the Anglo-German Antagonism, 1860–1914*. London: Allen and Unwin, 1980.

———. *The Samoan Triangle: A Study in Anglo-German-American Relations*. New York: Barnes & Noble, 1974.

Kershaw, Ian. *Der Hitler-Mythos. Volksmeinung und Propaganda im Dritten Reich*. Stuttgart: Deutsche Verlags-Anstalt, 1980.

———. "How Effective Was Nazi Propaganda?" In David Welch, ed., *Nazi Propaganda: The Power and the Limitations*. London: Croom Helm, 1983, 180–205.

———. *Popular Opinion and Political Dissent in the Third Reich: Bavaria, 1933–1945*. New York: Clarendon Press-Oxford, 1983.

Khoury, Philip S. "Factionalism among Syrian Nationalists during the French Mandate," *International Journal of Middle East Studies*, 13 (1981): 441–69.

Kieser, Rolf. *Englands Appeasementpolitik und der Aufstieg des Dritten Reiches im Spiegel der britischen Presse (1933–1939). Ein Beitrag zur Vorgeschichte des Zweiten Weltkrieges*. Winterthur: Verlag P. G. Keller, 1964.

Kimball, Warren F. "Dieckhoff and America: A German's View of German-American Relations," *The Historian*, 27 (1965): 218–43.

Kimmich, Christoph M. *Germany and the League of Nations*. Chicago: University of Chicago Press, 1976.

Kirk, George. *Survey of International Affairs, 1939–1946: The Middle East in the War*. London: Oxford University Press, 1953.

Kramer, Thomas W. *Deutsche-ägyptische Beziehungen in Vergangenheit und Gegenwart*. Tübingen and Basel: Horst Erdmann Verlag, 1974.

Krecker, Lothar. *Deutschland und die Türkei im zweiten Weltkrieg*. Frankfurt/Main: Klostermann, 1964.

Krüger, Peter. *Die Aussenpolitik der Republik von Weimar*. Darmstadt: Wissenschaftliche Buchgesellschaft, 1985.

Krüger, Peter and Hahn, Eric J. C. "Der Loyalitätskonflikt des Staatssekretärs Bernhard Wilhelm von Bülow im Frühjahr 1933," *Vierteljahrshefte für Zeitgeschichte*, 20 (1972): 376–410.

Kuhn, Axel. *Hitlers aussenpolitisches Programm. Entstehung und Entwicklung 1919–1939*. Stuttgart: Klett Verlag, 1970.

Kühne, Horst. "Die Fünfte Kolonne des faschistischen deutschen Imperialismus in Südwestafrika (1933–1939)," *Zeitschrift für Geschichtswissenschaft*, 8 (1960): 765–90.

Kulka, Otto Dov. "Die Nürnberger Rassengesetze und die Deutsche Bevölkerung im Lichte Geheimer NS-Lage- und Stimmungsberichte," *Vierteljahrshefte für Zeitgeschichte*, 32 (1984): 582–623.

Lachmann, Günter. "Der Nationalsozialismus in der Schweiz 1931–1945. Ein Beitrag zur Geschichte der Auslandsorganisation der NSDAP." Unpublished Ph.D. dissertation. Freie Universität Berlin, 1962.

Landes, David S. *Bankers and Pashas: International Finance and Economic Imperialism in Egypt*. Cambridge, Mass.: Harvard University Press, 1958.

Lang, David M. *A Modern History of Soviet Georgia*. Westport, Conn.: Greenwood, 1975; first pub. 1962.

Langer, William L. *The Franco-Russian Alliance, 1890–1894*. New York: Octagon, 1967; first pub. 1929.

Langer, William L. and Gleason, S. Everett. *The Undeclared War, 1940–1941*. New York: Harper, 1953.

Laqueur, Walter. *A History of Zionism*. New York: Holt, Rinehart and Winston, 1972.

Lauren, Paul Gordon. *Diplomats and Bureaucrats: The First Institutional Responses to Twentieth-Century Diplomacy in France and Germany*. Stanford: Hoover Institution Press, 1976.

Leopold, John A. *Alfred Hugenberg: The Radical Nationalist Campaign Against the Weimar Republic*. New Haven: Yale University Press, 1977.

Levin, N. Gordon. *The Zionist Movement in Palestine and World Politics, 1880–*

1918. Lexington, Mass.: D. C. Heath, 1974.

Levine, Herbert S. "A Jewish Collaborator in Nazi Germany: The Strange Career of Georg Kareski, 1933–37," *Central European History,* 8 (1975): 251–81.

Lührs, Hans. *Gegenspieler des Obersten Lawrence.* Berlin: Büchergilde Gutenberg, 1939.

McCane, Eugene R. "Anglo-German Diplomatic Relations, January 1933–March 1936." Unpublished Ph.D. dissertation. University of Kentucky, 1982.

McCann, Frank D., Jr. *The Brazilian-American Alliance, 1937–1945.* Princeton: Princeton University Press, 1973.

McClelland, Charles E. *State, Society, and University in Germany, 1700–1914.* Cambridge: Cambridge University Press, 1980.

McKale, Donald M. *The Nazi Party Courts: Hitler's Management of Conflict in His Movement, 1921–1945.* Lawrence: The University Press of Kansas, 1974.

———. *The Swastika Outside Germany.* Kent, Ohio: Kent State University Press, 1977.

Macmunn, George and Falls, Cyril. *The History of the Great War.* 4 vols. London: His Majesty's Stationery Office, 1928.

Mahrad, Ahmad. "Die deutsch-persischen Beziehungen, 1918–1933." Unpublished Ph.D. dissertation. Freie Universität Berlin, 1973.

Maier, Charles S. *Recasting Bourgeois Europe: Stabilization in France, Germany, and Italy in the Decade after World War I.* Princeton: Princeton University Press, 1975.

Mansfield, Peter. *The British in Egypt.* London: Weidenfeld and Nicolson, 1971.

Marks, Sally. "The Myths of Reparations," *Central European History,* 11 (1978): 231–56.

Martin, Bernd. *Deutschland und Japan im Zweiten Weltkrieg. Vom Angriff auf Pearl Harbor bis zur deutschen Kapitulationen.* Göttingen: Musterschmidt, 1969.

Massey, Robert F. *Personality Theories: Comparisons and Syntheses.* New York: D. Van Nostrand Co., 1981.

Massing, Paul W. *Rehearsal for Destruction: A Study of Political Antisemitism in Imperial Germany.* New York: Harper, 1949.

Mastney, Vojtech. "Stalin and the Prospects of a Separate Peace in World War II," *American Historical Review,* 77 (1972): 1365–88.

Melka, R. L. "Max Freiherr von Oppenheim: Sixty Years of Scholarship and Political Intrigue in the Middle East," *Middle Eastern Studies,* 9 (1973): 81–93.

Merkes, Manfred. *Die deutsche Politik gegenüber dem spanischen Bürgerkrieg 1936–1939.* Bonn: Rohrscheid, 1961.

Michalka, Wolfgang. *Ribbentrop und die Deutsche Weltpolitik 1933–1940. Aussenpolitische Konzeptionen und Entscheidungsprozesse im Dritten Reich.* Munich: Wilhelm Fink, 1980.

Mommsen, Hans. *Beamtentum im Dritten Reich. Mit ausgewählten Quellen zur nationalsozialistischen Beamtenpolitik.* Stuttgart: Deutsche Verlags-Anstalt, 1966.

Monroe, Elizabeth. *Britain's Moment in the Middle East, 1914–1971.* Baltimore: Johns Hopkins University Press, 1981.

Morsey, Konrad. *T. E. Lawrence und der arabische Aufstand 1916/18.* Osnabrück: Biblio-Verlag, 1976.

Mosse, George L. *Crisis of German Ideology: Intellectual Origins of the Third Reich.* New York: Grosset & Dunlap, 1964.

————. *Germans and Jews: The Right, The Left, and the Search for a "Third Force" in Pre-Nazi Germany.* New York: Howard Fertig, 1970.

Mühlmann, Carl. *Das Deutsch-Türkische Waffenbündnis im Weltkriege.* Leipzig: Verlag Köhler und Amelang, 1940.

Nevo, Joseph. "Al-Hajj Amin and the British in World War II," *Middle Eastern Studies,* 20 (1984): 3–17.

Nicosia, Francis. "Arab Nationalism and National Socialist Germany, 1933–1939: Ideological and Strategic Incompatibility," *International Journal of Middle East Studies,* 12 (1980): 351–72.

————. *The Third Reich and the Palestine Question.* Austin: University of Texas Press, 1985.

de Nogales y Mendez, Rafael. *Vier Jahre unter dem Halbmond: Erinnerungen aus dem Weltkrieg.* Berlin: R. Hobbing, 1925.

Oendra, Zehra. *Die türkische Aussenpolitik im Zweiten Weltkrieg.* Munich: R. Oldenbourg, 1977.

Paucker, Arnold. *Der jüdische Abwehrkampf gegen Antisemitismus und Nationalsozialismus in den letzten Jahren der Weimarer Republik.* Hamburg: Leibniz-Verlag, 1968.

Petersen, Jens. *Hitler-Mussolini. Die Entstehung der Achse Berlin-Rom 1933–1936.* Tübingen: Max Niemeyer Verlag, 1973.

Petter, Wolfgang. " 'Enemies' and 'Reich Enemies': An Analysis of Threat Perceptions and Political Strategy in Imperial Germany, 1871–1914." In Wilhelm Deist, ed., *The German Military in the Age of Total War.* Warwickshire, U.K.: Berg, 1985, 22–40.

Pick, Walter. "German Railway Constructions in the Middle East." In Jehuda L. Wallach, ed., *Germany and the Middle East, 1835–1939.* Tel-Aviv: Israel Press, 1975, 72–84.

Pickar, Eberhard. "Berufsbeamtentum und Parteienstaat: Eine Fallstudie," *Zeitschrift für Politik,* 7 (1960): 225–40.

Pommerin, Reiner. *Das Dritte Reich und Lateinamerika. Die deutsche Politik gegenüber Süd- und Mittelamerika 1939–1942.* Düsseldorf: Droste, 1977.

Post, Jr., Gaines. *The Civil-Military Fabric of Weimar Foreign Policy.* Princeton: Princeton University Press, 1973.

Prager, Dennis and Telushkin, Joseph. *Why the Jews? The Reason for Anti-semitism.* New York: Simon and Schuster, 1983.

Pulzer, Peter G. J. *The Rise of Political Anti-Semitism in Germany and Austria.* New York: Wiley, 1964.

Rathmann, Lothar. *Berlin-Baghdad. Die imperialistische Nahostpolitik des kaiserlichen Deutschlands.* [East] Berlin: Dietz Verlag, 1962.

Reichmann, Eva G. "Der Bewusstseinswandel der deutschen Juden." In Werner

E. Mosse and Arnold Paucker, eds., *Deutsches Judentum in Krieg und Revolution 1916–1923*. Tübingen: Mohr, 1971, 511–612.

Reynolds, David. *The Creation of the Anglo-American Alliance, 1937–41: A Study in Competitive Co-operation*. Chapel Hill: University of North Carolina Press, 1982.

Rich, Norman. *Friedrich von Holstein: Politics and Diplomacy in the Era of Bismarck and William II*. 2 vols. Cambridge: Cambridge University Press, 1965.

Richards, Guy. *The Hunt for the Czar*. Garden City, N.Y.: Doubleday, 1970.

Richmond. J. C. B. *Egypt 1798–1952: Her Advance Towards a Modern Identity*. New York: Columbia University Press, 1977.

Robertson, Esmonde M. "Hitler and Sanctions: Mussolini and the Rhineland," *European Studies Review*, 7 (1977): 409–35.

————. *Mussolini as Empire-Builder: Europe and Africa, 1932–36*. London: Macmillan, 1977.

Robinson, Ronald and Gallagher, John. *Africa and the Victorians: The Official Mind of Imperialism*. London: Macmillan, 1974; first pub. 1961.

Röhl, John C. G. "Beamtenpolitik im Wilhelminischen Deutschland." In Michael Stürmer, ed., *Das kaiserliche Deutschland. Politik und Gesellschaft 1870–1918*. Düsseldorf: Droste, 1970, 287–312.

Rosen, Klaus-Henning. "Vorurteile im Verborgenen: Zum Antisemitismus in der Bundesrepublik Deutschland." In Herbert A. Strauss and Norbert Kampe, eds., *Antisemitismus. Von der Judenfeindschaft zum Holocaust*. Frankfurt: Campus Verlag, 1985, 256–79.

Rosenbaum, Kurt. *Community of Fate: German-Soviet Diplomatic Relations, 1922–1928*. Syracuse: Syracuse University Press, 1965.

Ruhl, Klaus-Jörg. *Spanien im Zweiten Weltkrieg. Franco, die Falange und das 'Dritte Reich'*. Hamburg: Hofmann und Campe Verlag, 1975.

Ryder, A. J. *The German Revolution of 1918: A Study of German Socialism in War and Revolt*. London: Cambridge University Press, 1967.

Safran, Nadav. *Egypt in Search of Political Community: An Analysis of the Intellectual and Political Evolution of Egypt, 1804–1952*. Cambridge, Mass.: Harvard University Press, 1961.

Salewski, Michael. *Die deutsche Seekriegsleitung 1935–1945*. 3 vols. Frankfurt/Main: Bernard and Graefe, 1970–75.

Sanke, Heinz, ed. *Der deutsche Faschismus in Lateinamerika 1933–1943*. [East] Berlin: Humboldt-Universität, 1966.

Scheffler, Wolfgang. "Wege zur 'Endlösung.' " In Herbert A. Strauss and Norbert Kampe, eds., *Antisemitismus. Von der Judenfeindschaft zum Holocaust*. Frankfurt: Campus Verlag, 1985, 186–214.

Schieder, Theodor. "Die Entstehungsgeschichte des Rapallo-Vertrages," *Historische Zeitschrift*, 204 (1967): 545–65.

————. *Die Probleme des Rapallo-Vertrags. Eine Studie über die deutsch-russischen Beziehungen 1922–1926*. Cologne: Westdeutscher Verlag, 1956.

Schleunes, Karl A. *The Twisted Road to Auschwitz: Nazi Policy Toward German Jews, 1933–1939*. Urbana: University of Illinois Press, 1970.

Schoenbaum, David. *Hitler's Social Revolution: Class and Status in Nazi Germany, 1933–1939*. New York: Norton, 1980; first pub. 1966.

Schröder, Bernd Philipp. *Deutschland und der Mittlere Osten im Zweiten Weltkrieg*. Göttingen: Musterschmidt, 1975.

Schröder, Hans-Jürgen. *Deutschland und die Vereinigten Staaten 1933–1939. Wirtschaft und Politik in der Entwicklung des Deutsch-Amerikanischen Gegensatzes*. Wiesbaden: F. Steiner, 1970.

Schuker, Stephen A. *The End of French Predominance in Europe*. Chapel Hill: University of North Carolina Press, 1976.

Schultz, Duane. *Theories of Personality*. 2d ed. Monterey, Calif.: Brooks/Cole, 1981.

Schwarz, Urs. *The Eye of the Hurricane: Switzerland in World War Two*. Boulder, Colo.: Westview Press, 1980.

Seabury, Paul. *The Wilhelmstrasse: A Study of German Diplomats under the Nazi Regime*. Berkeley and Los Angeles: University of California Press, 1954.

Shamir, Haim. "The Middle East in the Nazi Conception." In Jehuda L. Wallach, ed., *Germany and the Middle East, 1835–1939*. Tel-Aviv: Israel Press, 1975, 167–74.

Sharfman, Glen. "Next Year in Jerusalem? The Question of Assimilation and Palestine for German Jews in the Weimar Republic." Unpublished M.A. thesis. University of North Carolina, 1984.

Sheehan, James J., ed. *Imperial Germany*. New York: Franklin Watts, 1976.

Snell, John L. *Illusion and Necessity: The Diplomacy of Global War, 1939–1945*. Boston: Houghton Mifflin, 1963.

Sontag, Raymond James. *Germany and England: Background of Conflict, 1848–1894*. New York: Norton, 1969; first pub. 1938.

Stegmann, Dirk. " 'Mitteleuropa' 1925 bis 1934: Zum Problem der Kontinuität deutscher Aussenhandelspolitik von Stresemann bis Hitler." In Dirk Stegmann, Bernd-Jürgen Wendt, Peter-Christian Witt, eds., *Industrielle Gesellschaft und politische System. Beiträge zur politische Sozialgeschichte. Festschrift für Fritz Fischer zum 70. Geburtstag*. Bonn: Verlag Neue Gesellschaft, 1978, 203–11.

Stein, George H. *The Waffen SS: Hitler's Elite Guard at War, 1939–1945*. Ithaca: Cornell University Press, 1966.

Steinberg, Jonathan. *Yesterday's Deterrent: Tirpitz and the Birth of the German Battle Fleet*. London: MacDonald, 1965.

Steiner, Zara S. *The Foreign Office and Foreign Policy, 1898–1914*. Cambridge: Cambridge University Press, 1969.

Steinert, Marlis G. *Hitler's War and the Germans: Public Mood and Attitude during the Second World War*. Ed. and trans. Thomas E. J. DeWitt. Athens: Ohio University Press, 1977.

Stern, Fritz. *The Politics of Cultural Despair: A Study in the Rise of the Germanic Ideology*. New York: Anchor Doubleday, 1965.

Stokes, Lawrence D. "The German People and the Destruction of the European Jews," *Central European History*, 6 (1973): 167–91.

Strauss, Herbert A. "Der Holocaust: Reflexionen über die Möglichkeiten einer wissenschaftlichen und menschlichen Annäherung." In Herbert A. Strauss and Norbert Kampe, eds. *Antisemitismus. Von der Judenfeindschaft zum Holocaust.* Frankfurt: Campus Verlag, 1985, 215–33.

Sykes, Christopher. *Troubled Loyalty: A Biography of Adam von Trott zu Solz.* London: Collins, 1968.

————. *Wassmuss: "The German Lawrence."* London/New York: Longmans, Green & Co., 1936.

Taylor, A. J. P. *Germany's First Bid for Colonies: A Move in Bismarck's European Policy.* New York: Norton, 1970.

Tignor, Robert L. *Modernization and British Colonial Rule in Egypt, 1882–1914.* Princeton: Princeton University Press, 1966.

Tillmann, Heinz. *Deutschlands Araberpolitik im Zweiten Weltkrieg.* [East] Berlin: VEB Deutscher Verlag der Wissenschaften, 1965.

Trumpener, Ulrich. "German Officers in the Ottoman Empire, 1880–1918: Some Comments on their Backgrounds, Functions, and Accomplishments." In Jehuda L. Wallach, ed., *Germany and the Middle East, 1835–1939.* Tel-Aviv: Israel Press, 1975, 30–43.

————. *Germany and the Ottoman Empire, 1914–1918.* Princeton: Princeton University Press, 1968.

Tuohy, Ferdinand. *The Secret Corps: A Tale of 'Intelligence' on All Fronts.* New York: Thomas Seltzer, 1920.

Vogel, Renate. *Die Persien- und Afghanistanexpedition Oskar Ritter v. Niedermayers 1915–1916.* Osnabrück: Biblio-Verlag, 1976.

Voigt, Johannes H. *Indien im Zweiten Weltkrieg.* Stuttgart: Deutsche Verlags-Anstalt, 1978.

Wallsdorf, Martin. *Westorientierung und Ostpolitik. Stresemanns Russlandpolitik in der Locarno Ära.* Bremen: Schuenemann Universitätsverlag, 1971.

Wavell, A. P. *The Palestine Campaigns.* 2d ed. London: Constable, 1929.

Wehler, Hans-Ulrich. *Das Deutsche Kaiserreich 1871–1918.* 5th ed. Göttingen: Vandenhoeck und Ruprecht, 1983.

Weidenfeld, Werner. *Die Englandpolitik Gustav Stresemanns. Theoretische und praktische Aspekte der Aussenpolitik.* Mainz: V. Hase & Koehler Verlag, 1972.

Weinberg, Gerhard L. "The Defeat of Germany in 1918 and the European Balance of Power," *Central European History,* 2 (1969): 248–60.

————. *The Foreign Policy of Hitler's Germany.* Vol. 1. *Diplomatic Revolution in Europe, 1933–36.* Chicago: University of Chicago Press, 1970. Vol. 2. *Starting World War II, 1937–1939.* Chicago: University of Chicago Press, 1980.

————. "Hitler and England, 1933–1945: Pretense and Reality," *German Studies Review,* 8 (1985): 299–300.

————. *World in the Balance: Behind the Scenes of World War II.* Hanover, N.H. and London: University Press of New England, 1981.

Whaley, Barton. *Codeword Barbarossa.* Cambridge, Mass.: MIT Press, 1973.

Wollstein, Günter. *Vom Weimarer Revisionismus zu Hitler. Das Deutsche Reich und die Grossmächte in der Anfangsphase der nationalsozialistischen Herrschaft in Deutschland.* Bonn: Voggenreiter, 1973.

Wrigley, W. David. "Germany and the Turco-Italian War, 1911–1912," *International Journal of Middle Eastern Studies,* 11 (1980): 313–38.

Yisraeli, David. "Germany and Zionism." In Jehuda L. Wallach, ed., *Germany and the Middle East, 1835–1939*. Tel-Aviv: Israel Press, 1975, 142–64.

———. "The Third Reich and Palestine," *Middle Eastern Studies*, 7 (1971): 343–55.

Zechlin, Egmont. *Die Deutsche Politik und die Juden im Ersten Weltkrieg*. Göttingen: Vandenhoeck und Ruprecht, 1969.

Zeine, Zeine N. *The Emergence of Arab Nationalism: With a Background Study of Arab-Turkish Relations in the Near East*. 3d. ed. Delmar, N.Y.: Caravan Books, 1976.

Zimmermann, Ludwig. *Deutsche Aussenpolitik in der Ära der Weimarer Republik*. Göttingen: Musterschmidt, 1958.

Index

114; and Tunisia, 170; and Turkey, 11,
14, 18, 19–20, 25, 50–52, 64, 68–70,
80–81, 117–18, 122; and United States,
94–95, 103–04, 142, 150, 151, 156; universities
of, 4, 7–8; and World War I,
33–38, 47–50; and World War II, 144,
146, 153, 156, 157, 160, 164–65, 167,
168, 172; and Zionism, 41, 105, 107–
09, 113. *See also Auswärtiges Amt; Abteilung III;* Prüfer, Curt
Ghali, Butrus, 20
Al Ghayali, 19
Glock, Gustav, 149
Goebbels, Joseph, 100, 137, 162, 167,
173, 179, 183
Goeben, 27
Goering, Hermann, 104, 116, 132, 137
Góes Monteiro, Pedro, 140, 146, 147,
148, 154, 159
Gondos, Ungar, 32
Gooch, G. P., 105
Gorst, Eldon, 15
Granow, Ulrich, 169, 172
Greece, 75
Grey, Edward, 22, 31
Grobba, Fritz, 60, 66, 113, 114, 138, 169–
72
Grossdeutsche Rundfunk ("Greater German radio network"), 172
Grünau, Werner Otto Freiherr von, 102,
129
Guadalcanal, 164
Guatemala, 140
Guinle, Guilherme, 151
Gustloff, Wilhelm, 130
Gutehoffnungshütte firm, 118
Guttmann, Herbert, 66

de Haas, Walter, 70, 76
Haas, Wilhelm, 133
Haavara Company, 107, 113, 134
Hakki, Topal Ismail, 74
Haldane, Lord, 198 n. 41
Hall, David, 86, 125–26, 183–84
Hamad, Gaafar Bey, 20
Hamburger Montagsblatt, 18
Hamza, Fuad, 138
Haniel von Haimhausen, Edgar, 60
Hassan (Syrian nationalist and army officer), 114

Hassell, Ulrich von, 101, 125, 228 n. 2
Hatzfeldt, Hermann Count von, 13, 17,
18–20, 22, 23
Havana conference of foreign ministers
(1940), 147
Heemskerck, Hans-Eduard von, 49, 100
Heeren, Victor von, 131
Heiden, Erich, 49, 185
Hejaz, 32, 43, 47
Hempel, Eduard, 136
Hencke, Andor, 176
Hentig, Werner Otto von, 26, 54, 66, 113,
121, 133, 138, 139
Hermann Goering mining company, 151
Herzegovina, 175
Hess, Rudolf, 102, 129, 132, 136
Hilfsverein der deutschen Juden ("Welfare
Association of German Jews"), 108
Hilfsverein der Juden in Deutschland
("Welfare Association of Jews in Germany"), 108
Himmler, Heinrich, 100, 101, 111, 132,
133, 137, 138, 167, 172, 173, 175
Hindenburg, Paul von, 89, 95, 99, 101,
104, 129
Hirsch, Paul, 61
Hirschfeld, Gustav Wilhelm, 101
Hitler, Adolf, 93; and diplomats, 98–99,
101, 103, 129–30, 132, 135–36, 191 n.
2; and domestic crisis, 89, 96; and England,
110–13, 127, 139; and Ethiopia,
123–27; and Latin America, 142, 151,
163; and Middle East, 113, 139, 142,
168, 171; and plans for war, 138; and
plot against, 182, 187; racism of, 94,
115–16, 157, 168; and rearmament,
111–12; and Ribbentrop, 102, 129, 130,
135–36, 167; and seizure of power, 100;
and United States, 142, 157; and war
aims, 142
al-Hizb al-Watani, 16
Hoesch, Leopold von, 104, 111, 129, 130
Holocaust, 175, 180, 182, 183
Holstein, Friedrich von, 196–97 n. 10
Honduras, 140
Hrugrzka, Herr von, 55
Hugenberg, Alfred, 191 n. 1, 193 n. 8
Humann, Captain, 27
al-Husayni, Haj Amin, 113–14, 122, 168–
72, 175–76, 177, 179